The Antitrust Paradox

THE ANTITRUST PARADOX

A Policy at War with Itself

ROBERT H. BORK

Basic Books, Inc., Publishers   *New York*

Library of Congress Cataloging in Publication Data

Bork, Robert H.
  The antitrust paradox.

  Includes bibliographical references and index.
  1. Antitrust law—United States. 1. Title.
KF1649.B67   343'.73'072   77-74573
ISBN: 0-465-00369-9 (cloth)
ISBN: 0-465-00370-2 (paper)

All that is meant, and that will be understood,
cannot be expressed in a dedication.
This book is for Claire.

CONTENTS

PART III
SUMMATION

PREFACE

This book grows out of long experience with the antitrust laws as student, practitioner, and teacher. Its appearance has been delayed perhaps six or seven years by a series of unexpected events. The first draft was finished in 1969, at the completion of a sabbatical year, and in the ordinary course the book would have been rewritten during 1970 and published, probably, in 1971. The turbulence of the campus during those years and certain personal concerns, however, precluded serious work. I had returned to my work and almost completed it when my entry into government in June 1973 once more put a stop to the effort. Since leaving government, I have been able, with some very generous assistance, to bring the project to a close. This is the result.

My intellectual indebtedness is particularly heavy. Much of what is said here derives from the work of Aaron Director, who has long seemed to me, as he has to many others, the seminal thinker in antitrust economics and industrial organization. His reputation is immense among those who know him; that it is not more widespread is entirely due to his choice to publish little and rest content with the establishment of a strong oral tradition at the law school of the University of Chicago, where he taught economic theory. I had the good fortune to be his student in 1953 and 1954, the latter year as a graduate research associate, and our discussions permanently and substantially altered my ways of thinking about much more than antitrust. It is impossible to capture the impressiveness of the man for the reader who does not know him: he depended for his results not at all upon pedagogical fireworks but rather upon a quiet manner and a remorseless logic. He gave the impression of absolute intellectual integrity, a very rare quality and so immensely impressive when encountered. Perhaps his genius lay in that, and in his capacity for examining what appeared the most ordinary propositions of law and perceiving at length that the shibboleths were empty. He is my idea of what a real intellectual is like.

Closely associated with Director in those days was Edward H. Levi, without question the most brilliant classroom teacher I have ever seen. He heavily influenced all my views of antitrust and of law generally. It was his capacity to dazzle, to entrance, to see more rapidly than anyone else the ramifications of ideas that attracted many of us to antitrust, because he taught it. There is much more to be said of Levi and his intellectual influence in the law school at that time, but that is another story.

At Yale for eleven years I benefited immeasurably from discussions with Ward S. Bowman, Jr., so much so that I cannot begin to identify all of the things in this book that could be traced to him. He, too, has acknowledged the powerful influence of Aaron Director during the years Bowman spent at Chicago. Bowman's own book, *Patent and Antitrust Law*,[1] is so good and so definitive that I have not even attempted in this book to comment upon that branch of the law. There is nothing more to say. His comments on my manuscript have been of enormous assistance.

Ralph K. Winter, Jr., another Yale colleague, also has read the manuscript and made many helpful comments and corrections. So, too, has Frederick M. Rowe, a prominent lawyer in Washington, himself the author of the exhaustive and excellent *Price Discrimination Under the Robinson-Patman Act*.[2] Antonin Scalia, a former colleague at the Department of Justice, now a professor of law at the University of Chicago, read and was particularly helpful with the last chapter. Midge Decter has been as encouraging, skilled, and perceptive an editor as everyone told me she would be.

I have never fully understood the custom of exonerating everybody who reads an author's manuscript from any complicity in its errors and shortcomings, but I am willing to follow the tradition. One and all, they are absolved. (Formally and in public, at least.)

I wish to acknowledge with gratitude the support of grants from Yale University made possible by the generosity of the Relm Foundation and the General Electric Foundation. I also wish to thank William J. Baroody and the American Enterprise Institute for Public Policy Research, of which he is president. AEI housed and supported me during the spring of 1977 so that the book could at long last be finished.

A comment upon one other matter seems appropriate. On several occasions in this book, and particularly in Chapter 8, I have used the automobile industry and the General Motors Corporation to illustrate my argument. These passages were written in 1968–1969. In 1977, I agreed to represent General Motors in connection with an investigation involving some of the issues discussed here. I have decided to let the text stand. To change it now in order to discuss a different company in a different industry would not only delay completion of the book once again, a prospect neither I nor my family could bear to contemplate, but would also be disingenuous. My analysis and conclusions would remain the same and would be completely transferable to the context of the automotive industry. The general position taken here is one I have held for many years and first took publicly, I believe, in dissenting from the Report of the White House Task Force on Antitrust Policy (the Neal Report) in 1968.

ROBERT H. BORK

New Haven, 1978

ACKNOWLEDGMENTS

I acknowledge the kind permission of the editors and publishers to use material that first appeared under their auspices:

"The Crisis in Antitrust," with Ward S. Bowman, Jr. *Fortune* 68 (1963): 138.

"The Supreme Court Versus Corporate Efficiency." *Fortune* 76 (1967): 92.

"Antitrust In Dubious Battle." *Fortune* 80 (1969): 103.

"Legislative Intent and the Policy of the Sherman Act, *Journal of Law and Economics* 9 (1966): 7–48.

"Vertical Integration and the Sherman Act: The Legal History of An Economic Misconception." *University of Chicago Law Review* 22 (1954): 157–201.

"The Rule of Reason and the Per Se Concept: Price Fixing and Market Division." Part I. *Yale Law Journal* 74 (1965): 775–847.[*]

"The Rule of Reason and the Per Se Concept: Price Fixing and Market Division." Part II. *Yale Law Journal* 75 (1966): 373–475.

"A Reply to Professor Gould and Yamey." *Yale Law Journal* 76 (1967): 731–743.

"Resale Price Maintenance and Consumer Welfare," *Yale Law Journal* 77 (1968): 950–964.

[*] Articles from *Yale Law Journal* by permission of The Yale Law Journal Company and Fred B. Rothman and Company.

The Antitrust Paradox

INTRODUCTION: THE
CRISIS IN ANTITRUST

Improbable as the statement may seem, antitrust today is almost an unknown policy. It is ubiquitous: Antitrust constitutes one of the most elaborate deployments of governmental force in areas of life still thought committed primarily to private choice and initiative. It is popular: There is some intellectual but almost no political opposition to its main features. And it is even exportable: This supposedly peculiarly American growth has spread to and taken at least equivocal root in Europe and even in Asia. Yet few people know what the law really commands, how its doctrines have evolved, or the nature of its ultimate impact upon our national well-being. Even among the specialized and elite corps of lawyers who operate the antitrust system there is remarkably little critical understanding of the policy.

This state of affairs is curious, and certainly unfortunate, but perhaps it is understandable. Antitrust is a subcategory of ideology, and by the time a once militant ideology triumphs and achieves embodiment in institutional forms, its adherents are likely long since to have left off debating first principles. "The antitrust movement," as Professor Richard Hofstadter remarks, "is one of the faded passions of American reform." [1] But Hofstadter goes on, and probably it is not a paradox—"the antitrust enterprise has more significance in contemporary society than it had in the days of T.R. or Wilson, or even in the heyday of Thurman Arnold." The very nearly simultaneous "collapse of antitrust feeling both in the public at large and among liberal intellectuals" and our arrival at a state of affairs in which "the managers of the large corporations do their business with one eye constantly cast over their shoulders at the Antitrust Division" are probably to be explained, though Hofstadter does not quite make the causality explicit, by the fact that "antitrust as a legal-administrative enterprise has been solidly institutionalized in the past quarter-century." The waning of fervor with the growth of organization, bureaucracy, and effective power is a familiar occurrence in both secular and religious movements.

But the ideology remains, and its inner logic drives the antitrust enterprise—lawyers, economists, judges, and legislators—inexorably toward the conclusions implicit in the premises. This phenomenon, along with a modest resurgence of antitrust feeling, accounts for the current round of litigation and proposed legislation designed to dissolve many of America's most successful corporations. In all kinds of political weather the machinery of antitrust enforcement grinds steadily on, mindlessly reproducing both the policy triumphs and disasters of the past. Even when public and political enthusiasm for the harassment of business is at an ebb, the enforcement bureaucracy and the residual potency of the antitrust symbol remain strong enough to prevent the law's mistakes from being retracted.

The full range of modern rules that significantly impair both competition and the ability of the economy to produce goods and services efficiently is discussed in detail in the remainder of this book. Generally, these rules ignore the obvious fact that more efficient methods of doing business are as valuable to the public as they are to businessmen. In modern times the Supreme Court, without compulsion by statute, and certainly without adequate explanation, has inhibited or destroyed a broad spectrum of useful business structures and practices. Internal growth to large market size has been made dangerous. Growth by merger with rivals is practically impossible, as is growth by acquisition of customers or suppliers. Even acquisitions for the purpose of moving into new markets have been struck down, as the law evolves a mythology about the dangers of conglomerate mergers. Cooperative ventures between independent businesses are outlawed through a misapplication of the sound policy against price fixing and market division. The Court has destroyed the most useful forms of manufacturer control over the distribution of products, requiring higher-cost modes of reaching the public. It has needlessly proliferated rules about pricing behavior that have the effect of making prices higher and markets less effective allocators of society's resources. The Court has done these things, moreover, on demonstrably erroneous notions of the economics that guide the law.

So far as the Supreme Court is concerned, we appear at the moment to be between cycles of antitrust expansion. Extensions of old doctrine to new fields have been relatively infrequent the last half dozen years or so, but there is scant comfort in that. The situation will not last. A position based not upon settled ideology but rather upon an accidental equilibrium of forces is unlikely to prove stable. Unless the theory of antitrust is understood and the law brought into line with it, the law will surely move on again, becoming even more unnecessarily restrictive of business freedom. A majority of the current Supreme Court has recently taken a significant step toward reforming a part of antitrust, and prospects for an intelligible, proconsumer law may now be brighter than they have been for several decades. Still, there is a very long way to go. Existing case law incorporates principles that have not been extended to the full reach of their internal logic. Law grows by analogizing new situations to old, and antitrust may move still further away from a policy of competition simply by realizing the potentialities inherent in the principles it now espouses.

But there is more to fear than that, for the courts are of course not the sole generators of antitrust policy. A new era of antitrust expansion seems likely to begin in Congress, which is influenced by popular moods. There has always existed in this country a populist hostility to big business, a hostility that is currently reinforced by the suspicion that major corporations are somehow to blame for hardships that have their origin elsewhere, in the politics of OPEC, in federal regulation of natural gas prices—or in bad weather, for that matter.

The direction of new legislation is determined by the prevailing tone of public discourse. That discourse has in recent years been almost uniformly in favor of fresh antitrust assaults on business. Ralph Nader, though rather more voluble than most, expresses not untypical attitudes. "Antitrust," Mr. Nader informed us a few years back, "is going to erupt into a major political issue because it is not just an esoteric issue for lawyers." Rather, it is "going modern and will shed more and more of its complexities." He was a true prophet: shortly thereafter, a Nader Study Group filed a report on something called "The Closed Enterprise System" [2] which shed the complexities of antitrust so completely that the reader is given no hint of their existence. Indeed, both the tone and the message of the report are best paraphrased by Professor Richard Posner as suggesting "that if we would only stop thinking so much about the problem and throw the book at the bastards our monopoly problem would be solved." [3]

Nader's essentially nihilistic attitude might perhaps be little to the point except that he and his Study Group are by no means alone, and some of their company is quite distinguished. I have heard an eminent professor of antitrust law argue that the economic problems of antitrust are too difficult and that the government should, for that reason, eschew policy analysis and just keep bringing lawsuits in order to keep

businessmen "shook up." Several hundred lawyers at a meeting of the
Antitrust Section of the American Bar Association listened to a nationally
prominent attorney, who subsequently became an Associate Justice of
the Supreme Court, contend that it was fruitless to worry about antitrust's
intellectual problems. Antitrust, the attorney said, is in the good old
American tradition of the sheriff of a frontier town: he did not sift
evidence, distinguish between suspects, and solve crimes, but merely
walked the main street and every so often pistol-whipped a few people.

Such attitudes have, of course, found reflection in Congress. Recently, for example, Congress enacted legislation allowing each state to
sue on behalf of all persons residing within its borders for triple the
damage done them by antitrust violations. The same legislation made
mergers more difficult by requiring advance notification to government,
and greatly expanded government's power to compel information
without resort either to a lawsuit or a grand jury investigation. The
Petroleum Industry Competition bill, which won astonishingly wide
support in the Senate in 1976, was designed to destroy vertical integration in the major oil companies by requiring that each company confine
itself to one of three phases of the industry: production, transportation,
or refining and marketing. That bill is, as of this writing, scheduled for
reintroduction, along with other bills that would prevent oil companies
from entering or remaining in any other energy field, such as coal or
solar energy. There is no reason to believe that the destruction of national wealth involved in the enactment of these bills or other recent proposed legislation * would be compensated by any social gain.

We are urged, then, by persons in and out of Congress, to throw the
antitrust book at business in order to improve the quality of American
life. One could wish that those who want to throw the book had taken
the time to understand it. In the pages that follow, I attempt to contribute to that necessary understanding by reading the antitrust book in
light of the disciplines of law and economics, in order to show that the
policy is not what it seems. Antitrust presents itself as a body of developed knowledge and principle worked out over years of investigation,

* A few years ago, the late Senator Philip Hart, then chairman of the Antitrust
Subcommittee of the Senate Judiciary Committee, introduced a proposed Industrial Reorganization Act. Reflecting the current shibboleth that monopoly is
everywhere, the bill would have directed antitrust attack at about 140 of the nation's largest 200 companies in seven industries. More recently, Senator Hart
introduced a bill that would make it no defense in a civil monopolization action
that defendant's monopoly power was "due to superior product, business acumen,
or historic accident," thus proposing to break up market positions based on
superior efficiency.

thought, and litigation. That image is misleading. Antitrust is not all of a piece.

Because antitrust's basic premises are mutually incompatible, and because some of them are incorrect, the law has been producing increasingly bizarre results. Certain of its doctrines preserve competition, while others suppress it, resulting in a policy at war with itself. During the past twenty years or so, the protectionist, anticompetitive strain in the law has undergone a spectacular acceleration, bringing to pass what Ward Bowman and I have termed the "crisis in antitrust." [4] The resolution of this crisis will determine antitrust's future. The law must either undergo a difficult process of reform, based upon a correct understanding of fundamental legal and economic concepts, or resume its descent to the status of an internal tariff against domestic competition and free trade.

Given the pace and direction of its development, the overriding need of antitrust today is a general theory of its possibilities and limitations as a tool of rational social policy. Yet there exists among those professionally concerned with antitrust a surprising lack of agreement concerning the most basic questions. The disagreement, though variously phrased, is finally about two issues: (1) the goals or values the law may legitimately and profitably implement; and (2) the validity of the law's vision of economic reality. I have attempted in this book to resolve both of those issues. A consideration of the virtues appropriate to law *as* law demonstrates that the only legitimate goal of antitrust is the maximization of consumer welfare. Current law lacks these virtues precisely because the Supreme Court has introduced conflicting goals, the primary one being the survival or comfort of small business.

A consumer-oriented law must employ basic economic theory to judge which market structures and practices are harmful and which beneficial. Modern antitrust has performed this task very poorly. Its version of economics is a mélange of valid insights and obviously incorrect— sometimes fantastic—assumptions about the motivations and effects of business behavior. There are many problems here, but perhaps the core of the difficulty is that the courts, and particularly the Supreme Court, have failed to understand and give proper weight to the crucial concept of business efficiency. Since productive efficiency is one of the two opposing forces that determine the degree of consumer well-being (the other being resource misallocation due to monopoly power), this failure has skewed legal doctrine disastrously. Business efficiency necessarily benefits consumers by lowering the costs of goods and services or by increasing the value of the product or service offered; this is true whether the business unit is a competitor or a monopolist. When efficiency is not counted, or when it is seen as a positive evil, it appears that no business structure of behavior has any potential for social good, and there is consequently no reason to uphold its legality if any remote danger can be imagined. The results could not have been worse, and would probably have been better, if the Court had made the opposite mistake and refused to recognize any harm in cartels and monopolies. Yet neither mistake need have been made. The hopeful development in the current Supreme Court's approach to antitrust, referred to a few pages back, is a single case weighing in favor of a business practice its capacity to create efficiency.[5] That approach seems obvious, but against the background of the jurisprudence of the last two decades it appears revolutionary. Applied generally, it could save antitrust as useful and respectable policy. It is too soon to tell whether the Court will follow up its new beginning.

This book attempts to supply the theory necessary to guide antitrust reform. Such an attempt assumes that reasonable certainty concerning basic issues is possible. I believe it is. Because the issues of goals and of economic means must both be faced, antitrust is necessarily a hybrid policy science, a cross between law and economics that produces a mode of reasoning somewhat different from that of either discipline alone. I use the words "science" and "discipline" deliberately. Basic microeconomic theory is of course a science, though like many other sciences it is by no means complete in all its branches. Were it not a science, rational antitrust policy would be impossible. We are too little accustomed, however, to thinking of law as a science, and indeed in current practice there is little enough to suggest the concept. Yet it should be obvious that the very idea of the rule of law requires some degree of certainty and logical rigor. Though its theory is not, and cannot be, nearly so highly developed as that of economics, law does have requirements that are distinctively its own. When these are ignored, as they increasingly have been in antitrust adjudication, law that is bad as law, quite apart from its substantive content, necessarily results.

There are many ways to organize a book such as this. I have elected to begin with fundamental economic and legal concepts before outlining and evaluating the law of various antitrust topics. By proceeding in this fashion, I hope to make the argument clear both to the lawyer unfamiliar with economics and to the economist innocent of law, as well as to those unsuspecting persons, perhaps businessmen or students, who have previously escaped formal involvement in either field.

Part I is devoted to an explication and evaluation of the basic ideas of the law. It begins with an account of the period, primarily the years 1890 to 1914, when the foundations of today's law were laid down. What is wrong today went wrong then, just as what is sound today was then correctly decided, for developments since have been almost entirely the extrapolation of principles adopted close to the outset of the policy. Those principles had to do with the goals the law seeks and the economic theories by which the law moves toward those goals. Both of these were confused issues, and they have remained so in modern discourse. Chapters 2 and 3 take up the crucial issues of goals and argue that antitrust policy, as expressed in our present statutes, cannot properly be guided by any goal other than consumer welfare.

Whether or not it is true, as I contend, that this must be the exclusive goal of antitrust, the law is universally admitted to have at least something to do with competition and the well-being of consumers. The remaining chapters of Part I, therefore, sketch the relationship between competition and consumer welfare and consider the implications of that relationship for law. Chapter 4 sets out the relationship of price theory to consumer welfare. Chapter 5 explains the elements of consumer welfare in the antitrust context, a concept rather different from the usual economist's view of welfare. A discussion of the mode of economic reasoning appropriate to antitrust is the subject of the sixth chapter. Finally, Chapter 7 consists of an examination of the basic economic theories employed by antitrust, theories of the ways in which competition may be injured. These theories underlie all of antitrust policy, and their flaws, which are readily apparent upon analysis, explain the present deformities of the law.

With basic concepts explained, we turn in Part II to the main subject headings of the law: monopoly and oligopoly created by the internal growth of the leading firms; mergers—horizontal, vertical, and conglomerate; price fixing and market division; price discrimination. Each chapter attempts to summarize the state of the law and then to evaluate it in light of economic analysis.

Part III contains just two chapters, one summarizing the major recommendations of this book for the substantive reform of the law, the other consisting of an overview, an attempt to suggest some broader implications of antitrust in its relation to society and ideas about society.

The reader will find in this book from time to time a note of dismay or of disappointment about the path that antitrust has taken. Since it may seem odd or inappropriate that emotion should be expended on such a topic, perhaps I had better explain why antitrust seems to me worth study and concern. If this were a law having to do only with the efficiency of one sector of the economy, if its sole function were to make consumers marginally richer, the law's current plight would hardly be a matter for even "faded passion." At best it would be a stimulating intellectual puzzle. But antitrust is much more than that. Its mystique, its legends, its celebration by all branches of the federal government constitute an exceptionally potent educative force that affects our thought, for better or for worse and in ways we do not fully realize, about all the aspects of society the law touches. I have referred to it as a subcategory of ideology; it is not far-fetched to view antitrust as a microcosm in which larger movements of our society are reflected and perhaps, in some small but significant way, reinforced or generated. The walls of ideological subcategories are permeable; battles fought and won or lost in one are likely to affect the outcome of parallel struggles in others. It is important, therefore, to recognize the aspects of society upon which this law impinges.

Antitrust is, first and most obviously, law, and law made primarily by judges. We are right to be concerned about the integrity and legitimacy of that lawmaking process, both for its own sake and because ideas about the power and discretion proper to courts in one field of law will inevitably affect their performance elsewhere. At issue is the question central to democratic society: Who governs?

Antitrust is also a set of continually evolving theories about the economics of industrial organization. These theories affect the thought of laymen about business and its behavior, of course, but it is nothing short of extraordinary to see how powerfully the enshrinement of an economic theory in a Supreme Court opinion affects the thought even of economists. For this and other reasons the political fate of the competitive, free-market ideal is heavily involved with developments in antitrust. The capture of the field by anti-free-market theories will have impact far beyond the confines of antitrust itself.

The struggle between economic freedom and regulation also reflects and reacts upon the tension in our society between the ideals of liberty and equality. Neither of these can be an absolute, of course, but the balance between them and the movement of that balance are crucial.

Within the limited frame for observation provided by antitrust, therefore, it is worth noting that the general movement has been away from legislative decision by Congress and toward political choice by courts, away from the ideal of competition and toward the older idea of protected status for each producer, away from concern for general welfare and toward concern for interest groups, and away from the ideal of liberty toward the ideal of enforced equality. No one can know how far these trends may go, but if, as I believe, they have already gone much too far in antitrust as elsewhere in our polity, they should be recognized and reversed, for they are ultimately incompatible with the preservation of a liberal capitalist social order. Antitrust should not be permitted to remain an unknown policy.

PART I

THE THEORY

1

The Historical Foundations of Antitrust Policy

ONE of the uses of history is to free us of a falsely imagined past. The less we know of how ideas actually took root and grew, the more apt we are to accept them unquestioningly, as inevitable features of the world in which we move. One reason for the stifling solidity of received opinion about antitrust, why counterargument makes so little headway, is that most of us accept our first principles and even our intermediate premises uncritically, as given, because we assume that they were established theoretically and confirmed empirically by legislators and judges long ago. Discussion begins from there.

What we all "know" is wrong. We are working from an intellectual base that does not exist. What *is* true is that our ideas are old; they carry whatever credentials time alone can confer. The years 1890 to 1914 witnessed the origin of every major theory that drives and directs the evolution of antitrust doctrine to this day. What the courts, the Congress, and the enforcement agencies have wrought since is little more than the working out of the implications of those early hypotheses. If modern results often appear sensational, that is less because anything fundamentally new has occurred than because we are diverted by new vocabulary from seeing continuity in superficial diversity and, more importantly, because we never really understood the sweeping implications of the old ideas.

But it is *not* true, as we trustingly assume, that these ideas were ever demonstrated theoretically or confirmed empirically. In that sense, the intellectual history we rely upon is false, in antitrust as in so much else of the law. The accepted view is well expressed by a concurring opinion in *White Motor*. "The *per se* rule of prohibition," the opinion said, "has been applied to price-fixing agreements, group boycotts, tying arrangements, and horizontal divisions of markets. As to each of these practices, experience and analysis have established the utter lack of justification to excuse its inherent threat to competition." [1] The eye passes easily over these sentences; they express antitrust wisdom so conventional as to appear obvious. And yet they are clearly, though unintentionally, misleading. Later chapters will attempt to show what is wrong about the statement that all practices in any of the four categories either are or should be illegal. The point here is that the history cited does not exist. Never has "experience" demonstrated the anticompetitive nature of any of these practices. Experience may demonstrate that a practice raises prices or that it injures a rival, but that is all, and many competitive practices do the same things. Only theory can separate the competitive from the anticompetitive, and as for that, the rules referred to were not established on a foundation of "analysis."

For this reason alone it is important to recapture the real foundations of modern policy: it will free us to think again about basic questions that have never been satisfactorily answered. The great problems were not solved but were shelved by the almost casual introduction and acceptance of concepts that were neither defined nor tested by rigorous analysis and adversary debate. This history should constitute a warning about the weaknesses of the adjudicative process and the danger of relying upon courts to evolve major social policy. If the course of antitrust is typical—and familiarity with other fields of law suggests that it is—courts are unlikely to work carefully toward adequate theory, and they require much more rigorous criticism and evaluation by an informed profession than they have ever received.

Law tends to arrive at basic answers before the right questions have been asked. Disputes that must be decided arise before there is a theory to handle them, so that the participants in the litigation often do not perceive the implications of a decision either way. By the time the real question is perceived, if it ever is, an answer has not only been given but has become dogma, and it is too late. If the answer given was wrong or irrelevant, the damage is then spread to new legal and business contexts through the law's habit of reasoning by analogy, extrapolating from principles without reexamining their validity.

There are other benefits and fascinations in a study of antitrust's formative period. The great early cases, for one thing, are not merely history or the exemplifications of a process; they are also precedent, and inconsistent precedent at that. Some of them contain themes and principles that run counter to much of today's law, and so, for the lawyer or the judge, they provide a tool of legal reform. They can add new flexibility and resourcefulness to legal argument.

The themes to be discerned in the legislation and judicial decisions from 1890 to 1914 are numerous, but there are three major ones that deserve especial attention. These consist of ideas about the goals of antitrust policy, about industrial structure and organization, and about the conceptual apparatus of the law.

Sometimes legislators and courts were explicit about the goals of antitrust—Senator Sherman and Chief Justice White both were highly articulate about the goal of the Sherman Act—but more often goals must be inferred from the substantive rules that men proposed or created. In the early period of the law the dominant goal was the advancement of consumer welfare, though Justice Brandeis introduced, or at least was the first to give operative weight to, the conflicting goal of small-business welfare. Brandeis's approach grew in importance in the later evolution of antitrust until, in the era of the Warren Court, it often became the dominant, though not the exclusive, goal.

Antitrust's economic theories about business structure and behavior also took shape in this early period. Congress and the courts believed that competition could be injured to the detriment of consumers by the agreed elimination of rivalry (through, for example, cartel arrangements or monopolistic mergers) or by a powerful firm's attack upon rivals with the purpose of driving them from the market (by predatory local price wars or control of raw materials or transportation). These remain our theories of the means by which competition may be destroyed. But at the end of the period under examination, each of these theories, and particularly the theory of aggression, was given enormous impetus by Congress's introduction of the concept of *incipiency*—the idea that courts could identify and catch anticompetitive activity in its very early stages, before its effects had become serious. We shall see in later chapters that the incipiency concept has proved to be an anticompetitive virus, working together with the Brandeis value strain to protect the inefficient from competition.

During this period, too, antitrust began to work out theories concerning the three forms of structure that it deals with today. In antitrust's vocabulary, a structure is *horizontal* when it involves only one market.

Thus, when we speak of a firm's market share we are speaking of horizontal structure, and phenomena such as price fixing by rivals or the merger of rivals are horizontal because the rivals operate in the same market. Structure is *vertical* when it links two markets in the same chain of manufacture and distribution, usually through the linkage of two firms that either do or could stand in the relationship of supplier and customer. Vertical structures include a manufacturer's ownership of retail outlets, his exclusive contracts with independent outlets, or his control of independent outlets' resale prices. Structure is *conglomerate* when it links two separate markets in any manner that is not vertical. Thus, a firm that operates in two distinct product markets is conglomerate, as is a firm that operates in distinct geographical markets; often there are contracts that link such markets and hence deserve to be termed conglomerate. Most of the law developed in the early cases involved horizontal structures, but much was decided about vertical structures, and the seeds of conglomerate theory were present. The law supposed that each of these types of structure was capable of being used to suppress competition.

The law's conceptual apparatus, or mode of analysis, is conventionally known as the "rule of reason," and its outlines and categories were fully developed during the period discussed. It may be no exaggeration to say that this apparatus attained its most perfect form by 1911 but was then thoroughly misunderstood and has deteriorated since. The rule of reason consisted of two major categories: (1) business behavior (or structure) that was illegal per se; and (2) business behavior that was judged by standards of the party's intent or the effect his behavior was likely to have, considering the market context.

Behavior is illegal per se when the plaintiff need prove only that it occurred in order to win his case, there being no other elements to the offense and no allowable defense. Justice Thurgood Marshall has well described the rationale of this legal category:

> *Per se* rules always contain a degree of arbitrariness. They are justified on the assumption that the gains from imposition of the rule will far outweigh the losses and that significant administrative advantages will result. In other words, the potential competitive harm plus the administrative costs of determining in what particular situations the practice may be harmful must far outweigh the benefits that may result. If the potential benefits in the aggregate are outweighed to this degree, then they are simply not worth identifying in individual cases.[2]

Behavior not placed in the per se category is properly judged by the criteria of the intent which accompanies it and its probable effect upon competition. The per se rule judges behavior by its inherent effect. Where the inherent effect is not clearly bad in the sense Justice Marshall described, the other criteria must be employed. Thus, the rule of reason, as a categorizing system, aids in clarifying thought and in ordering trials.

Finally, running through the arguments and decisions of this early period was a recognition of the need to eliminate the evils of monopoly without hampering business efficiency. It is only in recent times that we see the Supreme Court announcing that efficiency is no concern of the law, or even that efficiency is anticompetitive.

The attempt to isolate the main themes of antitrust in this early period involves an element of artificiality, but not one fatal to the enterprise. I do not for a moment suppose that the legislators and judges whose views are discussed possessed fully articulated philosophies. Since Congress and the courts were feeling their way through confusing problems, the main lines of reasoning did not always display sharply defined edges. Yet it is still useful and legitimate to attempt analytical classifications. The problems these men dealt with required a number of basic distinctions, and the necessary assumptions and implications of these distinctions, whether fully perceived by their authors or not, may now be discerned and properly said to constitute identifiable themes or philosophies.

The period begins with the passage of the Sherman Act in 1890 and ends with the adoption of the Clayton Act and the Federal Trade Commission Act in 1914. We will step outside this period only to discuss the *Chicago Board of Trade* case (1918), which develops and establishes an idea plainly adumbrated before 1914.

THE PASSAGE OF THE SHERMAN ACT

Federal antitrust policy began when President Benjamin Harrison signed Bill S. 1, which later became known as the Sherman Act,[3] on July 2, 1890. The main provisions of the new statute proclaimed, somewhat enigmatically:

Section 1. Every contract, combination in the form of trust or otherwise, or conspiracy, in restraint of trade or commerce among the several States, or with foreign nations, is hereby declared to be illegal. . . .

Section 2.   Every person who shall monopolize, or attempt to monopolize, or combine or conspire with any other person or persons, to monopolize any part of the trade or commerce among the several States, or with foreign nations, shall be deemed guilty of a misdemeanor. . . .

The language of the statute, which is singularly opaque, was chosen not merely because it employed familiar common law terminology but also to allay fears that the law might go beyond the then narrowly conceived commerce power of Congress.[4] The act's reach would be coextensive with the Supreme Court's demarcation of commerce. This common law phraseology has caused no end of confusion, however, since there was no unitary body of common law doctrine that could give meaning to the statute. The common law of restraints of trade and monopolies has been a variable growth, composed of diverse and contradictory strains, many of them obviously irrelevant or even hostile to the policy of fostering competition. Yet Sherman and many of his colleagues repeatedly assured the Senate, without objection by anyone, that they proposed merely to enact the common law.

There is no mystery, for Sherman and the others also repeatedly stated what their version of the common law was. The statute's ultimate use of common law terms thus carried with it the substantive rules that Sherman and others thought appropriate to the policy they sought to enact. The cases discussed by Sherman as representative of the common law held illegal the predatory extraction of railroad rebates by the Standard Oil Co., cartel agreements, and monopolistic horizontal mergers. Cases going the other way he simply ignored. The fact that the statements of Sherman and his colleagues did not accurately portray the actual confusion of common law precedent at the time does not obscure what they intended to accomplish. It is clear from the debates that the "common law" relevant to the Sherman Act is an artificial construct, made up for the occasion out of a careful selection of a few recent decisions from different jurisdictions, plus a liberal admixture of the senators' own policy prescriptions. It is to this "common law," holding full sway nowhere but in the debates of the Fifty-first Congress, that one must look to understand the Sherman Act.

The statute was intended to strike at cartels, horizontal mergers of monopolistic proportions, and predatory business tactics. Wide discretion was delegated to the courts to frame subsidiary rules, but it was also clear, as we shall see more fully in the next chapter, that the delegation was confined by the policy of advancing consumer welfare. Sherman's draft of the statute outlawed arrangements "designed, or which tend, to advance the cost to the consumer." And in the debates Sherman demonstrated his understanding that higher prices were brought about by what an economist today would call a restriction of output, as when he asked whether Congress had not the power to "protect commerce, nullify contracts that restrain commerce, turn it from its natural courses, increase the price of articles, and thereby diminish the amount of commerce?" The wide variety of other policy goals that have since been attributed to the framers of the Sherman Act is not to be found in the legislative history.

THE SHERMAN ACT IN THE COURTS: THE ESTABLISHMENT OF THE RULE OF REASON

The rule of reason, as we have seen, is simply a set of general categories that are given content by ideas about the proper goals of the law, economics, and the requirements of the judicial process. As ideas about these matters change, the substantive law—the content of the categories —also changes.

Divergent strains in the rule of reason appeared in the very first case to be decided upon the merits by the Supreme Court, and these irreconcilable traditions persist in the law to this day. These traditions are defined primarily by their view of the goals of policy, and it does little credit to the law's reputation as an intellectual discipline that the dispute has not only remained unresolved but its continuation in slightly altered contexts generally goes unrecognized.

The main outlines of antitrust policy are illuminated by the opinions of six men: Justice Rufus Wheeler Peckham, who wrote the Supreme Court's first substantive antitrust opinions; Judge (later Chief Justice) William Howard Taft, who wrote one of the law's most brilliantly suggestive and neglected opinions; Justice Oliver Wendell Holmes, who usefully destroyed the idea that the law can outlaw all eliminations of competition; Justice (later Chief Justice) Charles Evans Hughes, who set the law of vertical price fixing on the course it has followed ever since; Chief Justice Edward Douglass White, who, after a false start in dissenting from Peckham's first opinions, recovered to write the monumental *Standard Oil* and *American Tobacco* opinions of 1911; and Justice Louis Dembitz Brandeis, who brought to prominence the idea that judges in antitrust cases could forward values opposed to consumer welfare.[5]

JUSTICE PECKHAM AND THE INCEPTION OF ANTITRUST POLICY

In the Supreme Court's first substantive Sherman Act decisions, Justice Peckham led a narrow majority that chose consumer welfare as the law's guiding policy, created the category of agreements illegal per se, and began to work toward a formula for excepting efficiency-creating integrations from the statute's interdiction. That, despite these achievements, he has since been repeatedly assessed as a mere literalist who took from the statutory text an unworkably rigid test of illegality can only be the result of a superficial reading of his opinions.

The *Trans-Missouri* case [6] of 1897 provided the occasion for a Peckham-White debate concerning the new statute's interpretation that was at bottom a debate about the law's goals. The government had sought to enjoin the members of a railroad association from agreeing upon rates. The case was complicated by the requirement of the Interstate Commerce Act, which nobody claimed the defendant roads had violated, that all rates be "reasonable and just." The government did not contest defendants' allegations that they fixed only "reasonable" rates. The trial court dismissed the bill, and a majority of the court of appeals affirmed, agreeing with "the proposition that it is not the existence of the restriction of competition, but the reasonableness of that restriction, that is the test." [7] Since the restriction in this case operated upon prices, this test proposed to judge the "reasonableness" of the prices set by cartel agreement. White adopted this version of the law when the case • came to the Supreme Court. Peckham saw that a reasonable-price standard was no standard.

Peckham proposed to judge the legality of the restraint by its character, White by its degree. This underlay Peckham's insistence in the majority opinion that the act could not be interpreted to legitimate a category of "reasonable" restraints since it explicitly outlawed every restraint of trade.[8] Everything depended upon the definition Peckham gave to the forbidden category. And in *Trans-Missouri* he gave notice that he would redefine that common law term to fit the different concerns of the Sherman Act. Thus, he declined to fix the definition of the term and suggested that a contract by the seller of property not to compete with the purchaser—clearly classified as a contract in restraint of trade at common law—"might not be included within the letter or spirit of the statute in question." Peckham was clearly not committed to a wooden literalism, as White and the generality of subsequent commentators believed, and he made clear that his objection to White's reasonable-price standard rested upon policy grounds. He argued persuasively and correctly that a reasonable-price standard was inherently uncertain (what rate of return must the courts allow the cartelists?) and, in fact, that the only price that can meaningfully be called reasonable is the price set by competition. He said of the railroad rate agreement that "there can be no doubt that its direct, immediate, and necessary effect is to put a restraint upon trade or commerce as described in the act," and that it was therefore illegal "no matter what the intent was on the part of those who signed it." It is clear that Peckham, like Sherman, defined a restraint of trade as that suppression of competition in the general market that was likely to create a restriction of output. By deciding the case against the railroads without a trial, he framed a rule of per se illegality for cartel price fixing.

The *Joint Traffic* decision [9] the following term made Peckham's proconsumer orientation clearer. Here the majority struck down another railroad rate agreement, but Peckham had to meet defendants' argument that his per se approach would destroy the most ordinary and indispensable contracts and integrations. After pointing out that no such cases were before the Court, he said that the following transactions would be difficult to bring within the statutory category of contracts in restraint of trade: (1) "the formation of a corporation to carry on any particular line of business"; (2) "a contract of partnership"; (3) "the appointment by two producers of the same person to sell their goods on commission"; (4) "the purchase by one wholesale merchant of the product of two producers"; and (5) "the lease or purchase by a farmer, manufacturer or merchant of an additional farm, manufactory or shop." This list is highly instructive, for each example involves both the agreed elimination of actual or potential rivalry and the integration of the parties' productive economic activities or facilities. The rate agreements declared illegal per se in *Trans-Missouri* and *Joint Traffic* involved only the first of these elements. Thus, Peckham seemed to be saving from the per se rule any agreement with the capacity for creating efficiency. Two aspects of Peckham's opinions are, therefore, consistent only with a goal of consumer welfare: the per se rule against cartel agreements and his solicitude for efficiency-creating agreements. If other goals, such as small-producer welfare, are admitted, cartel price fixing cannot be illegal per se: a defense is possible and a full trial is necessary in order to weigh the interests of producers against those of consumers. Similarly, efficiency-creating integrations cannot be automatically lawful, since their effect will be to harm some rivals. The approach Peckham took, then, necessarily implies an exclusive concern with consumer well-being. We will see in a moment, however, that Peckham slipped once in this approach.

White's *Trans-Missouri* dissenting opinion [10] (he and the other three dissenting justices merely noted their disagreement in *Joint Traffic*) did not suggest how the reasonableness of cartel prices was to be judged. Peckham's argument required the dissent to specify what criteria were available for deciding how far above the competitive level a price might be raised before it became unreasonable. White attempted no answer, probably because there is no answer that can sensibly be given. He contented himself with arguing that a law striking down all contracts that restrained trade or the freedom of traders regardless of reasonableness would destroy "all those contracts which are the very essence of trade, and would be equivalent to saying that there should be no trade, and therefore nothing to restrain." White thus lumped together the main contending themes of the rule of reason that must be kept distinct if any clarity of analysis is to be achieved: the idea that some agreements are necessary to trade, though they also eliminate some rivalry between the parties; and the entirely different notion that some general suppression of competition might be desirable for its own sake. In order to preserve contracts of the former type, he was willing to permit those of the latter, thereby plunging the courts into the making of political choices. A standard that requires courts to determine how high cartel prices may be set requires judges to adjust the conflicting interests of consumers and producers in each case. The choice is "political" in that there are no principles to guide it; there is nothing more than a decision to favor one or another interest group. Yet this was what White meant when he employed the phrase "rule of reason" in his *Trans-Missouri* dissent. The choice of words was unfortunate because it helped obscure the fact that he later meant something very different by the same phrase in his famous 1911 opinions.

These are the main contrasts between Peckham and White: one enunciating rules and approaches that would commit the statute to an exclusively proconsumer policy, the other seizing a verbal formula that, whether he fully realized it or not, would have committed the courts to case-by-case compromises of the claims of consumers and producers. But such clarity is too much to expect of judges working for the first time with difficult and opaque matters, and Peckham did slip once. He suggested, by way of dictum, that business combinations

. . . may even temporarily, or perhaps permanently, reduce the price of the article traded in or manufactured, by reducing the expense inseparable from the running of many different companies for the same purpose. Trade or commerce under those circumstances may nevertheless be badly and unfortunately restrained by driving out of business the small dealers and worthy men whose lives have been spent therein and who might be unable to readjust themselves to their altered surroundings. Mere reduction in the price of the commodity dealt in might be dearly paid for by the ruin of such a class.[11]

With those few lines Peckham introduced a fundamental inconsistency into his argument. If the dictum is to be taken seriously—and there is strong internal evidence that the anticonsumer aspect was a slip rather than a deliberate policy statement—he seemed willing to give weight to the well-being of producers as against consumers. Yet the admission of that consideration into the law would have destroyed the rule of per se illegality for price-fixing cartels. That Peckham framed and adhered to that rule is the strongest evidence he did not take his dictum about small producers seriously. But it is significant both that this theme should have been sounded in the first antitrust case decided on the merits in the Supreme Court (for that establishes its ancient lineage in antitrust) and that Peckham gave it voice (for that shows that not even the consumer-oriented tradition of the law has been entirely consistent). We shall hear more of these "small dealers and worthy men" that Peckham loosed upon us, for they are the widows and orphans of antitrust debate, and they may yet sweep the field.

Despite this lapse, if lapse it be, Peckham occupied a crucial position in the formation of basic antitrust policy, and he deserves a better reputation than he has been accorded. If he did not work out a completely consistent and fully articulated rule of reason, neither has anyone else; and Peckham made the attempt without prior legal tradition or scholarship upon which to rely. Yet he had three major achievements. First, he framed a rule in which agreed eliminations of rivalry (in both cases, price fixing) without any other element of economic integration were illegal regardless of their asserted purpose, but in which agreed eliminations, even if explicit, could be lawful if they were an aid to the integration of economic activities. This is a necessary distinction that the modern law has lost sight of. Second, by his insistence that in outlawing "every" restraint of trade the statute did not enact the common law, Peckham saved the Sherman Act from a stultifying effort to incorporate a body of confused and inappropriate precedent. Finally, his rejection of a reasonable-price standard of legality may have saved the statute from becoming a judicially administered version of the National Recovery Administration, allowing cartels but policing their prices and behavior. Given the administrative impossibility of the task, the result of such a misstep would surely have been the effective retirement of the courts from the field. He thus helped prevent the statute from becoming a license to cartelize. Perhaps even more important, he helped shape a law that became, and for a long time remained, the politically potent symbol of the virtues of free and unregulated markets. Whatever the artistic shortcomings of his opinions—and they are fewer than those who read superficially suppose—at a crucial point in antitrust history Peckham and the four justices who joined him made the right decision.

JUDGE TAFT: THE *ADDYSTON* CASE

Between the Supreme Court's *Trans-Missouri* and *Joint Traffic* decisions, Judge William Howard Taft, writing for the Sixth Circuit Court of Appeals in *Addyston Pipe & Steel*,[12] made a remarkable attempt to settle the issue of goals and to provide the Sherman Act with a workable formula for judging restraints. The opinion is one of almost unparalleled suggestiveness, and yet its potentialities, after more than seventy years, remain almost entirely unexploited. Indeed, given the time at which it was written, *Addyston* must rank as one of the greatest, if not the greatest, antitrust opinions in the history of the law.

The government's case was brought against six manufacturers of cast-iron pipe who had agreed to fix prices and divide territories. Defendants attempted to avoid the *Trans-Missouri* precedent by arguing that stricter law governed railroad cases and that the common law, which they claimed imposed a reasonable-price test, applied to their agreement. Taft elected to show that even at common law, and therefore certainly under the statute, their agreement was unlawful. He chose to argue the common law, one suspects, as a way of joining the debate between Peckham and White without a directness that might have seemed presumptuous in a lower court judge. He chose his common law cases carefully, however, and imposed upon them his own ideas. What emerged was not the restatement it pretended to be so much as a new structure.

Taft's view of the proper goals of the law was heavily influenced by his view of the types of issues that are fit for judicial determination. On this ground he rejected, in the guise of a discussion of common law cases, White's reasonable-price standard as a "sea of doubt":

> It is true that there are some cases in which the courts, mistaking, as we conceive, the proper limits of the relaxation of the rules for determining the unreasonableness of restraints of trade, have set sail on a sea of doubt, and have assumed the power to say, in respect of contracts which have no other purpose and no other consideration on either side than the mutual restraint of the parties, how much restraint of competition is in the public interest, and how much is not.

Like Peckham, Taft thought "the manifest danger in the administration of justice according to so shifting, vague, and indeterminate a standard would seem to be a strong reason against adopting it." Earlier in the opinion he had said that, in cases where restriction of competition is the sole aim of the agreement, "there is no measure of what is necessary to the protection of either party, except the vague and varying opinion of judges as to how much, on principles of political economy, men ought to be allowed to restrain competition."

This argument, which is juridical rather than economic, led Taft to propose a rule of per se illegality for what have been called "naked restraints," agreements in which the parties engage in no significant dealings other than the elimination of competition. But Taft recognized that some restrictions upon rivalry are socially valuable, and to provide the necessary guidelines for judging these he offered, supposedly from the common law, the concept of the "ancillary restraint." To be ancillary, and hence lawful, an agreement eliminating competition must be subordinate and collateral to a separate, legitimate transaction. The ancillary restraint is subordinate and collateral in the sense that it makes the main transaction more effective in accomplishing legitimate purposes.

Taft used the illustration of a partnership. This, it will be recalled, was one of Peckham's examples of a nonrestraint in *Joint Traffic*. Though writing before that case, Taft was clearer about the reasons for permitting partnerships, and he went a step further and explained the

reasons for the validity of an agreement "by a partner pending the partnership not to do anything to interfere, by competition or otherwise,
with the business of the firm":

> ... when two men became partners in a business, although their union might
> reduce competition, this effect was only an incident to the main purpose of a
> union of their capital, enterprise, and energy to carry on a successful business,
> and one useful to the community. Restrictions in the articles of partnership
> upon the business activity of the members, with a view of securing their
> entire effort in the common enterprise, were, of course, only ancillary to the
> main end of the union, and were to be encouraged.

This insight is, or should be, central to modern antitrust. It is useful,
therefore, to put Taft's reasoning in modern terms and to generalize it.
The integration of economic activities, which is indispensable to productive efficiency, always involves the implicit elimination of actual or
potential competition. We allow it—indeed, should encourage it—because the integration creates wealth for the community. We should
equally encourage those explicit and ancillary agreed-upon eliminations
of rivalry that make the basic integration more efficient. To distinguish
between the basic, implicit elimination of competition and the ancillary,
explicit elimination would be a pointless contradiction in policy. This, in
essence, was Taft's economic argument. His juridical argument was that
the legality of ancillary restraints could easily be judged, for "the main
purpose of the contract [i.e., the purpose of the main transaction] suggests the measure of protection needed, and furnishes a sufficiently
uniform standard by which the validity of such restraints may be judicially determined." To put the matter roughly, lawyers forming a partnership could lawfully agree on fields of exclusive specialization (which
is market division) and the fees each should charge (price fixing),
while the same lawyers, if they were not in partnership, could not do
these things lawfully. We will return to these matters in discussing price
fixing, market division, and concerted refusals to deal. Only an application of Taft's rubric is capable of rescuing those fields of law from
their present difficulties.

Taft went beyond Peckham in two other ways. First, he improved
upon Peckham's simple dichotomy by suggesting that even restraints
ancillary in form would be illegal if they were part of a general plan to
gain monopoly control of a market. Second, he applied his theory to
vertical restraints. This point is worth examining, for it too has been
overlooked and is badly needed by modern law.

Defense counsel tried to justify the "naked restraint" disclosed by the facts of the *Addyston* case by citing *Chicago, St. L. & N.O. R.R. v. Pullman Southern Car Co.*[13] There the Supreme Court had upheld at common law a contract by which a sleeping-car company, Pullman Southern, had agreed to supply the cars and service required by the sleeping-car business of the railroad, in return, among other considerations, for the promise that no other sleeping-car company would be permitted to engage in that business on the same line. Taft justified this vertical arrangement in terms similar to those he had used in connection with the partnership agreement:

> The main purpose of such a contract is to furnish sleeping-car facilities to the public. The railroad company may discharge this duty itself to the public, and allow no one else to do it, or it may hire someone to do it, and, to secure the necessary investment of capital in the discharge of the duty, may secure to the sleeping-car company the same freedom from competition that it would have itself in discharging the duty. The restraint upon itself is properly proportioned to, and is only ancillary to, the main purpose of the contract, which is to secure proper facilities to the public.

This forgotten but enormously provocative passage contains the seeds of much useful law. Taft's argument would validate all vertical arrangements. In a vertical case there is always economic integration between the parties, the transaction of supplying and purchasing, so that the main condition of the ancillarity test is satisfied. Moreover, the argument that the railroad could provide the sleeping cars and services itself and so lawfully exclude all competition may also be generalized for all vertical cases. A manufacturer, for example, could always perform the retailing function itself; therefore, nothing is lost if, instead, it requires of independent retailers the maintenance of their resale prices, or sales only within prescribed territories, or exclusive dealing in the manufacturer's products. These forms of vertical elimination of competition are all analytically identical to the arrangement between the railroad and the sleeping-car company. For reasons that will be expounded in later chapters, I think Taft was correct and that, by precise analogy, all other vertical arrangements should be lawful as well. This, of course, is almost the reverse of the law today.

Taft's accomplishments in *Addyston,* then, were quite remarkable, not only when one considers the time at which he wrote but also in comparison with the judicial performances that were to come after. He indicated clearly why, for juridical reasons, courts must not "set sail on a sea of doubt" by trying to balance the interest of consumers in competition against that of producers in monopoly. This committed him to a consumer welfare standard. His doctrine of naked and ancillary restraints offered the Sherman Act a sophisticated rule of reason, a method of preserving socially valuable transactions by defining the scope of an exception for efficiency-creating agreements within an otherwise inflexible per se rule. Finally, he gave us the core of correct law about vertical arrangements. It is both startling and discouraging to realize that, in view of what came later, the *Addyston* opinion of 1898 may well have been the high-water mark of rational antitrust doctrine.

JUSTICE HOLMES IN *NORTHERN SECURITIES*

The *Northern Securities* decision [14] of 1904 would be thoroughly unimportant but for Justice Harlan's ineptitude in doctrinal disputation,* which misled Justice Holmes into a famous, though very uneven, dissent, and has misled generations of lawyers into thinking the case a precedent for the illegality of all horizontal elimination of rivalry. The case concerned the formation of the Northern Securities Company to take control, as holding company, of the Great Northern Railway Company and the Northern Pacific Railway Company. The roads operated, according to Harlan's opinion, "parallel and competing lines across the continent through the northern tier of states between the Great Lakes and the Pacific." A majority of the Court held the plan illegal. Holmes, supposing a merger or fusion of interests to be involved, demonstrated that a rule of per se illegality was nonsensical. Harlan's argument seemed at times to rest upon nothing more substantial than the typographical arts, as in his insistence, complete with italics, upon propositions like this one: "*every* combination or conspiracy which would extinguish competition between otherwise competing railroads engaged in *interstate trade or commerce,* and which would *in that way* restrain *such* trade or commerce, is made illegal by the act." His real answer, which must be quarried from the opinion, was that Northern Securities, as a mere holding company, was not a true merger but only a profit-pooling

---

* Harlan's style of dogmatic analysis, displayed here and in his *Standard Oil* and *American Tobacco* dissents, gives point to a remark Holmes made about him elsewhere: "That sage, although a man of real power, did not shine either in analysis or generalization and I never troubled myself much when he shied. I used to say that he had a powerful vise the jaws of which couldn't be got nearer than two inches to each other" (2 Holmes-Pollock Letters, 7–8 [Howe ed., 1941]).

scheme equivalent to a cartel. He stressed the absence of real fusion when he said, for example, that the holding company was "to manage, or cause to be managed, both lines of railroad *as if* held in one ownership." (Emphasis in original.) In Harlan's view, therefore, the case was properly governed by the per se rule of *Trans-Missouri* and *Joint Traffic.* *

In dissent [15] Holmes attempted his one general structuring of the Sherman Act—and a curiously inconsistent piece of work it is, announcing that the statute "says nothing about competition" and yet construing selected parts of it in terms of competition.† His version of the statute deprives it of any general policy goal and, almost, of any intelligible reason for existence. Yet, because he mistook Harlan's meaning, Holmes performed the valuable task of demonstrating in vivid terms that no rule making the elimination of competition between rivals illegal per se is even thinkable. Since he saw *Northern Securities* as a fusion of interests, a merger, Holmes argued that to strike it down as a combination in restraint of trade under a rule of per se unlawfulness would "require all existing competitions to be kept on foot, and, on the principle of the *Trans-Missouri Freight Association*'s case, invalidate the continuance of old contracts by which former competitors united in the past."

He had hold of a crucial economic distinction, that between cartels and mergers, when he said that "to suppress competition in that way [by a contract with a stranger to one's business] is one thing; to suppress it by fusion is another." Repeatedly he picked up the theme of the devastating effect of a per se rule for integrations:

To see whether I am wrong, the illustrations put in the argument are of use. If I am, then a partnership between two stage drivers who had been competitors in driving across a state line, or two merchants once engaged in rival

---

* This explains why Harlan thought the case required no more than the broad slogans extracted from such prior decisions as *Trans-Missouri* and *Joint Traffic* (naked restraint cases), and why he failed to discuss issues such as market dominance that would have been relevant to a merger case. The "combination" he referred to as illegal, moreover, was not the holding company itself but the antecedent agreement and cooperation of the stockholders of the two roads. 193 U.S. at 335. The holding company was seen not as an efficiency-creating integration but only as the implement of that illegal combination. Id. at 327.

† His insistence that the statute must be interpreted in strict accordance with the common law whose terms it employed, without reference to any supposed policy of preserving competition, is difficult to reconcile with *Trans-Missouri* and *Joint Traffic,* decisions which Holmes said he accepted "absolutely, not only as binding upon me, but as decisions which I have no desire to criticize or abridge." 193 U.S. at 405.

commerce among the States whether made after or before the act, if now continued, is a crime. For, again I repeat, if the restraint on the freedom of the members of the combination caused by their entering into a partnership is a restraint of trade, every such combination, as well the small as the great, is within the act.

He said that this interpretation "would make eternal the *bellum omnium contra omnes* and disintegrate society so far as it could into individual atoms."

Holmes also queried the application of the statute to mergers on one additional ground: Since a single corporation could lawfully have constructed the lines of both railroads, how could it be unlawful for a single corporation to purchase them both after they were built? Here he raised the question of the distinction between size by growth and size by merger which has puzzled the law for years, and anticipated the difficulties that faced Judge Learned Hand years later in the *Alcoa* case. It is a problem to which the law continues to return.

Holmes's contribution to the rule of reason was quite limited. The interpretation of the statute he suggested, keyed to no particularly coherent policy, has lapsed into an oblivion that seems deserved. Yet, because he was ultimately unable to keep the concept of competition, and hence economic reasoning, out of his argument, he put basic questions that remain provocative today.

JUSTICE HUGHES, *DR. MILES*, AND THE LAW OF VERTICAL RESTRAINTS

It is rarely possible to identify one decisive misstep that has controlled a whole body of law. A single paragraph in Justice Hughes's 1911 *Dr. Miles* opinion [16] is such an instance, however, and the law of resale-price maintenance and vertical market division has been rendered mischievous and arbitrary to this day by the premise laid down there. The Dr. Miles Medical Co., a manufacturer of proprietary medicines, maintained the resale prices of its products through a great network of contracts with wholesalers and retailers. John D. Park & Sons Co., a noncontracting wholesaler, cut the specified prices on products it obtained by inducing other wholesalers to sell to it in violation of their contracts with Dr. Miles. Dr. Miles's tort suit against Park & Sons was dismissed upon demurrer, and the Supreme Court affirmed, holding the price-maintenance scheme illegal under the Sherman Act. Because of the view the Supreme Court took of the economics of the situation, it does not appear from the opinion whether the arrangement was truly vertical (i.e., imposed by the manufacturer downward in its own interests) or the result of pressure upward from a horizontal agreement among the resellers. Taft's *Addyston* rationale would have validated the first but not the second. To Dr. Miles's assertion that a standard retail price was beneficial to the company, Justice Hughes, writing for the Court, replied that the defense was insufficient even if true:

If there be an advantage to the manufacturer in the maintenance of fixed retail prices, the question remains whether it is one which he is entitled to secure by agreements restricting the freedom of trade on the part of dealers who own what they sell. As to this, complainant can fare no better with its plan of identical contracts than could the dealers themselves if they formed a combination and endeavored to establish the same restrictions, and thus to achieve the same result, by agreement with each other. If the immediate advantage they would obtain would not be sufficient to sustain a direct agreement, the asserted ulterior benefit to the complainant cannot be regarded as sufficient to support its system.

Hughes thus equated horizontal cartel behavior with vertical price fixing. Since the former was per se illegal, it followed that the latter was also. His error lay in the implausible assumption that a manufacturer's interest in eliminating price rivalry among its resellers must have the same motives and consequences as the interest of resellers in forming a cartel. Yet if anything is certain, it is that Dr. Miles, unless it was being coerced by a reseller cartel, could have had no interest in creating a monopoly profit for its resellers at its own expense. A rule of per se illegality was thus created on an erroneous economic assumption.

CHIEF JUSTICE WHITE'S 1911 RULE OF REASON: *STANDARD OIL* AND *AMERICAN TOBACCO*

The 1911 *Standard Oil* [17] and *American Tobacco* [18] cases, handed down by the Supreme Court on the same day, are among the most important decisions in antitrust. Their direct economic results—the dissolution of two monopolistic combines—were significant, but probably less so than the tendencies, good and bad, that they impressed upon anti-trust doctrine. Certainly Chief Justice White's opinions must rank among the most artful in the field. The need for a restatement of the law must have seemed compelling. Peckham's opinions had been largely misunderstood. The consternation their seeming rigidity caused can hardly have been much allayed by the famous debate in *Northern Securities* between Harlan and Holmes, which must have suggested that the Sherman Act was unworkable or unintelligible or, more likely, both.

The major virtues of White's opinions were numerous. The monopolies before the Court were held illegal, while the business community was reassured by the explicit adoption of a "rule of reason" that not every elimination of competition was unlawful. The Sherman Act was related in a plausible way to the common law, whose terms it used, without being subjected to future distortion by the application of a largely inappropriate mass of precedent. The goal of the law was clearly defined as the maximization of consumer welfare, and a dynamic principle was built into the rule of reason so that the interpretation of the law could change and adjust in its pursuit of that goal as economic understanding advanced. Concern was shown that the statute not interfere with means of creating efficiency or with market structures that resulted from efficiency. Finally, the rule of reason became a three-part test, incorporating the per se concept; this test was both fully adequate to the tasks of antitrust policy and completely manageable by counsel and courts in the litigation process. These were very considerable accomplishments, and had they not been badly, perhaps fatally, flawed, the Sherman Act might have remained our only antitrust statute and antitrust policy might have had an unambiguous career as a guarantor of free markets.

Two faults in the 1911 opinions prevented this. The first—and it is nonetheless grievous for being in part the work of others—is that the *Standard Oil* and *American Tobacco* opinions were capable of being, and therefore were, so thoroughly misunderstood that many people believed the Supreme Court had subverted the Sherman Act.[19] This was due not only to Harlan's demagogic and thoroughly uncomprehending dissent, but also to the tortuousness and opacity of White's prose and to his unfortunate use of the phrase "rule of reason" to signify a set of criteria wholly opposed to the lack of criteria he had urged with the same phrase in his 1897 *Trans-Missouri* dissent. The Court was alleged to have claimed the power to make subjective choices between "good trusts" and "bad trusts." This misunderstanding was a very substantial factor in the demand for more legislation, a demand that culminated in 1914 with the adoption of the Clayton Act and the Federal Trade Commission Act. These statutes, as we shall see, have had thoroughly pernicious results.

The second fault in the 1911 opinions is that White and the Court adopted uncritically the idea that it is easy for one firm to injure another by means other than superior efficiency, and they accepted the notion, again almost without examination, that vertical integration, local price cutting, bargaining for preferences from suppliers, and the like provide the means by which such injury is improperly inflicted. These ideas, of course, were among those incorporated in the Clayton Act, but they have, even more importantly, remained part of antitrust's conceptual equipment, guiding courts to indefensibly restrictive results that are not compelled by any statute.

Before reaching the facts, White attempted in *Standard Oil* to give the Sherman Act a generally applicable doctrinal structure. He deftly converted the vexing question of the supposed common law origin of the statute's terms—restraint of trade and monopolize—into a strong point of his interpretation. Leading up to a textual demonstration that the law was based on an "existing practical conception of the law of restraint of trade," [20] he was able to base his reading of the statute not on an elaborate consideration of the precedents but on his version of "the elementary and indisputable conceptions of both the English and American law on the subject prior to the passage of the antitrust act." From a review of the growth of these conceptions he derived the policy goal of the common law and hence of the Sherman Act:

The evils which led to the public outcry against monopolies and to the final denial of the power to make them may be thus summarily stated: 1. The power which monopoly gave to the one who enjoyed it to fix the price and thereby injure the public; 2. The power which it engendered of enabling a limitation on production; and 3. The danger of deterioration in quality of the monopolized article which it was deemed was the inevitable resultant of the monopolistic control over its production and sale.

These evils, against which, according to White, the Sherman Act was directed, are each reducible to the single evil of restriction of output. The second—limitation of production—is obviously that. The first— the power to fix prices—can be wielded only by restricting output. The third—deterioration in quality—is merely another form of output restriction: putting less in each item made rather than making fewer items. A statute directed against the restriction of output is, as we shall see in

the next chapter, controlled by the policy of maximizing consumer welfare. The maximization of consumer welfare, therefore, is the only
policy goal White ascribed to the Sherman Act.

As might be expected of a law concerned with economic evils, "practical common sense caused attention to be concentrated not upon the
theoretically correct name to be given to the condition or acts which
gave rise to a harmful result, but to the result itself." In bringing this
mechanism attributed to the common law into the statute, White built
into the Sherman Act a principle of evolution controlled by the progress
of economic understanding. Thus, the Sherman Act becomes not a set
of specific rules, still less a body of precedent, but a direction to enforce
the law's rationale. Precedent is not ultimately controlling; economic
argument is.

White created a three-part rule of reason, which he stated most clearly
in *American Tobacco:* "The words 'restraint of trade' . . . only em-
braced acts or contracts or agreements or combinations . . . which, either
because of their inherent nature or effect or because of the evident purpose of the acts, etc., injuriously restrained trade." [21] There are thus
three tests to be applied to any practice or structure. The "inherent
nature" test results in what we would call today the category of practices
illegal per se. When economic analysis shows that a practice can have
no significant beneficial effects but is solely a means of restricting output,
the "inherent nature" of the practice is injuriously to restrain trade.
The practice then is labeled illegal per se, which means that there is no
defense and that the court need not examine either intent or market
power before pronouncing the behavior unlawful. White placed in the
per se category pure cartel agreements, as is shown by his explicit acceptance of the *Trans-Missouri* and *Joint Traffic* decisions as correctly
decided against the defendants without trial.[22] This, along with the
phrase "inherent nature," demonstrates that since 1897 White had
abandoned his idea of judging a restraint by its degree and accepted
the idea of judging it according to its character.

The remaining two tests were those of "inherent effect" and "evident
purpose." When economic analysis does not reveal that a practice is
always harmful by nature, as are pure cartel arrangements, the court
must pass on to these tests. White thought mergers not inherently, or
per se, illegal. What additional facts, then, must be examined to determine a merger's legal status? Proof of an "evident purpose," or an
actual intent, to inflict the evils of monopoly would render the merger
unlawful. This means an intent to gain or maintain monopoly through
means other than superior efficiency. Bad intent can be shown by admis-

sions, documents, the employment of abusive or predatory practices, or by other behavior inconsistent with efficiency. White did not define the "inherent effect" test, but it almost certainly refers to the inference of bad effects from some fact additional to the character of the restraint. This additional fact, almost surely, is the market share of the parties. Not only is this sound economics, but White repeatedly laid stress on market share in the two cases. He did not attempt the futile direct study of actual effects; rather, in keeping with the implications of the word "inherent," he inferred effects from the fact of market control.

White's rule of reason, then, may be phrased as a three-part test: (1) "inherent nature" or the per se concept; (2) "inherent effect" or market power; and (3) "evident purpose" or specific intent. The rule of reason was thus not composed of any particular substantive rules but was entirely a mode of analysis, a system for directing investigation and decision. This was in keeping with the dynamic principle of the law, by which substantive rules would evolve and alter as economic understanding progressed. The only constant elements were the goal (consumer welfare) and the mode of analysis (the three-part rule of reason). The rule of reason was also eminently suited to the litigation process. It completely avoided lengthy industry studies of actual performance. Court and counsel need only understand the most basic economics and concern themselves with facts such as market shares and actual intent. There is in this system no complete safeguard against mistaken economic theorizing, but no system can entirely avoid the risk of that. The 1911 rule of reason did as much as is possible to set the goal and the method of approach.

White's opinion on the legality of the Standard Oil and American Tobacco combines was less satisfactory. There seems little room for doubt of the correctness of the decisions that these two "trusts" violated the Sherman Act, but the Court's argument was unfortunate. White appears to have been moved by his concern that the statute not interfere with efficiency to place the emphasis of the case upon the trust's predatory behavior. In so doing, he gave impetus to doctrines whose main effect has been the needless destruction of business efficiency. This is the irony of the cases.

The *Standard Oil* decision turned upon defendants' bad intent. Perhaps it would have gone the same way regardless of their intent because of the "inherent effect" of the combination—defendants had achieved a 90 percent market share at the refining level largely through the acquisition of rivals—but White did not choose to face that issue. Instead he argued that the method of the most recent unification, the placing of all the associated corporations under the control of New Jersey Standard (which acted like a holding company, suspect at least since *Northern Securities*), raised a "prima facie presumption" of wrongful intent. The nature of wrongful intent is crucial. White said the intent was not to maintain market size through "normal methods" (superior efficiency)—which would have been proper—but to do it by "new means of combination" that gave greater control and power to exclude others. The presumption was of an intent to hold a monopolistic market share by means that were not more efficient but gave market size improperly. Even this presumption was apparently rebuttable because it arose, he said, in the "absence of countervailing circumstances," which can only mean a failure by defendants to show affirmatively that the intent underlying the unification was the "normal" one of creating efficiency. White said that the presumption was made conclusive by the showing that the power created was intended to be and was used abusively. The opinion goes on to state that there were "acts and dealings wholly inconsistent with the theory that they were made with the single conception of advancing the development of business power by usual methods, but which, on the contrary, necessarily involved the intent to drive others from the field and to exclude them from their right to trade, and thus accomplish the mastery which was the end in view."

The *Standard Oil* opinion is thus preoccupied with abuses, predatory practices, coercion, unnatural means of gaining and maintaining market power. The intent inferred from such practices is important because it reassured the Court that the size attained by the company whose dissolution was demanded was not due to superior efficiency. If efficiency would have produced comparable results, why resort to such practices? A very similar process of reasoning was used to decide the *American Tobacco* case.[23]

The weakness of the opinions—indeed, their capacity for mischief—lies precisely in this attempt to preserve efficiency by distinguishing it from unnatural economic conduct. The distinction between "natural" and "unnatural" has plagued the law with respect to types of behavior of more general and intense interest than economic conduct. But it has its problems here, too, and they cannot be made to disappear with any easy cliché along the lines of "two consenting corporations in private." White gave us no general guide to what behavior was abnormal other than, perhaps, the suggestion that it involved an intent "to drive others from the field and to exclude them from their right to trade." This is about as useful as defining normal sexual conduct as that engaged in to express love and abnormal sexual conduct as that engaged in for personal gratification. Whenever a competitor competes he intends to take business away from rivals, which involves excluding them. If he were completely successful in a market, he would thereby exclude them completely, and he would have intended to do so. Some test other than an intent to exclude must be framed, one that distinguishes exclusion through efficiency from exclusion by means unrelated to efficiency. We will come in the following chapters to what we mean by efficiency and what exclusion by predation means. Suffice it to note here that White raised a distinction that was potentially harmful if courts and legislators were unable to distinguish correctly between efficiency and other means of exclusion, and a distinction that has, in the event and for that reason, proved harmful.

One of the most important aspects of the *Standard Oil* case is that it solidified the dubious Standard Oil legend. The Court's opinion lent weight, substance, and seeming historical veracity to the oft-told tale of Standard's use of predatory techniques to gain and hold monopoly. From this derived much of the support not only for the Clayton and Federal Trade Commission acts but also for the Robinson-Patman Act and the continuing judicial hostility to competitive vigor. The theoretical case for the existence of most predatory tactics, as we shall see, is so confined as to make their common occurrence doubtful. John S. McGee has demonstrated that the record of the case shows "Standard Oil did not use predatory price discrimination to drive out competing refiners, nor did its pricing practice have that effect." [24] Yet local price cutting is one of the central charges against the old Standard Oil company, and its use of other predatory practices is no more probable on theoretical grounds than this. We badly need a similar investigation of other alleged cases of predatory behavior, particularly of the factual accuracy of the American Tobacco legend.

Whatever their theoretical or factual infirmities, we can nonetheless see almost every one of the modern law's economic theories foreshadowed in these cases. They were, first of all, horizontal: specifically, they were concerned with monopoly control of petroleum refining and the various branches of tobacco product manufacture. American Tobacco's market share is not clear, but Standard had achieved, it was said, control of 90 percent of the nation's refining capacity. That figure alone, since it was created by merger, would have justified dissolution. But, as in many modern horizontal cases, the Supreme Court relied upon nonhorizontal aspects and thereby laid down the basis for our modern law of

vertical and conglomerate arrangements. The law of both of these relationships goes back farther than we usually think—at least to 1911, in
fact.

The antitrust theory of conglomerate arrangements is the same as the
theory of vertical arrangements. Both involve a connection between two
markets and a theory of how power in one market can be used to aug-
ment power in the second. The only difference, and it is not very important, is that in one case the two markets are vertically related and in the
other they are not.

The seeds of law about conglomeration may be found, for example,
in the Court's acceptance of the tales of predatory local price cutting.
This is, supposedly, a tactic by which a firm uses money gained in one
market to wage a price war in a second. Power is transferred from one
market to another through the transfer of cash to subsidize war. This
theory was picked up by Section 2 of the Clayton Act, but, as we shall
see in later chapters, other forms of law about conglomerateness evolved
long before the term became fashionable with the 1950 amendment to
Section 7 of the Clayton Act.

Vertical law appeared throughout the opinions. In *Standard Oil,*
White's reasoning on the subject contained a curious internal contradiction. Thus, in a theory employed by the law today, White seemed
to argue that ownership of pipelines was a means of foreclosing rival
refiners and so extending the refining monopoly. He spoke of "the slow
but resistless methods . . . by which the means of transportation were
absorbed and brought under control" as one of the combination's unnatural, monopoly-gaining techniques.[25] The idea was that a transportation monopoly was sought, not so much for itself, but as a weapon
in the fight for a refining monopoly. Yet, in answer to defendant's argument that the combination controlled only a very small percentage of
crude production, White said that "substantial power over the crude
product was the inevitable result of the absolute control which existed
over the refined product, the monopolization of the one carried with it
the power to control the other." This observation, though quite correct,
undercuts not only the pipeline argument but much of the reasoning
about vertical integration in *American Tobacco* as well. If monopoly in
refining gives the power to control the crude level, even though the
latter is not owned, then (by a parity of reasoning) monopoly over
transportation would give control over refining without the necessity
of owning the refining level. In that event, there would be no particular reason to use the monopoly in transportation to gain a second,
vertically related monopoly in refining. We will see that this argument is

correct. White did not see its implications, however, and went on viewing vertical integration as a means of using one monopoly to gain a second at another level.

In *American Tobacco,* White was even more severe with vertical integration. Defendants owned suppliers of tinfoil and licorice paste, each itself a combination of previous rivals. The licorice firm supplied 95 percent of the market for paste, the foil company more than half the market for its products. White observed that no one unable to obtain licorice paste could compete in the manufacture of plug tobacco.[26] And later he listed, as a factor showing wrongful intent, "the gradual absorption of control over all the elements essential to the successful manufacture of tobacco products, and [the] placing [of] such control in the hands of seemingly independent corporations serving as perpetual barriers to the entry of others into the tobacco trade." Here was the use of another concept that we sometimes think of as new: "barriers to entry."

ANTITRUST POLICY ACCORDING TO JUSTICE BRANDEIS

In the 1918 *Chicago Board of Trade* case [27] Justice Brandeis picked up and developed the strain of policy suggested in Peckham's remark about "small dealers and worthy men." Because of his willingness to balance the interests of small producers against the interests of consumers, Brandeis was necessarily hostile to the per se rule and inclined to subjective judgments. Indeed, Brandeis's *Chicago Board of Trade* opinion is more like White's 1897 *Trans-Missouri* dissent than any other prior case. Since this strain of antitrust thinking is now so strong, the opinion of its first major spokesman is worth examining.

It is well known that a strong underlying policy orientation of Brandeis' approach was sympathy for small, perhaps inefficient, traders who might go under in fully competitive markets. His rule thus spoke for the desirability of tempering competition by private agreements. Such sympathy is, of course, an enduring strand in antitrust policy, reflecting a strong anticompetitive strain in our national social policy. But the staying power of Brandeis's approach in the presumably hostile environment of antitrust probably owes a very great deal to its lack of conceptual clarity. Brandeis was not explicit about what his approach would mean for the law generally. Its unadmitted anticompetitive elements are often difficult to isolate and identify. When they are so isolated and identified, they cannot stand scrutiny.

The *Board of Trade* case arose on the government's suit to enjoin enforcement of the price-fixing portion of the board's "call" rule. The "call" was a special session of the board held immediately after the close of each day's regular session. The regular session was taken up with spot sales and future sales (respectively, sales of grain already in Chicago in railroad cars or elevators for immediate delivery, and agreements for delivery later in the current month or in some future month). The "call" was occupied with sales "to arrive" (agreements to deliver on arrival grain which was already in transit to Chicago or was to be shipped there within a specified time). Purchases of grain "to arrive" were made not only at the "call" from members who offered it on behalf of others but also directly from country dealers and farmers; sometimes the bids were by telephone or telegraph, but most often the offers to purchase were sent out to hundreds of country dealers by the afternoon mail, subject to acceptance before 9:30 A.M. on the next business day.

For an understanding of Brandeis's performance in the case, it is crucial to understand that the "call" rule did two quite separate things. First, the rule established the trading session named the "call" in order to provide a public competitive market to supplement and partially replace the private, unorganized market that had grown up. Second, and quite distinctly, the rule also prohibited members of the board from purchasing or offering to purchase during the period between the close of the "call," usually at about 2 P.M., and the opening of the regular session at 9:30 A.M. on the next business day, any wheat, corn, oats, or rye "to arrive" at a price other than the closing bid on the "call." The result, of course, was to confine price competition to a portion of the day and to fix prices for the remaining hours.

The significance of the rule, on these facts, is certainly equivocal. Conceivably, the price agreement served some legitimate purpose; more probably, it was anticompetitive in intent and effect. Unfortunately, the government had, and persuaded the district court to adopt, a trivial theory of the case. Offering no evidence to show the purpose or effect of the price-fixing provision, the government rested upon the proposition that it later, unsuccessfully, offered to the Supreme Court as dispositive: "An agreement between men occupying a position of such strength and influence in any branch of trade to fix the prices at which they shall buy or sell during an important part of the business day is an agreement in restraint of trade within the narrowest definition of the term." [28] The district court struck from defendants' answer allegations concerning the purposes underlying the rule, and excluded much evidence on this issue. When defense witnesses testified in general terms to the benefits flowing from the rule, government counsel did not press the cross-examination to determine how the price-fixing segment of the rule and the benefits described were causally related. In fact, however, as the government's brief in the Supreme Court pointed out, most of the benefits claimed for the rule—claims that Brandeis nevertheless seemed to accept at face value—were not related to the price-fixing provision at all, but to the other aspect of the rule, the establishment of the "call" as a public market.

Brandeis, writing an opinion upholding the agreement, began his argument by rejecting "the bald proposition" of per se illegality. In a passage that has become famous, he went on to hold that it had been error for the district court to strike the allegations and exclude evidence concerning the history and purposes of the "call" rule:

. . . the legality of an agreement or regulation cannot be determined by so simple a test, as whether it restrains competition. Every agreement concerning trade, every regulation of trade, restrains. To bind, to restrain, is of their very essence. The true test of legality is whether the restraint imposed is such as merely regulates and perhaps thereby promotes competition or whether it is such as may suppress or even destroy competition. To determine that question the court must ordinarily consider the facts peculiar to the business to which the restraint is applied; its condition before and after the restraint was imposed; the nature of the restraint and its effect, actual or probable. The history of the restraint, the evil believed to exist, the reason for adopting the particular remedy, the purpose or end sought to be attained, are all relevant facts. This is not because a good intention will save an otherwise objectionable regulation or the reverse; but because knowledge of intent may help the court to interpret facts and to predict consequences.

This dictum is often quoted as the quintessential expression of the rule of reason. There is much in it that is clearly correct, and apparently it struck the rest of the Court at the time as sufficiently orthodox. Given Brandeis's apparent equation of "competition" with any business activity, so that every contract restrains competition, much of what he said was only good sense. His catalogue of relevant inquiries may be taken as no more than examples of the kind of investigations into purpose and effect of the sort White had called for in *Standard Oil* and *American Tobacco*. Such inquiries would certainly have made sense here, since the "call" rule's price-fixing aspect was neither obviously a cartel agreement nor clearly not one.

Yet there is more to Brandeis's intention than that; there is a cast to the passage that is not entirely conventional. Most significant, perhaps, is his entire omission of any suggestion that there exists any category of restraints illegal per se. Such a category follows naturally from the policy goal of consumer welfare. Restraints whose only effect can be to restrict output are per se illegal, as Peckham, Taft, and the White of 1911 had made clear. But the per se concept does not fit an approach that balances other values (e.g., the welfare of small traders) against that of consumers.

The conviction that Brandeis was advocating a deviant rule of reason, what Taft would have called a "sea of doubt" because the judge must undertake to decide how much competition is a good thing on grounds other than consumer welfare, is reinforced by the remainder of the *Board of Trade* opinion. Brandeis did an extraordinary thing. Not only did he hold that the trial judge had erred in excluding evidence of intent and effect, which should have required a remand for a new trial, but he went on to state that, even so, enough evidence had been admitted to demonstrate affirmatively the lawfulness of the regulation. That was not so. He asserted, without anything resembling adequate record support, that "the rule had no appreciable effect upon general market prices; nor did it materially affect the total volume of grain coming to Chicago." Such questions had been passed over at the trial, and there was no basis for this conclusion in the record, nor could there have been.

Brandeis went on to insist that the result of the price fixing had actually been to improve market conditions. He appears to have culled from the record, and accepted at face value, conclusionary and often ambiguous statements made by defendants' witnesses. These statements had not been tested at the trial, apparently because of the position taken by the government and the trial court that such evidence was immaterial and not an adequate defense. This makes it all the more remarkable that Brandeis should have accepted these unexamined assertions as conclusive proof of his own views. Many of the improvements in market conditions that Brandeis cited appear, if taken seriously, to have been due not to the price-fixing provision of the rule but to its establishment of the "call" as an organized, public trading session, or to other irrelevant

factors.* Worse, some of the claimed benefits are inherent in any cartelization. Thus: "It [the restraint] distributed the business in grain
'to arrive' among a far larger number of Chicago receivers and commission merchants than had been the case there before." This example
must be taken to indicate, because so offered, one of the ends that
Brandeis considered ought to help justify an agreement on prices. Yet

* ". . . within the narrow limits of its operation the rule helped to improve
market conditions thus:

"(a) It created a public market for grain 'to arrive.' Before its adoption bids
were made privately. Men had to buy and sell without adequate knowledge of
actual market conditions. This was disadvantageous to all concerned, but particularly so to country dealers and farmers.

"(b) It brought into the regular market hours of the Board sessions, more of
the trading in grain 'to arrive.'

"(c) It brought buyers and sellers into more direct relations, because on the
call they gathered together for a free and open interchange of bids and offers.

"(d) It distributed the business in grain 'to arrive' among a far larger number
of Chicago receivers and commission merchants than had been the case there
before.

"(e) It increased the number of country dealers engaging in this branch of
the business; supplied them more regularly with bids from Chicago; and also
increased the number of bids received by them from competing markets.

"(f) It eliminated risks necessarily incident to a private market, and thus
enabled country dealers to do business on a smaller margin. In that way the
rule made it possible for them to pay more to farmers without raising the price
to consumers.

"(g) It enabled country dealers to sell some grain 'to arrive' which they would
otherwise have been obliged either to ship to Chicago commission merchants or
to sell for 'future delivery.'

"(h) It enabled those grain merchants of Chicago who sell to millers and
exporters, to trade on a smaller margin and by paying more for grain or selling
it for less, to make the Chicago market more attractive for both shippers and
buyers of grain.

"(i) Incidentally it facilitated trading 'to arrive' by enabling those engaged
in these transactions to fulfill their contracts by tendering grain arriving at Chicago on any railroad, whereas formerly shipments had to be made over the
particular railroad designated by the buyer" (246 U.S. at 240–41).

This was a most unhappy performance by Justice Brandeis. Of the claimed
improvements, (a) through (h), insofar as they may be taken seriously, appear
to be entirely due to the establishment of the call as a public market rather than
to the price-fixing requirement of the call rule. Many of the cited advantages,
moreover, were plainly imaginary. There was, for example, no demonstration in
the brief record of the "fact" recited in (h) that grain merchants were able to
trade on a smaller margin and therefore paid more for grain or sold it for less.
Worse still, (i) had nothing whatever to do with the call rule in either of its
aspects but was due to a separate change in the contract form prescribed for such
transactions. It is difficult to believe that Justice Brandeis was unaware of these
matters.

every cartel tends to spread the business. Raising the rate of return always has the tendency to draw more persons into an endeavor and to
make it easier for the less efficient already there to remain. If given
operative weight, this kind of "benefit" makes the per se rule impossible. Brandeis clearly was introducing considerations of producer welfare into the law as a policy competitive with consumer welfare.

The case-by-case resolution of such conflicts is the great difficulty
in any approach that leaves conflicting policy goals in the hands of
judges. Brandeis's only indication of his solution was:

> Every Board of Trade and nearly every trade organization imposes some re-
> straint upon the conduct of business by its members. Those relating to the
> hours in which business may be done are common; and they make a special
> appeal where, as here, they tend to shorten the working day or, at least, limit
> the period of most exacting activity.

This solution seems to have been nothing more or less than judicial
subjectivism. This sort of restraint is common, we are told. But then
so are cartels, and their ubiquity would not seem enough to justify
them. The only other factor mentioned is that restraints of this tendency
"make a special appeal." Brandeis does not tell us what ends purchased by private agreement at the expense of consumer welfare might
"make a special appeal," but there is no a priori reason to limit the
class to gains in producer welfare. Later judges have not so limited it.

Milton Handler has justly suggested that Brandeis's eagerness to uphold many private regulations of competition led him to resort to consciously sophistical economic reasoning (of which *Chicago Board
of Trade* provides an example) when that seemed necessary:

> In interpreting this and other private agreements, Brandeis employed the
> same method he utilized in upholding state legislation against constitutional
> attack under the due process clause. Apparently, he implied a presumption
> of reasonableness to such agreements and required the Government to negate
> [demonstrate?] any anticompetitive purpose or effect by affirmative proof.
> As in the constitutional sphere, Brandeis buttressed the presumption by his
> ingenious ability to contrive a rational basis for the questioned arrangement.[29]

There is thus a thought-provoking contrast between Brandeis's willingness, on the one hand, to uphold state economic regulations and, on the
other, to lessen the impact of federal antitrust regulations upon private
agreements. This is not, however, a contradiction to Brandeis's philosophy of the proper role of judges vis-à-vis legislatures; he was, in
these areas at least, quite clearly an "activist" prepared to enforce his

own views of proper social policy. Any seeming anomaly disappears when it is realized that in both the due process clause cases and the antitrust cases Brandeis brought into play "his ingenious ability to contrive a rational basis" for the questioned statute or agreement in order to uphold restrictions on the operation of free markets. Brandeis was not so much a believer in competition as a believer in safety and smallness in the economic world. And, apparently, he also believed in a judge's right to force his policy views even against the tenor of a statute. These beliefs, for good or, as I think, for ill, are both prominent themes in later jurisprudence.

THE PASSAGE OF THE CLAYTON AND FEDERAL TRADE COMMISSION ACTS

With a brief analysis of the 1914 statutes our investigation of the foundations of antitrust policy will be completed. These laws entrenched one old idea and introduced two new ones that complete the roster of basic antitrust concepts. The rest of antitrust history is merely elaboration.

The reinforced older idea was, of course, that some economic practices are particularly suspect, somehow not normal, because they provide means, other than superior efficiency, by which a firm may gain or keep a monopoly position. But this notion, whose dangers have already been sketched, attained new potency because it was coupled with a second idea, the concept of incipiency. To recapitulate briefly, this consists of the theory that the anticompetitive potential of suspect practices may be discerned, and the practices stopped, well before they have actual anticompetitive consequences. The two ideas were interrelated in the preamble to the original Clayton bill, which asserted that the purpose of the legislation was

to prohibit certain trade practices which . . . singly and in themselves are not covered by the [Sherman Act] . . . and thus to arrest the creation of trusts, conspiracies and monopolies in their incipiency and before consummation.

This coupling of the ideas of suspect practices and incipiency was to have disastrous consequences for antitrust policy.

The practices specified by the Clayton Act [30] were price discrimination with intent to injure a competitor, exclusive dealing, and corporate stock acquisitions. Each of these was to be illegal "where the effect may be to substantially lessen competition or tend to create a monopoly." The incipiency theory was embedded in the superficially innocuous word "may," which has since been said by the Supreme Court to require a "reasonable probability" of a lessening of competition or tendency to monopoly. This verbal formula has proved meaningless. The fallacious economic theory employed by the courts makes the problem of forecasting the relevant economic events so intractable that there is no question of being able to estimate degrees of probability or possibility. The result has been that any imaginary threat to competition, no matter how shadowy and insubstantial, is sufficient to satisfy the "reasonable probability" test.

The third major idea of 1914 was that antitrust policy could best be developed by an administrative body that would gradually acquire an economic expertise that Congress felt itself and the federal courts to lack: hence the creation of the Federal Trade Commission by the Act of that name.[31] The Commission's mandate was contained in Section 5 of the Act, which gave it the power to order the cessation of a category of behavior identified only as "unfair methods of competition." It is difficult to say how much this idea of administrative expertise has affected the course of antitrust law. For a long time the Commission used its powers for little more than the enforcement of existing antitrust provisions, being content to follow the courts rather than lead them. This may have been due, at least in part, to the apparent disinclination of the courts to follow such leads as the Commission offered and the rather thinly disguised judicial suspicion that the Commission's expertise was more a legal fiction than a reality. Nevertheless, the Commission appears to have taken some bodies of law farther than the Antitrust Division would have, notably the law about price "discrimination" after the Robinson-Patman amendment to the Clayton Act in 1936.[32] The Federal Trade Commission has in fact proved less expert about economics and business realities, and more hostile to competition, than any other group connected with the operation of the antitrust system.

* * * *

Rather early in the history of antitrust policy, then, its intellectual foundations had been set in place. Looked at in the large, there were three main issues. The first was the conflict over the goals of antitrust

policy; this conflict was, as it remains today, not really about desirable
social policy but, first and foremost, about the proper decision-making
role of a judge in our system of government. The other two issues were
economic. The first of these was how to judge the legality of agreed
eliminations of competition. Here the law had made considerable progress in the opinions of Peckham, Taft, and White. But the second of the
economic issues was the identification of practices that injured rivals, not
as vigorous competition does, but somehow improperly. The law accepted the idea that there were such practices but found no general way
of identifying them theoretically. Had the law remained as it stood in
Standard Oil and *American Tobacco,* requiring monopoly size and other
manifestations of monopolizing intent, probably the economic theory
of predatory behavior, unsatisfactory though it was, would not have
done much harm. But the concept of incipiency added an energizing
element with unforeseen consequences. This concept empowered the
courts and the newly created Federal Trade Commission to identify practices that were believed inherently exclusionary, regardless of underlying
intent, even though the party employing them had no monopoly power.

This thrust a new and dangerously heavy burden upon the enforcement agencies and the federal courts. Competition is inherently a process in which rivals seek to exclude one another. Efficiency tends to
exclude firms that are less efficient. Since Congress was clearly not
passing the Clayton and Federal Trade Commission acts with the intent
of destroying competition and efficiency, the courts and the enforcement
agencies were necessarily given the task of distinguishing between those
exclusionary practices that were competitive, that created or reflected
efficiency, and those that were anticompetitive and not so related to
efficiency. This task was utterly beyond the economic competence of the
time, and it remains beyond the law's economic competence in our time.
Whether that is because the distinction does not exist in reality or because we have not learned to make it is a more difficult question, one
that will be taken up in several places in this book. For the moment,
the point to notice is that inability to make the distinction raises the
danger that the courts and the enforcement agencies will identify competition and efficiency as processes to be stopped in the name of preserving competition. That danger has been realized over great reaches of the
law.

2

The Goals of Antitrust: The Intentions of Congress

ANTITRUST policy cannot be made rational until we are able to give a firm answer to one question: What is the point of the law—what are its goals? Everything else follows from the answer we give. Is the antitrust judge to be guided by one value or by several? If by several, how is he to decide cases where a conflict in values arises? Only when the issue of goals has been settled is it possible to frame a coherent body of substantive rules.

Despite the obtrusive importance of this issue, the federal courts in over eighty years have never settled for long upon a definitive statement of the law's goals. Today the courts seem as far as ever from the necessary clarity of purpose. A survey of judicial opinions, not to mention the surrounding confusion of scholarly and professional commentary, is likely to leave the impression that antitrust is a cornucopia of social values, all of them rather vague and undefined but infinitely attractive.

A multiplicity of policy goals in the law seems desirable to some commentators,[1] though they do not address the question of whether the goals contradict one another and how such contradictions are to be resolved in deciding specific cases. Other commentators appear to think the question of goals essentially unsolvable, one of those ultimate value choices about which men can never be expected to agree. Thus Donald Dewey: "To criticize the courts for having the wrong antitrust goals is politics, not science." [2] These are positions I wish to dispute. The antitrust laws, as they now stand, have only one legitimate goal, and that goal can be derived as rigorously as any theorem in economics.

This chapter and the next advance a pair of related propositions:

(1) The only legitimate goal of American antitrust law is the maximization of consumer welfare; therefore,

(2) "Competition," for purposes of antitrust analysis, must be understood as a term of art signifying any state of affairs in which consumer welfare cannot be increased by judicial decree.

This chapter supports these propositions by an analysis of the legislative intention that underlies the various antitrust statutes. In the chapter following, the argument is even stronger: The responsibility of the federal courts for the integrity and virtue of law requires that they take consumer welfare as the sole value that guides antitrust decisions.

Clearly the law does employ other values, values that often conflict with consumer welfare, and occasionally, though not often, courts have been explicit about the fact. Justice Peckham suggested concern for "small dealers and worthy men" at the expense of consumers, but his opinion did not give any operative weight to that value. In *Chicago Board of Trade*, Justice Brandeis did give it operative weight. But the most articulate spokesman for the propriety of multiple values in antitrust adjudication was Judge Learned Hand. Values in conflict with consumer welfare played large and explicit roles in both his *Alcoa* and *Associated Press* opinions.

In *Alcoa* [3] the Court of Appeals for the Second Circuit judged illegal the large market position held in virgin aluminum ingot by Aluminum Company of America. In an assertion seemingly important to his argument, Judge Hand said:

We have been speaking only of the economic reasons which forbid monopoly; but . . . there are others, based upon the belief that great industrial consolidations are inherently undesirable, *regardless of their economic results*. In the debates in Congress Senator Sherman himself . . . showed that among the purposes of Congress in 1890 was a desire to put an end to great aggregations of capital because of the helplessness of the individual before them. [Emphasis added.]

Without pausing to explain, Judge Hand moved on to another formulation of the noneconomic values supposedly embedded in antitrust:

Throughout the history of these statutes [the antitrust laws, including the Sherman Act] it has been constantly assumed that one of their purposes was to perpetuate and preserve, for its own sake and *in spite of possible cost,* an organization of industry in small units which can effectively compete with each other. [Emphasis added.]

This passage was followed immediately by: "We hold 'Alcoa's' monopoly of ingot was of the kind covered by Sec. 2 [of the Sherman Act]."

Had he dealt with the case entirely in terms of consumer welfare, Hand might have had a difficult judgment to make: Alcoa had a monopoly position (on Hand's reckoning of the market), but it had maintained its size over a period of many years without merger or predation in the ingot market, so the possibility that its size was due to superior efficiency could not be discounted. The rhetoric of the social purpose of the antitrust laws saved Hand from a judgment about net effects on consumer welfare. But the rescue from such judgment was illusory, since Hand's argument does not withstand analysis.

In the first passage quoted above, Hand asserts that large market size is to be broken down regardless of cost to consumers because of the helplessness of the individual before the large firm. This helpless individual is evidently not a consumer, since his interests are said to outweigh economic results. It was essential to Hand's argument that he tell us who this individual is, at what point in firm size he begins to become helpless, and in what way he is helpless. But on these points Hand said nothing, perhaps because there is really nothing to say. Similarly, in the second passage, Hand does not tell us why effective competition is desirable, if not to get costs down for the benefit of consumers. In what sense is competition "effective" if we are not talking about effectiveness in serving consumers? How are we to know when the number of firms becomes sufficient for "effective" competition so that we can stop sacrificing consumer well-being through further dissolution? Nothing in Judge Hand's rationale provides any answer. There is, in fact, no discernible meaning to his remarks on this subject, and therefore no criteria for the prediction and decision of future cases. He seems to be asserting the right to trade off consumer welfare for unarticulated social values.

But Judge Hand went further even than this. In his *Associated Press* opinion [4] he asserted that the Fifty-first Congress had given the federal courts carte blanche to choose the values they would implement through the Sherman Act. Approaching his topic through a rapid survey of antitrust doctrine and using a cluster of trade association cases for his springboard, Judge Hand said:

. . . the injury imposed upon the public was found to outweigh the benefit to the combination, and the law forbade it. We can find no more definite guide than that.

Certainly such a function is ordinarily "legislative"; for in a legislature the conflicting interests find their respective representation, or in any event can make their political power felt, as they cannot upon a court. . . . But it is a mistake to suppose that courts are never called upon to make similar choices: i.e., to appraise and balance the value of opposed interests and to enforce their preference. The law of torts is for the most part the result of exactly that process, and the law of torts had been judge-made, especially in this very branch. Besides, even though we had more scruples than we do, we have here a legislative warrant, because Congress has incorporated into the Antitrust Acts the changing standards of the common law, and by doing so has delegated to the courts the duty of fixing the standard for each case.

The liberating potential of this judicial assumption of full legislative freedom was demonstrated as Judge Hand went on to note that Associated Press's bylaws made attainment of membership more difficult for newspapers in competition with present members; that nonmembers were disadvantaged to some extent by their inability to get Associated Press news; that the First Amendment expresses an important value in our society; and finally, that this value weighed against the Sherman Act legality of the bylaws. The method by which Judge Hand moved from First Amendment values to the illegality of the bylaws left a great deal—in fact, almost everything—to be desired. The point could have been argued the other way with equal, and probably greater, ease. Passing that, however, the important question is the propriety of the value-choosing role Judge Hand claimed on behalf of the federal judiciary. That claim is staggering in its scope, for, as described by Hand, it is the power to do everything Congress could do under the Commerce Clause in any case that falls within a conventional antitrust category.

Hand thus created an inexhaustible reservoir of major premises for courts to choose among, a warrant to do good as the judge sees the good, with no more guidance than that public injury is to be weighed against private benefit on scales that are not described, or rather are described merely as the judge's "preference." The warrant he claimed for this "ordinarily 'legislative'" function does not bear examination either, for the law of torts was not built through a process as unconfined as that, and certainly does not proceed in so liberated a fashion in these more democratic days, when the legislature is regarded as the major engine of social change. More importantly, Congress, by its use of common law terminology in the Sherman Act, most certainly did not delegate any such free value-choosing role to the courts. And if it had attempted to do so, the courts should have refused the commission.

No judge after Learned Hand openly claimed the degree of freedom he took, but that judicial reliance upon values conflicting with con-

sumer welfare has persisted is surely not in dispute. Sometimes the
preference for small producers over consumers is explicit, as in Chief
Justice Warren's *Brown Shoe* opinion;[5] more often it is implicit, the
only explanation for decisions that are otherwise incomprehensible.
Phil Neal notes, for example, that the Court in certain merger cases has
been "careful to cloak its judgment exclusively in terms of effects on
market shares but has used market definitions so plainly contrived for
the purpose of holding mergers unlawful that suspicion of motives
other than protection of competition cannot easily be suppressed."[6] Neal
suggests:

There appear to be two emerging themes in antitrust doctrine that rival competition as the central goal. . . . One is a preference for a system of industrial
organization that is fragmented as much as possible, both horizontally and
vertically. The other is a desire to protect participants in the competitive
process who are seen as somehow victimized by larger firms with which they
deal.

Fragmentation is sought as "an end in itself and not merely for the sake
of competition," while the second concept sometimes appears to be one
of "bondage" from which small businessmen who contract with larger
business units are to be freed.

These notions, which are examples of the theory of the "social and
political purposes of antitrust," are, to put the matter kindly, a jumble
of half-digested notions and mythologies. The vocabulary of the tradition is an attractive one, being, as Professors Carl Kaysen and Donald
Turner have remarked, loosely Jeffersonian.[7] Insofar as there can be said
to be a theory behind the tradition, it is that efficiency should sometimes
be curbed because of the social and political health supposedly engendered by the preservation of a sturdy, independent yeomanry in the business world. Thus, the Supreme Court attributed to Congress a policy of
protecting "viable, small, locally owned businesses" even if that resulted
in "occasional higher costs and prices."[8] Added to this is a generous
admixture of uncritical sentimentality about the "little guy"—though
why the small corporation is "littler" than a consumer no one has
troubled to explain.

The ideas are dubious on their merits. There is no persuasive evidence
that a middle-level corporate executive is socially or politically a less
desirable creature than he would be if he ran his own business. One may
be permitted to doubt, for example, that the moral fiber of Jones &
Laughlin's management would be appreciably stiffened if Ling-Temco-
Vaught had to sell its stock in the firm. Our national experience sug-

gests, in fact, that misuse of the political process, dependence upon government favor, and a marked distaste for competition are as characteristic of politically potent small-business, farm, and labor groups as they are of large corporations. Fragmentation for its own sake confers no clear gain, and it makes economic processes more costly. But the merits of such a policy are irrelevant to the argument, advanced in this and the next chapter, that in any case the policy is not properly found in the antitrust laws.

Neal describes the "bondage" strain in modern antitrust: "An increasing number of businessmen are seen [by the Court] as victims, for whom the antitrust laws should provide relief against ill-advised bargains or superior economic force." In the *Perma-Life Mufflers* case,[9] Neal states, the Court permitted recovery by "a franchised dealer who wished to take the benefits of his bargain without its burdens. There was no evidence of monopoly and no indication of how consumers might be disadvantaged. In the Court's words, 'Petitioners apparently accepted many of these restraints solely because their acquiescence was necessary to obtain an otherwise attractive business opportunity.' Still, as the Court said, 'even if [they] actually favored and supported some of the . . . restrictions, they cannot be blamed for seeking to minimize the disadvantages of the agreement once they had been forced to accept its more onerous terms as a condition of doing business.' Of course they cannot be blamed for trying," Neal remarks, "but this does not seem a wholly satisfactory explanation why the Court should permit them to succeed."

The "bondage" concept, exemplified by any number of cases that attempt to ensure the position of smaller firms in chains of distribution, and thus to reorganize at least a part of society on the basis of status rather than contract, has no ascertainable intellectual content. Manufacturers cannot engage in a policy of systematically binding their dealers to unfair arrangements. They must allow dealers at least a competitive rate of return or they will gradually lose their dealer organizations. Given that fact, it requires an extraordinarily unsophisticated sentimentality to perceive the dealer as so oppressed that the federal courts ought to rewrite his contract for him. Of course the dealer wants more; everybody does. But that is what bargaining, rather than antitrust litigation, should be about.

A variety of such themes may be discerned in antitrust case law; they may be referred to collectively as theories of social and political purposes of antitrust, to distinguish them from the proconsumer tradition of the law. No matter how they are characterized, however, they have this in common: the idea that the law properly expresses social and political purposes, purposes which should be taken into account by courts, always turns out to mean that there are some cases in which protection of inefficient firms or the subsidization of small firms should overrule considerations of efficient resource allocation through the free market. This is a tax upon consumers for the benefit of some producers—a tax levied not by Congress but by the Supreme Court of the United States. The point here is not that these ideas are dubious social policies (which they are), but rather, as our statutes now stand, that they make impossible antitrust law.

There are two general cases in which the goal of small-producer welfare conflicts with the goal of consumer welfare. The first is that in which a court permits small producers to lessen competition by cartel agreement, thereby gaining a profit above the competitive level. *Appalachian Coals* [10] appears to have been such a case. The second is the case in which a court prevents some firm or firms from achieving efficiencies, in order to protect less efficient, possibly smaller, firms. Here there is no profit above the competitive level, but consumers are denied the benefit of the efficiency. *Brown Shoe,* [11] *Proctor & Gamble,* [12] and *Von's Grocery* [13] are among the hundreds of cases like this. The law has sometimes countenanced the first result, but the strength of the rule against such cartel behavior as price fixing has made these cases relatively rare. However, the second result, judicial destruction of superior efficiency, is quite common. Both results, which arise out of admitting goals other than consumer welfare, are equally improper.

Their impropriety may be seen, first, upon consideration of Congress's presumed intent in enacting the various antitrust statutes.

THE INTENTIONS UNDERLYING THE ANTITRUST STATUTES

The problems and artificialities in attributing an "intent" to a sizable body of men are well known. We need not dwell upon them. The justification for ignoring the difficulties inherent in the very concept of legislative intention lies primarily in the fact that courts and lawyers do regularly "find," describe, and rely upon such intentions. Indeed, they must do so if law, which is never written so as to cover every specific case that could arise, is to have any coherence. The concept of legislative intent may be artificial, but it is also indispensable. Besides, the construct is not wholly arbitrary. A legislature may never address the issue of ultimate policy goals and yet write a law whose various categories and distinctions can be explained only by a particular policy. That policy may then quite legitimately be said to have been intended by the legislature, even though not a single member articulated it even to himself. A system of classifications has implications, and the legislature must be taken to intend not only what it says but also what is implied by what it does.

The language of the antitrust statutes, their legislative histories, the major structural features of antitrust law, and considerations of the scope, nature, consistency, and ease of administration of the law all indicate that the law should be guided solely by the criterion of consumer welfare.

THE LANGUAGE OF THE STATUTES

The bare language of the Sherman Act conveys little, though there are surely traces of policy in the fact, stressed by Chief Justice White in *Standard Oil*, that Section 2 outlaws not the condition of monopoly but only the process of monopolizing. A policy of rivalry for its own sake, and in spite of the costs of industrial fragmentation, would outlaw monopoly no matter how gained. The statute's focus upon the process by which monopoly is achieved suggests a different value premise, and the legislative history will make clear what that was.

The texts of the other major antitrust statutes are more enlightening. The Clayton Act of 1914 and all its subsequent amendments specify the same policy goal. Thus, Section 7, as amended in 1950, makes illegal corporate mergers only "where . . . the effect . . . may be substantially to lessen competition, or tend to create a monopoly." Section 3 employs an identical test with respect to tying arrangements, exclusive dealing contracts, and the like. Even Section 2, as amended by the Robinson-Patman Act of 1936, prohibits price discrimination only "where the effect of such discrimination may be substantially to lessen competition or tend to create a monopoly . . . or to injure, destroy, or prevent competition with any person who either grants or knowingly receives the benefit of such discrimination, or with customers of either of them." In analyzing these texts for the purpose of discerning the original congressional intent we must not unconsciously read into them the glosses that the courts and the Federal Trade Commission have placed upon them. We must stick to the words themselves as if these were newly minted statutes.

The polar models of the Clayton Act and its various amendments, therefore, are "competition" and "monopoly." Since these are models derived from economics rather than sociology or political science, this usage would seem to rule out all but economic goals. But which economic goals? Part of the confusion about goals arises from the ambiguity of the word "competition," and it is necessary to examine some of its possible meanings for their usefulness in antitrust. The fact that judges, like the rest of us, have used the word to mean very different things has resulted in the fruitless discourse of men talking past each other. There are at least five different meanings that deserve to be sorted out.*

1. "Competition" may be read as the process of rivalry. This is a natural mode of speech, because rivalry is the means by which a competitively structured industry creates and confers its benefits, and because the event that triggers the application of law is often the elimination of rivalry by merger or cartel agreement. Yet it is a loose usage and invites the further, wholly erroneous conclusion that the elimination of rivalry must always be illegal. This sort of slippage seems to have occurred, for example, in Justice Tom Clark's dissent in *White Motor:* "To admit, as does the petitioner, that competition is eliminated under its contracts is, under our cases, to admit a violation of the Sherman Act. No justification, no matter how beneficial, can save it from that interdiction." [14]

But this identification of competition with rivalry will not do for antitrust purposes. It makes rivalry an end in and of itself, no matter how many or how large the benefits flowing from the elimination of rivalry. And it is clear what those benefits are. Our society is founded upon the elimination of rivalry, since that is necessary to every integration or coordination of productive economic efforts and to the specialization of effort. No firm, no partnership, no corporation, no economic unit containing more than a single person could exist without the elimination of some kinds of rivalry between persons. Taken seriously, Justice Clark's policy would be what Justice Holmes believed to

---

* The object here is not to alter English usage. The word "competition" is properly used to mean quite different things, and indeed it is so used in this book. The purpose of the exercise here is to show that we must be careful of the meaning in the context and not allow reasoning to miscarry, as often happens, by beginning with an inappropriate meaning of the word.

be the policy of Justice Harlan in *Northern Securities,* a prescription for the complete atomization of society. That policy is unthinkable, of course, since it would call not only for general abject poverty but for the death by starvation of millions of people. We may assume the antitrust laws were not designed to place the United States in worse economic condition than Bangladesh. So long, therefore, as we continue to speak of antitrust's mission as the preservation of competition, we must be on guard against the easy and analytically disastrous identification of competition with rivalry.

2. "Competition" may be read as the absence of restraint over one person's or firm's economic activities by any other person or firm. So viewed, competition is the absence of what Neal referred to as "bondage." (This usage may have slipped into the thought patterns of lawyers because the Sherman Act was understood to be about competition and yet struck at "restraints of trade," a common-law term referring to contracts by which one man controlled the right of another to engage in a specified trade at a particular place for a given period of time.) This is not a useful definition, however, for the preservation of competition would then require the destruction of all commercial contracts and obligations. Brandeis adopted this meaning of "competition" in *Chicago Board of Trade* as a means of denying the possibility of a rule of per se illegality: ". . . the legality of an agreement or regulation cannot be determined by so simple a test, as whether it restrains competition. Every agreement concerning trade, every regulation of trade, restrains. To bind, to restrain, is of their very essence." If we wish both to speak of the law as requiring the preservation of competition and to maintain rules of per se illegality, we cannot use this definition. More fundamentally, we cannot use it because it requires either the destruction of contracts (an impossibility in anything recognizable as a society) or the introduction of some value more fundamental than the preservation of competition (a needless proliferation and complication of concepts).

3. "Competition" may be read as that state of the market "in which the individual buyer or seller does not influence the price by his purchases or sales. Alternately stated, the elasticity of supply facing any buyer is infinite, and the elasticity of demand facing any seller is infinite." [15] George Stigler, whose words these are, lists four conditions under which a competitive market will normally arise: perfect knowledge; large numbers; product homogeneity; and divisibility of output. This is an enormously useful model for economic theory, but it is utterly useless as a goal of law. The model deliberately leaves out considerations of technology (in the broadest sense) that prevent real markets from

approximating the model. For the law to move either national markets
(in such products as steel, automobiles, computers) or local markets (in
motion picture exhibition, newspapers, department stores, education)
as close as possible to the model of perfect competition (perfect knowledge could not be either required or supplied by the law) would entail
an unbelievable loss in national wealth for no particular purpose. The
economic model of perfect competition was never intended as a policy
prescription, and it is a basic, though extremely common, error to suppose that markets do not work efficiently if they depart from the
model. As we shall see, antitrust must use the model and its implications
as a guide to reasoning about actual markets, but the pure model must
never be mistaken for that "competition" we wish to preserve.

4. "Competition" may be read, in a meaning closely related to the
one just discussed, as the existence of "fragmented industries and
markets" preserved "through the protection of viable, small, locally
owned businesses." This was the meaning given the word by Chief
Justice Warren in the *Brown Shoe* case. It differs from the economist's
model of perfect competition primarily in that it lacks clarity (does
"fragmented" mean that there are so many sellers and buyers that the
elasticities of demand and supply are infinite, or something less than
that?) and in the introduction of a rather vague social value (the business units are to be "locally owned").

There are a number of objections to this definition. First, of course,
is its vagueness. "Fragmented" is a word without much content. Taking
the word literally, a market with two firms is fragmented—or, to
look at the other extreme, any merger between firms in the same market,
no matter how small, decreases fragmentation. The word has no assign-
able meaning unless we read it as a description of that number of units
which in the particular industry best serves consumers. But that is to
convert it to a consumer welfare test, which is not what the Chief
Justice had in mind. Second, "competition" in ordinary usage has
nothing to do with whether the business units are locally owned. Third,
the definition would lead, and in fact very nearly has led, the Court
to say that all horizontal mergers are illegal, which is clearly not the
statute Congress wrote. Fourth, the definition is specific to merger law
under amended Section 7 of the Clayton Act. It would not, for instance,
fit Section 3, which deals with vertical contracts, and we would be required to say that Congress meant quite different things by "competition" in the different provisions of the same statute. We would also be
required to say that the "competition" preserved by amended Section 7
is a wholly different thing from that intended by the Sherman Act; or

else read the Sherman Act, at enormous costs in national wealth and contrary to both its clear intent and years of interpretation, as requiring the fragmentation of all industries into small units that are locally owned. Aside from the presumption that Congress means the same thing by the same word in the various provisions of the same statute, having different meanings for "competition" in each statutory context would introduce intolerable complexities. The law has not arrived at one satisfactory definition of "competition." Requiring it to have two or three or four would indefinitely postpone any hope of coherence.

5. "Competition" may be read as a shorthand expression, a term of art, designating any state of affairs in which consumer welfare cannot be increased by moving to an alternative state of affairs through judicial decree. Conversely, "monopoly" and "restraint of trade" would be terms of art for situations in which consumer welfare could be so improved, and to "monopolize" or engage in "unfair competition" would be to use practices inimical to consumer welfare.

We are compelled, I think, to accept this definition of "competition" for reasons to be discussed shortly. Surely, on the face of it, this meaning is consistent with everyday speech. When we talk of the desirability of competition we ordinarily have in mind such things as low prices, innovation, choice among differing products—all things we think of as being good for consumers. Our understanding of the benefits of competition for consumers is somewhat inaccurate, but that does not affect the fact that this is usually the primary value we have in mind. Very likely this is the primary value Congress had in mind when it used the word. Moreover, because "competition" as a shorthand expression for consumer welfare enables us to employ basic economic theory, it avoids the pitfalls inherent in the other definitions surveyed. This understanding of the goal of antitrust policy accords with that of Chief Justice White's opinions in *Standard Oil* and *American Tobacco,* and as will be shown in this chapter and the next, only this reading is consistent with other indicia of congressional intent and with the requirements of the judicial function.

THE LEGISLATIVE HISTORY OF THE STATUTES

The legislative history of the Sherman Act, the oldest and most basic of the antitrust statutes, displays the clear and exclusive policy intention of promoting consumer welfare.[16] Both in the bills introduced and in the debates, there are a number of explicit statements that the purpose of the legislation was the protection of consumers. Sherman's original bill, which was the one debated and which was clearly carried forward into the redraft that became law, declared illegal two classes of "arrangements, contracts, agreements, trusts, or combinations": (1) those "made with a view, or which tend, to *prevent full and free competition*"; and (2) those "designed, or which tend, to *advance the cost to the consumer*" of articles of commerce. (Emphasis added) Many of Sherman's arguments before the Senate showed exclusive concern for consumer welfare, and he even demonstrated that he understood the inseparability of higher prices and what the modern economist would call restriction of output. In defending his bill's constitutionality he asked, wholly rhetorically, whether Congress had not the power to "protect commerce, nullify contracts that restrain commerce, turn it from its natural courses, increase the price of articles, and thereby diminish the amount of commerce?"

The rules of law foreseen in the debates—against cartel agreements, monopolistic mergers, and predatory business tactics—support the thesis. A per se rule against cartels is inconsistent with values other than consumer welfare because it permits no other value to interfere with competitive pricing. The other two rules were explained in proconsumer terms. Their significance is made even clearer by the concern, repeatedly stressed, that the law should not interfere with business efficiency. This concern was so strong, as will be shown later in this chapter, that it led Congress to agree that even complete monopoly should be lawful if it was gained and maintained only by superior efficiency. Thus, monopoly was to be legal or illegal depending upon the route by which it was reached. The route by which market size is reached determines the probable impact of that size upon consumer welfare, but it is not relevant to other values. Small producers would be as thoroughly removed by a rival on its way to monopoly through superior efficiency as by one that used mergers or predation. The noneconomic helplessness of the individual to which Judge Hand referred would, moreover, be the same regardless of the route to power taken by the monopolist. Only a consumer welfare value that, in cases of conflict, sweeps all other values before it can account for Congress's willingness to permit efficiency-based monopoly.

Congress also had a restricted view of its constitutional power in 1890. It assumed that the ends to be accomplished by an exercise of the commerce power must themselves be of a commercial nature and not attempts "to regulate the good order of society." Senator Edmunds, who proposed the final phrasing of the statute, expressed this view quite clearly. The Sherman Act was evidently designed to protect the flow of commerce and not to use commerce as a pretext for reaching other ends.

Congress recognized that it was delegating broad rule-making power to the courts, but those, such as Judge Hand, who think that delegation essentially unconfined are in error. Sherman was clear about this, not merely in his description of the common law to be enacted (a description completely at variance with Judge Hand's) but in such statements as the following: "The first section, being a remedial statute, would be construed liberally, with a view to promote its object. . . . [The courts] will distinguish between lawful combinations in aid of production and unlawful combinations to prevent competition and in restraint of trade." He could hardly have said more clearly that his statute would delegate to the courts the task of distinguishing between combinations that are lawful because they create efficiency and those that are unlawful because they restrict output. These are precisely the criteria appropriate to a consumer welfare policy.

The legislative histories of the subsequent antitrust statutes do not display the policy clarity of the Sherman Act, but there is much that points in the same direction. The original Clayton Act and the Federal Trade Commission Act were envisaged as reinforcements of the Sherman Act; they were designed to specify practices believed likely to undercut competition. These statutes were at least primarily intended to protect consumers from the exactions of monopolists. The claim of social purposes antithetical to the interests of consumers is made mainly in connection with the Robinson-Patman Act of 1936 and the amendment to Section 7 of the Clayton Act in 1950.

No doubt many of the backers of the Robinson-Patman Act were moved by an NRA-style philosophy and intended to protect independent merchants against chains and new methods of distribution. But it is not at all clear that the congressmen who voted for the bill knew that they were sacrificing consumers for the benefit of small merchants. Indeed, there is evidence—not only in the text of the law and in the structure of the statute, but also in the language of the bill's proponents—that many congressmen thought the law would serve consumers by preserving small merchants from depredations. Representative Patman claimed the bill preserved competition and was "in the interest of the consumers, wage earners, farmers, and the general welfare of the people." [17]

The Senate Judiciary Committee thought original Section 2 of the Clayton Act had been "too restrictive, in requiring a showing of general injury to competitive conditions in the line of commerce concerned;

whereas the more immediately important concern is in injury to the competitor victimized by the discrimination. Only through such injuries, in fact, can the larger general injury result, and to catch the weed in the seed will keep it from coming to flower." This is the conventional incipiency theory: protect the competitor only for the purpose of protecting competition. It may lead to disastrously anticompetitive law, but there is no reason to suppose that the senators who spoke in this way realized this or that they were not sincere in relating the statute to conventional antitrust concerns. The Senate Judiciary Committee stated its goal as

the preservation of equal opportunity to all usefully employed in the service of distribution comportably with their ability and equipment to serve the producing and consuming public with real efficiency, and the preservation to that public of its freedom from threat of monopoly or oppression in obtaining its needs and disposing of its products.

There is nothing here that suggests a preference for small merchants over consumers. Instead, the committee appeared to think their interests were coterminous in many cases. And it is important to remember that the statute requires a likelihood of injury to general competition, so that, as drafted, it would not appear to protect small merchants in any case in which there was not a threat to consumers. The House Judiciary Committee was even more careful to announce that the law would not interfere with efficiencies or harm consumers, but would protect consumers from monopoly.

We know better today. We know that in the hands of the Federal Trade Commission and the courts the act has been viciously anticompetitive, but that is not sufficient reason to impute an anticonsumer policy goal to a Congress that seems simply to have displayed a rather common form of bad economics. Nor does the argument change even if one is willing to impute some large measure of disingenuousness to many congressmen, to infer that they must have known better, that they must have realized (as Congressman Celler, to his credit, told them at the time) the law would harm consumers by protecting the inefficient. A court can hardly support a policy goal contrary to the one the congressional majority announced by insisting that the majority was really insincere. At worst, then, the policy goal of the Robinson-Patman Act is left unclear by the various statements made during the legislative history of the measure. More accurately, however, the legislative history shows predominant concern for consumers, with protection of small competitors intended only when that was a means of protecting consumers from monopoly not based on efficiency.

Amended Section 7 presents an even clearer case. Proponents of the bill discussed the alleged increase of overall concentration in the American economy, the increase in concentration in particular industries, the role of mergers in both types of concentration, the effects of big business on individuality and initiative, harm to civic responsibility, and so on, through a long catalog of the real and imagined economic and social consequences of mergers.[18] Many commentators and courts rather uncritically assume that it is the duty of the courts in some way to reflect these woolly congressional concerns in deciding particular cases. In *Brown Shoe,* in fact, the Supreme Court went so far as to attribute to Congress a decision to prefer the interests of small, locally owned businesses to the interests of consumers. But to put the matter bluntly, there simply was no such congressional decision either in the legislative history or in the text of the statute. As Donald Turner reports, there is "no credible support for the statement in *Brown Shoe* that Congress appreciated the possible efficiency cost of attempting to preserve fragmented industries and consciously resolved the competing considerations in favor of decentralization." [19] The Warren Court was enforcing its own social preferences, not Congress's.

Much of the confusion about what Congress intended probably arises from the failure to make the necessary distinction between what criteria Congress intended courts to use in applying the statute and what side effects might result from the application of the statute. It is perfectly proper to praise or support a law written in terms of effect upon competition because its enforcement will also tend to reduce smog. It is completely improper to confuse criteria and side effects by making speculations about smog the ground for applying or not applying the statute. Our concern is with the criteria intended to govern the application of the statute, and when that question was addressed, Congress phrased its intent in conventional consumer welfare terms. Thus, the House committee report:

The bill is intended to permit intervention in . . . [a series of mergers] when the effect of an acquisition may be a significant reduction in the vigor of competition, even though this effect may not be so far-reaching as to amount to a combination in restraint of trade, create a monopoly, or constitute an attempt to monopolize. Such an effect may arise in various ways: such as elimination in whole or in material part of the competitive activity of an enterprise which has been a substantial factor in competition, increase in the relative size of the enterprise making the acquisition to such a point that its advantage over its competitors threatens to be decisive, undue reduction in the number of competing enterprises, or establishment of relationships between buyers and sellers which deprive their rivals of a fair opportunity to compete.

This may be vague; it may—in fact it does—reflect poor economic understanding; but nothing about the passage suggests courts are to take into account in deciding cases any goal other than the preservation of competition in a traditional economic sense.

The legislative histories of the antitrust statutes, therefore, do not support any claim that Congress intended the courts to sacrifice consumer welfare to any other goal. The Sherman Act was clearly presented and debated as a consumer welfare prescription. The same clarity may not be present in the history of the later statutes, but consumer welfare is a major component in the debates, and there is no indication of any congressional decision to sacrifice consumer welfare in any case to any other value. The most that could be made of the legislative history of these later statutes by a determined proponent of other goals is that Congress mentioned a variety of values besides consumer welfare and apparently never recognized or discussed the possibility of a conflict of values.

THE MAJOR STRUCTURAL FEATURES
OF ANTITRUST LAW

A more certain guide to the policy intentions of Congress can be found in the major structural features that Congress built into antitrust law. The major features or distinctions of a law are drawn in accordance with policy ideas, and those of antitrust law are consistent with no policy other than an overriding concern with consumer welfare. There are five such features: the per se rule against cartels; the distinction between cartels and mergers; the distinction between mergers and internal growth; the distinction between normal methods of competition and predation; and the cost-justification defense of the Robinson-Patman Act.

THE PER SE RULE AGAINST CARTELS

The Congress that enacted the Sherman Act intended to make naked price-fixing agreements illegal per se, and the courts from the beginning have, with only occasional aberrations, faithfully adhered to that policy. A rule of per se illegality for naked agreements not to compete means that no defenses are permitted once the agreement is proved to exist.

The judge is foreclosed from considering the appeal of a shorter working day, the hardships visited by competition on small traders and worthy men, or any other value that might arguably be forwarded by the cartel. The only value that the per se rule implements is consumer welfare, since it necessarily implies a legislative decision that business units should prosper or decline, live or die, according to their abilities to meet the desires of consumers. No considerations of fragmentation or local ownership enter in, although it is clear that permitting cartels to raise prices above competitive levels would permit more firms to enter and survive. The per se rule against naked price fixing and similar agreements not to compete is the oldest and clearest of antitrust doctrines, and its existence can be explained only by a preference for consumer welfare as the exclusive goal of antitrust.

THE DISTINCTION BETWEEN CARTELS AND MERGERS

Mergers eliminate rivalry between the participating firms even more effectively than do cartels, and they are much more permanent. Yet mergers were not intended to be illegal per se either under the Sherman Act or under the more stringent standards of amended Section 7 of the Clayton Act. This difference in treatment accorded cartels and mergers has been termed "one of the most provocative anomalies in the law." [20] The disparity is provocative but it is far from anomalous. It is explainable in terms of, and only in terms of, a policy of consumer welfare. The sole difference between these two forms of the elimination of rivalry that suggests a more lenient treatment for mergers is that mergers may lead to new efficiencies while cartels, which do not integrate the productive activities of their participants, have no or at best insignificant efficiency-creating potentials. A preference for efficiency is explainable only by a proconsumer policy. A policy designed to preserve producers would reverse the law's distinction and outlaw mergers while permitting cartels.

THE DISTINCTION BETWEEN MERGERS AND INTERNAL GROWTH

In enacting the Sherman Act, Congress made it clear that merger to monopoly position was to be illegal but that growth to the same size, based upon superior efficiency, would be lawful. By tightening the merger law in amended Section 7 of the Clayton Act, Congress increased the disparity of treatment between merger and growth. This disparity cannot be explained on sociological grounds or by the helplessness of the individual before great aggregations of capital. The means by which size is gained does not affect those values. The disparity can be explained on the basis of differing presumptions about the presence of efficiency. Merger to monopolistic control of a market does not necessarily reflect the expectation of new efficiencies from the integration; the merger may have been motivated entirely by the anticipation of monopoly profits. Growth to the same size, however, demonstrates the presence of superior efficiencies. The premium thus placed upon efficiency, here as elsewhere in the structural features of the law, can rest only upon a consumer welfare policy.

THE DISTINCTION BETWEEN COMPETITION AND PREDATION

The Congress that adopted the Sherman Act also made a sharp distinction between size achieved by normal means, thought to reflect superior efficiency, and size gained by unfair practices that prevented competition.* The latter were unfair precisely because they were means of winning without attaining superior efficiency. Again, the distinction in favor of efficiency imports a consumer welfare policy.

THE ROBINSON-PATMAN ACT'S COST-JUSTIFICATION DEFENSE

The Robinson-Patman Act strikes at price discrimination that may lessen competition, but it also provides a complete defense for the seller who can prove that the price differential did no more than make allowance for differences in costs of the two transactions being compared. The fact that the courts and the Federal Trade Commission have practically emasculated this defense through interpretation does not alter the obvious congressional intention to let lower costs be reflected in lower prices even when a rival was thereby injured and competition presumptively threatened. This willingness to let efficiency have its way in the market-

---

* In the debate over the final draft of the Sherman Act, Senator Kenna asked whether it was intended that "if an individual . . . by his own skill and energy, by the propriety of his conduct generally, shall pursue his calling in such a way as to monopolize a trade, his action shall be a crime . . . ?" Senator Hoar replied that the Judiciary Committee intended to strike at monopolizing and defined it as "the sole engrossing to a man's self by means which prevent other men from engaging in competition with him. I suppose, therefore, that the courts of the United States would say . . . that a man who merely by superior skill and intelligence . . . got the whole business because nobody could do it as well as he could was not a monopolist, but that it involved something like the use of means which made it impossible for other persons to engage in fair competition . . ." (21 Cong. Rec. 3152 [1890]).

place is not only proconsumer in itself but throws new light on the rest of the statute. Congress obviously thought that many of the price differentials in existence did not reflect real economies, but rather the predatory exercise of power. Both points indicate a basic consumer welfare rationale.

THE SCOPE, NATURE, CONSISTENCY, AND EASE OF ADMINISTRATION OF THE LAW

There must surely be a canon of statutory construction holding that, other things being equal, courts should attribute to the legislature a policy intent which, because of the scope and nature of a body of law, makes that law effective in achieving its goals, renders the law internally consistent, and makes for ease of judicial administration. These considerations all favor the attribution to the antitrust laws of an exclusive goal of maximizing consumer welfare.

SCOPE

Any law will, of course, be most effective if it deals with all or most of the instances of behavior that are directly relevant to the values it seeks to implement. The antitrust laws are, for that reason, better suited to implement a policy of consumer wealth maximization than one of small-producer survival or any broad, open class of values that the courts would be free to choose under the approach suggested by Justice Brandeis and Judge Hand. Antitrust scans only certain defined categories of behavior (cartels, mergers, price discrimination, exclusive dealing contracts, and the like), and these comprise only a minor segment of the full range of private actions that may advance or impede the variety of social goals that a judge like Brandeis or Hand might find appealing. The survival of less efficient but small and locally owned business units cannot be subsidized through the antitrust laws unless the more efficient business units express their superior efficiency through price differentials or create it through merger or exclusive dealing, for example, activities that the scope of antitrust's categories fortuitously permits the court to reach. But if the survival of such small and locally owned businesses is endangered through, say, others' superior innovation, better guesses about consumer tastes, or lower but nonpredatory prices, the judge is helpless. The same thing is even more true of other suggested values, such as free speech, the creation of leisure, and so forth. These values, if they are to be served, are better served by laws whose scope is appropriate to reach the full range of situations in which a given value is affected. Thus, Congress has available and has used such legislation as tax benefits, subsidies, tariffs, and the like to promote and protect small business. Though the antitrust laws are only a haphazard and inefficient means of promoting such values, they are well suited to the policy of consumer welfare because the categories of antitrust cover all those forms of behavior that are thought to be means of injuring competition. This is another argument for interpreting antitrust laws as devoted solely to maximizing consumer welfare.

NATURE

The antitrust laws are wholly prohibitory and passive in nature, so that they are effective only to screen conduct that private parties themselves initiate. Unlike many other laws, therefore, antitrust is wholly unable to serve values that must be implemented by requiring or inducing affirmative conduct which the self-interest or capabilities of private persons do not cause or permit them to undertake. Laws that affirmatively support investment are better suited to a policy like that of the preservation of small business. It does make sense, however, to use a prohibitory law when the goal is the maximization of wealth. The destruction of national wealth through restriction of output is accomplished by affirmative private action, such as cartelization or merger, that brings all relevant conduct to the passive screen of the law. The law must be drawn to serve as a mesh that stops output-restricting behavior and permits efficiency-creating activity to pass through. In fact, when the antitrust laws are seen as keyed to the goal of wealth creation, it becomes apparent that their passive and prohibitory nature is a necessity. Affirmative wealth-creating behavior cannot generally be commanded by law. The opportunities for efficiency creation are almost as numerous as the number of business decisions made in the economy and are therefore better left to the superior numbers, information, and incentive of entrepreneurs.

INTERNAL CONSISTENCY

Many features of antitrust law do serve the goal of consumer welfare. The most obvious example is the per se rule against cartel arrangements, though others have been discussed previously. So long as the per se rule and the other distinctions mentioned remain central features of policy, a presumption of consistency within the body of the antitrust laws should lead the courts, in the absence of compelling evidence of congressional intent to the contrary, to read the other branches of antitrust in the light of the same goal.

EASE OF ADMINISTRATION

Should consistency be sought by introducing values other than consumer welfare into the law about cartels, antitrust would lose much in ease of administration and therefore in effectiveness. A law that balances other values against consumer welfare has no natural role for a per se rule, since it requires examination of the effect upon the conflicting values and a balancing process in every case. Ease of administration could be regained only by creating new per se rules along other lines, but these rules would be necessarily arbitrary. Thus, a Brandeisian court might decide that agreements to close businesses on Sundays were always lawful but that agreements on prices were always unlawful. Aside from the fact that the administrative benefits of a per se rule would have been purchased at the expense of economic rationality, the effectiveness of this rule would be limited because cartelists could take their monopoly revenues in approved rather than disapproved currency.

* * * *

The conventional indicia of legislative intent overwhelmingly support the conclusion that the antitrust laws should be interpreted as designed for the sole purpose of forwarding consumer welfare. Yet there is another, even clearer reason for reaching that conclusion. We turn to that now.

3

The Goals of Antitrust: The Responsibility of the Courts

THE goals of antitrust policy are usually discussed as though they were determined entirely by the intentions of Congress. Yet equally important is an independent, and usually overlooked, factor: the responsibility of the courts for the integrity of the law and the lawmaking process. Even in statutory fields of law, courts have obligations other than the mechanical translation of legislative will, and these obligations are particularly important with statutes as open-textured as the antitrust laws. The process of antitrust lawmaking has largely been confided to the judiciary. Ideas about legitimate judicial roles and legitimate processes therefore inevitably affect the law's substance. Thus, the process by which antitrust is made and applied determines its proper goal.

The need of the law generally is for the systematic development of normative models of judicial behavior, models which, while they cannot attain, will at least distantly approach the rigor of the descriptive models of basic economic theory. Until we have such models, criticism of the courts for having the wrong goals will generally be empty, the mere assertion of a different set of personal preferences. That is a deplorable condition, since it means that we lack valid, objective standards for evaluating and controlling judicial performance. In such circumstances, we cannot attain a "rule of law."

A normative model consists of a system of understood constraints upon the values judges may consider in particular fields of law, the sorts of choices that are proper to the judiciary, and the methods by which they may reason from values to the decision of specific cases. Antitrust, unlike many other fields of law, already possesses the rudiments of such a model, but the failure to articulate its elements and to follow its principles consistently has led to much that is wrong and even perverse in current law. Several cases provide us with the rudiments of the model we seek. After analyzing those decisions we will be in a position to articulate some of the elements of judicial responsibility that determine the proper goal of antitrust under the laws as they are now written.

THE CASE LAW

As we saw in Chapter 1, the early Sherman Act courts rejected the reasonable-price test as a means of judging the legality of cartel agreements. They did so, not on grounds of legislative intent, but because that "test" provided no discernible standards for judging. The suggested reasonable-price test was in actuality an invitation to mediate between the interest of consumers in competitive prices and the interest of producers in monopoly prices. The courts, presumably, were to choose a price somewhere in between. In framing a rule of per se illegality, the courts necessarily opted for a complete consumer welfare stance, not necessarily because they were imbued with proconsumer sentiments, but because that position provided the only available firm criterion for deciding cases. The only other firm criterion in sight, the complete legality of cartels, was ruled out because the Sherman Act was understood to be about the preservation of competition. Other cases, in the early period and later, make it clear that this judicial need for standards rested on a profound though not fully articulated philosophy about the virtues of law, virtues that rise to the level of constitutional values.

The problem of standards is raised most explicitly in the constitutional context of the void-for-vagueness doctrine, and that doctrine is discussed primarily in terms of the need to give fair warning to the citizen who must obey the law. That is, of course, a valid consideration, but there are other values implicated in that doctrine. In these cases and in the cases discussed in Chapter 1, there is also apparent a concern about the inability of courts to function without standards. There is, too, a suggestion that the need for standards is closely linked to the question of which organ of government shall make essentially political choices.

Nash v. *United States* [1] involved a challenge to the Sherman Act for unconstitutional vagueness allegedly created by the reading given the law in the *Standard Oil* and *American Tobacco* cases. According to Justice Holmes's opinion for the Court, defendants' challenge was not that there were no standards but only that "the statute contains in its definition an element of degree as to which estimates may differ, with the result that a man might find himself in prison because his honest judgment did not anticipate that of a jury of less competent men." Holmes's answer was:

But apart from the common law as to restraint of trade thus taken up by the statute [as shown by *Standard Oil* and *American Tobacco*] the law is full of instances where a man's fate depends on his estimating rightly, that is, as the jury subsequently estimates it, some matter of degree. If his judgment is wrong, not only may he incur a fine or short imprisonment, as here; he may incur the penalty of death. "An act causing death may be murder, manslaughter, or misadventure according to the degree of danger attending it" by common experience in the circumstances known to the actor.

Holmes's remark about the statute taking up the common law is likely to be misleading unless read in the light of his remark, in the paragraph preceding the passage quoted above, that *Standard Oil* and *American Tobacco* "established that only such contracts and combinations are within the act as, by reason of intent or the inherent nature of the contemplated acts, prejudice the public interests by unduly restricting competition or unduly obstructing the course of trade." This is recognition that "restraint of trade" was to be interpreted in those economic terms which Holmes in *Northern Securities* had contended were largely lacking in the common law and hence in the statute. The availability of economic theory made the law's uncertainties only matters of degree, and hence tolerable.

The constitutional difference that a consumer welfare orientation makes, by placing the standards of price theory at the disposal of the court, may be seen by comparing *Nash* with *International Harvester, Cohen,* and *Cline.* The statutes struck down in those cases all contained a kind of vagueness very similar to that inherent in the approaches of Justice Brandeis and Judge Hand to antitrust.

International Harvester Co. v. *Kentucky* [2] came in 1914, just a year after *Nash.* The Court, in an opinion also written by Holmes, held invalid under the Fourteenth Amendment's due process clause the antitrust laws of Kentucky under which defendant had been convicted, essentially, for having agreed to sell and for having sold harvesters at a price in excess of their "real value." The state courts had held that "real value" was "market value under fair competition, and under normal market conditions." The result, Holmes pointed out, was to require the defendant combination to guess what the market price would have been if the combination had not been formed and nothing else violently affecting values had occurred. He found the problem beyond human ingenuity. "The reason is not the general uncertainties of a jury trial but that the elements necessary to determine the imaginary ideal are uncertain both in nature and degree of effect to the acutest commercial mind." The decision was consistent with *Nash,* which upheld the Sherman Act. *Nash,* Holmes said, went

. . . no further than to recognize that, as with negligence, between the two extremes of the obviously illegal and the plainly lawful there is a gradual approach and that the complexity of life makes it impossible to draw a line in advance without an artificial simplification that would be unjust. The conditions are as permanent as anything human, and a great body of precedents on the civil side coupled with familiar practice make it comparatively easy for common sense to keep to what is safe.

The conditions Holmes called "as permanent as anything human" seem to be the principles of economics, and the contrast he draws is one between a law that employs those principles and common business sense to mark the degrees between competition and monopoly and a law that uses a "real-value" test for which, like a reasonable-price test, there are no standards. The Kentucky statute held invalid thus employed a test similar to White's 1897 reasonable-price test and to Brandeis's or Hand's open class of appealing values.

The 1921 decision in *United States* v. *Cohen Grocery Co.*[3] made even clearer the contrast in constitutional validity between economic criteria and subjective criteria. The Supreme Court there employed the Fifth and Sixth amendments to strike down Section 4 of the Lever Act, a federal criminal statute, which provided: "That it is hereby made unlawful for any person willfully . . . to make any unjust or unreasonable rate or charge in handling or dealing in or with any necessaries;

to conspire, combine, agree, or arrange with any other person . . . (e) to exact excessive prices for any necessaries."

Chief Justice White, who had given the rule of reason its final phrasing in the 1911 cases, wrote the opinion for the Court invalidating this provision for reasons that are applicable equally to the Brandeis approach and to his own position in *Trans-Missouri*:

Observe that the section forbids no specific or definite act. It confines the subject-matter of the investigation which it authorizes to no element essentially inhering in the transaction as to which it provides. It leaves open, therefore, the widest conceivable inquiry, the scope of which no one can foreshadow or adequately guard against. In fact, we see no reason to doubt the soundness of the observation of the court below, in its opinion, to the effect that, to attempt to enforce the section would be the exact equivalent of an effort to carry out a statute which in terms merely penalized and punished all acts detrimental to the public interest when unjust and unreasonable in the estimation of the court and jury.

The Brandeis-Hand approach to the Sherman Act, with its license for the judge to choose appealing or preferred objectives, precisely corresponds to the description of the invalid statute characterized in the passage above as penalizing "all acts detrimental to the public interest when unjust and unreasonable in the estimation of the court and jury."

The opinion in *Cline* v. *Frink Dairy Co.*,[4] written by Chief Justice Taft, held the Colorado Anti-Trust Act unconstitutionally vague because it made the lawfulness of certain conspiracies and combinations turn upon a determination of "reasonable profit." Significantly, Taft quoted at length from his own opinion in *Addyston Pipe & Steel,* showing that he saw not only policy but constitutional objections to a law that required courts to say "how much restraint of competition is in the public interest, and how much is not." The per se rule against naked price fixing appears to have been required to make the Sherman Act constitutional.

United States v. *Trenton Potteries Co.*,[5] decided before *Cline* but in the same year, added a further element to the constitutional importance of an exclusively proconsumer orientation of the law of price fixing. Justice Stone's opinion disapproved of Justice Brandeis's dictum in *Chicago Board of Trade* concerning the nature of the rule of reason. Stone rejected the reasonable-price approach both because it would place too great a burden of administration and enforcement on the government, and because

in the absence of express legislation requiring it, we should hesitate to adopt a construction making the difference between legal and illegal conduct in the field of business relations depend on so uncertain a test as whether prices are reasonable—*a determination which can be satisfactorily made only after a complete survey of our economic organization and a choice between rival philosophies.* Compare *U.S.* v. *Cohen Grocery Co.,* 255 U.S. 81; *International Harvester Co.* v. *Kentucky,* 234 U.S. 216; *Nash* v. *United States,* supra. [Emphasis added.]

The first two cases Stone cited were instances in which the Court had not merely been reluctant to adopt so uncertain a test but had declared unconstitutional federal and state statutes that did expressly require it. The "choice between rival philosophies" which Stone wished to avoid was a choice between consumer protection and degrees of producer protection. He appeared to recognize that such a choice would force gross legislative decisions onto the Court, and his citation of *Cohen* and *International Harvester* connected that objection with both the per se rule and the void-for-vagueness doctrine.

It has been suggested by Anthony Amsterdam that the void-for-vagueness doctrine has usually been employed by the Supreme Court to create an added zone of protection around certain Bill of Rights freedoms.[6] *International Harvester* and *Cohen* are, under this view, reduced in large part to the status of historical curiosities left over from "an era when economic laissez faire was for the Court the sanctum sanctorum that free speech has become today." Since economic freedom is not noticeably a sanctum sanctorum for the modern Court, this theory may be read too broadly to mean that uncertainty in an antitrust statute, even a criminal antitrust statute such as the Sherman Act, would not today cause great concern, and, therefore, that Brandeis's rule of reason might now be acceptable. However, the Court's 1963 decision in *United States* v. *National Dairy Products Corp.*[7] indicates that this is not the case, and that the Court continues to refuse to tolerate lack of standards, when it recognizes the problem, even in an economic regulation.

The district court in *National Dairy* had dismissed an indictment laid under Section 3 of the Robinson-Patman Act, which makes it a crime to sell goods at "unreasonably low prices for the purpose of destroying competition or eliminating a competitor," on the ground that the statute was unconstitutionally vague and indefinite. A majority of the Supreme Court reversed, but read the statute to prohibit sales below cost made with a predatory intent. This was the familiar judicial device—an alternative to a declaration of unconstitutional vagueness—of gaining the necessary statutory certainty through interpretation.

The *National Dairy* opinion distinguished *Cohen* because neither the statute nor the indictment there specified a definite act that was prohibited, and, moreover, the standard held too vague in *Cohen* was without a meaningful referent in business practice or usage. . . . In view of the business practices against which § 3 was unmistakably directed and the specificity of the violations charged in the indictment here, both absent in *Cohen,* the proferred analogy to that case must be rejected.

Justice Clark's opinion for the majority, while it does not bear out the idea that *International Harvester, Cohen,* and *Cline* can be relegated to the historical ashpile, does suggest that vagueness problems may be approached differently in cases involving economic regulation and those involving First Amendment problems. In the latter, he said, the Court is

concerned with the vagueness of the statute "on its face" because such vagueness may in itself deter constitutionally protected and socially desirable conduct. . . . No such factor is present here where the statute is directed only at conduct designed to destroy competition, activity which is neither constitutionally protected nor socially desirable.

Put in terms of the danger of deterring socially desirable conduct, this distinction between statutes aimed at proscribable speech and at predatory pricing does not seem tenable. Just as protected speech lies next to that which may be outlawed, so does vigorous price competition adjoin that which goes too far and is predatory. It is not socially desirable that conduct in either of the two adjacent areas be deterred.

The constitutional importance of economic theory, however, is once more shown by Justice Clark's suggestion that a "meaningful referrent in business practice or usage" existed for Section 3 of the Robinson-Patman Act but not for the Lever Act. The distinction seems to rest on the assumption that there is an economic theory which distinguishes predatory price cutting from other kinds of price cutting, but none which distinguishes unreasonable from reasonable rates. Whether such price theory is correct (a matter we shall have reason to doubt) is irrelevant to the main point: the Court thought it was correct and relied upon it to lend the law the required criteria.

The Court's method of narrowing Section 3 of the Robinson-Patman Act as applied in the particular case may not be a wholly satisfactory solution to the vagueness of that statute, but it demonstrates the continuance of real concern over the problem of vagueness even when the freedoms at stake are economic. This suggests that it is not entirely the quality of the freedom that impels the Court, but also the problem of vagueness itself. The point is emphasized by the fact that Justice Black, dissenting in an opinion in which Justices Stewart and Goldberg joined —a group that cannot be described as committed to economic laissez faire as a constitutional value—contended that Section 3 of the Robinson-Patman Act was flatly unconstitutional under the rule established in *Cohen.*

We may now restate the problem of antitrust goals and then review the reasons why the responsibility of the courts for the integrity of the law requires adherence to the exclusive goal of consumer satisfaction.

THE NATURE OF THE PROBLEM

The problem may be stated as one of determining which types of trade-off decisions belong in legislatures and which in courts. Trade-offs, the sacrifice of one thing to gain another, are involved in the formulation of every legal rule; they cannot be avoided. An antitrust law devoted entirely to consumer welfare faces severe trade-off problems. There are many situations in which the destruction of monopoly power necessarily involves a sacrifice of business efficiency, and the task of economic analysis is to inform the court whether the gain or the loss is likely to be greater. The important point here is that the ultimate goal of consumer welfare provides a common denominator by which gains in destruction of monopoly power can be estimated against losses in efficiency, and economic theory provides the means of assessing the probable sizes of the gains and losses.

That is not true when the trade-off is one between values, such as the decision of how much consumer welfare is to be sacrificed for what amount of additional wealth for small dealers and worthy men, or for what degree of industrial fragmentation, or for what number of additional sources of news. The case law provides no guide whatever for judging such trade-offs. There is no common denominator between these values, and there is no economics, no social science, no systematized knowledge of any sort that can provide the criteria for making the trade-off decision. This is not to say that such decisions need not be made, or even that courts must never make them. Value trade-offs must be made, and to refuse to deal with them is to make the choice of letting the status quo decide the trade-off.

In constitutional law the trade-off choice is given to courts, but in areas where the legislature is not forbidden to make the choice, we think of such value trade-offs as the very essence of politics. We then typically reserve the choice for legislative determination and require the terms of the treaty—between rival interests, between manufacturers and consumers, laborers and consumers, farmers and consumers, or high-income groups and low-income groups—to be written down, with the resultant of the value trade-offs specified in tariff statutes, labor-management relations laws, farm programs, and internal revenue codes. Value trade-offs in antitrust litigation are of the same nature. The problem of a trade-off between consumer and producer welfare illustrates the point, but the analysis is the same no matter what value is weighed against consumer welfare.

Antitrust has attempted to deal with the consumer-producer welfare trade-off in two types of situations that are the same in principle. The classic case is the agreement by rivals to fix prices. When this case is brought before a court for a determination of legality, there is a head-on conflict between consumer and producer interests. Consumers would prefer a competitive price, i.e., a decision that the price-fixing agreement is illegal per se. Producers would prefer a monopoly price, i.e., a decision that they may agree upon any price they choose. The court can obtain a clear rule for decision making by choosing to be guided entirely by either group's welfare, though to choose producer welfare as the sole guide is forbidden by the entire thrust of the antitrust laws. But if the court attempts to give weight to both values, to arbitrate a price between the competitive and the monopolistic, it will find that there are no criteria whatever to guide its decision. By deciding what price the cartel may charge, the court decides how much each of the two groups "deserves" at the expense of the other. The judge can relate the decision to nothing more objective than his own sympathies or political views.

The problem differs in detail but not in principle in merger cases such as *Brown Shoe,* where the Supreme Court's objection was that the creation of new efficiencies threatened some rivals with a diminution of their market shares or, possibly, with extinction. The Court has not chosen to ignore the benefits of efficiency completely, or it would tolerate no mergers at all. Here the consumer interest favors the merger and the efficiency, as does the interest of the merged firms; the interest of other producers, at least those not capable of achieving similar efficiencies, is in having the merger declared illegal and dissolved. There is no danger of monopoly profit, but the opposition of interest groups is the same as in the price-fixing case, and there are again no objective criteria for striking a balance between them. Striking the balance is essentially a legislative task.

CONSUMER WELFARE AS AN
EXCLUSIVE GOAL

Stating the nature of the problem that arises when antitrust adjudication attempts to reconcile inconsistent values on a case-by-case basis should be enough to indicate the impropriety of courts undertaking such a function. Nevertheless, a multiple-goal antitrust law appears so attractive to many people that it may be worthwhile to suggest some of the ways in which the single goal of consumer welfare is superior. Exclusive adherence to a consumer welfare goal is superior in that it (1) gives fair warning, (2) places intensely political and legislative decisions in Congress instead of the courts, (3) maintains the integrity of the legislative process, (4) requires real rather than unreal economic distinctions, and (5) avoids arbitrary or anticonsumer rules. A multiple-goal approach can achieve none of these things.

FAIR WARNING

Looked at from the standpoint of those who must obey the law, the case for exclusive adherence to a consumer welfare standard is clear. That was a major basis of the cases establishing the per se rule for price-fixing, and of the void-for-vagueness cases we have just reviewed. No businessman can know what the law is if the "law" depends upon the sympathies and prejudices of any one of the hundreds of federal judges before whom he may find himself arraigned at some uncertain date in the future. He can know what the law is when the goal of the law is consumer welfare, because the major distinctions of such a system run along the same lines in which the businessman thinks, making lawful his attempts to be more efficient and making unlawful his attempts to remove rivalry through such improper means as cartelization, monopolistic merger, and deliberate predation. A consumer welfare goal, moreover, lends itself to relatively few and simple rules of substantive law, so that predictability is further enhanced. (This point is shown by the conclusions of this book.) Finally, a consumer welfare orientation makes change in the law predictable and less likely to produce unfairness.

A court attempting to apply the economic criteria appropriate to consumer welfare may, of course, make mistakes. It may, for example, erroneously approve a disguised cartel, as the Court may have done in *Chicago Board of Trade*. Yet if the basic objective of the law is kept clearly before the public and the legal profession by repetition and use in opinions, the mistaken precedent may be overturned with minimal unfairness. Persons who make such agreements in the future may be presumed to know the actual motivation of their own behavior, and their reliance, therefore, can only be upon the continuing erroneous application of known principles. Brandeis's version of the rule of reason, on the other hand, seems to have greater rigidity built into its doctrines. Producers would be invited to rely upon decisions that certain forms of monopoly income (e.g., leisure) are "appealing" in and of themselves. Later courts might find the attractive qualities of cartelization less apparent, but they would also feel less free to correct the law because it could not truthfully be said that persons who had relied on the prior case should have known it was unreliable as precedent and therefore had warning of the possibility of change.

LEGISLATIVE AND JUDICIAL ROLES

Alexander Bickel perceived another constitutional value at work in the void-for-vagueness cases:

. . . when the Court finds a statute unduly vague, it withholds adjudication of the substantive issue in order to set in motion the process of legislative decision. It does not hold that the legislature may not *do* whatever it is that is complained of but, rather, asks that the *legislature* do it, if it is to be done at all.[8]

This reflects a recognition that some kinds of determinations are appropriate *only* for the legislature, just as other kinds, particularly those arising out of the Constitution, are reserved for final determination by the courts. Our present antitrust laws do not contain any legislative determination that consumer welfare is to be sacrificed in any case to any other value, and they most certainly do not contain a decision of the degree of sacrifice or the circumstances under which it is to occur. With the law in this posture, it is utterly improper for courts to take on the task of adjusting the rewards to be allocated to consumers and those to be allocated to other groups. The degree of the impropriety of that process can be appreciated all the more if one realizes that it would be wrong for the courts to undertake it even if the Congress had in fact attempted to delegate it. We have seen this already in the void-for-vagueness cases in which Congress and state legislatures did attempt to delegate just such a function and the Supreme Court refused the task.

Some analogies may make the point clearer. Consider three other policy decisions with which we are familiar: the imposition of tariffs upon imported goods in order to protect domestic manufacturers at the expense of consumers; the encouragement of labor union formation to enhance the gains of some workers at the expense of consumers; and the collection of income taxes at progressive rates in order to benefit some income groups at the expense of others. Imagine the response of the Supreme Court if Congress enacted statutes explicitly delegating to federal judiciary the task of deciding: which imports should bear duties and in what amounts; which workers should be permitted to unionize and bargain collectively, and what tactics they might lawfully employ; and what rates of progression, if any, should be applied in the federal income tax. Surely the Court would, and clearly it should, announce that these were matters not suited for judicial determination, that Congress cannot delegate to the judiciary the basic political decisions of the society.

For some time, as a matter of fact, the federal courts, not perceiving the basic incongruity of the attempt, did try to govern labor-management relations through the Sherman Act. The incongruity lay in the attempt to permit labor unions as cartels fixing the price of labor but to regulate their behavior. This was identical with a decision to permit cartelization but to require that the cartel charge only "reasonable" prices, a course the Court refused to take in nonlabor cases. The result, in the antitrust labor cases, as we all know, was an incoherent body of law, and Congress and the Court both came to recognize the unsuitability of the judiciary for the task.[9]

Courts are the wrong institution for these unstructured interpersonal comparisons both because political choices of this nature should, in a society with our presuppositions about democracy, be made by elected and representative institutions, and because the courts do not have the facilities for fact-finding on a broad scale that are available to the legislature. The admission by a court of goals in conflict with consumer welfare into the adjudicative process, therefore, involves a serious usurpation of the legislative function by the judicial arm.

INTEGRITY OF THE LEGISLATIVE PROCESS

Courts that refuse to make basic policy choices for the legislature thereby force the legislature to face and decide questions they had previously been content to leave unanswered. In this way the courts help focus the issues to be addressed and make the legislative process more responsible. There are, of course, a variety of techniques, of which a declaration of void for vagueness is but one, by which courts engage the legislature in dialogues of this sort. One of the most useful is the ascription of legislative intent. In antitrust this purpose is best served by ascribing to Congress a consumer welfare goal in each of the antitrust statutes. It is sometimes suggested that the Supreme Court's anticonsumer interpretation of certain statutes, most notably amended Section 7 of the Clayton Act and Section 2 of the Robinson-Patman Act, is justified because, despite their textual demands for competition, they were really intended to protect small business from competition. It is maintained that the Court is rightly giving effect to an aura somehow seen as surrounding a law that on its face is proconsumer. There is in this view more than a suggestion of political manipulation by the courts. It is an assertion that Congress wanted to enact an anticonsumer policy but did not care to pay the political costs of making its choice explicit, and that the federal courts should assist Congress in this dubious enterprise by ignoring the straight-faced statutory command and enforcing the discreet congressional wink. Yet the purpose of a wink is to convey the opposite of one's words and thus to deceive a third party who hears only what is said. The third party to the dialogue between Congress and the federal courts is, of course, the electorate, and surely no argument can be accepted as respectable that assigns to the courts the role of assisting in a deception of this nature.

In any case, a more realistic version of Congress's performance in enacting statutes such as these is that few if any congressmen ever focused upon the possibility of a conflict between consumer and small business interests. It is impossible to say that, had Congress been forced to face that choice, it would have abandoned the mainstream of antitrust tradition for a protectionist stance. When statutes are clothed in the political symbols of consumer welfare, and when there are other good reasons to think that value basic to antitrust, the courts can best focus the issues for congressional determination by adhering to the consumer welfare goal in their application of the statutes. If Congress really wants different results, it can then face the issue openly and phrase its law in words that make the political decision and its costs apparent, not only to the courts but also to the electorate and to the legislators themselves.

AVOIDANCE OF UNREAL DISTINCTIONS

The policy of consumer welfare provides courts with the principles of basic price theory as their criteria for decision. This is not to suggest that all decisions will be automatic or easy. In some cases, the practice or market structure under examination will lie somewhere on a continuum between efficiency and restriction of output, and it will not be clear which is the more probable effect. But this sort of uncertainty is familiar to courts and inevitable whenever questions of degree arise. The choice involves an estimate; it differs fundamentally from a choice between opposing values that have no common denominator. In such cases, no common goal calibrates the continuum for the guidance of judgment. Where the common denominator of consumer welfare is abandoned, an antitrust court that attempts to avoid the appearance of complete subjectivism, that tries to explain its decision, will be driven to distinctions without any reality.

This process is illustrated by Justice Brandeis' opinion in *Chicago Board of Trade*. In that case, it will be recalled, Justice Brandeis approved an agreement fixing prices overnight on purchases of grain "to arrive" because, among other things, it spread the business to more firms and its limitation on the hours of active business activity was "appealing." Neither of these reasons distinguishes the agreement from any cartel agreement on prices. By eliminating rivalry and raising the rate of return, all naked price fixing tends to spread the business, since more firms can survive and more will find it profitable to enter the market.

The distinction in terms of "appealing" purposes, such as the creation of leisure, fares no better. Leisure and money are merely different forms of income for producers and different forms of payment by consumers. When they are obtained by agreed restrictions of output, there is no valid means of distinguishing between them. An example may make the point clear. It is, presumably, more likely that a judge in the Brandeis tradition would uphold an agreement by automobile dealers to close on Sundays than an agreement by the same dealers to add $200 to the price of each car. Yet there is no difference between the cases. Both are limitations upon competition whose sole purpose is to increase the dealers' income by restricting output. The output in one case is the number of cars sold (which will decrease with the raised price); the output in the other case is the provision of convenience of shopping to consumers (which will decrease with the Sunday closing). The identity is shown further by the ability of the dealers to switch the results of the two agreements. Auto dealers with Sundays off can work elsewhere on those days, converting leisure to money; and dealers with higher prices and profits can work fewer hours, converting money to leisure. The Brandeisian distinction between the two forms of agreement rests upon unanalyzed (and by no means universal) psychological associations relating to leisure and money. A court that takes the distinction seriously ought to decide the automobile dealer cases only after a trial of the issue of whether the free Sundays were used for laudable or for vicious purposes, and whether the increased income was given to charity and spent on the children's education or squandered in nightclubs. Aside from this sort of test, which we are unlikely to follow logically in the antitrust laws or to entrust to courts, there is no valid economic distinction on the producer side between any cartel and the agreement Justice Brandeis found attractive.

From the consumers' point of view such agreements are also indistinguishable. Consumers who lose the convenience of shopping on Sunday are deprived of something that is as much an economic good as is money. There is no acceptable way for a judge to decide that a restriction in the offering of a convenience is any less objectionable than a restriction in the number of automobiles sold.

Nor are the distinctions any more real when a judge, following Chief Justice Warren, disallows a merger because it may create efficiencies that threaten less efficient rivals. The increased output that would have resulted from improved efficiency and lower costs is prevented from occurring, and consumers are taxed by the court to that extent. Though there may be no monopoly profit, as there is in the cartel case, the result is the same. Some producers (the less efficient ones) make higher profits than they would otherwise, and consumers have fewer of their wants satisfied. There is, therefore, no valid distinction between outlawing a merger because of its efficiencies and permitting a cartel. Yet the present Court does one and not the other. The distinction is entirely subjective; it does not correspond to any real or significant difference between the phenomena.

AVOIDANCE OF ARBITRARY OR ANTICONSUMER RULES

It is, as a matter of fact, quite unlikely that courts which admit into the adjudicative process goals in conflict with consumer welfare will engage in balancing, in case-by-case compromises between the values. They are much more likely to arrive at rigid rules which will either be arbitrary or completely anticonsumer.

The judicial need for standards appears to be basic and intrinsic. It seems to go deeper even than the constitutional requirement of fair warning, and to rest upon something either in the nature of courts or so deeply embedded in tradition that it amounts to the same thing. This is suggested in a variety of legal contexts and may be illustrated both by the historical progression of the Supreme Court's treatment of the problem of legislative reapportionment and by the Court's development of merger law under amended Section 7 of the Clayton Act.

A major element in the opposition of some members of the Supreme Court to that institution's entry into the field of legislative apportionment was the inherent lack of

accepted legal standards or criteria or even reliable analogies to draw upon for making judicial judgments. To charge courts with the task of accommodating the incommensurable factors of policy . . . is to attribute, however flatteringly, omnicompetence to judges.[10]

Justice Frankfurter repeated "the caution not to undertake decisions where standards meet for judicial judgment are lacking."

It seems significant that when the Court did undertake the reapportionment of state legislatures it moved speedily to the only firm criterion available—"one person, one vote"—which had the overwhelming virtue, despite considerable defects as history or as political or constitutional theory, of seeming to be at least a standard, and the only standard available.[11] That the Court subsequently allowed larger deviations from the rule of absolute equality in state legislative reapportionments, though not in congressional districting, does not alter the point that an essentially arbitrary standard was chosen because it *was* a standard.

The subjective approaches of Brandeis and Hand lack "standards meet for judicial judgment." Therefore, it is to be expected that the explicit, full-scale adoption of such approaches would create uncertainties that the courts would not long tolerate. The progression of the legislative reapportionment cases suggests that a conscious adoption by the courts in cartelization cases of the Brandeis or Hand rule of reason would shortly be followed by the evolution of arbitrary rules concerning the purposes for which cartelization is allowable.

Something very much like that has happened in other fields of antitrust. Area after area has been taken over by harsh rules, and sometimes, as in the law of requirements contracts, the Court has pointed to the need for certainty as justifying a rigid rule that was, admittedly, not the best resolution of the economic considerations.[12] Merger law under amended Section 7 of the Clayton Act was set upon its course by the *Brown Shoe* decision, which admitted the value of small-business welfare into the adjudicative process. The result has been, not a process of balancing inconsistent goals from cases to case, but something like the abandonment of consumer welfare as a goal at all. Disregarding the value of efficiency, a majority of the Court for a long time struck down every merger that came before it. Subsequent decisions allowing some mergers have by no means repaired the damage. The result is a merger law that deserves to be called an antitrust statute about as much as the Smoot-Hawley tariff did.

The Supreme Court has thus achieved firm, manageable standards in both the price-fixing and merger fields. (That one is justified and that the other is not is beside the point presently being made.) It remains to be seen whether it can tolerate indefinitely the complete policy inconsistency between the two sets of rules.

* * * *

Though the courts have not satisfactorily handled the question of antitrust's goal, neither have they uniformly overlooked it or the issues that underlie it. From time to time the Supreme Court has handled the problem very well. Aside from the cases rejecting the reasonable-price test discussed in Chapter 1, it is well to remember that Chief Justice White in framing the modern rule of reason in the *Standard Oil* decision stated the Sherman Act's purpose to be entirely one of preventing restriction of output—and that is one way of stating a consumer welfare goal. And Judge Taft, in *Addyston Pipe & Steel,* clearly chose a proconsumer goal because of the need for judicial standards. Much later, in *Apex Hosiery Co.* v. *Leader,*[13] Justice Stone analyzed the legislative history of the Sherman Act and concluded:

The end sought was the prevention of restraints to free competition in business and commercial transactions which tended to restrict production, raise prices or otherwise control the market to the detriment of purchasers or consumers of goods and services, all of which had come to be regarded as a special form of public injury.

And, in a constitutional case, *Wickard* v. *Filburn,*[14] Justice Jackson perceived the basic point argued in this chapter:

The conflicts of economic interest between the regulated and those who advantage by it are wisely left under our system to resolution by Congress under its more flexible and responsible legislative process. Such conflicts rarely lend themselves to judicial determination.

Whether one looks at the texts of the antitrust statutes, the legislative intent behind them, or the requirements of proper judicial behavior, therefore, the case is overwhelming for judicial adherence to the single goal of consumer welfare in the interpretation of the antitrust laws. Only that goal is consistent with congressional intent, and, equally important, only that goal permits courts to behave responsibly and to achieve the virtues appropriate to law.

4

Business Behavior and the Consumer Interest: Some Rudiments of Theory

ANTITRUST is about the effects of business behavior on consumers. An understanding of the relationship of that behavior to consumer well-being can be gained only through basic economic theory. The economic models involved are essential to all antitrust analysis, but they are simple and require no previous acquaintance with economics to be comprehended. Indeed, since we can hardly expect legislators, judges, and lawyers to be sophisticated economists as well, it is only the fact that the simple ideas of economics are powerful and entirely adequate to this field that makes it conceivable for the law to frame and implement useful policy.

Consumer welfare is greatest when society's economic resources are allocated so that consumers are able to satisfy their wants as fully as technological constraints permit. Consumer welfare, in this sense, is merely another term for the wealth of the nation. Antitrust thus has a built-in preference for material prosperity, but it has nothing to say about the ways prosperity is distributed or used. Those are matters for other laws. Consumer welfare, as the term is used in antitrust, has no sumptuary or ethical component, but permits consumers to define by their expression of wants in the marketplace what things they regard as wealth. Antitrust litigation is not a process for deciding who should be rich or poor, nor can it decide how much wealth should be expended to reduce pollution or undertake to mitigate the anguish of the cross-country skier at the desecration wrought by snowmobiles. It can only increase collective wealth by requiring that any lawful products, whether skis or snowmobiles, be produced and sold under conditions most favorable to consumers.

The role of the antitrust laws, then, lies at that stage of the economic process in which production and distribution of goods and services are organized in accordance with the scale of values that consumers choose by their relative willingness to purchase. The law's mission is to preserve, improve, and reinforce the powerful economic mechanisms that compel businesses to respond to consumers. "From a social point of view," as Frank H. Knight puts it, "this process may be viewed under two aspects, (a) the assignment or *allocation* of the available productive forces and materials among the various lines of industry, and (b) the effective *coordination* of the various means of production in each industry into such groupings as will produce the greatest result." [1]

These two factors may conveniently be called *allocative efficiency* and *productive efficiency*.* (When, for convenience, the word "efficiency" alone is used, productive efficiency is meant.) These two types of efficiency make up the overall efficiency that determines the level of our society's wealth, or consumer welfare. The whole task of antitrust can be summed up as the effort to improve allocative efficiency without impairing productive efficiency so greatly as to produce either no gain or a net loss in consumer welfare. That task must be guided by basic economic analysis, otherwise the law acts blindly upon forces it does not understand and produces results it does not intend.

THE NATURE OF ALLOCATIVE EFFICIENCY

Both economics and law generally link business behavior to consumer welfare through the concepts of "competition" and "monopoly." But the two disciplines mean quite different things by those terms, and when the differences go unremarked—or, worse, when various common-speech

---

* It is important that the distinction be very clear. Allocative efficiency, as used here, refers to the placement of resources in the economy, the question of whether resources are employed in tasks where consumers value their output most. Productive efficiency refers to the effective use of resources by particular firms. The idea of effective use, as we shall see, encompasses much more than mere technical or plant-level efficiency.

meanings are inserted without notice—debate grows more and more
heated and less and less illuminating. The economist's models of competition and monopoly are descriptive. The lawyer's, if he thinks of
antitrust as designed to preserve competition and destroy monopoly,
must be normative. There is a wide gap in practical consequences. The
economist builds a pure model in order to clarify thought; such models
are indispensable starting places for policy analysis, but they are not
prescriptions for policy. They leave out too much. A determined attempt to remake the American economy into a replica of the textbook
model of competition would have roughly the same effect on national
wealth as several dozen strategically placed nuclear explosions. To say
that is not to denigrate the models but to warn against their misuse.

An understanding of the efficient allocation of resources, and hence
of the evils of misallocation, is best attained through simple models
of firm behavior under differing market structures. I will sketch the most
basic aspects of the conventional theories of competition, monopoly, and
oligopoly. Each of these terms describes an industry structure. Economic theory attempts to relate structure to performance, and performance to the goal of consumer welfare. The theories are listed in de-
scending order of rigor. The theory of competition states the way in
which firms *must* behave if they are to survive when the market is competitively structured. The theory of monopoly states the way in which a
firm possessing control of a market *can* behave in order to maximize
profits. Conventional oligopoly theory, however, is little more than a
guess about the ways in which firms might be able to behave in a market
composed of a few sellers.

COMPETITION

The operation of pure competition may be illustrated by an imaginary
widget industry (widgets are the customary product of hypothetical
industries) composed of 100 firms of equal size making a uniform
product, which is sold to 1,000 well-informed purchasers. Under these
conditions—as under a wide range of conditions we need not stop
to argue about now—no company would have power significantly to
affect the market price for widgets because both its output and the
variations in its output would be trivial with respect to total industry
output. The demand for the output of any individual manufacturer
would then be perfectly elastic, which is just a way of saying that any
manufacturer who quoted a price above the prevailing market price
would make zero sales, since every purchaser would turn to another

supplier. Any manufacturer who quoted a price below market would be offered all the business, but for reasons that will become apparent, he would not want it and could not afford to take it.

The demand faced by the individual manufacturer in a completely competitive industry is reflected in Figure 1 by a price line drawn flat to indicate that he will face the same market price no matter how he adjusts his own rate of output. Another way of saying this is that in a completely competitive industry the individual firm's marginal revenue (the revenue added by selling one more unit) is always the same as the market price. This is an extreme statement, since it may be that all sellers can affect market price somewhat, but it is conventional to ignore very small effects and to draw the individual firm's demand curve flat in fragmented markets.

Our hypothetical widget manufacturer also lacks short-run control over the costs of making his product. Costs are presented to him as brute facts of life in the prices of labor, raw materials, machinery, electricity, and so forth. His existing method of coordinating these factors of production determines his costs, and he cannot alter costs until he finds a better method of coordination, that is, a better method of production or distribution. He does, however, have power to affect one species of costs, those that vary with his rate of output. By changing his rate of output he can change his marginal cost (the cost, starting at any specified rate of output, of producing one more widget in the period of time under discussion). Thus, if he is producing 5,000 widgets per week, his marginal cost is the additional cost he would incur by increasing the rate to 5,001. This is important to the manufacturer, for though he cannot change market price or basic cost determinants, he can alter his rate of output and so choose the marginal cost associated with the new rate.

The manufacturer may or may not be completely aware of these facts, but in adjusting his rate of output until he arrives at the profit-maximizing solution, he will, whether he thinks of it that way or not, be working up and down his marginal cost curve.* The profit-maximizing

---

* Costs are, of course, affected by factors other than the rate of output. Absolute volume of output has important effects. See Armen A. Alchian, "Costs and Outputs," in *The Allocation of Economic Resources,* by Moses Abramovitz et al. (Stanford University Press, 1959). Increasing the rate of output tends to increase costs, while an increase of absolute volume, without an increase in rate, tends to decrease costs. Such complications are not, however, essential at the moment. The important fact is that marginal costs do rise at some point and that the firm operates at a point where they are rising. It is convenient here to speak of output rate as the determining factor, though the existence of other factors will become relevant in particular contexts.

solution may be described for all sellers, whether competitiors or monopolists, as the rate of output at which marginal cost is equal to marginal
revenue. For the competitor alone, however, marginal revenue is equal
to market price.

That profits are maximized by equating marginal cost and marginal
revenue (or price) is simply shown: if the firm produces one more
widget, the marginal cost will be greater than the marginal revenue
and the extra widget is sold at a loss; if it produces one less, marginal
cost is less than marginal revenue, and the firm is failing to pick up
profitable business. (Marginal cost includes normal return, so there is a
profit when marginal cost equals marginal revenue.) In the explanation
that follows, the distinction between the state of affairs in the short
run and in the long run is not made, both because it is unnecessary
to the analysis and because, given the dynamism of the market process,
it is quite unlikely that the long-run result of the textbooks is often
approached.

Let us assume that the individual widget manufacturer equates marginal costs and marginal revenue (price) at an output of 250,000 units
per year, and that market price is $30 per widget. The firm's position
may then be represented as in Figure 1. The graph makes it easy to see
why marginal costs are always rising at the rate of output chosen by any

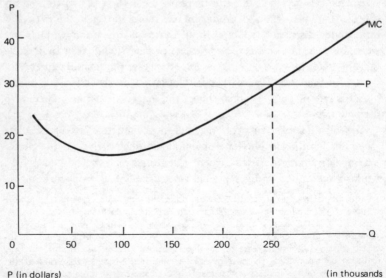

P (in dollars)   (in thousands
                                                         per year)

Figure 1.   The situation of the firm under pure competition.

competitive firm. We infer a rising cost curve from the existence of more than one firm, since if marginal costs were level or declining, the firm would continually increase its rate of output until it occupied the entire industry.

All of this has a clarity and precision that is spurious in one sense and quite real and useful in another. The clarity and precision are spurious if one is so misled as to conclude that the widget maker has a chart like this on the wall and has only to read off the correct output to earn his profit for the week. He has no such exact information and cannot, for a variety of reasons, including the imprecise nature of cost information and constant changes in both costs and demand. In fact, the analysis here is not even intended to represent the mental processes of businessmen.

The chart may mislead in other ways as well. It focuses attention exclusively on the price and cost aspects of competition, though competition in product characteristics is equally important. Moreover, the chart suggests a static situation, while the reality is one of shifting prices and costs, changing technologies and organizational structures, and attempts to alter and improve products, so that it is most unlikely that price equals marginal cost for long in most industries. Market rivalry is a much more complex and progressive process than can be represented on any chart. Fatal errors in analysis are easily made when the limitations of the diagram are forgotten.

The clarity and precision of the analysis are both valid and useful, however, when the model is understood to be a statement of the limiting condition of tendencies we know to be at work. Regardless of the ways in which management may choose to think about or to explain its decision making (and the explanations can be marvels of empty, public-relations-style prose), the model represents the ultimate situation toward which economic forces tend to drive the firm. The model, that is to say, resembles an equation showing how chemicals tend to combine, not a statement of the psychological predisposition of chemicals or an assertion that there are never factors that impede the reaction. Firms that achieve a poorer approximation of the ideal will have a lower rate of return and will, sooner or later, run short of capital: they must improve or die. This mechanism would work even if management decisions were made by flipping coins, though we do have the additional reassuring factor that men, unlike chemicals, generally prefer to succeed and will seek the solution to the economic equation that ensures their prosperity. Under the conditions hypothesized for the widget industry, we could predict with confidence that firms would arrive precisely at the solution shown here. Under more realistic conditions, with continual change and incomplete information built into the model, no firm might ever reach the ideal solution; firms would then thrive or decline according to the nearness of their approach. The model predicts the tendencies of business behavior, which is all that is possible and all that we need.

Public policy, however, is interested in the performance of the widget industry as a whole. For this analysis we require a new graph (see Figure 2). The demand curve facing the individual manufacturer is

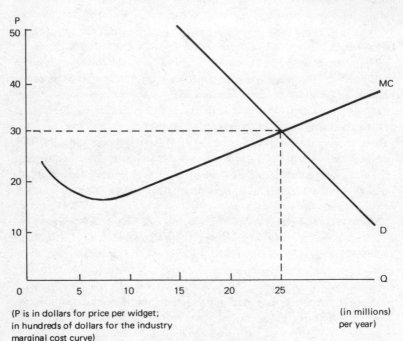

(P is in dollars for price per widget;   (in millions)
in hundreds of dollars for the industry   per year)
marginal cost curve)

Figure 2.   Hypothetical output and price for an entire industry under pure competition.

flat (perfectly elastic) because the widgets of 99 other manufacturers are perfect substitutes for his. There are no perfect substitutes for widgets as a commodity, however, and the demand curve for all widgets will display some inelasticity, sloping down and to the right to indicate that as price declines more widgets are demanded. It is an axiom of price theory that, other things being held constant, more units of a product can be sold only by lowering the price; conversely, if fewer units are offered, the price will be bid up. That is the relationship symbolized by the sloping demand curve *D*. (The demand curve is drawn as a straight line only to simplify the arithmetic.) The industry marginal cost curve is arrived at by summing the marginal costs of the 100 identical firms that constitute the industry. (This ignores, as an unnecessary complication, the possibility that changes in industry output may affect the prices of input factors and so give an industry supply curve different from the sum of the individual firms' marginal cost curves.) The graph reflects the fact that the efforts of all firms to maximize their profits result in an industry output of 25 million widgets per year at a price of $30 each.

This solution is not merely "correct" for the industry but also for consumers. The forces of competition have balanced social desires and costs through the intermediary of the widget industry. The demand curve expresses the amounts that consumers are willing to pay for widgets as against all other uses of their purchasing power; it expresses, at all prices shown, their desire for widgets at different prices relative to their desire for all other things the market has to offer: automobiles, bubble gum, education, sweet potatoes, whiskey, medical services, ski lessons, or what have you. The demand curve thus expresses a social ranking of wants. Similarly, the marginal cost curve expresses the cost not merely to the firm or the industry but to the society of producing widgets. We are talking here about real costs, not historical costs or bookkeeping costs, and the cost of using a unit of a resource is the maximum amount that unit could earn elsewhere. Real costs are thus forgone alternatives or opportunities, and so they are often called alternative or opportunity costs. These are brought home to the widget maker through the price he must pay for factors of production. If he must pay $50 for a ton of steel, that is the price of bidding that ton away from alternative uses. And his cost is also the real cost to society, because the ton of steel was valued in the alternative use at $50. Thus, when the widget firm and the widget industry equate demand and marginal cost, they also equate social desire and social cost. The closer the members of the industry come to maximizing their profits, the closer they come to maximizing the welfare of consumers.

This process goes on not only within firms and industries but also between industries. Should the automobile industry experience an increased demand and bid up the price for steel, that higher price will be reflected in the marginal cost of the widget industry. In Figure 2 a higher marginal cost curve would mean a new intersection with demand to the left of and higher than the old intersection, hence a lower rate of output and a higher price. This situation represents a new equilibrium in which production has adjusted to take account of a change in competing consumer desires.

Processes of this sort go on endlessly in the economy. Resources are combined and separated, shuffled and reshuffled, in the endless pursuit of greater net revenues by persons who own resources and persons who employ them. Each productive resource tends to move to that employment where the value of its marginal product (the sum of money added to the firm's net receipts by the employment of an additional unit of the input or resource per unit of time), and hence the return paid to it, is greatest. If equilibrium were ever reached, the value of marginal product would be the same in all employments—which is the same as saying that the price put upon the resource by consumers would be the same in all its possible uses—and the distribution of resources would be ideal. Output, as measured by consumer valuation, would then be maximized, since there would be no possible rearrangement of resources that could increase the value to consumers of the economy's total output.

This condition has never been and can never be achieved. Changing wants and technologies are in themselves sufficient to prevent the attainment of such an equilibrium. But the forces of competition in open markets cause the actual allocation of resources to be ever shifting in pursuit of the constantly moving equilibrium point. And the more closely the economy approximates this limiting conditon, the more closely do we approach the maximization of consumer welfare. Indeed, the best practicable approximation to the limiting condition can realistically be called the maximization of consumer welfare.

MONOPOLY

We are now in a position to understand the case against monopoly. As we shall see, it is not an absolute case, for though monopoly may interfere with allocative efficiency, it may also rest upon productive efficiency. Whether a particular monopoly is, on balance, beneficial or detrimental to consumer welfare must take both types of efficiency into account. Later on, we shall see how that is done. For the moment, remember that the case made here is entirely in terms of allocative efficiency and is therefore one-sided.

Suppose that our hypothetical 100 widget manufacturers either merge into a single corporation or simply meet and agree to place the power to make output decisions for all firms in a central industry committee. Let us suppose also that neither course of action produces any change in costs. We would have, in one case, a monopolistic horizontal merger or, in the other, a cartel. In either case, the new management would have control of 100 percent of widget output. The new monopolist, whether corporation or committee (I will no longer distinguish, the principles being the same), will perceive at once that its output decisions do affect market price. Since the monopolist is the entire industry, it faces the sloping industry demand curve rather than the competitive firm's flat demand curve. More important, the monopolist does not maximize profits by continuing to run along at the old output rate of 25 million widgets annually. The reason is simple. For the competitor, marginal revenue was always the same at any output rate and always equaled market price. But for the monopolist, marginal revenue is always less than market price because his demand curve slopes. Should he decide to offer an additional 1 million widgets per year, the demand curve shows that he would have to accept a lower price, and the crucial point is that the lower price would apply not just to the additional million but to all his output. He would get less for the first 25 million widgets as well as for the additional million. The additional output has a drag effect upon his marginal revenues all the way along the line. The difference that a sloping demand curve makes is a matter of simple arithmetic, as shown by Table 1.

Now the widget monopolist, like the widget competitor and all bus-

TABLE 1

Effect of Monopoly on Total and Marginal Revenues

Rate of output (Q) (in millions)	Price (P)	Total revenue (in millions)	Marginal revenue (in millions)
10	60	600	—
11	58	638	38
12	56	672	34
13	54	702	30
14	52	728	26
15	50	750	22
16	48	768	18
17	46	782	14
18	44	792	10
19	42	798	6
20	40	800	2
21	38	798	-2
22	36	792	-6
23	34	782	-10
24	32	768	-14
25	30	750	-18

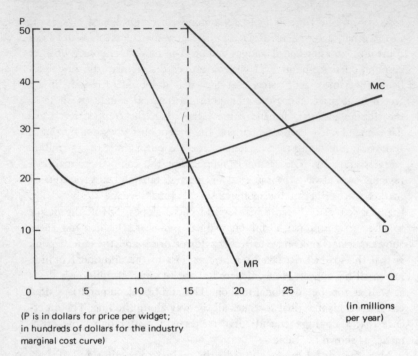

(P is in dollars for price per widget;
in hundreds of dollars for the industry
marginal cost curve)

Figure 3.   Hypothetical marginal cost, marginal revenue, and demand curves
for a monopoly.

inessmen under any circumstances, maximizes profits by producing at a
rate where marginal cost equals marginal revenue. As may be seen from
Figure 3, the intersection of marginal cost and marginal revenue is well
to the left of the intersection of marginal cost and demand.

This means that the monopolist will find it profitable to produce
fewer widgets annually than did the same industry when competitively
structured. This cutback in the rate of production and sale is what
economists call a "restriction of output." Here, the lowered rate is
15 million widgets annually. Fewer widgets on the market, the demand
curve informs us, means that purchasers will bid a higher price for
what is available, in this case $50 each. (Perhaps it should be stressed
again that these graphs and the table are not intended to be typical
except in the sense that they show the directions, though not the magnitudes, of movements in price and output when competition is converted to monopoly.)

But the higher price is not the root of the problem, nor is the lower output. Many unobjectionable developments could produce these. An increased demand for housing, and hence for steel, could have made the raw material for widgets more expensive, raising the marginal cost curve, so that even a competitive widget industry might have cut back to an annual production of 15 million, with a resulting $50 widget price. The distinctive feature of the monopoly situation is that the monopolist has created a gap between marginal cost and price, which means that social costs and social desires are no longer equated. Indeed, the monopolist has made his monopoly profit by creating an imbalance between cost and desire. With the restriction in output, moreover, the widget industry no longer needs as many resources as before. The unneeded resources must either lie idle, an obvious social waste, or migrate to other industries where the value of their marginal product will be less than it would be in the monopolized widget industry. The result, of course, is that they contribute less wealth as consumers define wealth, so that consumers would be better off if these resources could return to making widgets.

This is the mechanism by which restriction of output, made possible by monopolistic merger or cartel or any other means of controlling the market, creates a misallocation of resources and thereby makes society poorer. The evil of monopoly, then, is not higher prices or smaller production (though these are its concomitants) but misallocated resources, or allocation inefficiency.

It is a common misconception that a monopolist's increased efficiency redounds only to the monopolist's benefit. Figure 3 should dispel that notion. If marginal cost is lowered, the intersection with marginal revenue moves to the right, indicating a larger output and a lowered price. That benefits consumers as well as the monopolist.

One important caveat should be stated here. As the monopolist pushes the price of widgets higher, consumers may suddenly switch to a product that was not considered a substitute at lower prices. That is to say, the demand curve may suddenly approach the horizontal at some point. If this occurred at a price of $40 per widget, for example, the monopolist would not misallocate resources to the same extent as supposed here. This limitation may often be important and, as will be discussed, is probably important in the case of monopoly gained by superior efficiency.

OLIGOPOLY

Almost none of the markets with which antitrust law must deal resemble the atomized or monopolistic models just outlined. For the vast majority of actual markets, therefore, we may not automatically assume that business behavior has the effect upon resource allocation predicted by either model. To this intermediate range of market structures has been applied the theory of oligopoly, which attempts to predict the behavior of firms in markets where rivals are "few." The lack of rigor in that theory may be suggested by the observation that there appear to be about as many oligopoly theories as there are economists who have written on the subject. In fact, it is a most unsatisfactory branch of economic theory, and as I will attempt to show in Chapter 8, there is no very good reason to think that so-called "concentrated" markets behave in a less satisfactory manner than more fragmented ones.

The dominant, but by no means universal, opinion among economists and antitrust commentators holds that markets with few rivals (there is very little agreement as to how many firms may still be "few" enough for the theory to apply) will perform poorly because the firms will, without overt agreement, recognize their mutual self-interest and restrict output in order to behave, so far as possible, as if they had formed an actual cartel.

Now in their desire to achieve cartel results, though without collusion, the firms in a concentrated industry differ not at all from those in a fragmented industry. Rather, it is their ability that differs; this, the theory holds, is chiefly a matter of numbers and the effect of individual firm behavior on the market. The 100 widget manufacturers of our hypothetical competitive industry know as well as any economist that they would make more money if they could all restrict output and take higher prices. If businessmen did not know this principle, they would not form cartels. Being barred by law from agreeing explicitly, they would like to get the same results by each behaving as if he were in a cartel. That is, mutual forbearance in rivalry could approach a situation in which industry marginal cost and industry marginal revenue are equated, so that each firm takes 1 percent of a monopoly profit instead of 1 percent of a lower competitive return. No one thinks that will happen in a fragmented industry, for a variety of reasons: each firm will be severely tempted to take more sales at the higher price, letting the others make the sacrifice of holding price up by holding back on sales; costs will differ, so that the firms will not arrive at the same judgment as to the most profitable price; costs and demand will change, increasing the probability of differing responses; and so on.

But the situation is thought by many persons to be different if the industry becomes concentrated. Suppose that in the fragmented widget industry, over time, some firms grow and others decline, many leaving the industry altogether, so that eventually there remain only four firms. One of these has 50 percent of actual sales, another 30, a third 15, and the fourth is struggling somewhat at 5 percent. Almost all economists would describe such an industry as "oligopolistic" or "concentrated," and perhaps most would predict that its structure would cause it to behave noncompetitively. The basis for that prediction is the concept of *oligopolistic interdependence*. Each firm is aware that its price and output decisions are no longer insignificant with respect to total industry price and output. Sellers no longer face an impersonal market price but one they can, to a greater or lesser degree, affect.

This much is true. If the 50 percent firm, which, let us suppose, now makes 12,500,000 widgets annually, expanded its output by 10 percent, perhaps because it lowered its costs, to 13,750,000 widgets per year, the market price would drop initially from $30 to under $28 per widget. If the other firms adjusted by reducing output to equate marginal cost with the new price, the price would rise somewhat and after a series of adjustments would settle down perhaps above $28 but below $30. The point of all this is that the widget makers would be aware of their power over price and might separately decide to try raising it. The 50 percent firm might begin by announcing a new $35 widget price. If the others did not follow, the higher price would not last long. The theory supposes, however, that the 30 percent firm's management will realize that undercutting the largest firm is short-sighted, since that firm will drop its price and all firms will be back where they began. Why not follow the price up? If the other two firms reason similarly, all will be getting $35, a price above the competitive level, though not at the monopoly level. By such a process the rivals may work themselves up to the monopoly price (and the restricted output necessary to raise the price), jointly maximizing their profits, without ever once meeting surreptitiously at a country club or leaving the telltale evidence of long-distance calls to one another in the telephone company's records.

Devotees of oligopoly theory rarely claim that businesses' maneuvers and reactions will be adroit enough for the oligopolists to arrive at the monopoly output and price that a single firm occupying the entire industry would choose. Changing conditions of demand and technology will continually alter the profit-maximizing solution, and four firms are most unlikely to read an uncertain and fluid situation in an identical way. When costs differ, as they always do, the best price and degree of restriction will differ for each firm, making tacit cooperation still more difficult. When products are not identical, and particularly when product descriptions change, so that prices must vary, yet another unsettling factor is introduced. Moreover, there will always be a temptation to "cheat," to pick up a very profitable piece of extra business with a small price cut. Purchasers can play sellers against each other to break down the oligopoly price.

It will be urged, however, that the theory does not demand perfect formation flying. If oligopolists cannot achieve the complete monopoly solution, that does not mean they will necessarily arrive at the complete competitive solution with prices at marginal cost. No, it does not. But nothing in the theory compels the conclusion that oligopolists do not behave as competitors. The whole thing is speculation about how firms may or may not be able to behave. The theory has nothing like the definiteness and rigor of the theories of competition and monopoly. We will examine it more closely and attempt to gauge its usefulness for antitrust policy in Chapter 8.

The models described so far constitute the rudiments of the theory of allocative efficiency. So far as consumer welfare is concerned, they are only half the story. We turn next to the other half.

THE NATURE OF PRODUCTIVE EFFICIENCY

Productive efficiency is a simple, indispensable, and thoroughly misunderstood concept. Not one antitrust lawyer in ten has a remotely satisfactory idea of the subject, and the proportion of economists who do, though surely higher, is perhaps not dramatically so. The situation has deteriorated so badly that one can hear it hotly denied that efficiency has anything to do with antitrust. There even appears to be an impression among the more zealous antitrust enforcers that efficiency does not exist but is some sort of trick thought up by unscrupulous defense attorneys. Yet, as Frank Knight points out, this form of efficiency is one of the two that enter into the organization of production to meet consumer preferences, and it follows that antitrust policy cannot be rational unless productive efficiency is understood and weighed in the law's processes.

Productive efficiency is any activity by a business firm that creates wealth. The concept is symmetrical with that of allocative efficiency. Productive efficiency, like allocative efficiency, is a normative concept and is defined and measured in terms of consumer welfare. Since a free market system assumes that consumers define their own welfare, it follows that productive efficiency consists in offering anything, whether products or services, that consumers are willing to pay for. (The caveat that the goods or services concerned must not be ones that society outlaws for other reasons—addictive drugs or prostitution, for example, is obvious.) The relative efficiency of firms is therefore measured by their relative success in the market.*

Attention must be focused on this definition of productive efficiency rather than on the wide variety of factors that contribute to it. Economies of scale, specialization of function, ability to obtain capital, management skill—all of these and many more are elements that contribute to the firm's ability to please consumers, but they are causes rather than manifestations of efficiency. Efficiency is at bottom a value concept, not a description of mechanical or engineering operation. As Knight points out:

> There is a common misconception that it is possible to measure or discuss efficiency in purely physical terms. The first principles of physics or engineering science teach that this is not true, that the term efficiency involves the idea of value, and some measure of value as well. It is perhaps the most important principle of physical science that neither matter nor energy can be created or destroyed, that whatever goes into any process must come out in some form, and hence as a mere matter of physical quantity, the efficiency of all operations would equal one hundred per cent. The correct definition of efficiency is the ratio, not between "output" and "input" but between *useful* output and total output or input. Hence efficiency, even in the simplest energy transformation, is meaningless without a measure of usefulness or value. In any attempt to understand economic efficiency, the notion of value is more obviously crucial since most economic problems are concerned with a number of kinds both of outlay and of return, and there is no conceivable way of making comparisons without first reducing all the factors to terms of a common measure.[2]

In antitrust the required common denominator is provided by the goal or value of consumer welfare. In a system which permits consumers to define their own welfare by their purchases, it follows, that, with an important reservation to be mentioned shortly, a firm's efficiency is shown by its success. It is useless, for antitrust purposes, to study the minimum efficient size of the firm by studying the engineering efficiencies of the plant and production line because the important factor

---

* Exceptions to this will be discussed later, particularly in connection with the theory of predatory practices in Chapter 7.

is consumer response to what comes off the production line. (This subject is taken up at greater length in Chapter 6 in connection with proposals to make efficiency an explicit defense in antitrust litigation.)

Considerations such as these, perhaps, led George Stigler to define efficiency simply as "competitive effectiveness." That will do as well as any other brief definition, but it must be remembered that competitive effectiveness or productive efficiency is not a concept coterminous with profitability. A firm may be profitable because it forms a cartel, merges to monopolistic size, or employs predatory tactics successfully. Profitability based upon such tactics is not evidence of productive efficiency because consumer welfare is lessened rather than increased. Profitability in such cases is based upon the disruption of allocative efficiency rather than the enhancement of productive efficiency. The methods of distinguishing efficiency from mere profitability are discussed in Chapter 6, and their application takes up much of the remainder of this book.

It may be objected that I have created a false dichotomy by assuming that the effects of business behavior are always classifiable with respect to allocative efficiency or productive efficiency. There are other problems in the world; among them are income distribution, externalities, and the purchase of goods that society does not want consumers to have. Quite right. If it were asserted that all of society's concerns with business behavior can be summed up as the effect on allocative and productive efficiency, the dichotomy would be false. The claim, however, is only that the dichotomy is proper for the specialized purposes of antitrust law. The classification is not merely proper, for we shall see in Chapter 6 that it is essential to reasoning about antitrust.

This definition of productive efficiency—competitive effectiveness—must necessarily be left without more content at this stage. As we go along we shall see in a variety of contexts some of the elements that go to produce efficiency.

5

The Consumer Welfare Model

Wᴇ can now be more explicit about the factors that are included in antitrust's consumer welfare calculus and those that must be excluded from it. We may usefully illustrate the basic reckoning involved with a graph employed by Oliver Williamson [1] to represent the trade-off problem in a merger that both creates power to restrict output and cuts costs.

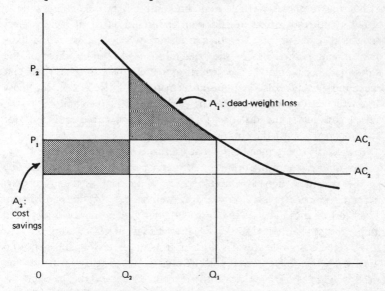

Figure 4.   Effects on consumer welfare of a merger that restricts output and cuts costs.

Williamson's graph (see Figure 4) compares the "dead-weight" loss (the amount above costs that consumers would be willing to pay for the lost output) to the gains to all consumers of cost reductions resulting from the merger. Cost reductions mean that the saved resources are freed to produce elsewhere in the economy.

The diagram assumes that the merger reduces the long-run average costs of the two firms from AC_1 to AC_2 but that the increased market power created by the merger results in a restriction of output so that the rate moves from Q_1 to Q_2. We then see that consumers have lost output—for which they would have been willing to pay an amount above cost equal to the area labeled A_1—and have gained in resource savings an amount equal to the area A_2. Obviously, if A_2, the cost savings, is larger than A_1, the dead-weight loss, the merger represents a net gain to all consumers. If A_1 is larger than A_2, a net loss results.

This diagram can be used to illustrate all antitrust problems, since it shows the relationship of the only two factors involved, allocative inefficiency and productive efficiency. The existence of these two elements and their respective amounts are the real issues in every properly decided antitrust case. They are what we have to estimate—whether the case is about the dissolution of a monopolistic firm, a conglomerate merger, a requirements contract, or a price-fixing agreement.

But the consumer welfare diagram must not be taken literally, as if one could read correct decisions off the graph paper. It merely illustrates a relationship; it does not quantify it. We do not know the location of any of the sides of the triangular area A_1 or of three of the sides of the rectangle A_2 (the fourth is merely the price axis), so that we cannot possibly calculate their areas mathematically. We do not know in any actual case the slope of the demand curve, the location of the initial cost curve, the distance (if any) the cost curve will shift, or the amount (if any) the output will change.

It must also be remembered that there need not always be a trade-off. In most cases, in my opinion, economic analysis will show that one of the areas does not exist, and decision of the case is therefore easy. Some phenomena involve only a dead-weight loss and no, or insignificant, cost savings. That is the case with the garden-variety price-fixing ring. Output is restricted so that Q_2 is to the left of Q_1, creating the area A_1, but there is no downward shift of costs, no line AC_2, and hence no area A_2. Other phenomena will involve only efficiency gain and no dead-weight loss. Examples of these include most of the mergers the Supreme Court strikes down and the price "discriminations" the Robinson-Patman Act is intended to stamp out. AC_2 drops below AC_1, creating the rectangle A_2, but Q_2 does not move to the left of Q_1, so there is no triangular area A_1. In fact, if the efficiency gain takes the form of a cost savings, Q_2 moves to the right of Q_1, signifying an increased rate of output due to lowered costs.

That raises a most important caveat which must accompany Williamson's diagram. The area A_2 represents only cost savings, and cost savings are but one element or form of increased efficiency. The area A_2, therefore, must be taken to symbolize any efficiency gain and not merely the reduction of costs.

Perhaps this representation of the consumer welfare model contains too many traps for the unwary, but I have adopted it because it illustrates so clearly the relationship between allocative and productive efficiencies in determining consumer wealth. It makes plain the error committed by the Supreme Court in holding either that efficiency is irrelevant or that it is actually a reason to strike down a merger. When efficiency is deemed irrelevant, there can never in any case be an area labeled A_2. Thus the merger can only be neutral, if no market power whatsoever is created (so that there is no area A_1), or harmful (if there is any area A_1 at all). When efficiency is deemed harmful, the merger is almost certainly bad, because it will almost certainly create either market power or efficiency. Otherwise, there would be very little reason to merge. The result of ignoring or outlawing A_2 is outlandish antitrust law. As Williamson says in arguing that the value of efficiency must be recognized: "if neither the courts nor the enforcement agencies are sensitive to these considerations, the system fails to meet a basic test of economic rationality. And without this the whole enforcement system lacks for defensible standards and becomes suspect." [2]

Williamson refers to his diagram as a "naïve model" and suggests a number of possible qualifications. Some relate to the elements of efficiency and the method of weighing the two kinds of efficiency. These are reserved for discussion in the next chapter. Here we will discuss possible qualifications that would either destroy the model or require its very substantial modification. Williamson raises two possibilities, the topics of income distribution and "second-best" theory,[3] and we may add for completeness the cost of gaining monopoly and the subject of externalities. Each of these qualifications should be rejected, and antitrust should concern itself solely with allocative and productive efficiency. This is a subject closely related to the goals of antitrust policy, which we have examined already in Chapters 2 and 3. Here we are discussing from a slightly different vantage point the inability of antitrust to accommodate, along with allocative and productive efficiency, these three additional economic considerations.

INCOME DISTRIBUTION

The model outlined addresses the total welfare of consumers as a class. It says nothing of how shares of consumption should be allocated through changes in the distribution of income. Yet all economic activity has income effects and, in particular, restriction of output by the exercise of monopoly power has income effects not taken into account by weighing only changes in allocative and productive efficiency. If the reader will look once more at Figure 4 he will see that at the competitive price, P_1, there is a large area under the demand curve that lies above the market price. This area represents the amount above the actual price that consumers would be willing to pay rather than go without the product; it is generally called the "consumer's surplus," perhaps on some notion that the consumer gets surplus value for his money.

Those who continue to buy after a monopoly is formed pay more for the same output, and that shifts income from them to the monopoly and its owners, who are also consumers. This is not dead-weight loss due to restriction of output but merely a shift in income between two classes of consumers. The consumer welfare model, which views consumers as a collectivity, does not take this income effect into account. If it did, the results of trade-off calculations would be significantly altered. As Williamson notes, referring to his diagram: "The rectangle . . . bounded by P_2 and P_1 at the top and bottom respectively and o and Q_2 on the sides represents a loss of consumers' surplus (gain in monopoly profits) that the merger produces. . . . Inasmuch as the income distribution which occurs is usually large relative to the size of the dead-weight loss, attaching even a slight weight to income distribution effects can sometimes influence the overall valuation significantly." [4]

The issue is not crucial, perhaps, since most antitrust cases do not involve a trade-off. The law's mistake has generally consisted of seeing restriction of output where there is none, and in such cases there will be no loss of consumer surplus. But even in cases where the trade-off issue must be faced, it seems clear the income distribution effects of economic activity should be completely excluded from the determination of the antitrust legality of the activity. It may be sufficient to note that the shift in income distribution does not lessen total wealth, and a decision about it requires a choice between two groups of consumers that should be made by the legislature rather than by the judiciary. This argument in its general form was developed in Chapter 3.

This conclusion is reinforced by the recognition that disapproval of the income redistribution could only rest upon a tenuous moral ground. Let us see where the income distribution criterion, if it were employed, would bite. It would never be important in any case in which dead-weight loss exceeds efficiency gain, because the business behavior in question would be unlawful on consumer welfare grounds alone. The income distribution criterion would be superfluous. That criterion could only play a role where the behavior under examination—a merger, for example—creates an efficiency gain that is larger than the dead-weight loss, but where dead-weight loss and consumer-surplus loss together are larger than efficiency gain. Such a merger would have the net effect of benefiting consumers, and its legality would turn upon the inclusion or exclusion of income redistribution as a factor. It would be improper to include income redistribution as a factor *because* we disapprove of monopolistic restriction of output, for that would really be to count the dead-weight loss against the merger twice. The dead-weight loss has already been subtracted, and we must now consider whether the remaining net efficiency gain is to be overcome by income redistribution.

Once the issue is refined to that point, it becomes difficult to distinguish between this merger and a merger that creates only efficiency gain. The pure efficiency-gain merger also redistributes income. The new efficiency will divert income to the merged firm from less efficient rivals, and all firms using resources of the type released will gain at the expense of the owners of such resources because the new efficiency means that demand for the resources has declined relative to supply.

I am unable to distinguish the pure efficiency-gain merger from the net efficiency-gain merger. Both increase consumer welfare and redistribute income. If income redistribution is not counted against one, why should it be counted against the other? There seems no reason. The impulse to count income redistribution arises from an excessive and uncritical moral aversion to the existence of *any* dead-weight loss, an aversion transferred to income redistribution. There is no basis for that aversion, at least no basis that courts can adopt, when the dead-weight loss is inseparable from a greater efficiency gain that benefits society at large.

Williamson suggests that the income transfer could be regarded unfavorably "because it produces social discontent." [5] He means not that it will certainly produce social discontent but that it *may,* and that such a possibility is an appropriate factor to weigh. It certainly is, but the question is what institution should weigh it and in what context. Income redistribution due entirely to increased efficiency may, and often does, produce social discontent, as when computers replace file clerks, but that would not be a reason for a court in an antitrust case to enjoin the progress of automation. The problem of social discontent is one for Congress and not the federal judiciary to address.

Other objections to income redistribution as an antitrust criterion could be elaborated. If income redistribution were to be weighed against cases of net efficiency creation on the ground that consumers are generally poorer than producers (which would be a most dubious ground), then the principle would seem to require that income redistribution be weighed in favor of any economic behavior when producers of a product had generally lower incomes than consumers. This would justify price fixing by poorly remunerated producers. If the criterion is to be taken seriously, moreover, courts really ought to attempt to trace all the income effects as they spread to rival firms and to the owners of competitive and complementary resources. These efforts would introduce horrendous complexities in which it is surely undesirable to mire the processes of antitrust.

There is every reason, therefore, to conclude that courts should ignore income distribution in deciding antitrust cases and stick to the criteria of the consumer welfare model.

COSTS OF GAINING AND MAINTAINING MONOPOLY

Richard Posner makes an observation that may be taken as suggesting a major qualification in the trade-off model used here. He points out that traditional analysis of the costs of monopoly

ignored the fact that an opportunity to obtain a lucrative transfer payment in the form of monopoly profits will attract real resources into efforts by sellers to monopolize, and by consumers to prevent being charged monopoly prices. The costs of the resources so used are costs of monopoly just as much as the costs resulting from the substitution of products that cost society more to produce than the monopolized product.[6]

The statement appears true, and it reinforces the case for having an antitrust policy. The statement does not, however, appear very relevant to the question of what rules should implement the policy. Resources used to gain monopoly power improperly (as by forming a cartel, for example) are wasted and may be added to the dead-weight loss, but that changes no rule, since illegality was required by the dead-weight loss alone. Resources expended in achieving monopoly power through superior efficiency, on the other hand, cannot be added to dead-weight loss because they are not wasted. The costs of achieving efficiency would have to be taken into account if an estimation of net benefit were attempted, but for reasons given in Chapter 6 that is not a real possibility. Antitrust rules must track inferences about whether a particular practice or structure creates or reflects a restriction of output or efficiency. There will be a few mixed cases, but Posner's observation about the additional costs of monopoly will be seen to make little difference there.

THE THEORY OF SECOND BEST

The model used here assumes that consumers are always better off if restrictions of output can be lessened or eliminated without offsetting losses of productive efficiency. The theory of second best, however, suggests that this may not always be the case. The theory states that so long as there are certain to be some monopolies in an economic system, it may or may not be worthwhile destroying others. If we attack vulnerable monopoly A, thereby equalizing the value of the marginal products of the resources used by both A and competitive industries, the possibility remains that the resources required for A's expansion to a competitive level of output may come from invulnerable monopoly B where the marginal products of the resources were higher. If that should prove to be the case, we have done consumers a disservice by worsening the allocation of resources. We know, as a matter of fact, that there are many monopolies that are invulnerable to antitrust attack: patents, labor unions, natural monopolies, and so forth.

Fortunately, at least for the author, we need not examine the theory in detail. The theory does not address itself to the probability of the bad result, but states it merely as a possible outcome. The legislative decision to promote competition rules out the adoption of the theory as the general rule of antitrust, since its adoption would require judicial repeal of the laws in their entirety, and the theory provides no criteria that could be applied by a court to the decision of individual cases.

In order to take into account second-best's caution in a price-fixing case, for example, the court would first have to measure the gap between price and marginal cost—in itself an all but impossible task. Next, the court would have to inquire whether there existed divergences between marginal cost and price in any industry making substitutes for or complements of the products produced by the cartel, or in any industry to and from which resources might move if the cartel were outlawed, and whether such divergences in any such industry would probably be increased or lessened by outlawing the price agreement. Finally, the court would have to judge whether the new equilibrium, across all affected industries, would be better or worse for consumers than the present equilibrium. The objection is not merely that every price-fixing case would take ten or fifteen years to try, but that the task itself is beyond the capacity of any court or of any other institution.

An occasional antitrust scholar has taken the possibility of second best as destroying the rationality of the consumer welfare basis of the law (which it does not) and therefore freeing the courts to evolve new rules based on other social and political values. The suggestion is little short of preposterous. Aside from the political-jurisprudential and constitutional objections to any such unconfined role for the courts, canvassed in Chapters 2 and 3, it would be utterly improper for the courts to decide that Congress had made a policy error in choosing to promote competition and deciding, for that reason, to take the statutes as authority to enforce different values of their own choosing.

If the possibility pointed out by the theory of second best were judged to be a probability (and most economists doubt that very much), we could use it only for making judgments in gross. It would call for the end of antitrust policy. There is no reason to accept that conclusion. Posner points out that the second best objection is further weakened when the additional costs of gaining and maintaining monopolies are added to the resource misallocation costs.[7] This makes it more likely that it is worth preventing the formation of vulnerable monopoly A even though monopoly B remains invulnerable. If we are to proceed with our present statutes, we may, with unfeigned relief, simply forget the topic of second best.

EXTERNALITIES

Economic activity creates social costs in the form of externalities that, by definition, are not taken into account through the price mechanism. Thus, an expansion of output through increased efficiency would appear as pure gain in the consumer welfare model but might impose other welfare losses upon the society, e.g., by an increase in atmospheric pollution. Once more, however, we face a problem whose solution lies with the legislature rather than the judiciary. Every decision to permit pollution or to require that it be lessened is a decision about income distribution. Thus, a legal rule that requires automobile manufacturers to reduce pollutant emissions imposes costs that raise the price of automobiles. The effect, of course, is to lessen the number of persons who purchase new cars (a redistribution of real income) and to provide an incentive to keep old cars in use longer (with adverse results for considerations such as safety). A trade-off in values is required, and that is properly done by the legislature and reflected in specialized legislation. It cannot properly form the stuff of antitrust litigation.

6

The Method of Antitrust Analysis

To read antitrust literature or to participate in the numerous conferences convened to discuss policy is to become convinced that antitrust is less a discipline than a buzzing confusion of unrelated opinion. Even agreement on conclusions is usually superficial, papering over fundamental disagreement about reasons. One cause of this eminently unsatisfactory state of affairs lies in a failure to focus and settle the question of the form of reasoning, or argument, proper to the subject matter.

The mode of correct antitrust analysis is determined by the strengths and weaknesses of price theory. Once these are understood and respected, we should achieve greater agreement on substantive issues.

This chapter will advance several related propositions.

First, price theory assures us that economic behavior is not random but is *primarily* directed toward the maximization of profits.

Second, attempts to maximize profits can stand in only three relationships with respect to consumer welfare. Economic behavior is primarily efficiency creating, primarily output restricting, or neutral in its consumer welfare impact.

Third, price theory enables us to identify, with an acceptable degree of accuracy, those activities whose primary effect is output restricting, leading to the inference that all other activity is either efficiency creating or neutral.

Fourth, antitrust must avoid any standards that require direct measurement and quantification of either restriction of output or efficiency. Such tasks are impossible.

Finally, in all cases in which behavior is neutral or in which analysis does not provide a basis for predicting effects upon consumer welfare, tie-breaking considerations indicate that the law should not intervene.

THE RELATION BETWEEN
PRICE THEORY AND ANTITRUST

The basic assumptions and doctrines of conventional price theory will be used throughout this book. To those who object that economics is not a sufficiently certain discipline upon which to rest major policy conclusions, the answer given here is not (though it could be) that they misunderstand the nature and strength of the theory, but rather that such reliance is inevitable. There is no body of knowledge other than conventional price theory that can serve as a guide to the effects of business behavior upon consumer welfare. To abandon economic theory is to abandon the possibility of a rational antitrust law.

Since the argument of this book will disagree rather strongly with some economists, it had better be explained that such disagreement does not of itself contradict my claim to rely upon basic economic postulates. The layman is likely to think that economic theory is what any economist theorizes, but of course it is not. If it were, we should have to believe that there are dozens or hundreds of mutually incompatible versions of economic theory, each as good as any other. Basic economic theory is an intensely logical subject, and much of it consists of a drawing out of the implications of a few empirically supported postulates. When I speak of economic theory, therefore, I mean those statements which, judged by the evidence available and the quality of the argument which supports them, appear to be the most probably correct statements at the moment. That way of stating the matter may make some theory appear more tentative than it really is. In many cases the theory is so well grounded that we can be certain, or virtually so, of its reliability. Economists differ on particular subjects for a variety of reasons, some of which it would be invidious to discuss. To mention a few of the others, it is quite easy to make mistakes in the process of creating and applying a detailed logical system, and it is particularly easy in fields where emotions and political and social attitudes vie with reason to control men's beliefs. There are, moreover, special difficulties in applying theory to business practices. It is easy to overlook the existence of alternative theoretical explanations for a single practice, or to neglect a seemingly minor aspect of behavior that will not fit the theory being imposed.

All of this means that the judge, legislator, or lawyer cannot simply take the word of an economist in dealing with antitrust, for the economists will certainly disagree. Unless we would be driven to a sterile agnosticism, therefore, we must work through the arguments and make up our own minds. And we will find that on most subjects there is a better view which we ought to accept until fresh analysis provides yet a superior position.

Several of the first principles of antitrust methodology derive from an aspect of the market system that has often been expressed in the analogy to the Darwinian theory of natural selection and physical evolution. The familiarity of that parallel, and the overbroad inferences sometimes drawn from it, should not blind us to its important truths. The environment to which the business firm must adapt is defined, ultimately, by social wants and the social costs of meeting them. The firm that adapts to the environment better than its rivals tends to expand. The less successful firm tends to contract—perhaps, eventually, to become extinct. The Stanley Steamer and the celluloid collar have gone the way of the pterodactyl and the great ground sloth, basically for the same reasons. Since coping successfully with the economic environment also forwards consumer welfare (except in those cases that are the legitimate concern of antitrust), economic natural selection has normative implications that physical natural selection does not have. At least there seems to me more reason for enthusiasm about the efficient firm than about the most successful physical organisms, the rat and the cockroach, though this view is, no doubt, parochial.

A key factor in evolution is death, and that holds true in economic as in physical evolution. The firm has an advantage over the animal because it can consciously change not just its behavior but its structure and so avoid or postpone death, but the threat is there and it becomes an actuality for many firms every year. There is in the literature much loose talk by people who should know better to the effect that the large modern corporation can escape the forces of the market through internal financing. Internal financing may often be a means of lowering the costs of acquiring capital, but it does not insulate the firm from the demands of the market. To expand, or even to survive, every firm requires a constant flow of capital for employees' wages, raw material, capital investment, repairs, advertising, and the like. When the firm is relatively inefficient over a significant time period, it represents a poorer investment and greater credit risk than innumerable alternatives. If the firm is dependent upon outside capital, the firm must shrink and, if no revival in its fortunes occurs, die. That fate cannot be averted by financing out of retained earnings. There is, in the first place, no reason for a firm to throw its own money into a losing proposition rather than invest elsewhere. Even if one postulated a management that did so, and also postulated an ability to escape stockholder revolts, takeover bids, and so forth, internal financing could only delay the end. The firm would be incurring expenses that were not recovered, and it could continue only so long as it was willing and able to go on giving away its capital to consumers. There is no theoretical, empirical, or intuitive reason to suppose that such conduct is at all common.

The need to make profit produces the search for it. Profit motivation is patently ubiquitous and overwhelming, and it matters little whether we view it as entirely a conscious motivation, merely the type of behavior selected for survival by the economic environment from random forms of behavior, or, perhaps most realistically, as something of each. It is a common observation of biologists that whenever the physical environment provides a niche capable of sustaining life, an organism will evolve or adapt to occupy the place. The same is true of economic organisms, hence the fantastic proliferation of forms of business organization, products, and services in our society. We turn out everything from the most sophisticated electronic equipment to chartreuse compact cars to hair sprays, from business executives to field goal specialists to psychiatrists for disturbed household pets to rentable conversationalists for sagging dinner parties. The yellow pages of the telephone book do not begin to tell the story. The strength of the driving force that sends persons and firms into every crevice capable or even just possibly capable of sustaining profitable economic activity can hardly be overestimated.

This assumption of price theory is so crucial—and yet so insistently misunderstood by, among others, businessmen and antitrust lawyers—that elaboration may not be amiss. It is commonly objected that businessmen are not purely, or perhaps even primarily, rational profit seekers, that they could not in any case master and apply the complex calculations that such a goal requires, and that they employ guidelines to behavior that are inconsistent with profit maximization. None of these is a valid objection. Though if required I should not hesitate to impute conscious profit maximizing to businessmen—experience with businessmen and, even more, with antitrust lawyers and consulting economists should convince anyone that profit is a goal not only consciously but constantly borne in mind—price theory requires no such assumption. The validity of its tenets depends upon their success in predicting behavior, and the basic tenet of price theory, as Milton Friedman points out, states that businessmen generally behave *as if* they were engaged in maximization, just as a theory of physical science might state that leaves position themselves on trees "as if each leaf deliberately sought to maximize the amount of sunlight it receives." [1]

Thus, "firms behave *as if* they were seeking rationally to maximize their expected returns . . . and had full knowledge of the data required . . . ; *as if,* that is, they knew the relevant cost and demand functions, calculated marginal cost and marginal revenue from all actions open to them, and pushed each line of action to the point at which the relevant marginal cost and marginal revenue were equal." [2]

Friedman uses an analogy that effectively disposes of the objections both that profit maximization is too complicated a goal and that businessmen often do not talk like profit maximizers:

Consider the problem of predicting the shots made by an expert billiard player. It seems not at all unreasonable that excellent predictions would be yielded by the hypothesis that the billiard player made his shots *as if* he knew the complicated mathematical formulas that would give the optimum directions of travel, could estimate accurately by eye the angles, etc., describing the location of the balls, could make lightning calculations from the formulas, and could then make the balls travel in the direction indicated by the formulas. Our confidence in this hypothesis is not based on the belief that billiard players, even expert ones, can or do go through the process described; it derives rather from the belief that, unless in some way or other they were capable of reaching the same result, they would not in fact be *expert* billiard players.

. . . Now, of course, businessmen do not actually and literally solve the system of simultaneous equations in terms of which the mathematical economist finds it convenient to express this hypothesis, any more than leaves or billiard players explicitly go through the complicated mathematical calculations or falling bodies decide to create a vacuum. The billiard player, if asked how he decides where to hit the ball, may say that he "just figures it out" but then also rubs a rabbit's foot just to make sure; and the businessman may well say that he prices at average cost, with of course some minor deviations when the market makes it necessary. The one statement is about as helpful as the other, and neither is a relevant test of the associated hypothesis.[3]

Friedman's point is not that firms maximize perfectly, any more than expert billiard players plan and execute every shot correctly. Perfection is the limiting condition to which the more successful come closer than their rivals. As Armen Alchian observes, business success is measured against rivals rather than the ideal: "Realized positive profits, not *maximum* profits, are the mark of success and viability. . . . Positive profits accrue to those who are better than their actual competitors, even if the participants are ignorant, intelligent, skillful, etc. The crucial element is one's aggregate position relative to actual competitors, not some hypothetical perfect competitors." [4] Profit maximization is the limiting point toward which success tends.

The fact that businessmen talk in terms not always equatable with profit maximization is of no particular importance, though it does mislead those who look no further. There are a variety of explanations: the simplest is that businessmen are no more self-conscious and articulate than the rest of the human race about their real motivations and conduct. Moreover, in a society whose intellectual leaders seem often not to understand the social value of self-seeking business behavior, the ability to talk vaguely about broad "social responsibility" while actually engaged in profit maximizing may be an important adaptive technique. Besides, many businessmen are as confused as other people about the morality of profits. Stigler reports that "in one field study, when [businessmen] were asked whether they maximized profits, they indignantly rejected the suggestion and pointed out that they were sincerely religious, public-spirited, and so on—as if these traits were inconsistent with profit-maximizing. But when the question was reformulated as: would a higher or lower price of the product yield larger profits?, the answer was, usually, no." [5]

The unsophisticated observer may also mistake for irrationality, or as indicating a goal other than profits, those rules of thumb that businessmen use to cope with uncertainty or to avoid the impossible task of rethinking every problem every time it arises. "Thus," according to Alchian, "the urge for 'rough-and-ready' imitative rules of behavior is accounted for. What would otherwise appear to be merely customary, 'orthodox,' nonrational rules of behavior turn out to be codified imitations of observed success, e.g., 'conventional' markup, price 'followship,' 'orthodox' accounting and operating ratios, 'proper' advertising policy, etc." [6] Such rules serve the function that habit and custom perform in other areas of life. Without them, moment-to-moment behavior would pose insuperable complexities. The firm will do better or worse as its rules of thumb prove to have survival value or not, and as it has or lacks the ability to alter them to meet circumstances.

We come now to a crucial point. To carry out its mission, antitrust must classify varieties of profit-maximizing behavior with respect to their probable impacts upon consumer welfare. Obviously, only three relationships are possible, and these correspond to three quite different ways of making money. A business firm may seek to increase its profits by achieving new efficiency (beneficial), by gaining monopoly power and restricting output (detrimental), or by some device not related to either productive or allocative efficiency, such as taking a bookkeeping advantage of some wrinkle in the tax laws (neutral).

The task of antitrust is to identify and prohibit those forms of behavior whose net effect is output restricting and hence detrimental. It should, of course, leave untouched behavior that is beneficial or neutral. The available resources of price theory dictate the manner in which this task must be accomplished. The best-developed branch of price theory is the theory of the ways in which firms may profit by interfering with allocative efficiency. Though we know something of the subject, there is no comparably clear, reliable, and general theory of the ways in which they may create productive efficiency. It follows, therefore, that antitrust analysis, if it is to be successful, must proceed primarily by elimination. We must appraise any questioned practice—say, a merger or a requirements contract—in order to determine whether it contains any likelihood of creating output restriction. If it does, and if it also contains the possibility of efficiency, we have a mixed case, which raises problems that will be discussed in a moment. If a practice does not raise a question of output restriction, however, we must assume that its purpose and therefore its effect are either the creation of efficiency or some neutral goal. In that case the practice should be held lawful.

It makes some people uneasy to have to rely entirely upon theory to infer the nature of a reality that is not directly observed. Yet I am convinced both that the theory is good enough to make the task doable and, equally important, that there is no other possible way to proceed. An economist once called this the "Philo Vance approach to antitrust"; he was not, one gathered, one of that detective's greatest admirers. (As a matter of fact, he was probably thinking of Sherlock Holmes's dictum: "When you have eliminated the impossible, whatever remains, *however improbable*, must be the truth." [7]) The characterization is not without justice, but the objection it implies is wide of the mark. Philo (or Sherlock) did not have the advantage of the tight, logical system provided by price theory. If he had, his method of deduction would have been perfectly practical.

This is not by any means to suggest that it is not possible and desirable to go further and to specify the nature of the efficiencies created or intended by various forms of business behavior. Such an effort may serve as a valuable double-check upon conclusions arrived at by the process of elimination, and it is certainly likely to be more persuasive. But it is not logically necessary.

The application of this technique to particular situations will not be completely error free. But that is not a fatal objection. No system of laws is error free. The legal system makes mistakes in perceiving reality in the decision of every kind of case, from torts and contract disputes to homicide prosecutions. To demand perfection is to demand the abolition of law. The question is whether a method of applying the law can give an acceptable degree of accuracy and whether this method is better than any alternative method. The method of reasoning by elimination in antitrust cases passes both these tests. Indeed, no other method of antitrust analysis is even possible, since the only alternative, that of quantifying both efficiency and restriction of output, is well beyond the present powers of economic analysis and is likely forever to remain so.

Before we turn to the question of alternative modes of analysis, a possible misunderstanding should be cleared up. A moment ago it was said that when a practice does not have the capacity to restrict output, we should assume that its purpose (and therefore its effect) is either the creation of efficiency or some neutral result. It is proper to infer purpose from the objective possibility that a firm faces (unless we have clear evidence of a different purpose), and it is also proper to infer effect from purpose, even though we know that the effect will not always be what the firm intended. Businessmen make mistakes, and a particular efficiency-motivated contract or merger may, in fact, turn out miserably for the firm and hence be a poor use of society's resources. Antitrust cannot concern itself with this possibility, however, because prosecutors and courts simply cannot replace management by attempting to make business decisions through the litigation process. Antitrust must content itself with the identification of attempts to restrict output and let all other decisions, right or wrong, be made by the millions of private decision centers that make up the American economy.

There remains the difficult problem of the mixed case, the business practice that seems likely to produce both output restriction and efficiency. This is the case represented by Oliver Williamson's trade-off model, discussed in the preceding chapter. Horizontal mergers provide a primary example (indeed, almost the only example). If we disallow all horizontal mergers, no matter how small, we shall make a great sacrifice of productive efficiencies. If we allow all horizontal mergers, no matter how large, we shall make large sacrifices in allocative efficiencies. Somewhere on the spectrum between large and small mergers lies a range of mixed cases, and in these we do not know with certainty whether the efficiency or the trade restraint element predominates. How is the law to make a sensible decision in such cases?

The temptation is to reply: by making a showing of efficiencies an affirmative defense. But that is a temptation to be resisted, although its superficial plausibility lends the idea a certain attractiveness. After all, it might be said, facts are better than conjectures. They are, but only if you are sure that what you are dealing with are facts, and, unfortunately, the relevant ultimate facts for antitrust purposes cannot be perceived directly or quantified.

Making the existence and size of efficiencies a matter for proof, moreover, misleads the courts and the enforcement agencies into thinking that such direct proof is the only way efficiencies can be taken into account in antitrust litigation. Not surprisingly, they react by denying that efficiencies have any relevance to the law; this disastrous conclusion usually flows from a realization of what direct proof of efficiency would entail. Thus, it is customary to denounce proposals for performance tests as likely to plunge antitrust enforcement into "economic extravaganzas" or as being "prescriptions for the nonenforcement of the antitrust laws." Such invective misses the point.

If performance tests or efficiency defenses were the only way to reach intelligent decisions, then we ought either to stage economic extravaganzas or give up enforcing the laws. As Williamson says, "Filing (and winning) however many bad cases does not make for effective antitrust enforcement." [8] Simplicity of law enforcement is not worth having if the cost is law that does harm. We would not convict a man accused of theft without evidence on the argument that insistence upon unobtainable evidence is a prescription for the nonenforcement of the larceny laws.

The real objection to performance tests and efficiency defenses in antitrust law is that they are spurious. They cannot measure the factors relevant to consumer welfare, so that after the economic extravaganza was completed we should know no more than before it began. In saying this I am taking issue with some highly qualified authorities. Carl Kaysen and Donald Turner proposed that "an unreasonable degree of market power as such must be made illegal," and they suggested that all the relevant dimensions of performance be studied.[9] Their idea, essentially, is that a court or agency determine, through a litigation process, whether there exists in a particular industry a persistent divergence between price and marginal cost; the approximate size of the divergence; whether breaking up, say, eight firms into sixteen would reduce or eliminate the divergence; and whether any significant efficiencies would be destroyed by the dissolution. The White House Task Force headed by Phil Neal came up with a similar proposal for litigating the desirability of restructuring concentrated industries.[10] Williamson thinks an efficiency defense is required if the trade-off relationship is to be recognized.[11]

These commentators are all entirely correct in perceiving the trade-off relationship and the crucial importance of efficiencies. There can be no rational antitrust policy that does not recognize and give weight to productive efficiency, and wide areas of present law are irrational precisely because they do not. The issue between these commentators and myself is simply the way in which efficiencies are to be given weight by the law.

A statement of what must be done in any direct measurement approach is sufficient to make its impossibility apparent. The court would have to make a reasonably accurate estimate of efficiency and deadweight loss in an actual situation, and then make the same estimates of those two quantities in a hypothetical situation, in order to determine whether the real or the hypothetical situation is more favorable to consumers. Suppose that a merger is proposed and the government seeks to prevent its consummation. In order to explore the trade-off problem by direct study, trial would have to be had on the present contribution of the two firms to consumer welfare, their level of efficiency as separate firms, and the degree, if any, to which they were presently able to restrict output. As we shall see, that task is itself impossible. But trial would then have to proceed to the measurement of efficiency and restriction of output under an imaginary set of conditions: what would the net contribution to consumer welfare be if the two firms were merged into one? Judgment would be rendered according to a comparison of the two situations.

Passably accurate measurement of the actual situation is not even a theoretical possibility; much less is there any hope of arriving at a correct estimate of the hypothetical situation. Consider two of the factors that would have to be known: the demand curve over all possibly relevant ranges of output and the marginal cost curve over those same ranges. Only by knowing where marginal cost and demand intersect could one know whether there was a restriction of output and what its size was. Nobody knows these curves. Even the companies involved do not. The clarity of the graphs of firm behavior misleads many people. Companies do not compute these curves and then adjust output to equate marginal cost and marginal revenue. Rather, by a process of groping, by trial and error, they continually attempt, under constantly changing conditions, to make as much money as possible (or to lose as little as possible). The graph is a statement that in the process the firm will be driven toward the solution shown on the graph. Management may never think of demand curves or marginal cost curves. It may think in terms of a "fair return" and average costs, but rivalry and profit maximization will push it toward the solution shown by the graph.

There is a good reason why firms do not know these things, and it is the same reason why they cannot be known through an antitrust trial. The demand curve is not known because it changes continually and because the company is not constantly plotting it by running its prices up and down. The attempt to do so might make a minor contribution to science, but quite a research grant would be required, since the losses incurred in an attempt by a major company might make serious inroads on the resources of even the Ford Foundation.

But it is the quantification of the productive efficiency factor that renders the problem utterly insoluble. The point may be clarified by examining that class of efficiencies known as economies of scale, efficiencies related to the size of the firm. The variety of such efficiencies is suggested by E. A. G. Robinson's list of five forces that affect firm size:

The forces which determine the best size of the business unit, assuming that the market is sufficient to absorb the whole production of at least one firm of optimum size, may be divided into five main categories: *technical forces,* making for a technical optimum size; *managerial forces,* making for an optimum managerial unit; *financial forces,* making for an optimum financial unit; the *influences of marketing,* making for an optimum sales unit; and the *forces of risk and fluctuation,* making for a unit possessing the greatest power of survival in the face of industrial vicissitudes. [Emphasis added.] [12]

A noteworthy aspect of Robinson's list, for those who think of efficiency as an engineering concept and, therefore, of more importance to plant than firm size, is that only one of the influences mentioned, technical forces, is related at all closely to engineering or to the size of the plant (rather than the size of the firm).

The problem of technical efficiencies alone is likely to be beyond the capacities of the law. Imagine a large firm making several products and operating in distinct product and geographic markets. This would mean the study of not one but a number of technical marginal cost curves. For each of these, one would face the complex problem of separating fixed and variable costs and the insoluble problem of segregating and allocating joint costs. These things can be and are done by artificial accounting conventions, but that process, however useful it may be to a firm that wishes to compare its own performance during two different time periods, has little validity for the issues of real costs that antitrust policy must decide. Moreover, real marginal costs include a "normal" return to the various resources employed which includes opportunity costs, the latter being the return various resources could earn in the most profitable alternative use in the economy. We should be very skeptical, therefore, of any marginal cost curve that purported to reflect merely the technical efficiencies of a firm, particularly a large and complex firm.

Skepticism should turn to utter disbelief at the sight of cost curve purporting to reflect all the efficiencies of a firm. What could a court do when faced with a management claim that a merger would improve financial efficiency and a government contention that it would not, or with a claim that the merger would improve the new firm's chances of riding out unforeseen risks and fluctuations? And how could a court attach a number to such claimed efficiencies, for the firms separately and for the as yet hypothetical merged firm? Worse, a crucial component in any firm's efficiency is the skill of its management. How does one quantify judgment and imagination? We cannot begin to assign a quantitative value to a claimed future improvement (or decline) in the performance of firm A resulting from its acquisition by firm B, because that would require, among other impossibilities, precise statements about differences in the effects of unspecified future decisions concerning problems that cannot now even be identified. This unmeasurable factor may be the most important element of efficiency.

Williamson concedes that measurement of economies is difficult, but he thinks that admitting an economies defense would create an incentive to improve techniques. "To dismiss an economies defense on the prevailing state of the art is to employ an unacceptably narrow horizon." [13] I think it is the other way around: to admit an economies defense that proceeds by measurement would force us to an unacceptably narrow horizon. Economists, like other people, will measure what is susceptible of measurement and will tend to forget what is not, though what is forgotten may be far more important than what is measured. Williamson himself seems to have engaged in such a narrowing process. He speaks of an "economies defense" and seems to think of it as a cost-cutting defense. That in itself throws out those contributions to consumer welfare which arise from the conception and introduction of new products, new services, and variations of products and services.

The most important thing about the Ford Motor Co. in its early years was the genius of Henry Ford, just as the most important efficiency of General Motors Corp. in later years was the organizational genius of Alfred Sloan. The acquisition by one of those companies of a rival would have extended to a new group of resources a management that was enormously superior, even if there were no cost cuts to be expected but only the doing of better things at higher costs.

The economies defense necessarily focuses on only half the problem, the cost-cutting side. And even within that half it will disallow efficiencies that are not easily proved. Thus Williamson: "if economies in both production and distribution expenses are claimed, and if the former are better specified than the latter, distribution economies would have to reach a higher threshold than would production economies to be admissible." [14]

Fortunately for both the time and cost of enforcement and the rationality of decisions, we can avoid attempts to measure dead-weight losses and efficiencies directly in order to compare a real situation with a hypothetical situation in terms of consumer welfare. We can avoid it because price theory tells us that many practices the law now views as dangerous do not contain any potential for restriction of output. In such cases there is no trade-off problem. The trade-off problem arises primarily in the context of horizontal mergers, and there we can take it into account by framing rules about allowable percentages that reflect the probable balance of efficiency and restriction of output.

Williamson criticizes this position (which I have taken previously):

Lacking a tradeoff relation, Bork is forced to assert that "Economic analysis does away with the need to measure efficiencies directly. It is enough to know in what sorts of transactions efficiencies are likely to be present and in what sorts anticompetitive effects are likely to be present. The law can then develop objective criteria, such as market shares, to divide transactions [into those predominantly one type or another]." But this obviously leaves the mixed cases, which are the hard ones, unresolved.[15]

He says that without an economies defense "the mixed case which involves both scale economy and market power effects can only be handled arbitrarily—and this is satisfactory to no one." [16] But the nature of the problem shows that some degree of arbitrariness will have to be accepted as satisfactory by everyone because direct measurement of the conflicting factors cannot conceivably handle the trade-off dilemma. Indeed, it is precisely the introduction of an attempt to quantify economies that would make the law even more arbitrary than it need be, by eliminating the most important efficiencies from consideration.

This book will try to show that rules can be devised which reflect and resolve the tension between productive efficiency and allocative inefficiency accurately enough for the law to confer a net benefit. I hope it has already shown that performance tests and efficiency tests would multiply the costs of antitrust enforcement and defense without conferring any compensating advantage.

SUGGESTED QUALIFICATIONS

It is not surprising that Williamson, whose articles on the crucial but neglected subject of antitrust methodology are the best and most provocative of which I am aware, should also have suggested important qualifications to the trade-off model. Even though we must reject his suggestion of an economies defense, these qualifications require discussion because, to the degree they are significant, they also may affect an attempt to balance the tradeoff considerations through general legal rules.

TIMING

The first proposed qualification is that of timing. Williamson argues that

significant economies will ordinarily be realized eventually through internal expansion if not by merger. Growth of demand can facilitate this internal adjustment process; the necessity for part of the industry to be displaced in order that efficient size be achieved is relieved in a growing market. Thus, although a merger may have net positive effects immediately (cost savings exceed the dead-weight loss), when allowance is made for the possibility of internal expansion these effects can become negative eventually (the cost savings persist, but these could be realized anyway, and the dead-weight loss could be avoided by prohibiting the merger). . . . By contrast with a growing market, to force economies to be realized by internal expansion in a static market is generally without merit. The market power effects will occur here anyway, and the internal expansion route merely delays and may upset the market adjustment.[17]

This consideration seems entirely too speculative to deserve weight in framing rules. In the first place, the same economies may not be achieved by internal expansion. If merger was the preferred route, that preference may rest upon the lower cost of merger in achieving the new efficiencies. Blocking that route may very well impose higher costs, which must be subtracted from the efficiencies, and the costs may be high enough to prevent the achievement of the efficiencies altogether. Second, as Ward Bowman points out in this connection, the dead-weight loss may be reduced with the passage of time, both by the entry of new firms and because demand tends to become more elastic in the long run. This tends to counterbalance the prospect of achieving efficiency by growth. Finally, it is difficult to see that internal expansion is preferable in a growing market. It is true that internal expansion may have upsetting effects in a static market, but it should also be true that merger in a growing market would be unlikely to have lasting market power effects because of the greater likelihood of entry.

INCIPIENCY

Ward Bowman and I once argued that applying the incipiency concept to halt a trend toward greater market concentration in its early stages is unfortunate because the existence of the trend constitutes evidence that greater concentration is desirable. The trend necessarily arises from emerging efficiencies.[18] Williamson comments:

Their evaluation of the social desirability of a trend suggests a certain insensitivity to the relevant scale economy–market power tradeoff considerations, and they appear to read the significance of a trend somewhat too loosely. That a trend necessarily implies emerging efficiences is incorrect: it may also indicate an emerging awareness that market power advantages might be realized through a series of combinations. Moreover, whereas they seem to suggest that to disallow a merger is to prevent the realization of scale economies altogether, ordinarily it is not a question of whether economies will be realized but when and with what market power effects. Thus, while Bork and Bowman may be correct in charging that scale economy justifications have not been given sufficient weight in the recent enforcement of the merger law, they are also guilty of a certain heavy-handedness in their own treatment of the incipiency question.[19]

To balance all this, Williamson drops a footnote to the second sentence in which he notes that I concede the possibility of an emerging awareness of market power advantages but that my "principal emphasis, which is probably correct, is that a trend signals emerging economies." [20] The upshot appears to be that I, along with Bowman, am insensitive and heavy-handed but probably correct. I will settle for that. I don't know about Bowman.

The incipiency concept appears to have no value whatever, and when the concept is applied to halt a trend (toward concentration, vertical integration, or what have you) in the early stages, it seems plain that the only effect is to halt (or perhaps only to delay and make more costly) the achievement of emerging efficiencies. It is altogether too much to believe that scores or hundreds of firms in a fragmented industry would at the same time begin growing by merger in the expectation that one day they would work the industry down to a highly concentrated state and achieve the power to restrict output. Each of them must rely upon all of the others to do the same thing and keep on doing it for a very extended period of time. More importantly, if we suppose there are not economies to be achieved by merger, we must, in order to accept the counterhypothesis, also suppose that there are no diseconomies, for if there were the process would be much too costly. Thus, we must imagine scores or hundreds of firms with perfectly flat marginal cost curves that permit expansion by merger to sizes perhaps twenty or more times their original sizes without diseconomy. And since we are asked to imagine that the beginning of the trend is not due to a change in cost conditions, we must wonder why, with marginal cost curves like that, the industry ever was fragmented in the first place.

It seems impossible to conclude that a merger trend signifies anything but emerging efficiencies unless the trend started from a condition so concentrated that one or two mergers would be sufficient to make output restriction a profitable course of action. That was not the case Bowman and I had under discussion, and the incipiency concept is not necessary to guard against that situation.

WEIGHTING

"The economies that a merger produces are usually limited strictly to the combining firms. But the market power affects of a merger may sometimes result in a price increase across a wider class of firms." Where this occurs, Williamson suggests, the balancing of cost savings and dead-weight loss should be adjusted accordingly.[21] This seems clearly correct in any case in which the other firms can be expected to behave as conventional oligopoly theory predicts—that is, to cooperate in maintaining the new higher price rather than to erode it through rivalry. So clarified, this is a consideration to be taken into account in the framing of rules about allowable market shares. It will be argued later, however, that conventional oligopoly theory is not credible, and that argument, if it is accurate, greatly diminishes the consideration of "weighting."

TECHNOLOGICAL PROGRESS AND MANAGERIAL DISCRETION

Williamson suggests that technological progress may be related to market structure.

Presently, however, neither the arguments nor the evidence relating market structure to progressiveness is unmixed. Provisionally, it may only be judicious to withhold judgment on this dimension. But, as the evidence accumulates, sharper definition is ordinarily to be expected; and operational integration of progressiveness within the efficiency standard might, therefore, eventually be achieved.[22]

There can be no objection to the integration of effects upon progressiveness into the weight given efficiency when enough is known to predict the effects of structure upon progressiveness. My objection to progressiveness as a goal of antitrust,[23] an objection to which Williamson was responding, was to its consideration as a goal independent of consumer welfare. It is a component of consumer welfare. There is, moreover, a more fundamental difficulty with the notion of counting progressiveness as a goal of policy: it is not clear how much progressiveness is desirable. Progress requires the sacrifice of other resources, it costs something, and no one thinks it worth paying any price, no matter how great, for faster progress. We are, therefore, necessarily ignorant of the "proper" rate of progress, and it may be wisest for that reason not to give the matter any weight in antitrust analysis.

Market power is also said to provide a firm "the opportunity to pursue a variety of other-than-profit objectives." This, if true and significant, would require that the efficiency component of a merger creating substantial market power be discounted because it would not be fully realized. Williamson characterizes this qualification, as well as that concerning technological progress, as "highly conjectural," [24] and it too must await further evidence before being taken as a serious factor in the framing of legal rules.

The upshot of this consideration of the qualifications advanced as appropriate to the naïve consumer welfare model is that weighting (the third suggested qualification) alone deserves to be worked into the trade-off relationship, but only in cases involving horizontal size. The argument of Chapter 8 suggests that this qualification is very minor and perhaps verges on non-existence.

TIE BREAKERS

Cases may occur, primarily in the fields of horizontal mergers and horizontal ancillary restraints, in which chances seem roughly equal that the activity is beneficial or harmful. Instances of such uncertainty should be treated like cases of behavior that is neutral. The law should not intervene. One frequently hears the opposite contention: when in doubt "play safe," by banning the conduct in question. This is the sheerest folly. There is no way to "play safe." If the dead-weight loss and efficiency are not in fact equally balanced, then the conduct is either beneficial or detrimental. Assuming the odds are equal where we are unable to be sure, the would-be safe player is doing good in half the cases and inflicting harm in the other half.

A cluster of considerations require nonintervention in doubtful cases. First, antitrust enforcement is a very costly procedure, and it makes no economic sense to spend resources to do as much harm as good. There is then a net loss. Second, private restriction of output may be less harmful to consumers than mistaken rules of law that inhibit efficiency. Efficiency that may not be gained in one way may be blocked because other ways are too expensive, but a market position that creates output restriction and higher prices will always be eroded if it is not based upon superior efficiency. Finally, when no affirmative case for intervention is shown, the general preference for freedom should bar legal coercion.

7

Injury to Competition:
The Law's Basic Theories

THE root trouble with modern antitrust, more damaging even than the confusion over goals, is the unsophisticated, indeed primitive, state of the law's economic doctrines. The seeming complexity of this topic is spurious. The ideas at work are of ancient lineage, few in number, and easily comprehended. To understand them is to understand the otherwise apparently bewildering course of the law and the unity that underlies its surface diversities. To grasp the nature of their error is to perceive the route to reform.

The early period of antitrust laid down two theories of the ways in which competition may be injured that continue to shape and drive the law today:

(1) Competitors may agree to remove the rivalry existing between themselves and thereby injure the competitive process; or

(2) Competitors may inflict injury on their rivals and thereby injure the competitive process.

Each of these theories has an important core of truth, but each has been egregiously overextended so that the law regularly strikes at and destroys normal business practices whose only consequence is enrichment of the community. The mistake is the same in both cases. Each theory contains an obvious dilemma: the agreed elimination of rivalry and the infliction of injury upon rivals are not merely means of injuring the competitive process; they are, even more importantly which productive efficiency is created and by which the for petition allocate resources. Because the law has not resolve lemma, has not found ways of separating the beneficial eli, of rivalry and inflictions of injury from the detrimental, it forced to ignore the claims of productive efficiency. The law is fore, driven by only one economic consideration: fear of injury to allocative efficiency. Considering only one vector in a two-vector situation is bound to give results far off the mark.

If the principles of law made by the courts were consistently applied, not only would competition be outlawed, but a modern (or almost any) economic system would be impossible. This has not happened, of course, but the law is saved from demanding impossible results only by applying its principles erratically and inconsistently. Vigorous and consistent enforcement of present antitrust doctrines would be a national disaster. There is no chance that we will ever see it occur, but that is no reason to be content with the wealth destruction that now takes place within the areas where antitrust's irrationalities are allowed free scope.

Examination of the two basic theories of injury to competition discloses the cause of the law's waywardness.

THE AGREED ELIMINATION OF RIVALRY

The first theory—that competition is injured by the agreed elimination of rivalry—is less than a half-truth. Competition, in the sense of consumer welfare, is in fact injured by such agreed eliminations of rivalry as price-fixing rings, exemplified by the agreements in *Trans-Missouri* [1] and *Addyston Pipe & Steel*,[2] or, very probably, by monopolistic horizontal mergers, as in *Standard Oil*.[3] But it is also true that productive efficiency absolutely requires the agreed elimination of rivalry in many more cases. When men join together in corporations or partnerships, or in any economic unit of more than one person, they either explicitly or tacitly accept the elimination of market rivalry between themselves. Joint effort organized by administrative direction replaces the forces of the marketplace.

Since cooperation and division of labor within such economic units is essential to the tasks of production and distribution, it is impossible to enforce a legal rule that makes the agreed elimination of rivalry unlawful. If the agreed elimination of rivalry were always illegal, the resulting economic system, should one remain, would be unable to support the present population of the United States, much less provide what we have come to regard as a civilized living standard.

It is wrong, therefore, to accept a rule of law that purports to do what it cannot: strike down all agreed eliminations of rivalry. That was Holmes's point in his *Northern Securities* dissent.[4] The correct distinctions for the law are two. Agreed eliminations of rivalry should be illegal when they do not accompany and make more effective the integration of persons or business units in productive economic activity. Thus, price-fixing cartels are properly declared unlawful per se, but partnerships are not. Second, even when economic integration is present, the arrangement may be unlawful if the parties control the market so that restriction of output appears to be the primary effect. These considerations impinge upon current law in several areas: price fixing, market division, and boycotts, among others. Their application requires elaboration which must be deferred to the appropriate chapters.

THE INFLICTION OF INJURY UPON RIVALS

The second theory employed by the law—that competition is harmed by injury inflicted upon rivals, their exclusion from the market or some segment of it—is more complex, and it has also proved more harmful to the integrity and rationality of antitrust. Though we will be dealing with aspects of this theory in various chapters—those, for example, on vertical mergers, conglomerate mergers, exclusive dealing, and price discrimination—a general statement of the argument will be useful at this point.

The law employs a rich, diverse, and confusing vocabulary to describe what it perceives as the problem of market exclusion. We read in the cases not only of "exclusionary practices" but also of "predation," "abuses," "coercion," "foreclosure," "unfair competition," "fencing out," and "barriers to entry." These words all reflect or assume a theory of practices that improperly exclude rivals and hence injure the competitive process.

The problem is to know what exclusion is improper. All business activity excludes. A sale excludes rivals from that piece of business. Any firm that operates excludes rivals from some share of the market. Superior efficiency forecloses. Indeed, exclusion or foreclosure is the mechanism by which competition confers its benefits upon society. The more efficient exclude the less efficient from the control of resources, and they do so only to the degree that their efficiency is superior.

Such exclusion is proper and beneficial. It is the task of antitrust to see that it continues to operate. Antitrust, therefore, must be able to distinguish efficiency exclusion from improper exclusion. The conceptual apparatus now in use is incapable of making that crucial distinction.

The law's theory of exclusionary practices contains two branches. The more modern, and more important, strikes at practices *because* they exclude, without asking whether they exclude through efficiency or improperly. No showing of wrongful intent is required. This will be referred to as the *theory of automatic exclusion.* The older, and nowadays less significant, branch required some indication of wrongful intent as a means of separating normal and efficient behavior from that which inhibits competition improperly. This is the *theory of predation.*

THE THEORY OF AUTOMATIC EXCLUSION

The theory that there exist business practices which are automatically exclusionary, that the exclusion is improper and anticompetitive, and that the law can usefully identify and prohibit them is probably the single most important economic idea in antitrust today. It controls the interpretation of most of the Clayton Act, including the Robinson-Patman Act, and now much of the Sherman Act as well. To cite but a single example: vertical mergers are today all but completely illegal, on the theory that the manufacturer who acquires a retailer also acquires the ability to shut rival manufacturers out of that segment of the market. It is not necessary to a successful government suit to enjoin the merger that the manufacturer display any wrongful or anticompetitive intent in making the acquisition or that the retailer represent a very large share of the market. Vertical mergers are believed inherently exclusionary and are dealt with severely, as are such things as exclusive dealing contracts, requirements contracts, and price differentials. Yet it is clear that the theory of automatically exclusionary practices is utterly without merit.

Inherent in the concept of automatically exclusionary practices are two major fallacies, each of them fatal. The first is the postulation of a category of economic motivation or behavior that does not exist. The second is the simple arithmetical error of counting the same market power twice.

The first fallacy is nowhere more clearly displayed than in Judge Wyzanski's renowned opinion in *United States* v. *United Shoe Machinery Corp.*[5] Judge Wyzanski decided that United had monopolized the shoe machinery market and thus violated Section 2 of the Sherman Act. His determination rested in major part upon the presumed exclusionary effect of United's system of leasing its machines to shoe manufacturers. The leases were thought to make it more difficult for other machinery manufacturers to compete. Yet this exclusionary effect was found not to be predatory, for Judge Wyzanski stated that "United's power does not rest on predatory practices. Probably few monopolies could produce a record so free from any taint of that kind of wrongdoing." But such a finding was unnecessary, Judge Wyzanski thought, because the alternative to predation was not necessarily efficiency. The Sherman Act, therefore, must take account of another possibility.

When they proposed the legislation, Senators Hoar and Edmunds thought it did little more than bring national authority to bear upon restraints of trade known to the common law, and it could not apply to one "who merely by superior skill and intelligence . . . got the whole business because nobody could do it as well" [21 Cong. Rec. 3146–3152]. They did not discuss the intermediate case where the causes of an enterprise's success were neither common law restraints of trade, nor the skill with which the business was conducted, but rather some practice which without being predatory, abusive, or coercive was in economic effect exclusionary.

The difficulty with this, and hence with all law that rests upon the idea of automatic exclusion, is that the intermediate case described by Judge Wyzanski simply does not exist. It is an idea that has no counterpart in reality, and so law based upon the idea has no relation to reality.

To be clear on this point it is necessary merely to examine the assumptions underlying the notion of the intermediate case. By definition it is a case in which the company has engaged in market behavior with neither the expectation nor the result of making money. The defendant is assumed not to be attempting to do business more efficiently and also not to be attempting to exclude rivals on some basis other than efficiency. But the excluded purposes exhaust the possible motivations for profit-maximizing behavior. There are no other categories of behavior that create revenue for the firm. To postulate an "intermediate case," therefore, is to assume that there is a class of market conduct that is motivated by nothing in particular. Further, it requires us to assume that the conduct, whatever its motivation, does not prove efficient nonetheless.

Judge Wyzanski's concept of the intermediate case asks us to believe that the executives of the United Shoe Machinery Corp. (and every other shoe machinery manufacturer in the history of the industry) spent decades working out and continuously modifying a complex leasing system (and that United, at least, defended that system against repeated antitrust attacks) with no particular purpose in mind. That is flatly impossible. The concept of the "intermediate case," which is the theory of automatically exclusionary practices, thus describes a null set.

Employment of the theory leads the court to deny without investigation the possibility that the questioned practice creates efficiency. Thus Judge Wyzanski:

In one sense, the leasing system and the miscellaneous activities just referred to (except United's purchases in the secondhand market) were natural and normal, for they were, in Judge Hand's words, "honestly industrial." They are the sort of activities which would be engaged in by other honorable firms. And, to a large extent, the leasing practices conform to longstanding traditions in the shoe machinery business. Yet, they are not practices which can be properly described as the inevitable consequences of ability, natural forces, or law. They represent something more than the use of accessible resources, the process of invention and innovation, and the employment of those techniques of employment, financing, production, and distribution, which a competitive society must foster. They are contracts, arrangements, and policies which, instead of encouraging competition based on pure merit, further the dominance of a particular firm. In this sense, they are unnatural barriers; they unnecessarily exclude actual and potential competition; they restrict a free market.

This passage is not an investigation of the efficiency hypothesis (there is no such investigation anywhere in the opinion) but only an insistence that, for reasons not cited, the leasing system cannot be efficient, that it is "something more"—the intermediate case. And once the system is not efficient, a proposition resting on nothing more than assertion, it becomes an "unnatural barrier" and "unnecessarily" exclusionary. Hence its exclusionary effect is improper, and a market share resting upon improper exclusion is itself improper. The real, the only, issue in the case—was United trying to be efficient or predatory?—was never even discussed.

The theory of automatically exclusionary practices achieves truly spectacular results when it is coupled with the theory of incipiency, as it is in litigation under the Robinson-Patman Act and Sections 3 and 7 of the Clayton Act. The incipiency concept authorizes courts to catch monopolies and restraints of trade in their infancy, before they have matured to Sherman Act size. Thus, the firm employing a practice identified as suspect by the law need not possess a market share anywhere near United's 85 percent in order to run afoul of the law. In these categories of behavior, the possibility of efficiency is eliminated by hypothesis, and any exclusion that seems possible is necessarily improper. Thus, vertical mergers with a mere potential for excluding rivals from less than 1 percent of the market are struck down, as are exclusive dealing contracts. In some Robinson-Patman Act litigation, exclusion itself is inferred from the mere fact of a minor price differential. In all of these cases, as in *United Shoe Machinery*, the real problem is resolutely ignored.

The second major fault in the theory of automatic exclusion is its necessary adoption of the fallacy of double counting. When a court assumes that a firm forecloses its rivals without predatory intent and without creating efficiency, the court also assumes that the firm gets "something more" without noticing it. That can be explained only if the firm pays nothing for the something extra. *United Shoe Machinery* may again be used to illustrate the error.

United was successful in getting most shoe manufacturers to accept its leases, and yet Judge Wyzanski said the effect of the leases was artificially to exclude rival machinery manufacturers, thus preserving United's monopoly position. Such exclusion would of course be detrimental to the shoe manufacturers. They would prefer not to have to deal forever with a monopolist. United could charge for its machines only what they were worth to the shoe manufacturers, and we may call that amount X. If X was taken by United entirely in rental dollars, it had no power left over to force any disadvantageous terms upon the shoe manufacturer lessees. Yet, by Judge Wyzanski's hypothesis, United must have done just that. We cannot suppose that United lowered its dollar rentals in order to buy the exclusionary lease terms from the lessees, for that would be conscious predation, which is excluded by hypothesis and, for good measure, by explicit finding. Nor can we suppose that United took less in dollars without realizing the fact, for that would mean, first, that its executives over a period of several decades never perceived that they could charge more if they did not impose disadvantageous terms and, second, that no lessee ever pointed out that it would be willing to pay more if some of those terms were relaxed or removed. Such a supposition denies elementary business ability to any of the companies involved. Judge Wyzanski must have assumed that United could capture X in rental dollars and capture it a second time in exclusionary lease terms. Implicit in his reasoning, therefore, is the elementary fallacy of counting the same degree of market power twice. There is no way the theory of automatic exclusion, which ignores the possibilities of efficiency and predation alike, can avoid that additional error.

Double counting is present, for example, in all the vertical merger cases under amended Section 7 of the Clayton Act. Courts assume that a manufacturer can buy a retailer, force the new retail subsidiary to take the manufacturer's products, and thereby foreclose rival manufacturers. For this behavior to work an anticompetitive result, it is necessary to assume that the manufacturer is able to transfer the retailer's market position to itself at the manufacturing level while the retailer retains that same market position at the retail level. Double counting is clearly involved. If a manufacturer with 10 percent of its market buys a retailer with 5 percent of the retail market and forces its products upon the retailer, the theory supposes that the manufacturer winds up with 15 percent of manufacturing, and that the added 5 percent is not based on competitive merit. The theory works only if the retailer continues to enjoy 5 percent of the retail market, and that cannot be, since we started with the assumption that the manufacturer could not have earned that 5 percent on competitive merit. The manufacturer's competitive weakness has been forced upon the retailer along with the products. To assume that improper exclusion flows from such a merger is to assume that the retailer can give its market position to a manufacturer, who does not deserve it, and still retain the market position for its own enjoyment.

A particularly clear double-counting error occurs in the Supreme Court's decision in *United States* v. *Griffith*.[6] The Court found illegal monopolization in a motion picture theater chain's practice of negotiating with each distributor a master agreement for all its theaters. The crucial characteristic of the master agreements, according to Justice Douglas (who wrote the majority opinion), was that "they lumped together towns in which the appellees [defendants] had no competition and towns in which there were competing theatres." Accepting the district court's finding that the chain had no intent to restrain trade or monopolize, Douglas held that even though no threat was made, it was nevertheless likely that the distributor would give the chain exclusive rights in towns where competitive theaters existed, because of the monopoly power of the closed towns.

To exclude the possibility of predation and still to attribute this result to the linking of the towns through the master agreement is to embrace the double-counting fallacy. Again, call the monopoly power of the closed town X. The chain comes to the negotiation armed with X, and only X, for each closed town. It would normally pay the competitive price for films in competitive towns and that same price, minus the dollar value of X, in each closed town. If the distributor charged the chain the competitive price in both open and closed towns but gave it preferential rights worth X in the open towns, the chain would surely notice what was happening. It would be giving up money in the monopoly market for preferential terms that no competitor would be willing to pay for in the competitive market. The only point in that would be to destroy rivals in the competitive market. But that would be predation —excluded by hypothesis. Therefore, the reasoning assumes that the chain gets X in dollars in the closed town and gets X again in preferential terms in the competitive towns—and without noticing it. Aside from the stupidity gratuitously attributed to the chain (the alternative to stupidity is knowledge and therefore predation), the argument assumes that the distributor, unlike the rest of the human race, is willing to pay $2X$ for a thing worth only X, and to do it without even being asked. The fact that a legal theory with such a premise has gained ascendancy is a tribute both to antitrust as an art form and to the bar's capacity for the willing suspension of disbelief.

Notice that double counting requires the linking of two markets by lease, contract, merger, or ownership of two units. The leases in *United Shoe Machinery* are the equivalent of the master agreement in *Griffith*, of vertical mergers, and of exclusive dealing contracts. Both the use of a conduit for the transfer of power from one market to another and the fallacy of counting the same power twice, once in each market, are essential to the automatic exclusion cases.

The theory of automatic exclusion, then, contains two fatal defects: reliance upon a nonexistent motivation for economic behavior and reliance upon the fallacy of double counting. The theory cannot be accepted upon the terms in which the courts present it.

There remains for examination, however, the possibility that the theory is a "legal fiction" not intended to make sense according to its own terms—just as the old action of ejectment conclusively presumed that the defendant was in possession of the disputed property, no matter that he was standing before the court hotly denying possession. The legal fiction of automatic exclusion might be defended by arguing that it rests upon a judicial intuition that predatory business behavior is extremely common but very difficult to prove so long as wrongful intent is a required element of proof. The law, therefore, may drop the element of specific intent and so arrive at a presumption of automatic exclusion in order to frame a prophylactic rule, believing it more important to block predation than to avoid an occasional injustice and the social disservice of destroying some efficiency. In this view, to demonstrate that the theory of automatic exclusion is fallacious is to miss the point.

The prophylactic justification will not withstand analysis, however. Aside from the fact that it would attribute to the courts a disingenuous willingness to disguise a major, and very debatable, policy judgment, there are two conclusive objections to it: an effective prophylactic rule would require the suppression of all competition; and predation is not more common than efficiency.

The first objection is easily stated. To return to *Griffith,* a court applying a prophylactic rule on the assumption that the chain was demanding preferential rights in order to monopolize the competitive towns could avoid the fallacy of double counting only by assuming that the chain was giving up X, in the form of dollars, in each monopoly town in return for X, in the form of preferential terms, in a corresponding number of competitive towns. But such a transfer of power through the master agreement could easily be duplicated, without the master agreement, by transferring cash from one town to the other. The chain would need only a checking account or a black satchel to get X dollars from a closed town to an open town and purchase preferential terms there.

All the transfers of power assumed in the cases can be converted to transfers of equivalent cash, and that poses an insuperable problem. To do any good the prophylactic rule would have to be applied to all uses of money. But money has the same purchasing power whether it comes from a theater monopoly, a competitive haberdashery, a rich aunt, frugal living, or a day at the races. It can all be used, if any can be used, for predation. Since the point of a theory of automatically exclusionary practices (viewed as a prophylactic rule) is to avoid examining intent or otherwise having to distinguish between predation and normal competition, there is no alternative but to prohibit any use of money that could be predatory. This means, to use motion picture exhibition as the example, that courts would have to regulate amounts paid for films, admission prices, interior comfort and décor, and so forth, to ensure absolute equality between theaters in the same town. That is true whether the theaters belong to a chain or are independent. The same reasoning applies to all other types of business. The manufacturer, forbidden to acquire retailers and force its products at a loss to the wholly owned outlets, could accomplish the same result at the same loss by cutting the price to independent retailers. A prophylactic rule would require regulation of both price and quality.

Thus, if we adopt the theory of a prophylactic rule in our anxiety to preserve free competition, we end with the necessity to suppress every vestige of free competition. We cannot, therefore, justify the theory of automatic exclusion as a legal fiction disguising a prophylactic rule.

The second objection—that predation is less frequent than efficiency, so that a prophylactic rule would do more harm than good—is best taken up in the context of the theory of predation.

THE THEORY OF PREDATION

Antitrust law has never clearly defined what it means by predation, but the concept clearly contains an element of wrongful or specific intent, of a deliberate seeking of market power through means that would not be employed in the normal course of competition. We need something a little more definite for purposes of analysis. Predation may be defined, provisionally, as a firm's deliberate aggression against one or more rivals through the employment of business practices that would not be considered profit maximizing except for the expectation either that (1) rivals will be driven from the market, leaving the predator with a market share sufficient to command monopoly profits, or (2) rivals will be chastened sufficiently to abandon competitive behavior the predator finds inconvenient or threatening. Since these results are detrimental to consumer welfare, predation is not to be classed as superior efficiency.

Unsophisticated theories of predation abound, leading to drastic overestimations of its likelihood. The most common "theory" views firms in the market as if they were thugs in a dark alley; evidently a large firm has more muscle and can beat smaller firms to death. Sometimes the figure is changed, as in ominous references to the "law of the jungle" or the sarcasm frequently offered to rebut arguments for market freedom: " 'Everyone for himself,' cried the elephant as he danced among the chickens." Such remarks, though they represent popular "learning" on the subject, do not reflect theory but are only foolishly inapposite metaphors that ignore the constraints the market places upon firm behavior.

An equally foolish theory holds that predation is possible for a multimarket or conglomerate firm because it can lower prices to uneconomic levels in one market and avoid the costs of predation by raising its prices elsewhere. This theory rests upon the often-exploded recoupment fallacy. The predator would already be maximizing profits in all markets and so would have no way of increasing profits elsewhere to finance predation. That statement holds, of course, whether or not the predator has a monopoly position in the other markets.

Any realistic theory of predation recognizes that the predator as well as his victims will incur losses during the fighting, but such a theory supposes it may be a rational calculation for the predator to view the losses as an investment in future monopoly profits (where rivals are to be killed) or in future undisturbed profits (where rivals are to be disciplined). The future flow of profits, appropriately discounted, must then exceed the present size of the losses. So stated, there seems nothing inherently impossible in the theory. The issue is the probability of the occurrence of predation and the means available for detecting it.

A growing body of economic literature contributes to our understanding of the problem. For reasons that will become obvious, however, this literature does not completely solve the problem for modern antitrust.

There was a time not so long ago when everybody knew that the great American trusts had established and maintained monopoly positions by the ruthless extermination of smaller rivals. The prize exhibit was, of course, the known conduct of the Standard Oil Trust, and for that reason a very large crack appeared in what had appeared solid knowledge when John S. McGee published his careful and startling reevaluation of the Standard Oil legend, showing that Standard had not used predatory price cutting in its march to monopoly.[7] McGee's study was done to test Aaron Director's hypothesis, founded entirely upon the logic of price theory, that would-be monopolists would always prefer merger to predation. The study bore out that prediction. After a careful analysis of the entire trial record of the *Standard Oil* litigation, McGee concluded that "Standard Oil did not use predatory price discrimination to drive out competing refiners, nor did its pricing practices have that effect. . . . I am convinced that Standard did not systematically, if ever, use local price cutting in retailing, or anywhere else, to reduce competition. To do so would have been foolish; and, whatever else has been said about them, the old Standard organization was seldom criticized for making less money when it could readily have made more." Standard attained its market share by merger rather than predatory pricing.

Morris Adelman examined the facts underlying the government's successful prosecution of A&P, including the charge that the chain employed predatory price cutting in local markets in order to gain monopolies and the ability to raise prices.[8] He showed theoretically why such behavior would have been foolish and demonstrated empirically that it most certainly never occurred. Yet the Antitrust Division's charges, and judicial acceptance of them,[9] established still another legend of deliberate predation by a large multimarket firm.

Another study of a legend of predatory price cutting is Kenneth Elzinga's review of the history of the Gunpowder Trust.[10] Taking fourteen companies the government had alleged to be victims of such tactics, Elzinga concluded: "the evidence is quite clear six of these . . . suffered no such fate, it is my impression that another . . . was not subjected to this pricing strategy, the evidence does not allow any conclusion as to five of the companies . . . , and possibly two . . . were in fact subjected to the practice, though even here the evidence is hardly conclusive." The Trust "actually relied upon mergers and loose-knit agreements" for the market dominance achieved.

A theoretical analysis of predation by Lester G. Telser starts with the "assumption that the law does not hinder monopoly by merger or predation" and proceeds to evaluate these practices as "alternative means to monopoly return."[11] Telser concludes that, where the merger route is open, "predatory pricing . . . remains a threat and not an actuality among reasonable men, regardless of conditions in the capital market. The carrying out of the threat indicates a mistake either in the valuation of assets, in the cost of predatory pricing, or in the probability of winning." Telser suggests, however, that the threat may be used by either party, the acquiring firm or the firm to be acquired, to affect the price of the merger, which is to say, the share of the monopoly returns to be anticipated from the merger.

These studies, valuable as they are, do not directly address the question of appropriate rules concerning predation today. They leave open at least two major issues. First, the Standard Oil and Gunpowder trusts had merger and cartelization available as alternative routes to monopoly profits, and Telser's analysis begins with the assumption that these paths are available. Modern antitrust law, however, completely closes the merger option and makes cartelization a costly, dangerous, and much less effective method than it once was. We need to estimate, therefore, the likelihood that the closing of alternatives makes predation an attractive form of behavior for would-be monopolists. Second, these studies dealt with only one form of predation, price cutting, and we need to know whether other forms may be more effective.

Predation is a war of attrition, with its outcome determined by the combatants' relative losses and reserves. The war will be a blitzkrieg only if the predator has greatly disproportionate reserves or is able to inflict very disproportionate losses.

The factor of reserves is probably the less important. For our purposes, a firm's reserves may be defined as its liquid assets plus outside capital available to it at a price justified by expectations of future income. It is plausible to assume that the reserves of various firms in one industry will usually be in proportion to their relative degrees of competitive success, hence in proportion to their market shares. The predator, presumably the largest firm, will thus typically have the largest reserves in absolute size, but its reserves are likely not to be much larger in proportion to market share, and this, as we shall see, will usually be the important factor. When reserves are proportionally equal or even close to equality, the large firm will not find predation profitable if it must employ a technique that inflicts proportionally equal losses upon itself and the victim, and it will certainly not employ a technique that inflicts proportionally larger losses upon itself. The likelihood that reserves will be proportionally equal increases when we realize that available outside capital is included.

It is common to hear objections that the victim will not be able to find outside capital because "the capital market is imperfect." George Stigler aptly characterizes this as a "Gabriel-horn phrase": "Not only is imperfections-in-the-capital-market a popular concept, but what is more important, it is a terminal concept. Once this phrase has been written or spoken, the economist has finished with *that* strand of analysis." [12] The general idea of the capital market being more imperfect than other markets is, of course, patently implausible, since, as Stigler notes, "capital (or general credit) is the most fungible, the most divisible, the most mobile of all productive resources."

The difficulty with the concept of imperfections in the capital market is worse than this, however, for it is not evidence of imperfection if a lender refuses to make an unprofitable loan. If resisting predation is a profitable activity, the imperfection theorist would have to explain why capital will not flow to profitable uses, not just because of occasional mistakes in appraisal, but by a systematic refusal to invest in profitable resistance to predation. Nobody has troubled to explain that form of irrationality in capital suppliers, and we are justified in believing that it does not exist.

If the potential victim would find resistance to predation a profitable use for his liquid assets, a lender should find it equally profitable to lend the required capital. In fact, in any case in which the predator must use a technique that inflicts proportionally equal or greater losses upon himself, the victim would merely have to show the predator his new line of credit to dissuade the predator from attacking.

There are costs in raising capital, of course, and a major cost is likely to be the provision of information to potential investors. That cost is likely to loom largest when the amount of capital required is small and the industry is little known. The cost of convincing lenders may then create a sharply rising cost of outside capital and so provide some opportunity for predators. Yet there are also innumerable small investors in our society, and it seems doubtful that any industry is so unknown to any source of funds. And when we speak of industries operating at regional or national levels, we find both widespread information and many corporate and institutional sources of capital. Here the costs of borrowing to resist predation should not be great, and these are the most important markets.

The technique of predation, rather than the question of reserves, is likely to be decisive in the success of the tactic, and the law should focus upon this issue. Stigler states that "all systems of disciplining rivals by imposing losses require that the rival have inferior access to capital." If I understand that proposition, I think it is incorrect. Given equal access to capital, rivals can be killed or disciplined if the predator is able to inflict disproportionately large losses on his victim. This is required not merely so that the predator may be able to outlast the victim in a war, but also so that the predator can win quickly and thus have a reasonable expectation that future gains will outweigh present losses.

TECHNIQUES OF PREDATION

We must, therefore, attempt to classify forms of business behavior according to their capacities to serve as techniques for predation. If that can be done, the law enforcement agencies will be able to concentrate their attention on activities that have a potential for predatory use, and drop their harmful habit of seeing predation in behavior that is actually vigorously competitive.

To illustrate the theory of predation we will discuss three strategies that businesses may employ. The first, price cutting, though conventionally viewed with grave suspicion, does not provide a likely means of predation because it requires the predator to bear losses that are much larger, both absolutely and proportionally, than those inflicted on the intended victim. The second, the disruption of distribution patterns, is a more complex phenomenon. It may be manifested in a variety of ways, from demands for exclusive dealing (which is an extremely unlikely form of predation) to expulsion from cooperative business groups (e.g., boards of trade), a tactic which may enable predators to inflict losses upon victims that are not merely absolutely and proportionally larger than their own but so crushing as to be instantly and completely decisive. The third predatory strategy consists of misuse of courts or other agencies of government. This strategy may well succeed, since the predator will often be able to inflict upon his victim costs that are in absolute terms equal to or larger than his own, and proportionally larger in either case. These techniques are discussed as examples of a general theory; other possible cases will be mentioned under appropriate chapter headings in this book.

Price Cutting. A firm contemplating predatory price warfare will perceive a series of obstacles that make the prospect of such a campaign exceedingly unattractive. The losses during the war will be proportionally higher for the predator than for the victim; merger law will make it all but impossible for the predator to purchase the victim, so the campaign will have to last until the victim's organization and assets are dissolved; ease of entry will be symmetrical with ease of exit; and anticipated monopoly revenues, being deferred, must be discounted at the current interest rate.

Losses during a price war will be proportionally higher for the predator because he faces the necessity of expanding his output at ever higher costs, while the victim not only will not expand output but has the option of reducing it and so decreasing his costs.

The nature of the problem may be illustrated with a hypothetical case. The particular figures used are arbitrary, but their relationship is not. We may assume that a firm with 80 percent of a market wishes to kill a rival w.th 20 percent in order to achieve the comforts and prerogatives of monopoly status. We shall assume also that these respective shares of the market were determined by the shapes of the firms' marginal cost curves and that each firm is selling where marginal costs equal price.* The situations of predator and victim are shown in Figure 5. (Figure 5 does not show fixed contractual obligations, such as obligations to repay loans, and we may realistically suppose that the predator

---

* Many persons might suppose that the demand curves of duopolists would slope and that prices would be set above marginal costs. Introducing nonmarginal cost pricing, however, would complicate Figure 5 without changing the nature of the problem.

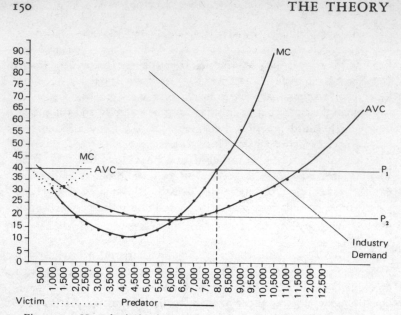

Figure 5. Hypothetical price, output, and cost for predator and victim.

has obligations amounting to $40,000 per week and that the victim's total $10,000.)

The market price is $40 and 10,000 units are being sold per week, of which the large firm sells 8,000 and the small firm 2,000. Let us suppose the predatory large firm opens warfare with a cut in price to $20. This price will cover neither firm's average variable cost,* and neither firm would remain in business if it expected that situation to continue for a long time. Indeed, the predator hopes to convince the victim of the futility of staying in the industry by indicating that $20 will be the price so long as the victim hangs on. But we must analyze the possible adjustments that may be made. These depend largely on the shape of the victim's average variable cost curve and on the feasibility of his closing down altogether until the price cutting ends. I have deliberately given the victim higher marginal and average variable costs than the predator at all relevant ranges of output, in order to

---

* Average variable cost is total variable cost divided by output. No firm will continue to produce if it does not expect to be able to cover its variable costs. It will continue if it covers variable but not fixed costs, though it will not replace equipment and plant as they wear out. This definition of average variable cost does not include expectations about the future. If it did, the illustration would require additional unnecessary explanation.

heighten the apparent probability of successful predation. If the victim's cost curves were as low as the predator's at any relevant output but rose more sharply (accounting for his lower share of the market), predation would fail even more certainly.

We may begin with the situation that is the worst for the victim, i.e., that he maintains his output at a rate of 2,000 per week. Halving the market price, however, has elicited a total demand of 12,500, which seems a modest enough increase; the predator, if he wishes to keep the price down to $20 for his victim's products, must satisfy this new demand by increasing output from 8,000 to 10,500 units per week. (The precise figures used in the example that follows are taken from a table on which Figure 5 is based. The table is not shown here because Figure 5 shows the relationship, and nothing depends on the exact numbers.)

The price received by the victim is $14.56 below his average variable cost. Given an output of 2,000, he is losing $29,120 in variable costs each week, to which must be added fixed expenses of $10,000, giving a total loss of $39,120. If losses were proportional to the starting market shares, the predator would be losing $116,480 in variable costs. But losses are not proportional, because the predator has had to expand output and because his average variable costs rise with that expansion. Average variable cost at the new output stands at $32.76, still below his victim's, but giving a loss of $12.76 on each of 10,500 units for a loss of $133,980 per week. Adding fixed obligations, he is losing $173,980. These assumptions produce a result so far that is not too bad for the predator, though they are certainly not favorable. If we assume, as is plausible, that the reserves of the two firms are in proportion to their original market shares—that is, in the ratio of 4 to 1—it is apparent that the predator is using up his reserves slightly faster than the victim. The ratio of losses is just over 4.4 to 1. That is not necessarily disastrous, of course. The predator may have reserves proportionally larger. On the other hand, the anticipated blitzkrieg has not materialized.

Yet this is by no means the worst that may happen to the hapless predator. The victim has options he has not begun to use. He may be able to close down operations for the time being, paying only $10,000 in fixed obligations and letting the predator supply the entire demand of 12,500 units at the price of $20. In Figure 5 the predator's average variable cost is $47.52 at that output, bringing his weekly variable costs to $344,000, and total losses to $384,000. The ratio of losses is then 38.4 to 1. A lower rate of increase in average variable cost would reduce the loss, but it would remain considerably higher than the loss necessary where the victim maintains his prewar output. The predator cannot raise the price because the victim would reopen, so he must take his losses as long as the victim retains the capacity to reopen.

But let us imagine a situation not quite so catastrophic for the predator. The victim may wish to avoid certain start-up costs, to keep a nucleus of staff on the job, to retain trade contacts, etc. He may, therefore, cut back to 1,000 units per week, where average variable cost is $33.60; then the loss per unit is $13.60, total loss in variable costs is $13,600 per week, and total losses are $23,600. The predator must now sell 11,500 units at an average variable cost of $39.50; he fails to recover weekly variable costs of $224,250, and absorbs a total loss of $264,250. Thus, while the predator's and the victim's reserves stand roughly in a ratio of 4 to 1, their losses per week stand in a ratio of almost 11.2 to 1. The unsophisticated observer might believe that the predator was winning the battle, since he appears to have "captured" 92 percent of the market, but it is that very fact that is defeating him.

A variety of factors may alter the magnitudes discussed here. Some of these would improve the predator's position somewhat; some would make it much worse. Thus, the predation would fail even more rapidly and disastrously if the victim had lower average variable costs below an output of 2,000, a not unreasonable possibility; or if the industry demand were more elastic, so that the predator had to produce, say, 13,000 units to hold the price down to $20.* However one varies the figures, one essential tendency will always be present: the predator must increase output, both to satisfy the new demand that comes forth at lower prices and to take up the market share relinquished by his victim, so he will sell many more units at a loss than will the victim. Moreover, the predator must move to higher average variable costs, while the victim can move to lower. The predator, therefore, will be taking higher losses, both absolutely and proportionally, than the victim. It looks as if the best method of predation is to convince your rival that you are a likely victim and lure him into a ruthless price-cutting attack.

This analysis is confirmed by the common sense of one Mr. Todd, the manager of a refinery allegedly threatened with price cutting by Mr. Moffett, the manager of the Standard Trust's Whiting refinery. John McGee quotes Todd's testimony:

---

* The victim might, of course, be driven from the market if he had very high levels of debt that had to be serviced. While this would be unfortunate for the owner, it would not harm competition. If the creditors either took over the business or sold it, the predator would find himself faced with a better-capitalized victim. Driving a company into bankruptcy turns out to be a way of eliminating what some might describe as an imperfection in the capital market.

Well, I says, "Mr. Moffett, I am very glad you put it that way, because if it is up to you the only way you can get it [the business] is to cut the market, and if you cut the market I will cut you for 200 miles around, and I will make you sell the stuff," and I says, "I don't want a bigger picnic than that; sell it if you want to," and I bid him good day and left.[13]

McGee notes, "The Standard threat never materialized."

The costs of predatory price cutting appear prohibitive, but three related considerations make such a tactic even more unattractive and improbable.

First, the modern law of horizontal mergers makes it all but impossible for the predator to bring the war to an end by purchasing his victim. To accomplish the predator's purpose, the merger must create a monopoly, and the law currently forbids mergers forming market shares of 5 percent or less. Even the much less stringent merger law advocated elsewhere in this book would preclude the attainment of the monopoly necessary to make predation profitable. This means that the price war must be protracted until the victim's facilities are entirely driven from the industry, without possibility of return, and there will always be the danger, until the victim's organization and facilities are irretrievably scattered, that an outside purchaser may appear; then the costly war will have been for nothing. Indeed, by depressing the value of the victim's business, the predator makes that business an attractive investment for any purchaser with adequate reserves. The substitution of such a purchaser for the victim will bring the war to an end, since its continuation would be pointless.

Second, as Ward Bowman points out, ease of entry will be symmetrical with ease of exit. The easier it is to drive a firm from the market, the easier it will be for that firm or another to reenter once the predator begins to collect his monopoly profits. Conversely, the more difficult entry is, the more difficult and expensive it will be to drive a rival out. A shoe retailer can be driven out rapidly, but reentry will be equally rapid. Railroading, which involves specialized facilities, is difficult to enter, but the potential victim of predation would be difficult to drive out precisely because railroad facilities are not useful in other industries. The railroad's management would have to be convinced that the long-run prospects, because of the predation, reduced the value of their facilities to little more than they would bring if sold as scrap. This symmetry of entry and exit means that predation by price cutting is a poor investment even if the predator has the reserves to bear the disproportional losses required.

Finally, while costs are immediate, the anticipated monopoly return is in the future, perhaps far in the future, and must be discounted by the rate of interest. This adds to the poor prospects for the firm contemplating predation by price cutting. (It may be added, if a fourth factor is wanted, that demand tends to become more elastic over time, thus further reducing the size of the anticipated future stream of monopoly payments.)

These considerations do not demonstrate that price cutting could never under any circumstances be a successful method of predation. We need more studies such as those by McGee, Adelman, and Elzinga of cases in which such predation is said to have occurred. But the analysis does demonstrate that predation by such techniques is very improbable.

It seems unwise, therefore, to construct rules about a phenomenon that probably does not exist or which, should it exist in very rare cases, the courts would have grave difficulty distinguishing from competitive price behavior. It is almost certain that attempts to apply such rules would do much more harm than good. For this reason, I am unpersuaded by the arguments advanced by Phillip Areeda and Donald Turner,[14] and even less so by F. M. Scherer's response [15] to them.

Areeda and Turner concede that predatory pricing seems highly unlikely and that extreme care must be taken that the rules formulated not deter competitive pricing. Yet they argue that it is well to have rules all the same. The rule they propose is that "a monopolist pricing below marginal cost should be presumed to have engaged in a predatory or exclusionary practice." (Presumably, the rule should apply to any large, established firm, and not merely to monopolists.) Since it is very difficult to ascertain marginal cost, they say, the rule can be applied by using average variable cost, which is shown in conventional business accounts, as a proxy for marginal cost. The suggestion poses a variety of problems.

The most worrisome is that true average variable costs cannot be reconstructed adequately from business records in a firm of any complexity. Areeda and Turner seem to be discussing plant-level costs, which are themselves sufficiently troublesome; but when we move to the level of the firm, particularly a multiplant, multiproduct firm, problems of costs estimation and allocation will ensure that the costs the law uses are only coincidentally related to real economic costs. There is a high probability of mistake, and hence of harassment, by enforcement authorities and private plaintiffs that would harm consumers by inducing noncompetitive price behavior.

We need not examine the theoretical points Scherer disputes with

Areeda and Turner because they lead him to an unworkable proposal, judicial inquiry into such matters as "the relative cost positions of the monopolist and fringe firms, the scale of entry required to secure minimum costs, whether fringe firms are driven out entirely or merely suppressed, whether the monopolist expands its output to replace the output of excluded rivals or restricts supply again when the rivals withdraw, and whether any long-run compensatory expansion by the monopolist entails investment in scale economy-embodying new plant." There could hardly be drawn a list of criteria less fit for judicial employment. Those items on the list that would not be altered by the monopolist's knowledge of the rules are unknowable by either courts or economists. It is a mistake to suppose that all of the questions posed by an abstract geometric representation of demand and cost phenomena can usefully be addressed in a court proceeding.

Roland H. Koller III studied twenty-three cases in which there were "convictions" for predatory price cutting and where the factual record was adequate to determine whether it had in fact occurred.[16] He thinks predatory price cutting was attempted in only seven cases, succeeded to some extent in four, and had harmful effects upon resource allocation in only three (and these three involved predation not to eliminate a rival but to precipitate merger or collusion).

If Koller's findings are accurate (any successful predation by price cutting is surprising and one should be wary of accepting at face value the assertion that even three cases exist), it is apparent at once how harmful the law has been. Twenty-three judge or jury findings of unlawfully low prices and only three cases of apparent harm to consumers. In sixteen cases firms were held liable for low prices when there was not even an attempt at predation. The result can only be to dampen the vigor of price competition. Moreover, in the three cases where Koller found harm to consumers, the mechanism (merger or collusion) is itself prohibited by law. It would appear safer for the law to concentrate on collusion and very large horizontal mergers in order to make predation ineffective than to jeopardize price competition by trying to prohibit predatory price cutting.

The theoretical argument presented here suggests that predatory price cutting is most unlikely to exist and that attempts to outlaw it are likely to harm consumers more than would abandoning the effort. The analysis also indicates that we should look for methods of predation which do not require the predator to expand output and incur disproportionately large costs. There are such techniques, and we turn to a consideration of some major examples.

Disruption of Distribution Patterns. In any business, patterns of distribution develop over time; these may reasonably be thought to be more efficient than alternative patterns of distribution that do not develop. The patterns that do develop and persist we may call the optimal patterns. By disturbing optimal distribution patterns one rival can impose costs upon another, that is, force the other to accept higher costs. This may or may not be a serious cost increase, but if it is (and the matter can only be determined empirically), the imposition of costs may conceivably be a means of predation. The predator will suffer cost increases, too, and that sets limits to the types of cases in which this tactic will be used for predation. There is a further complication, moreover, in that the behavior involved will often be capable of creating efficiencies. Thus, the law cannot properly see predatory behavior in all unilaterally enforced changes in patterns of distribution.

An example of a business practice carrying a very weak possibility of predation and a very strong probability of efficiency is the use of exclusive dealing contracts. Assume an industry with two manufacturers of equal size, ten retailers of equal size, and a pattern of distribution in which each of the manufacturers supplies half of each retailer's requirements. The pattern of distribution may be supposed to be optimal. Suppose that manufacturer *A* then imposes the condition that any retailer who buys from him must buy only from him. Contrary to some formulations of the problem, this does not threaten manufacturer *B* with foreclosure from the retailers. Since there was an equal demand for the products of the two manufacturers, should half of the retailers decide to accept *A*'s condition, the other half will be better off dealing exclusively in *B*'s product and not acceding to *A*. But the distribution pattern has altered, and it is possible that the new pattern is less efficient and hence imposes costs on *B*, though it is far more probable that *A* has merely perceived that exclusive dealing is more efficient and has adopted it for that reason. The law need have little difficulty with this case, however, for the patterns of distribution have changed to the same extent for both *A* and *B*, and each has suffered the same increase in costs, if there is an increase in costs and not a better mode of selling. The law should not interfere. Either *A* is a witless would-be predator and will retract his condition of exclusivity when he realizes his mistake, or, much more likely, he is trying to find a better mode of doing business.

The possibility of predation might arise if *A* started with 90 percent of the market and *B* with 10 percent, each of them selling in those proportions to each retailer. When *A* imposes its exclusive dealing condition, it will perhaps get nine of the retailers and *B* one. Assuming that benefits of the first pattern of distribution are proportional to the sales in each outlet, then A loses one retailer making X amount of sales and B loses nine whose sales also total X amount. Increased costs would again be equal, but if those costs impose a loss on each firm and their reserves are proportional to their market shares, A can bear the loss much better than B, and the result could be to drive B from the business. These assumptions can be altered in a variety of ways to give different results, but I want merely to note that the possibility of predation, however slim it may be, cannot be entirely excluded on theoretical grounds.

This analysis may be applied to *all* impositions of terms by a seller, which is one way of saying that the analysis alone is of no practical use whatever to antitrust law. Anybody who sells sets terms, and it seems a bit extreme to stop commerce on the ground that some minuscule proportion of it may theoretically involve predation. The search for predation may be narrowed somewhat, for the theory set out can work only if the predator has well over half of the relevant market. Even then it would not work unless the disruption of the distribution pattern imposed significant costs that could not be avoided. That narrowing is not sufficient, however. It would not make sense to deny the right to set terms to all firms with, say, a market share over 80 percent. Aside from the point that such a rule would really be a statement that no such market share should be permitted (a judgment that ought to be debated on other grounds), there is no reason to believe that the terms set, such as exclusive dealing, do not create efficiency far more often than they indicate predation.

The law can usefully attack this form of predation only when there is evidence of specific intent to drive others from the market by means other than superior efficiency and when the predator has overwhelming market size, perhaps 80 or 90 percent. Proof of specific intent to engage in predation may be in the form of statements made by the officers or agents of the company, evidence that the conduct was used threateningly and did not continue when a rival capitulated, or evidence that the conduct was not related to any apparent efficiency. These matters are not so difficult of proof as to render the test overly hard to meet. The real danger for the law is less that predation will be missed than that normal competitive behavior will be wrongly classified as predatory and suppressed.

It would be tempting to dismiss the whole topic on the ground that there is insufficient likelihood that predation of this sort ever occurs, but it seems clear that it can and does in certain classes of cases. It could

have occurred in *Griffith,* since purchasing unreasonable clearances over
rival theaters does not appear to require the predator to accept losses
disproportionately larger than those of his intended victim. We have
already canvassed the reasons why *Griffith*'s rationale of automatic exclusion was incorrect, and from this it follows that specific intent must
be shown if efficiencies are not frequently to be sacrificed. Moreover, it
should be noted that the theory of predation sketched here does not
suppose that power flowed from monopoly towns to competitive towns
but only that Griffith, being much larger than the independents singly
or collectively, had larger reserves than all other theaters in its area
and hence could have afforded a war that did not require it to accept
disproportionate losses. There was, of course, no evidence cited that
this was what happened.

But there is no doubt that predation can succeed when the distribution pattern is so much more efficient than the alternative that those
forced out of the pattern cannot compete. The technique of predation is
the denial of access to an essential economy of scale. Boards of trade,
for example, often control such access, and their members may often
easily destroy a troublesome rival by expelling him from membership
or, perhaps more commonly, may bring a rival into line with the mere
threat of expulsion.

The possible use of this technique may be illustrated by the factual
situation underlying *Chicago Board of Trade.*[17] The trial record is inadequate to permit determination of the real purpose of the board regulation fixing prices overnight on grain "to arrive." There is a suggestion in the Supreme Court's opinion, however, of what may have been
an unrecognized predatory design. Justice Brandeis noted that defendants averred the purpose of the rule was "to promote the convenience
of members by restricting their hours of business and to break up a
monopoly in that branch of the grain trade acquired by four or five
warehousemen in Chicago." That is an improper use of the word
"monopoly," and in any case Justice Brandeis, in arguing that the
price-fixing rule affected such a small fraction of total grain sales as
to have no adverse effect, indicated that even a real "monopoly" would
have had no market power. Yet breaking the grip of four or five traders
on this segment of trade may have been the purpose of the rule. Indeed,
Brandeis claimed as a benefit of the regulation that "it distributed the
business in grain 'to arrive' among a far larger number of Chicago
receivers and commission merchants than had been the case there before." If the effect of fixing prices overnight was to take business from
the four or five warehousemen and spread it to other grain traders, the

most probable explanation would seem to be that the four or five had efficiencies in overnight price making that the others lacked. Perhaps they had night staffs or better connections with the farmers and country merchants and were able to follow the market and make prices more rapidly and accurately. The price-fixing regulation may well have been a move by a political majority within the board to deprive these traders of the benefits of their efficiencies. The tactic would work because it was probably essential for a trader to use the exchange. Thus, the predatory majority could confront the more efficient minority with the alternatives of giving up the benefit of their superior price-making capacities or giving up their membership on the Board of Trade. Loss of membership would be intolerable for such traders. The predators thus had the ability to impose totally unacceptable losses while bearing insignificant losses themselves.

Misuse of Governmental Processes. Misuse of courts and governmental agencies is a particularly effective means of delaying or stifling competition. We are here speaking of legal processes undertaken without regard to the merit of the claim advanced, in order to harm an actual or potential business rival. Litigation can be framed so that the expenses to each party will be about the same, and expenses in complex business litigation can be enormous, not merely in direct legal costs and fees but in diversion of executive effort and disruption of the business organization's activities. Where the object of predatory litigation is to drive an existing rival from a market altogether, the technique will generally be useful only by a larger firm against a smaller, since equal absolute costs will be proportionally greater for the smaller firm. But where delaying the appearance of new competition is the objective, the predator may be any size relative to the victim. The cost of the litigation must be measured against the worth of delay in the appearance of a rival in a lucrative market. The object is not then to inflict unacceptable costs upon the victim but merely to tie him up in proceedings to preserve a market position for a few years more.

The ability of the antitrust laws to deal with predation through this technique is somewhat constricted by countervailing policies. In some part, regulation by administrative agencies is expressly designed to allow firms to suppress the appearance of rivalry. That is not usually true of the court system, but even there the policy of allowing access to the courts, a policy that at times takes on constitutional dimensions, somewhat curtails the ability of antitrust to strike at predation through litigation. There is reason to think, however, that antitrust can and will play a valuable role in punishing predation through this technique. The issues are discussed at greater length in Chapter 18.

* * * *

The argument of this chapter has sweeping implications for antitrust policy. We have examined all of the law's theories about the ways in which business practices or structures may injure competition and found all of them, in varying degrees, to be defective. This is a serious matter, for it means that the law now perceives threats to competition where none exists, and it follows that the law is destroying valuable business arrangements for no reason.

The details of the necessary reforms are worked out in the chapters that follow, but the analysis so far indicates the general nature of those reforms. The law of arrangements that remove rivalry by agreement (e.g., horizontal price fixing, market division, mergers, and the like) must be substantially revised to save those arrangements whose primary effect is an increase in efficiency.

More important are the changes required in the law concerning practices or arrangements thought to be exclusionary (e.g., vertical and conglomerate mergers, exclusive dealing, tying arrangements, price discrimination, and the like). The theories of automatic exclusion and incipiency, upon which the Clayton Act, the Robinson-Patman Act, and the Federal Trade Commission Act are now based, should be abandoned completely. Antitrust should attack no practice or arrangement on the grounds that it is exclusionary or foreclosing unless deliberate predation can be proved. Improper exclusion (exclusion not the result of superior efficiency) is always deliberately intended. There is no "intermediate case" of exclusion resulting from neither efficiency nor predation. The law must become more sophisticated about techniques of predation. Presently, it fears exclusion from such things as price cutting and exclusive dealing, which are very rarely if ever predatory, and tends to pay too little attention to misuse of governmental processes and organized exchanges, where opportunities for predation are plentiful.

These reforms would greatly alter the course of decisions under the antitrust statutes. Just how much will shortly be seen. That alteration would bring the antitrust laws into line with their professed purposes and would represent a clear net gain for consumers as well as for the integrity and intellectual respectability of the law.

PART II

THE LAW
AND THE POLICY

8

Monopoly and Oligopoly: The Problem of Horizontal Size by Internal Growth

ISSUES of industrial concentration —of monopoly and, more especially, oligopoly—hold center stage in current debates over antitrust policy. They seem likely to provide the main battleground of policy in the coming decade. There are two possible paths to that battleground: the continuing judicial transformation of basic Sherman Act doctrine, or the effort to adopt one of the increasingly serious proposals for new antitrust legislation.

The Department of Justice's suits against IBM and AT&T and the Federal Trade Commission's actions against the major oil companies and the cereal manufacturers follow the former route. They would break up large firms in the expectation that more competitive behavior would result. As we shall see, government suits seeking structural remedies are not soundly based in either law or economics. Nor was Ralph Nader's call for antitrust action against General Motors: "The history and attainments of GM's market power make it a classic candidate for antitrust enforcement under Sherman 2 and Clayton 7. In law and economics there are solid grounds for proceeding toward dissolution or divestiture of General Motors under the two antitrust laws." [1] This calls for a very considerable judicial expansion rather than an application of existing doctrine, doctrine which is itself already extended well beyond the bounds of economic reason. Yet very competent analysts, such as Donald Turner and Carl Kaysen [2] and the majority of the Neal Task Force appointed by President Johnson,[3] have called for new laws designed to break up concentrated industries. Bills to accomplish such restructuring have been introduced in Congress. Other proposed legislation would not mandate divestitures according to generally applicable criteria but would direct that firms in particular industries be broken up. Thus the proposals, rather closely resembling bills of attainder, that would effect horizontal and vertical divestitures of large oil companies.

Antitrust has historically dealt with large horizontal size according to the means by which it was achieved. Large market shares attained by horizontal merger have always been more vulnerable to legal attack than large shares achieved by internal growth, and this difference has been accentuated by the Supreme Court's harsh interpretation of amended Section 7 of the Clayton Act. Now the law is being urged to close the "gap" by attacking size itself, ignoring the route by which it was gained. This is fundamental error, since inferences about the economic effects of market shares properly flow from the origins of those shares.

The law of horizontal mergers and the reform it requires are discussed in a subsequent chapter. In this chapter we will deal with the topic of monopolistic and oligopolistic market structures created by the internal growth of the firms in those markets. My conclusion is that the law should never attack such structures, since they embody the proper balance of forces for consumer welfare. Before making the economic argument in support of that conclusion, however, I will sketch the present case law and some of the proposed legislation on the subject.

THE EVOLUTION OF EXISTING LAW ABOUT SIZE BY INTERNAL GROWTH

The framers of the Sherman Act were, as we have seen, prepared to allow any market share that was achieved by superior efficiency. They wished to ban horizontal mergers of monopolistic size and predatory behavior, which "involved," according to Senator Hoar, "something like the use of means which made it impossible for other persons to engage in fair competition." [4] And Chief Justice White was faithful to this legislative intention in *Standard Oil* and *American Tobacco*. Noting that the Sherman Act omitted "any direct prohibition against monopoly in the concrete," [5] he framed doctrine about size that rested upon monopolistic combination, bad intent, and predatory practices, in order that size gained by efficiency would not be hampered.

Two influences began gradually to wear away the law's requirement that size, to be illegal, be gained either by merger or predation. One was the osmosis into the Sherman Act of the theory, inspired by the Clayton Act, that exclusionary practices need not involve a deliberate intent to gain monopoly power and may, in fact, seem to the persons employing them to be perfectly normal behavior. The result, inevitably, was to expand the category of behavior that made large size itself impermissible.

The second influence that eroded the old doctrine was an illogical stress upon the importance of allocative efficiency without regard to productive efficiency. Once productive efficiency is dropped from consideration, there is no difference between means of gaining large size or monopoly. If the market share is the same, the danger of restriction of output appears to be the same. Indeed, once efficiency is ignored, there appears to be no difference between a cartel and a company. They both eliminate competition internally. Since cartels are illegal regardless of market power, companies should be outlawed, no matter how small. That the principle has not been taken to this logical conclusion does not make it intellectually more respectable, nor has it prevented the principle from wreaking havoc where it is applied.

Two famous opinions illustrate the alteration of the early law. Judge Hand's 1945 *Alcoa* opinion displays both of the influences cited, while Judge Wyzanski's 1953 *United Shoe Machinery* opinion shows the potentialities of the theory of exclusionary practices. These cases are so firmly embedded in modern antitrust jurisprudence and are so widely admired as examples of skilled judicial handling of economic issues that I had better state plainly that they seem to me clearly bad law. Yet there is real danger that they will be taken as bases for attempts to strike at oligopolistic market structures through the Sherman Act.

The major charge in the *Alcoa* case,[6] decided by the Court of Appeals for the Second Circuit because the Supreme Court could not muster a quorum, was that Alcoa had monopolized the market for virgin aluminum ingot. After a trial of just over two years the district court found for the defendant, but in an opinion by Judge Learned Hand the Court of Appeals reversed, holding that Alcoa had, as alleged, violated Section 2 of the Sherman Act.

Alcoa's market position originated in a patent monopoly that lasted from 1899 to 1909 and had, according to the opinion, been perpetuated in part by unlawful practices from 1909 to 1912. According to Judge Hand's reckoning, Alcoa's market share in 1940 was 90 percent. He laid down a dictum that has greatly influenced the course of the law since: "That percentage is enough to constitute a monopoly; it is doubtful whether sixty or sixty-four percent would be enough; and certainly thirty-three percent is not."

That much is clear, but it is quite difficult to follow the reasoning by which Hand demonstrated that 90 percent of a market achieved without predation or merger is monopoly within the meaning of Section 2 of the Sherman Act and, further, that its possessor had monopolized. This distinction between having a monopoly covered by the Act and having monopolized was necessary because a monopoly might be lawful, while monopolization is necessarily illegal. The main interest of the case lies in the gap between the two concepts: what monopoly can a firm possess without having monopolized?

Hand proceeded by a syllogism whose major premise is that price-fixing agreements are "unconditionally prohibited" and whose minor premise is that "monopoly necessarily involves an equal, or even greater, power to fix prices" than does agreement. Thus, the inexorable conclusion: "It would be absurd to condemn such contracts unconditionally, and not to extend the condemnation to monopolies; for the contracts are only steps toward that entire control which monopoly confers: they are really partial monopolies."

Two observations should be made about that syllogism. First, the minor premise leaves out a crucial factor: a firm, even though a monopolist, is economically integrated and so has internal efficiencies that a price-fixing ring does not. When that is admitted, Hand's conclusion does not follow. Second, even though Hand buttressed his economic reasoning by arguing that the alleged noneconomic purposes of the Sherman Act, which we have examined in Chapter 2, compelled the same conclusion of per se illegality for monopolies (which, it must be recalled, may range down to market shares of 60 percent), he then seemed to take back the conclusion, at least in part, in a very troublesome passage.

"It does not follow," said Judge Hand, that "because 'Alcoa' had such a monopoly that it 'monopolized' the ingot market: it may not have achieved monopoly; monopoly may have been thrust upon it." His distinction appears to be one between unlawful achievement and lawful passivity. He stressed this point again, before apparently contradicting it: "persons may unwittingly find themselves in possession of a monopoly, automatically so to say: that is, without having intended either to put an end to existing competition, or to prevent competition from arising when none had existed; they may become monopolists by force of accident." He gave three examples. The first was natural monopoly because of economies of scale; the second was changes in taste or cost that drive out all but one seller. The third example of a lawful monopolist was, in view of the achievement-passivity distinction, at first glance rather surprising: "A single producer may be the survivor out of a group of active competitors, merely by virtue of his superior skill, foresight and industry." This producer, one would have thought, has hardly had monopoly "thrust upon" him; he has not gained his position "by force of accident" or "unwittingly." If anybody has, he has "achieved monopoly."

There may seem a difficulty in reconciling this language with the outcome of the case, for Alcoa, according to Hand, had maintained its market position entirely by superior efficiency. It may be suggested, therefore, that the case is to be read as permitting monopoly gained over the bodies of active rivals but not monopoly that began as such and was maintained. The former, the argument goes, demonstrates superior efficiency, while the latter does not. There is, however, no difference in the inferences about efficiency in the two cases unless one posits artificial barriers to entry, so that a firm need not have superior efficiency to bar entrants. We will see that no such barriers exist. But the point of interest for the moment is not the wisdom of the distinction but whether Judge Hand intended to make it. In favor of that reading is the necessity of reconciling what seem to be utterly inconsistent statements in the opinion and the fact that Hand stated the issue in the case as including the origin of the monopoly: "the most important question in the case is whether the monopoly in 'Alcoa's' production of 'virgin' ingot, secured by the two patents until 1909, and in part perpetuated between 1909 and 1912 by the unlawful practices, forbidden by the decree of 1912, continued for the ensuing twenty-eight years; and whether, if it did, it was unlawful under § 2 of the Sherman Act." So one might read the case as holding only that it is unlawful to maintain a monopoly not originally won against competition, and perhaps unlawful as well to maintain a position originally tainted with some unlawful practices. This reading would make *Alcoa* a rather narrow and relatively unimportant precedent.

The weight of the internal evidence, however, appears to be against such an interpretation. The argument that a monopoly is the same economic phenomenon as a cartel applies regardless of the origin of the monopoly; so also does Hand's argument from the assumed noneconomic of the statute. Moreover, Hand often seemed to equate gaining and maintaining monopoly, as when he remarked, "Persons may unwittingly find themselves in possession of a monopoly, automatically so to say: that is, without having intended *either* to put an end to existing competition, *or* to prevent competition from arising when none had existed; they may become monopolists by force of accident" (emphasis added); or, earlier in the opinion, "We may start therefore with the premise that to have combined ninety percent of the producers of ingot would have been to 'monopolize' the ingot market; and, *so far as concerns the public interest, it can make no difference whether an existing competition is put an end to, or whether prospective competition is prevented*" (emphasis added). The distinction between getting and maintaining monopolies seems to be denied by Hand's own language.

If we return to Hand's remarks about lawful monopolies, we will see that he takes back what he seemed to say about the lawfulness of gaining a monopoly through "superior skill, foresight and industry." Immediately after that statement, Hand says,

In such cases a strong argument can be made that, although the result may expose the public to the evils of monopoly, the Act does not mean to condemn the resultant of those very forces which it is its prime object to foster: finis opus coronat. The successful competitor, having been urged to compete, must not be turned upon when he wins.

The second sentence is often read as though it were a policy conclusion adopted and advocated by Judge Hand. In context, it seems plain that it is not: it is merely Hand's statement of a position for which "a strong argument can be made," and he proceeds to suggest that it was once the law but is so no longer. He next says that the "most extreme expression of this view" occurred in the 1920 *United States Steel* decision,[7] and that it was repeated in the 1927 *International Harvester* opinion.[8] Not only may his readers be presumed to know that these were by 1945 regarded as shaky precedents, but Hand at once distinguishes them, pointing out that in both cases the defendant had a market share of less than two-thirds, so that even if the views expressed had not later been modified, they were not necessary to the outcome of the cases and did not have the authority of an actual decision. He then argues that "whatever authority" the cases did have was in fact modified by Justice Cardozo's language in the 1932 *Swift* decision: [9]

Mere size . . . is not an offense against the Sherman Act unless magnified to the point at which it amounts to a monopoly . . . but size carries with it an opportunity for abuse that is not to be ignored when the opportunity is proved to have been utilized in the past.

Thus, a two-part test: size is illegal if it is either large enough to be called monopoly or if it is abused. So much for the monopolist who gained his position by superior skill, foresight, and industry. He turns out to have violated Section 2 of the Sherman Act after all.

But the law is seen to be even more draconian when we discover what Hand means by abusing size, for in Hand's reasoning, the exercise of superior skill, foresight, and industry is itself an abuse. By this criterion Alcoa fell within both of Justice Cardozo's categories:

"Alcoa's" size was "magnified" to make it a "monopoly"; indeed, it has never been anything else; and its size, not only offered it an "opportunity for abuse," but it "utilized" its size for "abuse," as can easily be shown.

Judge Hand began his showing by telling Alcoa it was not "the passive beneficiary of a monopoly following upon an involuntary elimination of competitors by automatically operative economic forces." We seem to be all the way back to a requirement of utter passivity and lucky accident. For a moment it seems as though Hand is pinning his reasoning to the rather minor unlawful practices engaged in between 1909 and 1912, though that would be a spectacularly inadequate underpinning for a finding of illegal monopoly in 1940. Apparently this was not the gravamen, however, for the opinion then goes on to decry the means by which the monopoly was maintained after 1912, and later Hand specifically said: "We disregard any question of 'intent.'" Apart from the magnification of its size to monopoly, then, what conduct constituted "abuse" and prevented Alcoa from claiming the sanctuary of the "thrust-upon" defense?

The only question is whether it falls within the exception established in favor of those who do not seek, but cannot avoid, the control of a market. It seems to us that that question scarcely survives its statement. It was not inevitable that it should always anticipate increases in the demand for ingot and be prepared to supply them. Nothing compelled it to keep doubling and redoubling its capacity before others entered the field. It insists that it never excluded competitors; but we can think of no more effective exclusion than progressively to embrace each new opportunity as it opened, and to face every newcomer with new capacity already geared into a great organization, having the advantage of experience, trade connections and the elite of personnel. Only in case we interpret "exclusion" as limited to manoeuvres not honestly industrial, but actuated solely by a desire to prevent competition, can such a course, indefatigably pursued, be deemed not "exclusionary." So to limit it would in our judgment emasculate the Act. . . .

The message is unmistakable: monopoly (two-thirds of a market or more) is illegal unless the monopolist could not avoid it. Superior efficiency is not only no excuse, it is an "abuse" of large size. One is forced to believe that Hand meant what he said when he equated firms of large size with price-fixing cartels, the sole legal difference being that large firms might suffer their market share by accident but that one could hardly enter into a cartel agreement through sheer bad luck. The most accurate summation of Judge Hand's *Alcoa* rationale appears to be that suggested by Aaron Director and Edward Levi: [10] "Perhaps, then, the successful competitor can be turned upon when he wins, because he has been told not to compete." The *Alcoa* opinion, therefore, stands revealed as a thoroughly perverse judicial tour de force, contrary to the legislative intent of the Sherman Act, the great 1911 cases that formulated the "rule of reason," and the entire spirit of antitrust.

Judge Wyzanski's *United Shoe Machinery* opinion [11] upheld the government's contention that United had monopolized the manufacture and sale of shoe machinery. Judge Wyzanski found further that there were three sources of United's market control: (1) the original constitution of the company by merger in 1899; (2) "the superiority of United's products and services"; and (3) the system United employed of leasing its machines to shoe manufacturers. The merger, having been approved by the Supreme Court in 1918, was now beyond legal reproach; the superiority of products and services, being examples of "superior skill, foresight and industry," Wyzanski said were immune to attack; but the leasing system was regarded as vulnerable. There may seem to be in that reasoning some comfort, for Wyzanski was clearly interpreting *Alcoa* not to outlaw monopoly based upon superior efficiency. But the comfort is illusory, for it is clear that Wyzanski convicted United of superior efficiency under another name, "barriers to entry." The leasing system was held to create the objectionable "barriers."

The objection to the leasing system rested upon a very peculiar argument, one which we have examined in Chapter 7 but whose importance justifies a brief reexamination. Judge Wyzanski said that when Senators Hoar and Edmunds brought the final version of the Sherman Act before the Senate they thought it applied to restraints of trade known to the common law (which is largely true, if that refers to the common-law cases cited by Sherman in which cartels, monopolistic mergers, and predation were outlawed), but would not apply to the results of superior efficiency. Perhaps recognizing that Judge Learned Hand's apparent disapproval of efficiency did violence to this intended dichotomy, Judge Wyzanski suggested a new category of economic behavior not contemplated by Hoar and Edmunds: "They did not discuss the intermediate case where the causes of an enterprise's success were neither common law restraints of trade, nor the skill with which the business was conducted, but rather some practice which without being predatory, abusive, or coercive was in economic effect exclusionary."

In accepting the idea that such an intermediate category of behavior exists, Judge Wyzanski, as we have seen, made a serious economic error —an error that other courts, the Supreme Court, and many economists also make. If the intermediate class of cases does not exist, and it seems certain that it does not, then the judge must determine which of the other two classes—the desire to drive out rivals by improper tactics (which is unlikely) or the desire to create efficiency—explains the practice before him. Judge Wyzanski did not examine the possibility that the net effect of the leasing system was efficiency creation. He thus certainly decided the case against United on an incorrect rationale. Almost as certainly, the sole result of his complete reformation of the leasing system was to lessen the firm's efficiency.

The decree removed those features of the leases that Judge Wyzanski thought exclusionary, and also required that customers be given an option to purchase machines on terms about as attractive as leasing. The idea was that with the barriers to entry removed, the industry would become more competitive. Subsequent experience could not, of course, confirm Wyzanski's basic reasoning, since a decline in United's market share would be a totally ambiguous datum. The believer in barriers to entry would take the decline as evidence that artificial barriers had existed. But the destruction of an efficient mode of distribution would also tend to lower the handicapped firm's market share. Nevertheless, even on the theory that artificial barriers to entry existed, one might have said (though Judge Wyzanski did not) that once those barriers were removed, if United continued to hold a large market share, its position would be demonstrated to rest entirely upon superior efficiency.

From this standpoint, the aftermath was rather macabre. Ten years later the government petitioned for further relief, claiming that adequately competitive conditions had not been returned to the industry by the decree. Judge Wyzanski found that United's market share had declined to about 62 percent, and its share by value of recent machine shipments might be as little as 48 percent and was certainly not much over 50 percent.[12] He concluded that the decree had worked much as intended, but he also interpreted the law to deny him the power to modify the decree in these circumstances. The government appealed, and the Supreme Court reversed because of Wyzanski's mistaken view of his power.[13] But the Court also delivered a lecture on the function of relief that may easily be read as a virtual directive to dissolve United. In any case, United and the government soon entered into a consent decree by which United was required to divest itself of assets sufficient to reduce its market share to no more than 33 percent.

The case was thus ultimately revealed to be about United's size and nothing more. Judge Wyzanski's original reasoning was circular. He looked at United's size and declared that it was lawful unless maintained by practices that were exclusionary. He then identified the practices that largely accounted for United's success as exclusionary—as indeed they were: whatever a firm does that gives it a market share excludes rivals from that share of the market. But it would be possible, even having made that mistake, to accept its logical consequences. The exclusionary practices having been forbidden, any market share remaining after ten years would certainly be due to efficiency. The Supreme Court, however, indicated that it would not accept that logic; it was the size that was offensive, no matter how maintained. *United Shoe Machinery* turns out not to be so different from *Alcoa* after all.*

The application of these two precedents to oligopolistic markets is problematical. Judge Hand's dictum that 90 percent of a market constitutes monopoly, 64 or 60 percent is doubtful, and 33 percent is certainly not monopoly would prevent use of Section 2 of the Sherman Act to attack most markets that are thought of as concentrated or oligopolistic. Judge Wyzanski tended to reinforce that dictum. In dealing with the charge that United had also monopolized the markets for supplies used by shoe manufacturers, he held that monopolization existed where United had "much more than half the market" by virtue of its control

---

* The issue of the legality of size achieved by superior efficiency remains in doubt. The Supreme Court adopted a formulation in *United States* v. *Grinnell Corp.*, 384 U.S. 653, 570–71 (1966), that runs counter to the anti-efficiency themes of *Alcoa* and *United Shoe Machinery*: "The offense of monopoly under § 2 of the Sherman Act has two elements: (1) the possession of monopoly power in the relevant market and (2) the willful acquisition or maintenance of that power as distinguished from growth or development as a consequence of a superior product, business acumen, or historic accident." The key to the law's development will doubtless lie in the Supreme Court's ability to recognize the nature and diverse forms of business efficiency. The rhetoric of antitrust contains a variety of terms (e.g., "competitive advantage" and "barrier to entry") designed to label superior efficiency as an improper means of exclusion. Unless those semantic traps are ~voided, the second element of the test enunciated in *Grinnell* will prove a nullity, and *Alcoa* and *United Shoe Machinery* will turn out to express the law.

over the shoe machinery market. But monopolization in supplies did not exist, despite the power added by the shoe machinery market, "where United has not over 50% of the share of the market," since then "it has nothing more than a limited market power flowing from its generally long line of supplies, its many business relations with shoe manufacturers, and its competitors' comparative weakness in resources and variety of products." The Supreme Court's lecture ten years later, when United had lost market share, may be thought to suggest a readiness to lower the percentage threshold of monopoly, but that remains unclear.

Application of these cases in the future will also depend upon the position taken toward secondhand markets. In *Alcoa,* Judge Hand excluded from the relevant market ingot made from scrap. Though it competed with the virgin ingot sold by Alcoa, Hand reasoned that a farseeing monopolist would control the amount of secondary ingot returning to the market by its original decision about how much virgin ingot to produce. In *United Shoe Machinery,* however, Judge Wyzanski insisted upon offering customers the option of purchasing machines in order to create a secondhand machinery market that would compete with United. This certainly implies that the secondhand market must be counted to some extent in computing a firm's market share. Inclusion of secondhand sales in computing market shares would greatly reduce the number of firms that might otherwise be held to have illegally large market positions.

Wyzanski's insight appears to be closer to reality than Hand's. The foresighted monopolist imagined by Hand would realize that he could only alter the availability of secondhand items in the future by curtailing his production in the present. In making a decision he will realize that he is sacrificing present profits to gain future profits, which must be discounted by the current rate of interest and by some factor expressing the uncertainty that he will still have a profitable monopoly in the future time period. In addition, not all products sold now will last into the future time period, so that a decision to produce ten less now would prevent the return not of ten but of only, say, seven or eight. All these factors suggest that a monopolist who sells a product that lasts for any considerable period of time will have little incentive to curtail current production and profits in order to lessen future competition from secondhand products. Probably in most such cases the full or a very slightly discounted value of secondhand sales should be counted in the relevant market. Where the life of the product is only a year or two, the monopolist has greater incentive to take secondhand sales into account, and such sales should be discounted more heavily in computing the relevant market.*

When there are three or four or more sellers in a market, there seems no doubt that all secondhand sales should be included. That many sellers cannot be treated as though they were one. This consideration, plus the factors just discussed, makes Judge Hand's thesis inapplicable in such markets.

Some commentators have regretted Judge Hand's market share dictum because its acceptance seems to preclude dissolution of any corporation with less than 60 or 64 percent of the market. This makes it difficult to attack what such commentators regard as the "oligopoly problem," since few oligopolies have a leading firm with the requisite market share, and those that do obviously cannot have a second or third firm with such shares. Drastic restructuring of concentrated industries thus seems impossible under existing law.

A proposed solution to this doctrinal problem is to accumulate the shares of the two or three largest firms in an industry on the theory that oligopolists behave together as if they were a single firm. Thus, if an industry had three firms with market shares respectively of 40, 30, and 20 percent, and then a scattering of smaller companies, aggregating the shares of the three largest would give a 90 percent share, which is clearly enough to meet Hand's test. This theory of joint monopolization requiring dissolution depends upon the economic theory that oligopolists inevitably behave as a single firm because they cannot help taking each other's probable reactions into account. An injunction against such behavior would accomplish nothing, the theory goes, because the firms cannot behave otherwise in such a structure.

The primary difficulty with this theory is its assumptions (1) that oligopolistic structure leads naturally to monopolistic behavior, so that restriction of output occurs, and (2) that dissolution would produce results more favorable to consumers. We shall see that these economic assumptions are not true, so that there is no merit in the proposed legal innovation.

Richard Posner has advanced a more interesting proposal for dealing with oligopoly under present law.[14] He argues, correctly, that noncompetitive behavior does not follow inevitably from market concentration. He suggests further that where noncompetitive pricing does occur, it is

---

* Where costs of salvaging the secondhand product are high, one may properly exclude it from the relevant market on the theory that it merely sets an upper limit to the monopoly power of the seller, coming forth only at high prices. Judge Hand excluded foreign aluminum from the relevant market on a similar theory.

the result of collusion, explicit or tacit. Explicit collusion violates Section 1 of the Sherman Act, and Posner argues that there is no doctrinal difficulty in applying Section 1 to tacit collusion. He recognizes that the greatest difficulty with his approach is the problem of discerning and proving instances of tacit collusion, and I am even less sanguine than he about the possibility of devising criteria that will be useful in a litigation context. There may be evidence of market behavior that is consistent only with collusion, and that may of course be used to show agreement, but Posner is seeking to go beyond that to find means of showing subtler forms of tacit understanding, and that will prove, as he recognizes, a perilous enterprise.

A larger difficulty with Posner's approach is the uncertainty of the premise that tacit collusion is an important phenomenon, or even that it is a real phenomenon. Posner asserts that "the Sherman Act has proved to be ineffectual in dealing with forms of collusive pricing that do not generate detectable acts of agreement or communication among the colluding sellers." That is certainly true *if* any such collusive pricing actually occurs. It is hard to say with certainty that such collusive pricing does or does not occur, since, by definition, we have not detected it. The difficulty of maintaining small-number cartels based upon detailed communication and agreement should, however, make us dubious that concerted action without explicit collusion is likely to be at all common or successful. Moreover, Posner is really offering a way to strike at the pricing restraint said to be characteristic of oligopolists, and as will be argued shortly, there is good reason to doubt that such restraint exists in the absence of explicit and detectable agreement. The attempt to apply Section 1 with inadequate techniques for discerning tacit collusion is, therefore, likely to produce a series of convictions of firms that have in fact done nothing at all reprehensible.

PROPOSALS FOR NEW LEGISLATION

Perhaps the best-known proposal for new legislation to break up monopolies (which are rare in important markets) and oligopolies (which are very common on many definitions) is that put forward by Carl Kaysen and Donald Turner in their much-discussed book *Antitrust*

Policy.[15] Kaysen and Turner suggest a statute designed to identify and dissolve firms found to have "unreasonable market power." Some idea of their target area may be gathered from their classification of oligopolistic markets. "A structurally oligopolistic market is one in which the few largest sellers in the market have a share of the market sufficient to make it likely that they will recognize the interaction of their own behavior and their rivals' responses in determining the values of the market variables." Competition will probably not operate freely in such markets, they say, and restriction of output is likely to occur. The crucial question, of course, is how many sellers may be "few." "As our dividing point we have adopted, somewhat arbitrarily, a market share of one third of total market sales for the eight largest sellers, because in the majority of markets with which we are familiar, a smaller number of firms with larger shares of the market generally accompany, to a significant degree, the kind of behavior indicated above." Kaysen and Turner do not state the evidence which leads them to this conclusion.

They break the concept of oligopoly down further. In Type One oligopoly, "the first eight firms have at least 50 percent of total market sales and the first twenty firms have at least 75 percent of total market sales." Here, "recognition of interdependence by the leading firms is extremely likely, and the 75 percent share of the first twenty sellers makes it likely that the response of the smaller sellers will not limit the behavior of the larger firms." In Type Two oligopoly, the eight largest sellers have a market share of at least 33 percent and the rest of the market is relatively unconcentrated. The suggestion that industries structured like these will not behave competitively is startling, and it is unfortunate the assertion is not supported in any way.

Such market structures are the concern of the statute the authors propose, and though Kaysen and Turner would provide for some performance tests and a type of efficiency defense, it is clear that any major firm in an industry classified as oligopolistic would be in danger. Certainly any major firm in a market characterized as a Type One oligopoly would be a prime candidate for dissolution and would face an uphill legal battle to justify its size.

In 1968 a White House Task Force on Antitrust Policy, appointed by President Johnson and chaired by Phil C. Neal, then Dean of the University of Chicago Law School, recommended adoption of a Concentrated Industries Act designed to reduce concentration in any industry in which "any four or fewer firms had an aggregate market share of 70% or more during at least seven of the ten and four of the most recent five base years."[16] Though a type of efficiency defense is again provided, it seems unlikely to prove important, and the proposed statute would empower the court to require "oligopoly firms" (those whose market share exceeded 15 percent in a market of the sort just described) either to divest themselves of assets or to modify their contractual relationships and methods of distribution so that no firm had a market share of more than 12 percent. This statute was endorsed by eleven of the thirteen members of the Neal Task Force, and the majority contained eminent academic lawyers and economists as well as distinguished practicing attorneys.

These proposals are important because they are representative of the trend of thinking about problems of monopoly and oligopoly. The prospect that such proposals may one day be enacted should not be dismissed as fanciful. Major antitrust legislation has always been difficult to pass, but in 1890, 1914, 1936, and 1950 such legislation has been enacted, creating significant policy shifts. The history of antitrust and of other forms of regulation suggests that changes come in this way: a change in the intellectual climate, engendered by academic discussion and its popularization by reformers; the translation of the new ideas into the political sphere, assisted by the always potent dislike and distrust of large corporations; and finally, the implementation of such ideas through law. This progression is not, of course, inevitable or predestined, but a variety of indicators suggest that with respect to attacks upon monopoly and oligopoly we are already in the second stage and may be entering the third.

Another caution is suggested by the history of antitrust. Attacks upon concentrated market structures make sense only if they gain through improved resource allocation more than they cost through destruction of productive efficiency. For this reason, both the Kaysen-Turner and the Neal Task Force proposals provide efficiency defenses to actions for dissolution. The prospect of such defenses should not make anyone too sanguine about the impact of the proposed statutes. In the first place, as we have seen, efficiency cannot be quantified, and no one can prove the size of the losses that would be incurred through a projected dissolution. Defendants will be unlikely, therefore, to carry successfully the burden of persuasion on efficiency defenses, particularly since the thrust of the statutes will suggest that cases of doubt are to be resolved in favor of the government. In the second place, past antitrust enactments have almost invariably proved far more severe in operation than they had seemed likely to be in advance. Whatever comfort the cost justification, meeting competition, and other defenses of the Robinson-Patman Act may have given those dubious about the law's major thrust has proved largely illusory. And neither the language of the 1950 amendment to Section 7 of the Clayton Act nor the tenor of the debate in Congress gave clear warning of the exceedingly severe measure the statute was to become in the hands of the Supreme Court. (Many legislators seemed to think they were not doing much more than closing the "asset loophole" in the old Section 7.) Similar statements could be made about other antitrust statutes. There is good reason to believe that new legislation aimed at monopolistic and oligopolistic market structures would follow the general antitrust pattern of proving harsher and less discriminating in application than had been forecast in legislative discussion.

POLICY ANALYSIS

Antitrust should not interfere with any firm size created by internal growth, and this is true whether the result is monopoly or oligopoly. The high probability is that any such interference will lead to a net loss in consumer welfare. This thesis is one I advanced in dissenting from the Neal Task Force's deconcentration proposal. "If the leading firms in a concentrated industry are restricting their output in order to obtain prices above the competitive level, their efficiencies must be sufficiently superior to that of all actual and potential rivals to offset that behavior. Were this not so, rivals would be enabled to expand their market shares because of the abnormally high prices and would thus deconcentrate the industry. Market rivalry thus automatically weighs the respective influences of efficiency and output restriction and arrives at the firm sizes and industry structures that serve consumers best." Today I would add only two thoughts. First, I doubt that there is any significant output restriction problem arising from the concentration of any industry. Second, there is no coherent theory based on consumer welfare that supports a policy of industrial deconcentration when concentration has been created either by the internal growth of the firms or by merger more than ten or fifteen years old.

We may approach the topic by asking what proponents of industry restructuring, such as Kaysen and Turner and the majority of the Neal Task Force, must prove in order to carry their case. We ought not to invoke the coercive power of the law—to say nothing of spending resources in protracted litigation—unless we are reasonably sure that some beneficial result will be achieved. Proponents of industry restructuring must, therefore, show each of three things in order to make a case for dissolving firms whose size has been attained by internal growth. These three elements of the case for dissolution are that: (1) significant restriction of output is the probable result of the industry structure; (2) dissolution would not destroy significant efficiencies; and (3) artificial "barriers" prevent deconcentration of the industry through growth of smaller firms or entry of new firms. Unless significant restriction of output exists, there is no problem to be solved. If dissolution would destroy significant efficiencies, the cure may be worse than the disease. If no artificial barriers exist, the growth or entry of other firms will deconcentrate the industry, unless the larger firms' market positions actually rest upon superior efficiency.

Proponents of dissolution must, therefore, establish the probability of each of these elements in order to sustain their position. In the case of complete monopoly, they can show only the first of the three elements but not the other two. In the case of oligopoly, they cannot prove a single one of the necessary elements. The argument for dissolution is made even less tenable, if that is possible, by Oliver Williamson's observation that "it is evident that a relatively modest cost reduction is usually sufficient to offset relatively large price increases." [17] This means that any efficiencies associated with a firm's size are very likely to outweigh any restriction of output on the consumer welfare scale. The probabilities are overwhelmingly on the side of the proposition that consumers are best served by letting market structures created by internal growth strictly alone. We shall examine each of the three elements in turn.

RESTRICTION OF OUTPUT

The theories of the ways in which monopoly and oligopoly lead to restriction of output, and hence to misallocation of resources, is spelled out in Chapter 4. The reader is reminded that the theories are of very different orders of rigor. A monopolist has the power to restrict output. The theory does not say that he must, but clearly he may, and we expect that he will (though entry of new firms and substitution of other products at higher prices may severly limit the monopolist's degree of output restriction). Oligopoly theory, however, is much more speculative. It really says very little more than that if a few sellers who occupy most of a market were able to act in concert, without collusion, they would be able to achieve results in rate of output and prices very much like those a monopolist could achieve under the same cost and demand conditions. That statement is less a theory than a tautology. It says only that *if* sellers can behave that way, they can behave that way. But the theory itself does not tell us *whether* they can or do, and those are the things we need to know. As matters stand, one must agree, at a minimum with the summation of Harold Demsetz: [18]

> [T]he asserted relationship between market concentration and competition cannot be derived from existing theoretical considerations and . . . is based largely on an incorrect understanding of the concept of competition or rivalry. . . .
> [W]e have no theory that allows us to deduce from the observable degree of concentration in a particular market whether or not price and output are competitive. [Emphasis in the original.]

The subject of oligopoly is wide open, and we must employ such pieces of fact and theory as we can muster to determine whether oligopolistic markets behave more like monopolistic markets than like competitive markets. The available evidence strongly suggests that oligopolies do not generally result in substantial or significant restrictions of output. It is quite possible that they result in no restriction of output, but the evidence does not permit one to make that statement with complete confidence.

Support for this position is of various kinds, but before citing it we should get out of the way a variety of "evidence" that does not bear upon the issue. The Neal Task Force argued that

> the adverse effects of persistent concentration on output and price find some confirmation in various studies that have been made of return on capital in major industries. These studies have found a close association between high levels of concentration and persistently high rates of return on capital, particularly in those industries in which the largest four firms account for more than 60% of sales. . . . It is the persistence of high profits over extended time periods and over whole industries rather than in individual firms that suggest (sic) artificial restraints on output and the absence of fully effective competition.

The very existence of the correlations claimed nas been the subject of a lively debate involving Yale Brozen, the members of the Task Force majority, and a number of others.[19] Brozen looked at later evidence in the industries studied and found that the correlations did not persist. Instead, both high-profit and low-profit industries tended to move toward the average. He states that his "examination discloses a lack of persistence of 'high' rates of return in highly concentrated industries and denies the asserted basis for the deconcentration recommendation." In his excellent book *In Defense of Industrial Concentration,* John McGee analyzes the numerous difficulties with the studies of the sort the Task Force relied upon, and he concludes: "Given the conceptual and data problems underlying these statistical studies, and the weakness of the findings, the results may, or may not, be statistical curiosa or mere mirage." [20]

We need not follow this rather involved debate here, for even if it could be demonstrated (and probably it has not been) that there is a persistent correlation between industry concentration and profitability, that fact would be utterly ambiguous. High rates of return are consistent with other factors besides restriction of output, primarily superior efficiency, so that if these debatable correlations could be made to stand up, they would prove nothing of interest to antitrust policy.

We must look elsewhere for evidence concerning the likelihood of substantial restriction of output in oligopoly industries. I think the best conclusion, on present evidence, is that such restriction probably does not occur. First, observations taken from antitrust cases and from studies of economic regulation indicate that oligopoly does not give results close to monopoly. The discrepancy is so great that one may conclude the results are far more like competition. Second, conventional oligopoly theory predicts results that are not observable in markets to which the theory should apply if it applies anywhere.

Evidence supplied by antitrust cases reveals that: (1) a large price drop occurs when even one firm appears to challenge an established monopolist; (2) oligopolists are frequently discovered in overt collusion; and (3) even overt collusion among oligopolists frequently breaks down, so that prices drop to competitive levels. Such evidence severely damages the theory that oligopolists not in overt collusion can achieve significant restriction of output. Evidence supplied by studies of the effects of economic regulation indicates that regulation of monopolies produces little change in price levels, while regulation of oligopolies produces substantial increases in price levels. This suggests that oligopolists cannot achieve monopoly prices until organized by regulatory authorities into effective cartels.

If oligopoly produces results similar to monopoly, then a two-firm (duopoly) structure should produce results very close to monopoly price and output. Yet quite well-known markets indicate that this is not the case. In *United Shoe Machinery,* for example, Judge Wyzanski made quite a point of the fact that United charged a substantially lower price for its machines wherever it met competition.[21] United used a "10 year investment formula" as a rough guide in determining costs, fixing prices, and estimating the profitability of the shoe-manufacturing machines that it leased to shoe factories. In some markets United had complete monopoly; in others, fringe competition; and in still others it faced Compo Shoe Machinery Corp. as an equal rival. The rate of return varied inversely with the amount of competition faced. United had a complete monopoly in the market for its machine called the Welt Sewing K, and at 1950 rates was able to recapture its ten-year investment in 2.21 years. But where it had to meet the direct competition of Compo, in selling the Cement Sole Attaching B, six years were required to return the investment. Apparently, the rate of return was cut by almost two-thirds from a monopoly to a duopoly market. The *United Shoe Machinery* opinion rehearses a number of other instances of dramatic price drops, often accompanied by the issuance of an improved machine model, when even one other rival appeared to challenge United. (Ironically, Judge Wyzanski blamed United for lowering its price when it faced competition, referring to the practice as a form of price discrimination.) Compo had been in these markets for years; there was a rather stable two-firm situation. If ever the mutual forbearance predicted by conventional oligopoly theory should produce results approaching monopoly price and output, it would be here. But that was not the result.

Similarly, IBM made large price reductions in its equipment when Telex entered its market; again, the trial court thought the price cuts exclusionary, though the holding was reversed on appeal.[22] The important point is that IBM and Telex did not behave as oligopoly theory predicts. Instead of sharing the market at high prices, they competed at much lower prices.

Organized professional sports display the same phenomenon. When second leagues appeared in baseball, football, basketball, and hockey, salaries paid players skyrocketed. Conventional oligopoly theory would have predicted that the leagues would be able to avoid such "ruinous competition" by mutual restraint, but clearly they could not.

Network television is a highly concentrated industry and yet it is clear that ABC, NBC, and CBS are and have been engaged in hectic competition, causing certain dramatic changes in market positions. ABC's rise from a weak third place to first place does not fit the predictions of oligopoly theory, nor do the vigorous efforts of the other two networks to regain lost ground.

Also highly suggestive is the fact that sellers in oligopolistic markets are often found in price conspiracies. Well-known instances are the price-fixing conspiracies uncovered among electrical equipment and plumbing supply manufacturers, and collusion has occurred in various concentrated branches of the steel industry, including branches making absolutely uniform products. The Supreme Court's opinion in *American Tobacco II* [23] discloses that the three leading cigarette manufacturers, collectively supplying 90.7 percent of the market (an oligopoly tighter than that in most "concentrated" industries), engaged in obvious and detailed collusion to raise the price of cigarettes and lower the price of tobacco. The fact that oligopolists are willing to engage in overt conspiracies indicates that oligopoly behavior without collusion does not produce a satisfactory suppression of competition. Indeed, when one considers the enormous legal risks of collusion, as well as the effort and costs required to run an effective conspiracy, it seems obvious that firms willing to conspire must find that oligopolistic market structures are very poor substitutes for collusion. Conversely, it seems obvious that consumers have much less to fear from oligopoly than from collusion and, therefore, much less to fear from oligopoly than from monopoly.

Finally, price-fixing conspiracies themselves are often fragile. Changing market conditions and the temptation to "cheat" frequently result in outbreaks of price competition that either destroy the cartel or must be repaired by further meetings and agreements. Both the electrical equipment and plumbing supply conspiracies broke down at various times, and even the famous Gary dinners in the steel industry proved notably ineffective in holding prices up. The fragility of cartels is one of the things that makes them easy to detect, for the conspirators are forced to hold a number of meetings and to exchange telephone calls. The significance of this for our problem is twofold. First, it reinforces the preceding point: if even an intermittently effective cartel is thought to be worth the costs of operation and the legal dangers, this indicates that oligopoly does not come close to producing the results of monopoly. Second, if uncertainties and temptations break down even detailed and specific agreements on prices, what chance has an unspoken, undetailed, mutual restraint of surviving market pressures? The best guess seems to be: none.

A confirmatory line of evidence comes from recent studies of the effects of governmental regulation on prices in monopolistic and oligopolistic markets. Summarizing studies done of the effects of regulation on natural monopoly industries, William Jordan concludes that their price levels have been largely unaffected.[24] But studies of Civil Aeronautics Board regulation of interstate airline service, Interstate Com-

merce Commission regulation of railroads, and ICC regulation of motor
carriers produce different results. Airlines and railroads may be taken as
good examples of oligopolistic industries, while motor carriage is competitively structured. Jordan's conclusions are startling:

The available evidence regarding the effects of regulation on price level for
formerly oligopolistic industries is consistent and unambiguous. Regulatory
actions and procedures have allowed the carriers in each industry to reach
agreements regarding prices and to enforce adherence to these agreements.
The result has been substantial increases in price levels for the interstate airlines, the freight motor carriers, and the railroads. Without regulation prices
would be from 9 to 50 per cent lower than they are with regulation, with
many reductions in the long-run exceeding 30 per cent.

Jordan concludes, as anyone must, that the effects of price and entry
regulation have been primarily to allow the producers in oligopolistic
and competitive industries to cartelize. There have been few effects on
prices in regulated natural monopolies because "there is little a regulatory commission can do to protect a firm that already enjoys extensive
monopoly power."

Jordan uses these figures to support his hypothesis that the actual effect of regulation is to protect producers, but his findings, and the findings of others that he summarizes, have clear implications for our subject
as well. Regulation does not affect monopolists' price levels because they
are already set at the monopoly maximizing level. Regulation increases
oligopolists' prices dramatically because, prior to regulation, they were
nowhere near the monopoly or cartel maximizing level. There could be
no clearer evidence that oligopolies or concentrated industries do not
produce anything like the degree of output restriction characteristic
of monopolies.

Finally, a few comments should be made about the predictions of
conventional oligopoly theory. It is important at this point to draw out
these predictions in order to test them against reality and the premises
of the theory. There is a bit of a problem here, for some reputable
economist can be found to support almost anything. Most economists appear to predict that oligopoly markets will produce stable market shares
for the participants, rather rigid price levels, and rivalry through product
differentiation rather than price. But then one finds a well-known economist like John Kenneth Galbraith who is perfectly capable of turning the
analysis upside-down.

When General Motors responded to Ralph Nader's attacks with evidence that the automobile industry displayed dramatically shifting market shares, price rivalry, and product rivalry, Galbraith said that the corporation "as though to advertise its error, . . . cites some of the conventional features of oligopolistic rivalry and price interdependence to prove its case. Product rivalry, changing market shares, even price interdependence, are all commonplace characteristics of the oligopolistic market and are so cited in every text and classroom." [25] These outré assertions by Galbraith must be attributed to sheer perversity, or to a willingness to state theory that will fit any facts, like an adaptable batter who will "go with the pitch." While it is true that economists often speak of product rivalry (rivalry in differentiating products) as typical of oligopoly markets, hardly anyone other than Galbraith in a cantankerous mood would claim that constantly shifting market shares and price sensitivity were symptoms of the absence of competition.

Conventional oligopoly theory, to repeat, predicts stable market shares, rivalry through product differentiation, and rigid prices. It is easy to see why the theory predicts stable market shares and prices. Oligopoly theory is really a first cousin of the theory of overt collusion. Though oligopolists may not explicitly agree on prices and output (and therefore do not, under current interpretations, run afoul of Section 1 of the Sherman Act), they are assumed by the theory to be in tacit agreement, each counting upon the reaction and restraint of the others in order to reach results similar to those that would be reached by overt conspiracy. This means that noncollusive oligopoly behavior should require for its success conditions similar to those required by successful cartelization; moreover, the behavioral symptoms should be the same. We know something of cartels, and conditions or behavior that they would find unsettling would necessarily also be unsettling to the supposed mutual restraint of oligopolists. In fact, since tacit, uncommunicated agreement is far more fragile than a constantly communicated and administered agreement, any departure from ideal conditions is bound to be far more destructive to oligopoly behavior.

Since (if the theory is to stand up) the oligopolists must fly in formation without communicating, they must necessarily achieve a stability that reduces the variables and uncertainties each must take into account. Hence, as Robert Dorfman puts the argument, a "quite general tendency is for some kind of *modus vivendi* among the competing firms to be established; it is the only alternative to an intolerable state of perpetual brinkmanship. *Each firm is conceded its traditional share of the market.* . . . The firms must rely on a vague set of mutual understandings, never directly communicated, and therefore, clumsy and unenforceable. A peace founded upon such murky conventions is likely to be fragile (emphasis added)." [26]

Now there seems to be something distinctly wrong with conventional oligopoly theory. Let us address directly the automotive industry, which is one that Nader and many others repeatedly characterize as oligopolistic and requiring dissolution, and one that the proposed statutes of Kaysen and Turner and of the Neal Task Force would break up. That industry is oligopolistic by all definitions, and yet it challenges the postulates of the theory. It does not display a concession by the firms to each other of traditional market shares, and it appears to be characterized by fluctuating and interdependent prices. It does display product rivalry, but that, curiously enough, is something oligopoly theory should not predict, since the prediction is inconsistent with the theory's premises. We will take up these points in order.

Stable market positions are precisely what we do not see in the automobile industry, and they were not present even before the incursion of foreign makes became dramatic. According to the data General Motors presented to a congressional committee, which provoked Galbraith into his ingenious version of oligopoly theory, the corporation had 38 percent of industry sales in 1946 (when steel allocations were in effect), 51 percent in 1954, 43 percent in 1959, 52 percent in 1962, and 48 percent in the first eight months of 1968. Ford was down to 19 percent in 1948, up to 31 percent in 1954, and down again to 24 percent in 1968. Chrysler had 26 percent in 1946, slid to less than 10 percent in 1962, and rose again to 16 percent in 1968. American Motors, previously running at 2 or 3 percent of the market, went up to about 7 percent in 1959 and the early 1960's after it introduced its successful compact. Later figures show the fluctuations continuing. In 1973, General Motors' share was 45 percent; Ford's, 24.5; Chrysler's, 13.7; and American Motors', 3.5. [27]

That is no way to run a tight oligopoly. Ford increased its market share by more than 50 percent in six years, while Chrysler lost almost two-thirds of its share in sixteen years, and American Motors lost well over half its share. General Motors' fluctuations were less dramatic but still significant: a loss of over 15 percent of its share in five years, followed by a gain of almost 21 percent in three years. These shifts in market positions are completely inconsistent with a theory of mutual restraint.

In the longer term the picture is even more dramatic. In 1921, General Motors had less than 14 percent of the market and Ford had 60 percent. Had they been playing the oligopoly game, those shares would have remained relatively stable. Instead, by 1927, General Motors had captured about 42 percent of the market and Ford had dropped to about 12 percent. General Motors thus increased its share threefold and Ford had lost four-fifths of its share. Swings of this sort do not square with anybody's oligopoly theory.

Figures concerning overall market shares actually understate the rivalry in the industry because they balance out larger swings in various submarkets. Thus, Buick had a striking success in 1955, capturing about 10 percent of the national automobile market, but then dropped to 4 percent over the next four years. Similarly, Ford's later success with the Mustang tends to be understated when folded into the total sales of all Ford cars.

Price rigidity does not appear to be characteristic of the automotive industry, though I do not know of figures that demonstrate the movements of prices charged to dealers and by dealers as models exceed or fall short of sales expectations. The fact of price changes as market conditions alter, however, appears to be undisputed. Here, as in other industries with relatively few sellers, observers sometimes erroneously report price rigidity because they rely on list or quoted prices rather than the prices at which transactions actually take place.

The most baffling of the predictions of conventional oligopoly theory, however, is the occurrence of a high rate of product differentiation as a substitute for price competition. The explanation usually given is that product competition does not drive prices down to marginal cost and is therefore a safer form of rivalry for the oligopolists. If we match that against the behavior of overt conspirators, the explanation seems definitely peculiar. Cartels very often engage in product standardization precisely to secure stability. It seems perverse of oligopolists to engage in product differentiation for the same reason. Conventional oligopoly theory ought to predict a lessening of product competition, just as it predicts a lessening of price competition. Where product competition is observed, the correct inference is that the companies involved are not behaving as restrained oligopolists are supposed to; they are competing.

There are at least three reasons for concluding that product rivalry is a sign of competition. First, product rivalry introduces so many variables that the stability of oligopolistic peace becomes impossible. Second, product rivalry is just as capable of eating away profits above the competitive level as is price rivalry. Third, product rivalry is a prominent feature of industries that are obviously not concentrated in structure.

Mutual restraint aimed at stability and high prices requires that products be comparable. Ideally, from the oligopolists' point of view, products should be identical. It seems obvious that product differentiation would destroy the stability that oligopolistic restriction of output requires. A company that captures more of the market with a new product or a new model is just as much a competitive threat as one that does so through a price cut. There is no reason why an oligopolist should be happier about losing 20 percent of its share because of a rival's product change. The profit loss is identical. The threatened firm can be expected to respond either with a new product of its own or with a price cut.

This basic point has not been sufficiently observed. The same economist may assert that oligopolists prefer product rivalry to price rivalry because it is less unsettling, and then proceed to demonstrate that product rivalry is completely unsettling. Thus, Robert Dorfman speaks of "the firm determination with which oligopolists eschew the use of prices in maintaining and advancing their market positions. In lieu of this instrument, oligopolists rely on two others: competition through advertising and other merchandising efforts, and competition through style changes and product improvements." [28] He cites, as an example of the distaste for price competition: "At the beginning of the 1957 model season Ford discovered that it had announced prices that were about 3 percent below those of Chevrolet, the price leader. Ford promptly raised its prices. This episode occurred at a time when Ford and Chevrolet were vigorously contesting for market leadership, but evidently both recognized that price competition could do nothing but harm to them both." Yet it is true even in fragmented markets that a competitior may raise his price if observation of other prices shows he can. The observation here proves nothing about the presence or absence of price competition.

A few pages earlier, moreover, Dorfman employs an example that shows why product rivalry would be equally unsettling to the assumed truce. He says that "each firm knows that if unbridled competition should break out, its rivals are as strongly armed as it is with weapons of price reductions, aggressive advertising, and product improvement. Each firm, then, has the delicate task of advancing its position in the market without igniting an uncontrollable sequence of challenges and retaliations."

Dorfman says this sort of problem is the subject matter of "game theory." He supposes two automobile companies (called Chevrolet and Ford) who share a market but who each want the largest share possible. The game is played in terms of numbers of headlights on next year's models, with Chevrolet for some reason having to choose first in the knowledge that Ford will then choose the number of headlights for its models that will minimize Chevrolet's market share. So Chevrolet analyzes the best Ford riposte to its own decision and chooses the number of headlights that gives Chevrolet the largest market share.

But Dorfman makes two qualifications that utterly destroy any claim to realism that might be made for this analysis. He points out that "when opponents' reactions are unpredictable, decisions are far more difficult." In the automobile industry, as in other industries, reactions are largely unpredictable: in part, because all rivalrous actions are; in part, because the major firms make great efforts to keep their model changes secret; in part, because lead times on many model features often require that a manufacturer commit itself before it can know what its rivals are planning.

More damaging to the realism of this game theory example, however, is Professor Dorfman's own footnote:

In order to bring out the concepts easily, the text treats only the simplest version of the simplest kind of game. We have described a "minorant" game in which one player is privileged to know his opponent's course of action before he has to make his own choice. If Chevrolet could keep its secret or could hope to discover Ford's choice in time to revise its own, the analysis would be more complicated but still tractable. *In fact, any constant sum game with two players is solvable—i.e., has readily discoverable best choices for both players. More complicated games rarely are.* [Emphasis added.]

Automobile rivalry is a far more complicated game. Besides Chevrolet and Ford, and ignoring the possible complications added by other divisions of their companies, there are Chrysler, American Motors, and a variety of foreign car sellers. So there are many more players than in Dorfman's game. Worse, there are many more variables in the rivalry than numbers of headlights. The varieties both of models and features within models, not to mention price variations, are so numerous that it should be clear beyond any doubt that this game is not "solvable." Oligopolists who proliferate models and variations are making the "game" of oligopolistic restriction of output impossible.

Product rivalry thus turns out to be a much more unstable and unsettling form of competition than price rivalry, which has only a single variable. Looking at the problem another way, product differentiation, even if it were not a form of competition in itself, would make price matching much more difficult. Added to the normal uncertainties would be the question of how much difference in price should be allowed for all the variations in product. It is impossible to conceive that sellers could reach the correct margins without ever communicating with one another, particularly if the variations are both numerous and continually changing.

Oligopoly theory should, therefore, predict product standardization rather than differentiation. The presence of rapid product change and extensive product differentiation is, in fact, evidence that oligopolistic mutual restraint (leading to output restriction and higher-than-competitive prices) is not taking place. This theoretical argument finds empirical confirmation in Lester Telser's study of advertising, which shows that advertising, a means of differentiating products in consumers' minds, is more intensive in markets where product shares shift rapidly and brand turnover is high.[29]

This analysis seems sufficient to dispose of the claim that product rivalry suggests noncompetitive behavior. But the theory is deficient on yet another score. Some economists contend that oligopolists prefer product rivalry to price rivalry because the former does not so readily drive prices down to marginal cost, thus eliminating profits above competitive levels. That is, oligopolists can quickly erode greater-than-competitive profits by price cuts but not by product improvements. Therefore, it is argued, they will refrain from price cuts and compete with increased product changes. This common observation does not survive examination. There is first the question of why oligopolists, who are assumed to desire and be able to eliminate competition, should actually intensify competition in any aspect of their businesses. To state that they prefer product rivalry to price rivalry is to avoid the question of why they should put up with *any* rivalry. I can think of no persuasive reason.

The point to be addressed, however, is the claim that product rivalry is less likely to equate prices and marginal costs. The validity of that claim depends upon the proposition that product variations are not so flexible as price variations and that the marginal cost of providing variations rises so quickly that the seller will not use up all his extra profits in adding product. But this assertion runs contrary to the basic assumption of economics that amounts of products are infinitely divisible. This is particularly true when there is money to be made by contriving divisibility. Thus, if price were held constant, product improvements and differentiations could be added to equate marginal cost and price. Shifting from price rivalry to product rivalry would not introduce an inevitable discrepancy between price and cost. Product rivalry from this standpoint is the equivalent of price rivalry.

There is no difficulty in explaining the prevalence of product rivalry. Those who see in it the peculiar machinations of oligopolists overlook the obvious fact that consumers are sensitive to much more than price. Most products present a bundle of satisfactions, both functional and aesthetic; product rivalry is essential, particularly in complex products, if the variety of consumer tastes is to be satisfied effectively. Intense product rivalry, therefore, signals not lack of competition but its presence. This can be demonstrated empirically as well as theoretically. There is probably no business that has a more competitive structure and performance that the garment industry—no one in his right mind would classify it as displaying any of the characteristics of oligopoly—and there is also no industry in which product rivalry and variation are more important.

The automotive industry is also widely known, and even criticized, for the incessant attempt of the various producers to differentiate their products and to impress the differences upon consumers. Not only are there enormous variations in available equipment and features within model lines, but the number of domestic models increased from 265 to 386, or by more than 45 percent between 1958 and 1968. That would be strangely self-defeating behavior for companies supposed to be seeking market stability and absence of rivalry.

The automobile industry makes an excellent test case for theories of oligopolistic restriction of output. Its structure is what economists call concentrated, but its behavior does not comply with the predictions of a rational theory of oligopoly. Yet one hears again and again that this is an industry in which oligopolists have suppressed competition. One begins to suspect that oligopoly theory is less an intellectual construct than a frame of mind, a mood, a dogma that is ripe for thoroughgoing reexamination.

For a wide variety of reasons, therefore, we are entitled to be highly skeptical of the entire theory of oligopolistic interdependence, upon which rest all the proposals to dissolve leading firms in concentrated industries. I would, in fact, go further and claim it as a certainty that something is radically wrong with the conventional theory which underlies the deconcentration proposals of the Neal Task Force and of Kaysen and Turner. That theory seems to have neither theoretical nor empirical substance. The upshot of all this is not that we can demonstrate the complete absence of any restriction of output in all oligopolistic industries, but rather that any significant restriction of output is highly improbable. It follows that very little, if any, benefit would be likely to flow from the dissolution of so-called oligopolistic firms. We turn next to the proposition that a great deal would be lost by restructuring industries through law.

EFFICIENCY

Advocates of large firm dissolution must demonstrate that the process will not destroy significant amounts of efficiency. Otherwise, they ask us to risk doing consumers more harm than good. Both the Neal Task Force and Kaysen and Turner provide efficiency defenses in their proposed statutes, and I have suggested some reasons why those defenses may be predicted to be inadequate. But now I wish to take a step further and to argue that if the efficiency defenses were adequate to their task, the government would never obtain a decree dissolving any company that had grown to its challenged size. The defense would swallow the proscription. The reason is that any size a company achieves by internal growth is the most efficient size for that company, and dissolution would always impose a significant efficiency cost.

This conclusion follows from the nature of efficiency. We have already seen that efficiency cannot be studied directly and quantified, and that the best definition of the concept is George Stigler's term "competitive effectiveness." To avoid the objection that the definition may include the ability to employ predatory tactics, fraud, and restraints of trade, we may limit "competitive effectiveness" to behavior that both maximizes profits and contributes to consumer welfare. It follows that the most efficient firm is simply the firm that has, without collusion or predation, experienced the most success in the marketplace.

If efficiency is competitive effectiveness in this sense, then any size a firm attains by internal growth is necessarily an expression of its efficiency. It is important to grasp this point because it changes the emphasis in the way we usually talk about firm sizes. Economists are accustomed to speaking of efficiency in terms of economies of scale. Economies of scale are merely one form of efficiency. Focusing upon economies of scale as the predominant factor leads to serious error. A narrow version of the concept relates to the minimum efficient size of the firm. Stigler was dealing with this concept when he devised his "survivorship test," which judges optimal sizes by the relative market success of firms of different sizes.[30] As Stigler put it: "Classify the firms in an industry by size, and calculate the share of industry output coming from each class over time. If the share of a given class falls, it is relatively inefficient, and in general is more inefficient the more rapidly the share falls."

Application of his test to various industries convinced Stigler not only that there is "customarily a fairly wide range of optimum sizes," but also that "the long-run marginal and average cost curves of the firm are customarily horizontal over a long range of sizes." Another conclusion he drew was relied upon by the Neal Task Force in framing its proposals for deconcentrating industry: "In the manufacturing sector there are few industries in which the minimum efficient size of firm is as much as 5 per cent of the industry's output and concentration must be explained on other grounds." [31] If these conclusions were accepted, it would seem to follow that drastic dissolution of the larger firms in many of our more concentrated industries—automobiles, steel, tires, computers, etc.—could be accomplished with little or no loss in efficiency.

The first difficulty with taking Stigler's conclusions as a guide to public policy is the treacherous nature of the concept of "minimum efficient size." It may be perfectly true that the survivorship test shows a minimum efficient size in an industry of, say, 5 percent, and yet not at all true that a 50 percent firm in the same industry could be dissolved into ten 5 percent firms without serious efficiency losses. Efficient sizes may vary from firm to firm within the same industry, depending upon the degree and type of integration, differences in production processes, specializations as to products, the methods of management organization, and the character and abilities of management. Larger and smaller firms may be geared to operate in wholly different ways. This suggests that though Stigler may be quite correct in saying "there is customarily a fairly wide range of optimum sizes," he may be wrong in thinking that "long-run marginal and average cost curves of the firm are customarily horizontal over a long range of sizes." The second assertion does not follow from the first, and will not be true if, as seems often the case, the range of optimal sizes is achieved by different organizations, specializations, and the like. There is also the danger that Stigler's test may lead to incorrect results if the degree of product heterogeneity is underestimated, as I believe it frequently is. This danger can only be avoided by great familiarity with the industry and its operations.

The basic rationale of Stigler's survivorship test is completely sound. But, for the reasons given, it is misapplied when used to support a conclusion of flat cost curves for the individual firm over enormous ranges of output, and hence the possibility of dissolution without great efficiency loss. Moreover, such a conclusion requires us to explain industrial concentration on grounds other than efficiency, and that will prove difficult or impossible to do when the concentration is created by the internal growth of the larger firms in each industry.

How, for example, can we explain an industry that has become concentrated by the internal growth of some firms and the decline of others, except on the grounds of the superior efficiency of the larger firms? Such a performance is inconsistent with the notion that all firms have equal and flat cost curves and can make products equally appealing to the public. To say, as Stigler did, that there are few industries in which the minimum efficient size of the firm is as much as 5 percent, and that concentration must therefore be explained on other grounds, raises at once the question: what other grounds? Stigler himself dismissed the notion of artificial barriers to entry, so there appears to be a logical gap in his system.

It seems sounder to use Stigler's basic argument to reach somewhat different conclusions. The survivorship test is based on the idea that success proves efficiency, and the required conclusion from that premise is that *any size achieved by internal growth without predation is the most efficient size for that firm.* This, in turn, leads to the conclusion that *the dissolution of any such firm will always create an efficiency loss.* There may be a rare case in which dissolution coincides with changes in costs and demand that would comparably have eroded the firm's market share in any event, but that can never be known accurately and is sufficiently unlikely for us properly to ignore it. It follows that the Neal Task Force and Kaysen and Turner are wrong in thinking that dissolution can restructure oligopolistic industries without significant losses in efficiency.

The variety of efficiencies that may be destroyed by dissolution are too numerous and complex to be stated simply—they include all the types we have catalogued. But it may be useful to specify one of the most obvious, which is also one of the most frequently overlooked. A major component of a firm's efficiency, particularly in larger and more complex firms, is the ability of its management to make decisions about products, product design, manufacturing processes, distribution, financing, and so on, on a continuing basis—decisions that lead to consumer acceptance more often than the decisions made by other managements. When a firm has achieved 60 percent of a market by internal growth, it has done so because its management has made thousands of decisions, many of them invisible to the outside observer, which produced results leading over half the consumers to prefer to purchase that firm's products and services. The market share the firm commands is the range over which management's effectiveness is felt. If the firm is dissolved, say into five equal parts, that management team may be destroyed, and with it the capacity for making as many correct decisions. But even if the superior management survives and goes to one of the new firms, the area within which that management's superiority can be effective has been reduced to a fifth, and that is a clear loss to consumers.

BARRIERS TO ENTRY

All proposals to dissolve the leading firms in concentrated industries, whether through new interpretations of existing law or new legislation, require as logical support a theory of artificial barriers to growth and entry. If new firms of superior or equal efficiency were able to enter the industry and erode the monopolistic or oligopolistic profits, there would be no problem for public policy. The absence of entry or the lack of growth by the smaller firms already in the industry suggests that one of two things is true. Either there is no restriction of output, and hence no greater-than-competitive profit, to induce entry or the growth of smaller firms; or the large firms are so far superior in efficiency that, even if there is a restriction of output, no new firm would find entry profitable and no smaller firm is able to grow. Of course, there may be both superior efficiency and absence of output restriction. These conclusions are awkward for the oligopolyphobe, for they suggest that there is never a case for restructuring the market. The proponent of dissolution, therefore, must first assert that restriction of output exists, leading to above-normal profits, and then explain why equally efficient or more efficient firms are unable to enter or expand to enjoy these profits.

The conventional, and entirely misconceived, answer is supplied by the concept of barriers to growth and entry. The basic ambiguity of this concept has led to its misuse in antitrust analysis. If everything that makes entry more difficult is viewed as a barrier, and if barriers are bad, then efficiency is an evil. That conclusion is inconsistent with consumer-oriented policy. What must be proved to exist, therefore, is a class of barriers that do not reflect superior efficiency and can be erected by firms to inhibit rivals. I think it clear that no such class of artificial barriers exists. It is the same phenomenon as Judge Wyzanski's "intermediate cases"—practices that are neither deliberately predatory nor efficiency creating, but are nevertheless somehow exclusionary. The idea is so transparent, so obviously lacking in substance, that one suspects it would never have been devised but for the desperate need to shore up a crumbling theory that markets allow unwarranted market shares to persist. Stigler states: "Barriers to entry arise because of economies of scale, or differences in productive factors, or legal control of entry." [32] None of these, of course, is properly subject to attack by antitrust. There is in the list no "artificial barrier" other than legal control of entry by government, and since we want the more efficient firm to have the extra share of the market its efficiency commands, there is no reason for concern over the other barriers.

Since the subject of barriers to entry and to growth appears in several areas of antitrust analysis, a fuller discussion of the topic is postponed until Chapter 16. That chapter attempts to demonstrate that all of the "artificial barriers" complained of in antitrust are, in fact, activities that create efficiency.

*   *   *   *

We are now in a position to state the proper policy toward oligopoly and monopoly. Advocates of dissolution of oligopolistic firms cannot sustain any of the three propositions their position requires. In fact, it looks very much as though there is a high probability, amounting in fact to a virtual certainty, that dissolving any oligopolistic firm that grew to its present size would inflict a serious welfare loss. Oligopolistic structures probably do not lead to significant restrictions of output; firm sizes reflect comparative efficiencies; and firms of equal or greater efficiency are free to enter or to grow anytime restriction of output occurs. Proposals like those of the Neal Task Force and of Kaysen and Turner are, therefore, seriously ill-advised.

Complete monopoly, which is extremely rare, presents a somewhat different problem because in such cases we may expect restriction of output. Yet where the firm has grown to its monopoly size, its efficiency must outweigh its output restriction, or entry would erode its position. Moreover, when a firm has gained monopoly by superior efficiency, it has monopoly power only within the limited range of the superiority of its efficiency. If prices are pushed higher, entry will occur. This means that efficiency-based monopoly has only a limited ability to restrict output. Of particular force here is Williamson's statement, already noted, that a modest cost reduction is usually enough to counterbalance even a relatively large price increase. This means that efficiency-based monopolies are always better for consumers than any alternative antitrust can produce. The firm is better left alone. A second consideration supports this conclusion. If the law dissolved a firm having a 100 percent monopoly into five approximately equal parts, the economic forces that had led to monopoly would still be operative and would lead in that direction again. Let us suppose, however, that the law announced a policy of dissolution of any firm that exceeded 50 percent of the market. When one of the new firms approached that size once more, it would have every incentive to restrict its output in order to avoid the penalties of the law, and so the law would produce the evil of resource misallocation in the attempt to avert it.

I have argued the case for size achieved by internal growth. The same argument applies to any size that has persisted in the market over a number of years, even if it was originally produced by merger, for the maintenance of size against the eroding forces of the market over a long period of time also indicates either an absence of restriction of output or superior efficiency, or both.

These arguments demonstrate, I believe, not only that proposals for new legislation are ill-conceived but also that the *Alcoa* and *United Shoe Machinery* cases were wrongly decided. The law would do well to stand by the original understanding of the framers of the Sherman Act.

9

The Crash of Merger Policy: The Brown Shoe *Decision*

THE career of Section 7 of the Clayton Act, subsequent to its amendment in 1950, provides a fascinating example of the trends that have made large areas of modern antitrust a harmful policy. Clayton 7 deals with corporate mergers, condemning only those whose effect "may be substantially to lessen competition or tend to create a monopoly." Yet a majority of the Warren Court, ignoring these criteria, took the first occasion that presented itself, the *Brown Shoe* case of 1962, to convert the statute to a virulently anticompetitive regulation.[1]

It is important to understand the impropriety of this transformation, for it was produced by the application of erroneous ideas that date back to the earliest period of antitrust policy. The Court carried to drily logical extremes the notions of exclusionary practices, incipiency, and the social purpose of the antitrust laws. That this produced a result incompatible with any concern for competition appeared to bother the Court not at all. The issue is more important than the deformation of merger law, however, for the categories of antitrust are notoriously permeable. Ideas developed in one context have a way of spreading, of seeping into and altering law even in older, seemingly settled, areas. The most obvious threat posed by the anticompetitive doctrines incubated under amended Section 7 of the Clayton Act is that they will increasingly affect and make even worse the law about size by internal growth under Section 2 of the Sherman Act. Indeed, the Neal Task Force cited the "gap" between the law's treatment of internal growth and mergers as a reason for making legal restrictions on internal growth more severe.

The correct interpretation of Clayton 7 begins with the answer to a basic question: Why should the law apply more severe standards to corporate size achieved by merger than to the same size achieved by growth? A number of possible answers have been given, but only one is consistent with both the statute and the goal of consumer welfare: size by internal growth demonstrates superior efficiency, but merger that creates real market control will certainly have the effect of restricting output and may or may not create new efficiencies. Thus, it is intelligible, though not inevitable, social policy to apply stricter standards to mergers. This and the following three chapters will try to show that the only mergers properly limited by law are very large horizontal mergers.

The question is often raised, "If some mergers are deleterious to consumer welfare and internal growth is not, why not simply ban all mergers?" Donald Turner supplies the answer: [2]

The reasons for not making mergers unlawful per se or for not even coming anywhere near such a rule are plain. Widespread prohibition of mergers would impose serious, if not intolerable, burdens upon owners of businesses who wished to liquidate their holdings for irreproachable personal reasons. Moreover, economic welfare is significantly served by maintaining a good market for capital assets. By enhancing the value of assets when owners wish to sell, a strong capital assets market increases the rewards of successful entrepreneurial endeavor. In this way the possibility of mergers stimulates the formation and growth of new firms, though the extent of this effect is of course highly speculative. More importantly, a policy of free transferability of capital assets tends to put them in the hands of those who will use them to their utmost economic advantage, thus tending to maximize society's total output of goods and services.

Growth by merger, like internal growth, will often yield substantial economies of scale—in production, research, distribution, cost of capital, and management. Entry by merger, like entry by new growth, may stimulate improved economic performance in an industry characterized by oligopolistic lethargy and inefficiency. Finally, acquisition of diversified lines of business, by stabilizing profits, may minimize the risks of business failure and bankruptcy.

It would be possible to expand Turner's list of the advantages of mergers, but his forceful statement of the main point—mergers are an important mechanism in the creation of social wealth—can hardly be improved.

Rational law, therefore, must draw the appropriate line between mergers that create wealth and those that decrease it. This has not been the course adopted by a majority of the Supreme Court. Instead, the Court has adopted a series of demonstrably erroneous ideas which, if uniformly and logically applied, are capable of making all mergers illegal, something Clayton 7 clearly does not intend. For a time this meant, in effect, that the legality of any merger depended on the discretion of the Antitrust Division or the Federal Trade Commission, rather than on any distinctions to be found in the Warren Court's doctrines. The "law" of the recent past was accurately summed up in Justice Potter Stewart's *Von's Grocery* dissent: "The sole consistency that I can find is that in litigation under [Section] 7, the Government always wins." [3] The present Supreme Court has retrieved the situation somewhat, though not enough.

On its face the Celler-Kefauver bill that amended Section 7 in 1950 presaged no dramatic switch in the direction of merger law. The amendment merely cured a split infinitive in the old statute, extended coverage to corporate asset acquisitions as well as stock acquisitions, and through a small wording change actually seemed to increase the possibility of lawful mergers between competitors. The extension to mergers accomplished by asset acquisitions was the primary talking point of the bill's proponents in Congress. Even the Supreme Court, which has found revolutionary meaning in the amendment, conceded this: "Virtually every member of Congress who spoke in support of the amendments, indicated that this aspect of the legislation was its salient characteristic. Representative Kefauver, one of the Act's sponsors, testified, 'The bill is not complicated. It proposes simply to plug the loophole in sections 7 and 11 of the Clayton Act.' " [4]

Beyond this point the diffuse legislative history of the bill gives remarkably little guidance. As many commentators have noted, Congress talked about a variety of sociopolitical objections to industrial concentration, but when the talk was of what courts would actually do under the statute, the criterion was usually the preservation of competition. And, of course, the statute itself employs exclusively economic criteria, making mergers unlawful only according to their probable tendency to move toward monopoly and away from competition. One would have expected, then, that the courts would decide cases entirely according to their competitive impact upon particular markets.

The *Brown Shoe* decision shattered that expectation. This was the Court's first encounter with the amended statute, and Chief Justice Earl Warren's opinion began by discussing the general considerations that were to govern the law's application. The Chief Justice took the rather peculiar tack of ignoring Clayton 7's text and relying instead upon the inchoate legislative history:

A review of the legislative history of these amendments provides no unmistakably clear indication of the precise standards the Congress wished the Federal Trade Commission and the courts to apply in judging the legality of particular mergers. However, sufficient expressions of a consistent point of view may be found in the hearings, committee reports of both the House and Senate and in floor debate to provide those charged with enforcing the Act with a usable frame of reference within which to evaluate any given merger.

Now, it is quite true that Congress did not specify "precise standards" for the decision of merger cases, but that is a far different thing from saying that Congress did not indicate the *kind* of standards to be employed. Congress did the latter, both in the legislative history and, more importantly, in the text of the statute it passed. The statute was intended to be applied to preserve competition and avert monopoly in particular markets. These are goals capable of generating criteria deserving the name of law. But the Court, choosing selectively from the confusion of congressional rhetoric, nailed together a "frame of reference" that overlooked such matters and condemned the statute to economic incoherence.

This frame of reference, the background ideas cited to justify the Court's version of amended Clayton 7, deserves attention. Most of its elements appear in *Brown Shoe,* but several ideas appearing in later cases will also be discussed. The purpose is to demonstrate that they are inappropriate—indeed, necessarily disastrous—to the interpretation of a statute designed to judge mergers by their effects upon competition.

THE COURT'S "FRAME OF REFERENCE" FOR MERGER CASES: MAIN THEMES

Chief Justice Warren began his *Brown Shoe* opinion by citing a cluster of three themes as relevant to the decision of merger cases:

The dominant theme pervading congressional consideration of the 1950 amendments was a fear of what was considered to be a rising tide of economic concentration in the American economy. . . . Other considerations cited in support of the bill were the desirability of retaining "local control" over industry and the protection of small business.

These three themes may well have been in the minds of some congressmen who voted for the amendment to Clayton 7, and that is not necessarily inconsistent with their having voted for a bill that spoke only of "competition" and "monopoly" in any specific "line of commerce" in any specific "part of the country." A policy of preserving competition in particular markets would have *as side effects* the tendencies to lessen the supposed pace of overall concentration in the economy, maintain local control over some firms that would otherwise have been acquired, and preserve some small business. But it is obvious that these themes cannot be taken as criteria to be employed by judges in deciding individual cases. We will examine nine major ideas employed by the Court in the merger field, the first three of them coming from the *Brown Shoe* opinion.

(1) *There is a rising tide of concentration in the American economy.* The imminent concentration of all ownership in a few giant corporations, with the concomitant demise of small business, is the standard, Mark I, all-weather antitrust hobgoblin. This congealing of the economy has been prophesied freely at least since the debates on the Sherman Act in 1890, always on the basis of overwhelming current trends, and it never comes to pass. It also never ceases to frighten people. The evil of this predicted economy-wide concentration appears to be so enormous and self-evident that critical faculties are overwhelmed.

One might attack the Court's reliance upon this theme in a variety of ways. That overall concentration is increasing in the American economy is doubtful, and it is certainly not increasing at any very impressive rate.[5] This would not matter, however, if Congress had thought overall concentration a danger and had written a law striking at the supposed trend. But it is clear Congress did not. As Donald Turner said, there is "no credible support for the statement in *Brown Shoe* that Congress consciously appreciated the possible efficiency cost of attempting to preserve fragmented industries and consciously resolved the competing considerations in favor of decentralization."[6] In response to the suggestion that the fear of overall concentration, right or wrong, is somehow forever built into Clayton 7, Turner very sensibly remarked, "It is certainly in order for the courts to take into account the facts as they are in rejecting a policy choice that is contrary to the main thrust of antitrust law and that Congress never really made."

I would go a step further. The courts need not take into account the facts of overall concentration as they are because Congress did not make any policy choice on the topic and did not write a law that speaks to the subject. Thus, even if overall concentration were increasing at a frightening rate, Section 7 would be an inappropriate tool to deal with the problem. There is no way Clayton 7's criteria about competition in particular lines of commerce can be legitimately invoked to prevent mergers that may increase the total concentration in the American economy but do not threaten competition in any market. And if a merger does threaten competition, it should be illegal, regardless of the condition of overall concentration.

In Clayton 7 litigation the theme of (allegedly) increasing overall concentration is worse than irrelevant; it is pernicious. It tends to rewrite the statute to make all mergers illegal because every merger tends to increase economy-wide concentration. What factor could save a merger, and how could a court strike a principled balance between overall concentration and some beneficial factor? No court has even tried to calibrate such themes to make them manageable in the decision of cases, probably for the very good reason that it would be impossible. The attempt would merely reveal the emptiness of the concept and its divergence from the standards laid down in the statute.

If economy-wide concentration should appear both probable and undesirable, Congress, not the Court, should make the political decision, expressed in the form of a new statute, about how much concentration is to be avoided at how much cost in economic efficiency. But that statute, presumably framed in terms of the maximum asset sizes of mergers or of firms, is not Section 7 of the Clayton Act, and it is improper for the Court to read Section 7 as though it were.

(2) and (3) *It is desirable to retain "local control" over industry and to protect small business.* These versions of the ancient and disreputable "social purpose" theory of antitrust are flawed in the same way as the theme of rising economy-wide concentration: they do not correspond to the statute, and they push for the per se illegality of all mergers, thus nullifying the tests Section 7 actually prescribes. Almost every merger tends to remove control over one of the firms from the locality where control had previously existed. Every merger, moreover, contains a "threat" to small business. Either the small business is absorbed (in this sense the Court "protects" small business from its own desire to sell), or the merger promises increased efficiency which, of course, threatens injury to all rivals, some of whom are likely to be

small. (It is not at all clear that the rule encourages small business in any event, because small firms are more likely to enter the market if the possibility of merger provides a safety net in case of failure.)

More fundamentally, this concern with local control and the protection of small business runs directly counter to consumer interest in every case in which the merger may create efficiencies. The balancing of the conflicting and incommensurable interests of producers and consumers is, as we saw in Chapter 3, an improper task for courts, one akin to the writing of tariff laws.

The other ideas imposed upon Section 7 by the Supreme Court are fully consistent with the three just discussed.

(4) *The creation of efficiency by merger is irrelevant to the merger's legality.* Justice Douglas's opinion for the Court in *Procter & Gamble* [7] dismissed efficiencies as hardly worth consideration: "Possible economies cannot be used as a defense to illegality. Congress was aware that some mergers which lessen competition may also result in economies but it struck the balance in favor of protecting competition." As Turner noted, Congress did not strike any such balance. If anybody did, it was the Court, in the process of implementing its own social policy. The statement that efficiency is not relevant means that consumer welfare is not important, and that in turn means that the primary reason for preserving competition is to be disregarded. But Justice Douglas actually meant more than that efficiency is irrelevant, for he went on to make the transformation described in the next subsection.

(5) *Efficiency is really a "competitive advantage" or a "barrier to entry" and is therefore anticompetitive.* In *Procter & Gamble,* after declaring efficiency irrelevant, Justice Douglas's opinion proceeded to invalidate Procter's acquisition of Clorox Chemical Co., in large measure because of the barriers to entry that would be created in Clorox's market, household liquid bleach. Three barriers to entry were cited: (a) Procter's great capital resources could supplement Clorox's limited advertising budget; (b) Clorox would share in volume discounts on advertising rates supposedly granted Procter by television networks and magazines; and (c) Clorox would obtain, in advertising and promotion, the advantages of a multiproduct form (e.g., the ability to feature several products in a single promotional mailing or on a single network television show). Unless advertising and promotion are viewed as not legitimate activities—a claim Justice Douglas did not make—it is clear that the Court objected to Procter making Clorox more efficient. The opinion never once explained why doing advertising and promotion at lower cost was not an efficiency.

Professor Morris Adelman's remark about competitive advantages applies equally to barriers to entry: "The phrase, 'competitive advantages of larger firms' means nothing more nor less than 'economies of scale'; it only sounds different." [8]

(6) *When efficiency is not irrelevant and not a "barrier to entry," it is bad anyway because Congress wanted to protect competition by protecting small business from the increased efficiency of rivals.* Of this, one can only say that it is the statement made by Chief Justice Warren in the *Brown Shoe* opinion. Of that, more shortly.

Notice that all of the three foregoing positions about efficiency cut in the direction of illegality for all mergers. The position that efficiency is a simple irrelevancy means that mergers have no social benefit, so why not be cautious and strike all of them down? The two positions that count efficiency against a merger seem to close off the possibility of legality even more effectively. If the merger restricts output, it is illegal because it hurts consumers, even though the higher prices would help small businesses. If the merger creates efficiency, it is illegal because it hurts small businesses, even though the lower prices would help consumers. That is intelligible social policy only in the sense that one can understand the separate words.

(7) *An incipient lessening of competition (illegal) exists whenever there is a trend toward concentration in an industry, since if we extrapolate the trend far enough, we will always arrive at a state of concentration that Congress wanted to prevent.* In case after case, the Supreme Court has engaged in the unlimited extrapolation of trends in order to perceive an incipient lessening of competition. The trend need not have come anywhere near producing a state of concentration for the Court to see an incipiency. Stopping mergers is one way of at least slowing the trend, although in the *Von's Grocery* case the Court majority declared a merger illegal because of the decline of single-store grocery firms in Los Angeles, despite a demonstration that the decline was not attributable to mergers and that the merger struck down did not involve a single-store grocery firm. As Justice Stewart said in dissent, the "decline is made the end, not the beginning of analysis." Our discussion of *Brown Shoe* will show the amount of unwarranted extrapolation the incipiency concept is thought to allow.

The difficulty with stopping a trend toward a more concentrated condition at a very early stage is that the existence of the trend is prima facie evidence that greater concentration in that industry is socially desirable. The trend indicates that there are emerging efficiencies or economies of scale—whether due to engineering and production developments, new distributive techniques, or new control and management tools—which make larger size more efficient. There can be no other explanation for the growth of firms by merger when their sizes are still much too small to make the hope of output restriction a possible motive. By stopping trends in their early stages, the misused concept of incipiency prevents the realization of those very efficiencies that competition is supposed to encourage.

The Supreme Court is not, of course, to blame for the fact that the incipiency concept inheres in the Clayton Act. That was Congress' idea. But the Court did not have to make of the concept what it did. Clayton 7, in particular, offered legitimate scope for the concept. Congress intended to tighten the Sherman Act merger rules, and it expressed fear of oligopoly. The Court could have read the language *"may* be substantially to lessen competition or *tend* to create a monopoly" as authority to accommodate oligopoly theory to some degree by lowering the market shares that may lawfully be created by mergers. That would have provided a function for the incipiency concept and avoided the unjustifiable and injurious extrapolation of trends.

(8) *Internal growth is always preferable to growth by merger.* This curious but widely accepted notion was also expressed in *Brown Shoe*: "Internal expansion is more likely to be the result of increased demand for the company's products and is more likely to provide increased investment in plants, more jobs and greater output. Conversely, expansion through merger is more likely to reduce available consumer choice while providing no increase in industry capacity, jobs or output." In the first place, in common with almost all the other ideas discussed in this chapter, this notion is useless as an aid in interpreting Clayton 7, for its implication is that mergers should always be illegal. The statutory tests, moreover, do not permit a court to decide merger cases on speculations about relative probabilities of increases in jobs and investment. But the Court's claim is worth unpacking in detail, for it is, on its own terms, wrong in every particular.

Growth is preferable to merger only in one type of case: where merger would create a market share so large that the result would be restriction of output. There is no other general reason to prefer internal expansion to merger.

When the likelihood of output restriction is not present, we must assume that the firm makes the choice between internal expansion and merger on the basis of its estimate of the relative costs of the two routes to larger size. A choice made on such grounds should, of course, be respected by the law. For antitrust to block the merger route when that is the least expensive alternative is to force higher costs upon the firm. The firm may accept those higher costs and expand internally, but the cost differential is a loss both to it and to society. In some cases the cost differential may be so large that the firm blocked from merging will decide not to expand internally. The law has then needlessly prevented the increase in efficiencies that the firm anticipated from larger size.

It might be thought that the Court's list of advantages to internal expansion may properly be set off against the considerations just mentioned. But those advantages seem either illusory or subsumed in the firm's choice about relative efficiencies. The remark about increases in plants, jobs, and output falls in the former category. If demand conditions call for such increases in the industry in question, they will be forthcoming from the existing firms or from new entrants, whether or not a merger is allowed. If demand conditions do not call for such increases, then forcing a firm to reach larger size through internal expansion merely means that other firms will have to close plants, lay off workers, and reduce output. Forcing growth by banning mergers in such cases merely compels a waste of resources and unnecessary hardship. Thus, such a policy would never have any benefits and would often do harm.

Two corollary remarks—that internal expansion is more likely to be the result of increased demand for the firm's products, and that expansion through merger is more likely to reduce consumer choice—fall within the category of things that may or may not be true but in any case are properly left to the judgment of the firm concerned. Merger may be the least expensive means of gaining facilities to meet an increased demand for the firm's products; or the acquiring firm may continue the product line of the acquired firm, so that consumer choice is not reduced. But these decisions will be made by the acquiring firm on the basis of consumer demand and costs, which means that the firm is deciding in its own interests according to the criteria that also determine consumer welfare. The firm's interest here is identical to the consumer interest, so that the decision to replace or to keep the acquired firm's product lines should be left to the acquiring firm. The Court's remark about consumer choice provides no reason to prefer internal expansion to merger.

To recapitulate, the decision to merge or to expand internally should be left to the firms involved. The law should interfere only where merger would create a market share that raises the likelihood of a significant restriction of output. In all other cases, there is no reason to say that internal expansion is more competitive or more desirable than expansion by merger. The firm, in its own interests, will make the best choice for consumers.

(9) *The legality of a merger is decided on the facts existing at the time of the lawsuit, not on those existing when the merger occurred.* In the *du Pont-General Motors* case [9] the Supreme Court held that du Pont's purchase during 1917–1919 of a 23 percent stock interest in General Motors violated the original Clayton 7. The case was decided not on the market facts existing at the time of the acquisition, but on those prevailing thirty years later when the lawsuit was brought. The Court's theory was that du Pont's stock interest gave it an anti-competitive advantage in selling finishes and fabrics to GM. The law judges the seriousness of such "foreclosure" by the share of the market of the "captive" firm. During the years the acquisition was occurring, GM's market share rose from 11 to about 21 percent, and a few years later it was below 14 percent. The Court held, however, that the relevant market share was the 50 percent GM had attained by 1949.

Worse still, the Court did not require that the changed market conditions be traced in any way to any anticompetitive aspect of the merger. In fact, had the supposed illegality in the *du Pont-GM* case—du Pont's alleged ability to edge out competitive suppliers because of the leverage of its stock ownership—been true, it would have had the net effect of harming General Motors and making its market share smaller than it would otherwise have been. Thus, one cannot read the case as tracing the changed market share in any way to any evil inherent in the stock acquisition. Hopes that this decision was *sui generis*, resting upon the Court's determination to find a way to sever any connection between these industrial giants, were quickly dashed. The doctrine has been employed in other cases and relied upon by the enforcement agencies. How widely it will be used we do not yet know. But it offers a legal device for restructuring concentrated markets and dissolving large firms with mergers in their distant pasts.

The idea of judging mergers on market facts existing at the time of the lawsuit rather than at the time of the merger is so obviously improper that it hardly requires criticism. Suppose that two companies each having 5 percent of a market merged in 1928 to form a 10 percent firm, and that in the intervening fifty years the firm grew to 60 percent of the market. To bring a Clayton 7 case based on the present 60 percent share is to attack not the market structure created by the merger but the market share created by the internal growth of the firm. Internal growth after merger is like any internal growth; it can be explained only by the superior efficiency of the firm. And if the original merger made those efficiencies attainable, that is merely proof that the merger was socially desirable. The origin of efficiency does not alter its contribution to consumer welfare.

To attack mergers on market facts that developed after the merger is to subvert the longstanding policy of Section 2 of the Sherman Act with respect to internal growth. An antitrust law that said it was lawful to build a 10 percent company and grow to 60 percent, but unlawful to merge to a 10 percent company and grow to 60 percent, would lack any rationality.

There is a related danger in this doctrine. The Federal Trade Commission objected to Reynolds Metals' acquisition of Arrow Brands,[10] a firm engaged in decorating aluminum foil for resale to the florist trade, because Arrow received financial strength it had not had before and demonstrated that strength both by keeping its prices low from October 1957 to mid-1958 and by building a new plant valued at $500,000. The Commission thought it probable that Arrow's prices went below cost, though the record did not establish the point. The opinion relied heavily on the testimony of competitors that they were injured and might have been driven from the florist foil-embellishing business if the low prices had continued, as they had not. The Commission said it was irrelevant whether Arrow originated the price cutting: the important aspect was that "Arrow could lower its prices and maintain them at low levels for an extended period, which it could not have done before the merger." The Commission used the merger statute, Clayton 7, to convict a company of charging low prices and building a new plant. If these acts by Reynolds and Arrow sprang from an intent to monopolize, Section 2 of the Sherman Act should have applied. If they did not, Section 7 was used merely as a vehicle to attack lawful pricing behavior and plant investment policies the Commission happened not to like.

The idea of judging a merger by what happens afterward thus converts Clayton 7 from a statute about the effect of mergers on market structure to one about the subsequent internal growth or market behavior of any firm that happens to have committed a merger. Yet there is no basis in the statute or in common sense for treating the growth or competitive tactics of such a firm differently from those of any other firm. To do so is to require that firms with mergers in their history compete less vigorously than other firms.

The doctrine under discussion, then, treats the fact that Clayton 7 deals only with mergers as wholly without operative significance, as no more than an arbitrary jurisdictional prerequisite. Like the requirement of jacks or better to open, once it is satisfied it has no further bearing on the outcome of the proceedings.

We have examined nine ideas imposed by the Supreme Court upon amended Section 7 of the Clayton Act. None of those ideas is found in the statute's language, and none is compelled by the statute's legislative history. Not one of them, moreover, provides any answer to the basic question of why there should be a statute applying more severe standards to size by merger than to size by internal growth. All that these ideas do is create the appearance of a justification for the extraordinary severity with which the Supreme Court judges mergers. They tend to make the deficiencies of the Court's economic analysis of merger cases appear less serious, because there seem to be lots of other factors weighing on the side of illegality. That is why it is important to recognize that not one of these factors has any substance or validity.

The commingling of these ideas with the invalid theory of exclusionary practices produced the crash of antitrust merger policy in the *Brown Shoe* case. The case is worth examining because it not only established the main lines of the law of horizontal and vertical mergers but also contains the seeds of conglomerate merger law.

THE *BROWN SHOE* DECISION

It would be overhasty to say that the *Brown Shoe* opinion is the worst antitrust essay ever written. The connoisseur of bad antitrust opinions must take into account *Fortner Enterprises I*,[11] *Utah Pie*,[12] *Sealy*,[13] *Schwinn*,[14] *Procter & Gamble*,[15] *Von's Grocery*,[16] and many others, to cite only some of the more recent cases. Still, all things considered, *Brown Shoe* has considerable claim to the title. It is not merely a bad case, it is also a trend setter—as if the poems of E. A. Guest had determined the course of modern literature.

Original Section 7 of the Clayton Act having proved ineffective, for reasons that are of no particular interest here, mergers were governed up to 1950 by the Sherman Act. Except for the special category of railroad mergers, which were treated with greater severity, merger law

under the Sherman Act followed the course laid down by the 1911
Standard Oil and *American Tobacco* decisions. Judge Hand's 33–64–90
percent dictum in *Alcoa* was actually drawn from merger cases and
probably represents the law prior to the amendment of Clayton 7 well
enough. The 1950 amendment was understood to presage a change in
the law, a tightening of merger standards, but no one was certain how
far the change would go until the Supreme Court spoke. It was thought
that horizontal mergers (those between market rivals) might be questioned at market shares as low as 25 or 30 percent. Perhaps vertical
mergers (those between firms in the relation of supplier and customer)
that tied up a similar share of the market would also be challenged.
Hardly anyone expected what ultimately did happen.

In *Brown Shoe Co.* v. *United States* [17] the Supreme Court held illegal the acquisition by Brown, primarily a shoe manufacturer, of the
G. R. Kinney Co., primarily a shoe retailer. Their respective shares of
the nation's shoe output were 4 and 0.5 percent. Kinney had 1.2 percent
of total national retail shoe sales by dollar volume (no figure was given
for Brown), and together the companies had 2.3 percent of total retail
shoe outlets. With more than 800 shoe manufacturers operating in a
national market, the industry was as close to pure competition as is
possible outside a classroom model. Yet the seven Justices participating
in the case managed to see a threat to competition at both the manufacturing and the retailing levels, and they did so by using the concepts
already discussed.

The Court held the merger illegal for its vertical as well as horizontal
aspects. The Court generally views vertical integration, whether by
merger or contract, as a form of exclusionary practice, since it is always
possible that the manufacturing level will sell to the controlled retail
level. As Chief Justice Warren put it in *Brown Shoe*: "the diminution
of the vigor of competition which may stem from a vertical arrangement
results primarily from a foreclosure of a share of the market otherwise
open to competitors." Therefore, "an important consideration . . . is the
size of the share of the market foreclosed." When that share "approaches monopoly proportions" both the Clayton Act and the Sherman
Act are violated, but at the other extreme, "foreclosure of a *de minimis*
share" is not illegal. The present case, said the Chief Justice, fell between these extremes. It was, therefore, "necessary to undertake an
examination of various economic and historical factors in order to determine whether the arrangement under review is of the type Congress
sought to proscribe," and important here was the "very nature and purpose of the arrangement."

The Chief Justice then immediately rang the death knell for vertical mergers by analogizing them to tying arrangements. This merger would operate like a tying clause, he said, because Brown would force Kinney to fill some of its retail needs with Brown's shoes. This, of course, means that any vertical merger in which integration is expected—that is, any vertical merger capable of creating efficiencies—is like a tying arrangement, and tying arrangements, said Warren (relying upon a long line of clearly mistaken precedents), are "inherently anticompetitive." So much for vertical mergers. He need hardly have gone on. The rest was almost overkill.

Warren attributed the illegality of this vertical merger to two factors: ". . . the trend toward vertical integration in the shoe industry, [and] Brown's avowed policy of forcing its shoes upon its retail subsidiaries. . . ." It is enlightening to examine the facts upon which that conclusion rests. The "trend toward vertical integration" was seen in the fact that a number of manufacturers had acquired retailing chains. The district court found that the thirteen largest shoe manufacturers, for example, operated 21 percent of the census shoe stores.

Accepting that figure for the moment, it is impossible to see any harm to competition. On a straight extrapolation, there would be room for more than sixty manufacturers of equal size to integrate to the same extent, and that would result in competition as pure as is conceivable. In fact, since these thirteen were the largest shoe manufacturers, there would be room for many more. But that is by no means all; the category of census shoe stores includes only those that make at least half their income from selling shoes. It thus leaves out about two-thirds of the stores that actually compete in shoe retailing, including such key outlets as department and clothing stores. Even if, as there was no reason at all to expect, complete vertical integration took place in the industry, there would clearly be room for hundreds of shoe manufacturers and, given the ease and rapidity of entry into shoe retailing, no basis for imagining that any manufacturer could not find or create outlets anytime it chose. The Court's cited "trend toward vertical integration" was thus, even on the Court's own economic theory, impossible to visualize as a threat to competition.

Brown's "avowed policy of forcing its own shoes upon its retail subsidiaries" turns out, upon inspection of the Court's footnotes, to consist of the testimony of Brown's president that the company's motive in making the deal was to get distribution in a range of prices it was not covering. He also observed that as Kinney moved into stores in higher-income neighborhoods and needed to upgrade and add new lines, "it [the upgrading and adding of new lines] would give us an opportunity, we hoped, to be able to sell them in that category." The empirical evidence of coercion was no more impressive than this "avowal." At the time of the merger Kinney bought no shoes from Brown, but two years later Brown was supplying 7.9 percent of Kinney's needs. (Brown's sales to its other controlled outlets apparently had risen to no higher than 33 percent of requirements, except in one case in which Brown supplied over 50 percent.) The "trend toward vertical integration" and the "avowed policy of forcing its own shoes upon its retail subsidiaries" were thus wholly imaginary threats.

Yet even if we accept the Court's version of the facts at face value, it must be remembered that Kinney supplied about 20 percent of its own retail requirements before the merger and represented only 1.2 percent of the retail market in dollar volume. Therefore, less than 1 percent of the relevant national shoe market was open to "foreclosure" by Brown through this merger, and it had actually "foreclosed" slightly less than 0.1 percent. The Court's use of an erroneous theory of vertical integration as an exclusionary device, coupled with a heavily biased version of the facts and an almost unlimited extrapolation in the name of incipiency, thus yielded an incredible result on the vertical aspect of the case.

Aside from the factual weakness of the *Brown Shoe* opinion, it should be pointed out that the economic theory underlying the vertical aspect of the case was identical with that of the erroneous *Griffith* decision, discussed in Chapter 7. The Court's analogy between vertical integration and tying arrangements and its theory of forcing shoes on retailers display the double-counting fallacy in a new context. The Court's theory necessarily supposes that Kinney could retain whatever market position it had achieved in retailing and simultaneously transfer that market position to Brown. Thus, it is assumed, Kinney would still have 1.2 percent of national shoe retailing, while Brown's position in manufacturing would increase by almost 1 percent through "forcing" shoes on Kinney (the percentage difference being due to the amount of Kinney's requirements already supplied by Kinney's own plants), even though Brown had done nothing to deserve the accretion to its business other than coerce Kinney.

That theory, of course, states an impossibility. It completely ignores the fact that whatever considerations of price, quality, style, or other matters had led Kinney not to purchase Brown's shoes before the merger would remain just as valid afterward (unless Kinney's markets changed, as Brown's president said they would, or the merger lowered the cost of distributing shoes to Kinney). "Forcing" Kinney to take a product inappropriate to its business would, therefore, cost Kinney at least as much as it would benefit Brown. Since Brown now owned Kinney, it could gain nothing and might well lose from this imagined maneuver.

The problem can be stated another way. If the Court's naïve theory of "forcing" were correct, Brown would not have to acquire Kinney to employ the tactic. Since Brown, in common with almost every enterprise, was already integrated vertically, it could simply set up a separate profit and loss statement for all vertically related manufacturing operations and require each department to "force" more goods at higher prices upon the next, seriatim, all the way to the factory door. The last department might have some trouble selling all those high-priced shoes, but imagine the profits every previous department would report. Nobody has ever explained why this Rube Goldberg mechanism should suddenly become sensible if one more department, a retail outlet, is added and the shoes "forced" upon it.

The horizontal aspect of the case—the putting together of Brown's and Kinney's retail outlets—was held illegal on equally inadequate reasoning. The Court found the creation of market shares of as low as 5 percent of shoe retailing in any city illegal, stating: "If a merger achieving 5% control were now approved, we might be required to approve future merger efforts by Brown's competitors seeking similar market shares. The oligopoly Congress sought to avoid would then be furthered. . . ." On this reasoning, of course, every horizontal merger "furthers" oligopoly, no matter how small a share of the market is taken over. To imagine that every firm would then merge up to 5 percent is to indulge in sheer conjecture, and in any event the result would still be competition. Twenty firms in a market is far too many to behave other than competitively; given the further fact of the ease and rapidity of entry into shoe retailing, the Supreme Court's professed fear of oligopoly is simply incomprehensible.

But the Court offered two additional reasons for the illegality of 5 percent horizontal mergers. The first, its unexplained fear of chain operations, represented the seeds of conglomerate merger law under Section 7 and is reminiscent of the *Griffith* case's aversion to theater chains:

Furthermore, in this fragmented industry, even if the combination controls but a small share of a particular market, the fact that this share is held by a large national chain can adversely affect competition. Testimony in the record from numerous independent retailers, based on their actual experience in the market, demonstrates that a strong, national chain of stores can insulate selected outlets from the vagaries of competition in particular locations and that large chains can set and alter styles in footwear to an extent that renders the independents unable to maintain competitive inventories.

How a chain can conceivably "insulate" some outlets from competition is nowhere explained. We are told only that small competitors, reciting their "actual experience," are angry because they could not keep up with the style changes either initiated or followed by the large chains. We are not told that the style changes were unjustified or sinister or predatory, only that independent retailers did not like them. For all we know, the chains simply served consumers better. The fear of multimarket firms, the notion that they can somehow transfer power from market to market and so destroy their smaller rivals one at a time, is an enduring theme in antitrust. *Brown Shoe*'s uncritical acceptance of it in a Clayton 7 context foreshadowed the Court's hostility to conglomerate mergers. No one bothered to ask whether the discomfort of the independent retailers was due to improper chain behavior or superior chain efficiency. But in antitrust cases, as Professor Adelman said, "The unverified—and unverifiable—complaints of interested parties become not only evidence but proof positive." [18]

Then, seemingly without realizing the inconsistency with its earlier prediction that Brown would "force" its shoes upon Kinney, the Court suggested that the 5 percent share in retailing was also bad because Kinney's new ability to get Brown's shoes more cheaply would give it an advantage over other retailers. "The retail outlets of integrated companies, by eliminating wholesalers and by increasing the volume of purchases from the manufacturing division of the enterprise, can market their own brands at prices below those of competing independent retailers." The merger was therefore illegal both because Brown might "force" Kinney and because Kinney wanted to be "forced." This fascinating holding creates an antitrust analogue to the crime of statutory rape.

Apparently concerned that the achievement of efficiency and low prices through merger seemed to be illegal under this formulation, Chief Justice Warren explained:

Of course, some of the results of large integrated or chain operations are beneficial to consumers. Their expansion is not rendered unlawful by the mere fact that small independent stores may be adversely affected. It is competition, not competitors, which the Act protects. But we cannot fail to recognize Congress' desire to promote competition through the protection of viable, small, locally-owned businesses. Congress appreciated that occasional higher costs and prices might result from the maintenance of fragmented industries and markets. It resolved these competing considerations in favor of decentralization.

No matter how many times you read it, that passage states: although mergers are not rendered unlawful by the mere fact that small independent stores may be adversely affected, we must recognize that mergers are unlawful when small independent stores may be adversely affected.

The *Brown Shoe* case employed the theory of exclusionary practices to outlaw vertical integration that promised lower prices; the theory of incipiency to foresee danger in a presumably desirable trend that had barely started; and the theory of "social purpose" to justify the fact that the decision prevented the realization of efficiencies by a merger which, realistically viewed, did not even remotely threaten competition. One wondered, after reading the opinion's economic reasoning and the array of antimerger ideas that constituted the Court's "frame of reference," what evidence could conceivably save any merger in the Supreme Court as then constituted. Since no merger ever survived the Warren Court's scrutiny, we cannot be sure, but at the very end of the *Brown Shoe* opinion the Chief Justice touched on the subject: "Appellant [Brown Shoe] has presented no mitigating factors, such as the business failure or the inadequate resources of one of the parties that may have prevented it from maintaining its competitive position, nor a demonstrated need for combination to enable small companies to enter into more meaningful competition with those dominating the relevant markets."

These mitigating factors bespeak concern only for small companies and for the ideal of marketplace egalitarianism. Efficiency may be created by merger only to keep a firm from dying or to allow it to maintain its position. Efficiency sufficient to cause a gain in market share is permissible only to small companies, and then only when their gains are to be made at the expense of larger ones that dominate the market. In all other cases, one gathers from this and from the body of the opinion, efficiency gains weigh against the merger. Efficiency is valued not for its contribution to consumers, but only when it maintains the status quo in a market or aids small producers against much larger producers.

Brown Shoe was a disaster for rational, consumer-oriented merger policy. The incredible severity it forecast for horizontal and vertical mergers has been fully borne out, and the seeds of conglomerate merger policy have germinated. To those specific varieties of mergers and their analysis we turn in the following three chapters.

10

Horizontal Mergers

THE Supreme Court's refusal in
Brown Shoe to sanction a horizontal merger of as much as 5 percent in
a market characterized by easy, if not instantaneous, entry is representative of current doctrine. Perhaps the case even sets too high a
threshold figure for illegality, since in *Pabst Brewing Co.*[1] the Court,
through Justice Black, said that each of three figures, the lowest being
4.49 percent of national beer sales, was "amply sufficient" to show a
probable adverse effect on competition. But one tends to lose interest
in the Court's ability to see injury to competition in smaller and smaller
market shares. Once you have shaded 4.5 percent you are beginning to
approach an absolute limit to the process. Indeed, horizontal mergers
have all but disappeared from the economy.

The harmful effects of the present law on consumers are evident in
this analogy: by the Court's criterion, if there are a hundred lawyers in
a town, no partnership may contain as many as five. Such a rule obviously cuts far too deeply into the efficiencies of integration.

Perhaps the best example of Clayton 7's disorientation was the Court's
1966 decision in *Von's Grocery*[2] striking down a merger between two
grocery chains that, as Justice Stewart's dissent noted, "produced a
firm with 1.4 per cent of the grocery stores and 7.5 per cent of grocery
sales in Los Angeles." Between 1953 and 1962 the number of grocery
chains in the market increased from 96 to 150, with 173 entries and
119 exits. There was much evidence of market share changes, turnover
in firms, entries and exits, and all the other indicia of an intensely

competitive market, but none of this withstood the Court majority's observation that the number of single-store owners had declined from 5,365 in 1950 to 3,818 by 1961 and to 3,590 by 1963, three years after the merger. One would have thought that the existence of 150 chains (let alone the presence of 3,590 single stores) was more than enough to preserve competition, but Justice Black's majority opinion used the irresistible incipiency concept to foresee an inconceivable danger: "It is enough for us that Congress feared that a market marked at the same time by both a continuous decline in the number of small businesses and a large number of mergers would, slowly but inevitably, gravitate from a market of many small competitors to one dominated by one or a few giants, and competition would thereby be destroyed." Justice Stewart, whose dissent eliminated every possible factual and theoretical basis for the holding, observed justly that the decision was "contrary to the language of § 7, contrary to the legislative history of the 1950 Amendment, and contrary to economic reality."

It would be easy enough to parade the horrors of Clayton 7 case law in this field almost indefinitely. Clearly, the Supreme Court must rework the field if it is to be made rational. The Court has held against the government, narrowly, in recent merger cases, but these decisions stress the particular aspects of each situation in ways that do not reform existing doctrine. *United States* v. *General Dynamics Corp.*[3] upheld the merger of two coal-producing companies, but it is hard to tell what market share was approved. Current production was held not a useful measure because utilities buy coal on long-term contracts and one of the coal companies had few uncommitted reserves with which to compete for new contracts. The majority thought this meant competition was not injured, no matter how the product and geographic markets might be defined. *United States* v. *Marine Bancorporation,*[4] *United States* v. *Connecticut National Bank,*[5] and *United States* v. *Citizens and Southern National Bank,*[6] while generally adverse to government positions, rest so heavily upon facts and regulation peculiar to banking that they too appear to have little general significance. The most that can be said is that the current Court majority appears to display a less hostile attitude toward mergers but has not translated that mood into rules of general applicability that would undo the damage done by the earlier cases.

The interesting question is: In applying Clayton 7's injunction to judge mergers, what rules should the Court evolve so as to avoid monopoly and preserve competition?

In choosing the market shares that may be created by horizontal merger, we are dealing with a spectrum, and it must be confessed that the proper place to cut it is not entirely clear. The nature of the problem may be clarified if we start with the extreme cases. When companies each having 1 percent of a fragmented market merge, they cannot be supposed to have monopoly profit in mind. Their motivation, and hence the presumed effect of their action, must be either increased efficiency or some effect irrelevant to antitrust. Such a merger should be lawful without question. When companies each having 50 percent of a market merge to create a complete monopoly, however, the motivation and effect of their act are not free from doubt. The law is justified in striking down such a merger on the theory that restriction of output is certain and an offsetting increase in efficiency, so far as law enforcement officers can judge, is not. But in this case, unlike the merger of the two 1-percent firms, there is a problem of a welfare trade-off. The policy may incur some efficiency costs. As the law moves down the spectrum from the 100 percent merger, the problem of the trade-off between restriction of output and efficiency rapidly becomes severe. How far down the spectrum can the law go before it begins to inflict more welfare losses than it averts?

This issue has formed the subject of an interesting debate between Oliver Williamson on the one hand and Michael DePrano and Jeffrey Nugent on the other.[7] Williamson employed a diagram to represent the trade-off problem in a merger that creates market power and cuts costs. We have already examined that diagram and its uses as an expository tool in Chapter 5. In Chapter 6 it was argued that Williamson was wrong in proposing an efficiency defense in merger cases, since the elements of the trade-off between output restriction and efficiency gain cannot be studied directly. The trade-off must be estimated indirectly through economic reasoning. Market shares that may or may not be created by merger can then be expressed in general legal rules. If we are in fact dealing with a spectrum—if, that is, some noncollusive restriction of output actually occurs in markets with "few" firms—then general rules can at best be expected to do more good than harm on balance. That is a modest hope, but all, I believe, that the nature of the problem allows.

DePrano and Nugent attack Williamson's proposed efficiency defense from yet a different direction. Proceeding from his trade-off diagram, they attempt to demonstrate that very large cost reductions would be required to offset the associated price increases. The thrust of this demonstration is that "the required cost reductions would have to be so large that they are very unlikely to be forthcoming." They conclude that "it would seem that more rigorous activity on the part of antitrust authorities would be likely to serve both the goal of increasing net economic welfare, and that of equity in income distribution." Since we have already seen that antitrust should never concern itself with equity in income distribution, we will address here only their conclusions about net economic welfare.

It is not clear what size mergers DePrano and Nugent are talking about, but if they are familiar with the merger law already firmly established before they wrote, and if they are nevertheless advocating yet "more rigorous" merger policy, then they are suggesting, one must assume, that mergers creating market shares well below 5 percent be banned. This would require an extreme theory of oligopoly behavior, but perhaps their policy suggestion reflects only lack of knowledge of the laws' present severity.

Still, the question remains: What size horizontal mergers should be banned? Here it may be helpful to say a warning word concerning the trade-off diagram (Figure 4) about which the debate turned. It is disastrous to draw policy conclusions from that diagram. Its only valid use is to indicate the general relationship of loss and gain in cases in which both occur. In some mergers there will be a dead-weight loss and no efficiency gain; in others there will be an efficiency gain and no dead-weight loss; and in some both these effects will be present. One simply cannot read appropriate merger policy off a chart. The relative sizes of the dead-weight loss and the efficiency gain, in those cases where both exist, depend upon how one draws the diagram, and how one should draw the diagram depends entirely upon what economic analysis suggests about the reality the curves should reflect.

DePrano and Nugent make some assumptions about the probable slope of demand curves and proceed to derive a stringent merger policy from the graph paper. One can, of course, imagine a number of not unrealistic conditions that would modify their result. But that would be mere fencing. The fundamental difficulty with the line of argument employed by DePrano and Nugent is that the diagram from which they attempt to reason reflects a change from pure competition to pure monopoly. It tells us no more than that it would be unwise to allow a merger to create 100 percent market control where previously there had been no market power at all. The diagram and the authors' analysis of it tell us nothing of the wisdom of permitting or opposing mergers that create market shares of 10, 30, or even 75 percent. The diagram tells us nothing because there is nothing built into it that shows whether there will be any restriction of output in such cases or, if there is, what the amount will be. Without that information we have no idea of the size of the dead-weight loss, if any.

The needed data cannot be derived from the diagram but must be estimated according to our theory of the effects on output of particular degrees of concentration. A large merger that produces the economies represented by the lowering of the cost line on the diagram but which produces only a small degree of output restriction will move the vertical line only very slightly to the left, giving a much smaller triangle for dead-weight loss than that shown and a larger rectangle for economies. The net effect of the merger would clearly be beneficial. The question must be whether that is a more realistic way of drawing the diagram for mergers in any particular size range.

We have examined in Chapter 8 the reasons for thinking that non-collusive oligopolistic behavior, to the extent that it exists at all (and I am not persuaded that such behavior occurs outside of economics textbooks), rarely results in any significant ability to restrict output. If that estimate is substantially accurate, then most mergers would not involve any dead-weight loss, and even large mergers involving fewer than all significant rivals in the market would rarely increase the slope of the firm's demand curve enough to pose a serious problem. The effect would usually be outweighed by cost savings.

Since the amount of restriction of output seems to decrease greatly from one-firm markets to two-firm markets (though we do not know that there is any significant noncollusive restriction of output in two-firm markets), and since mergers may very well create substantial new efficiencies, we are in an area of uncertainty when we ask whether mergers that would concentrate a market to only two firms of roughly equal size should be prohibited. My guess is that they should not and, therefore, that mergers up to 60 or 70 percent of the market should be permitted—a figure that, curiously enough, resembles the old Sherman Act merger rule and Judge Hand's dictum in *Alcoa*.

Partly as a tactical concession to current oligopoly phobia and partly in recognition of Section 7's intended function of tightening the Sherman Act rule, I am willing to weaken that conclusion. Competition in the sense of consumer welfare would be adequately protected and the mandate of Section 7 satisfactorily served if the statute were interpreted as making presumptively lawful all horizontal mergers up to market shares that would allow for other mergers of similar size in the industry and still leave three significant companies. In a fragmented market, this would indicate a maximum share attainable by merger of about 40 percent. In a market where one company already has more than 40 percent, the maximum would be scaled down accordingly. For example, where one company already had 50 percent, it could not engage in any horizontal mergers, and no other company could create by merger a share above 30 percent (barring some exceptional circumstance, such as the imminent failure of one of the merger partners).

Even at these levels the law would certainly be preventing the realization of some efficiencies; since the law already strikes at even smaller horizontal mergers, it is surely exacting a large efficiency toll, and doing so, I think, for no particular reason. It is commonly said that the efficiency costs of banning mergers are not serious because the same efficiencies can be achieved through internal growth. But, as we have already seen, where merger is the less expensive method of reaching the size necessary for such efficiencies, the increased cost of growth is a social loss, and this increased cost may be large enough to preclude the attainment of the necessary size altogether.

It should also be noted that the reasoning which discounts the efficiency loss in banning mergers because growth may ultimately achieve the same results would support the idea that we might as well allow mergers to 95 percent size. There may be losses in allocative efficiency, but (to parallel the other argument) they are not serious because the internal growth of the smaller firms will erode them. The answer in this case, of course, is that there is no reason to wait for the market to remove allocative inefficiency when the law can cure it faster. An answer of the same nature can be made to the other argument: there is no reason for the law to force consumers to wait for the creation of productive efficiencies through internal growth when merger can create them faster.

But what of the law's application to ancient mergers? In *du Pont-GM* [8] the Supreme Court created the doctrine that Clayton 7 can reach back in time to undo old mergers and that it may judge them according to the market situation at the time suit is brought, rather than at the time the merger occurred. These notions form the peg upon which Nader hangs his proposal that General Motors be dissolved because it was formed by mergers dating back half a century. Chevrolet stock, for example, was first acquired in 1915, and the remainder in 1919. The impropriety of this doctrine has been discussed, but what is the correct rule? Let us take the two ideas of the *du Pont-GM* doctrine separately.

There should be a time limit within which a merger must be challenged. The Neal Task Force suggested a ten-year limitation, and that seems an excellent suggestion. There is, in the first place, the question of equity, of settled expectations that grow up about a state of affairs which has been permitted to continue without question for a long period. Second, it is desirable that enforcement authorities not have a club they can hold over a firm forever. They can at present control or influence a company's market behavior by threatening a merger suit, even though the merger is essentially irrelevant to the behavior and the behavior itself violates no antitrust statute. The *Reynolds Metals* case [9] shows that this is no idle menace. When that sort of thing occurs, Clayton 7 is converted from a law about the structure of markets to an open warrant for the enforcement authorities to engage in detailed regulation of the behavior of firms. Finally, and most important, there is no reason for the law to act if a market structure created by merger has persisted for years. The persistence of a market structure for years shows that it reflects the balance of market forces that best serves consumers. If it did not, the growth of smaller firms or the entry of new ones would erode and alter the structure. The Court is capable of adopting a ten-year rule on the basis of these considerations. If a dissolution suit is filed ten years after a merger and is contested, it will probably be another five years at least before a final decree can be enforced. Anything market forces have not done to the merger in ten or fifteen years, the law ought not to do.

Mergers should be judged on the market facts existing when the merger occurred, not those of the date of the lawsuit. Internal growth after a merger is the same as internal growth by a company that never merged. Both are demonstrations of efficiency. To apply Clayton 7 to the growth that occurs after a merger is to rewrite the statute as though it amended Sherman 2 in relation to internal growth. It did not. A statute that confines its reach to mergers must be applied only to the undesirable effects of mergers. As law, it cannot legitimately be applied to behavior identical to that which remains proper for unmerged firms. As economics, it cannot intelligently be applied to destroy consumer welfare. The drafting of Clayton 7 to strike only at anticompetitive effects caused by mergers must be viewed as essence rather than accident.

The rules suggested in this chapter might not completely prevent noncollusive restriction of output, and certainly will not completely avoid the destruction of efficiencies by law. Probably some welfare losses are inevitable in any policy that can be framed with respect to horizontal mergers. But we may be reasonably confident that this rule, whatever its imperfections, is at least in the proper range of the spectrum. And we may be certain that it strikes a much better balance between the factors impinging upon consumer welfare than the present judge-made proscription of horizontal mergers creating market shares as small as 5 percent or even less.

11

Vertical Mergers

ANTITRUST has been concerned about the effects of vertical mergers upon competition for over sixty years, but it has never evolved a satisfactory theory of the ways in which such integration could be harmful. The predominant fear has been that the acquisition of a customer or supplier would "foreclose" a market or source of supply to rivals and thereby fence out competition. That theory appeared in the 1911 *American Tobacco* decision,[1] which supposed that the acquisition of suppliers was a means of gaining or maintaining monopoly in tobacco manufacture.

But the law under the Sherman Act vacillated. Sometimes it appeared that vertical integration by merger was lawful unless the integration was used in a manner the courts regarded as coercive; at other times, as in *Yellow Cab I,* the Supreme Court appeared to say that vertical merger was illegal per se.[2] A wide range of possible abuses was imagined in various cases. The most accurate generalization of the Sherman Act decisions, perhaps, is that when the courts looked at vertical integration, they always thought it at least suspect and believed that in some manner it enhanced the power of the firm so structured.[3]

With the passage of the 1950 amendment to Section 7 of the Clayton Act and the subsequent draconian judicial interpretations, vertical mergers became, if not illegal per se, almost impossible to defend against government challenge. *Brown Shoe,*[4] it will be recalled, condemned a vertical merger that involved a potential foreclosure of less than 1 percent of a fragmented market and an actual foreclosure of less than 0.1 percent. The Department of Justice has issued guidelines for vertical mergers indicating somewhat higher threshold figures.[5] When the effect studied is upon the supplying firm's market, for example, "the Department will ordinarily challenge a merger or a series of mergers between a supplying firm, accounting for approximately 10 percent or more of the sales in its market, and one or more purchasing firms, accounting in toto for approximately 6 percent or more of the total purchases in that market, unless it clearly appears that there are no significant barriers to entry into the business of the purchasing firm or firms." In practice, however, the Department frequently attacks much smaller vertical mergers. The precise degree of the law's current severity may be in some doubt, given the less hostile attitude of the present Supreme Court toward antitrust defendants, but there seems no reason to doubt that vertical acquisitions remain subject to stringent limitation.

Antitrust's concern with vertical mergers is mistaken. Vertical mergers are means of creating efficiency, not of injuring competition. There is a faint theoretical case, hardly worth mentioning, that vertical mergers can be used by very large firms for purposes of predation under exceptional circumstances, but it is highly doubtful that that narrow possibility has any application to reality. In any event, the vertical mergers attacked by the law do not contain even that possibility. The vertical mergers the law currently outlaws have no effect other than the creation of efficiency.

It is conventional and useful to say, as Morris Adelman does, that vertical integration exists when a firm "transmits from one of its departments to another a good or service which could, without major adaptation, be sold in a market." [6] This definition calls attention to the choice of the firm to bypass a market transaction in favor of internal control. But the definition may lead us to overlook the ubiquity of such integration in our economy. Often there is no outside market for a good or service transmitted within a firm precisely because the efficiencies of vertical integration are so great that no firm would think of selling or buying at that stage. Every firm in the economy is vertically integrated in the sense that goods and services are transmitted within it and not offered on any market. This fact is important because it shows that vertical integration is indispensable to the realization of productive efficiencies. One can imagine the chaos and costs that would arise if the law were logically to extend its aversion to vertical integration by requiring, for example, an open market transaction every time goods moved from one worker or department to another or, indeed, by forbidding individuals to perform more than one task in the productive chain before selling. This is entirely fanciful, of course, but it is worth stressing that all economic activity displays vertical integration, because that tends to remove some of the sinister coloration this essential form of integration has undeservedly acquired.

The word "integration" means only that administrative direction rather than a market transaction organizes the cooperation of two or more persons engaged in a productive or distributive activity. The firm chooses between modes of organization according to their relative costs. On this basis, it chooses to perform particular tasks itself, to subcontract them to others, or to sell a finished or semifinished product to other firms which perform further functions in bringing a finished product to the final market. The firm itself is best defined for purposes of economic analysis as the area of operations within which administration, rather than market processes, coordinates work.[7]

What antitrust law perceives as vertical merger, and therefore as a suspect and probably traumatic event, is merely an instance of replacing a market transaction with administrative direction because the latter is believed to be a more efficient method of coordination. Vertical mergers may cut sales and distribution costs, facilitate the flow of information between levels of the industry (for example, marketing possibilities may be transmitted more effectively from the retail to the manufacturing level, new product possibilities may be transmitted in the other direction, better inventory control may be attained, and better planning of production runs may be achieved), create economies of scale in management, and so on. When such possibilities become apparent throughout an industry, a trend toward vertical integration will develop, as it did in shoe manufacturing and retailing, and as it has done in many other industries. Such trends are merely the responses of businessmen to changing circumstances. They are essentially no different from, and certainly no more cause for alarm than, countless other trends in product styles, types of outlets, automation, prices, and the like. What is incipient in any such trend is not the lessening of competition but the attainment of new efficiency, and it is the latter result at which amended Section 7 of the Clayton Act is actually striking in vertical merger cases.

It is thoroughly naïve of the law to suppose that vertical merger affects resource allocation adversely while vertical growth affects it not at all. The only difference between vertical merger and vertical growth is that in a specific situation at a particular moment one or the other will be the lower-cost way of achieving the efficiencies of integration. In fact, the sole difference between vertical merger and existing vertical integration within all firms is historical. In the latter case the efficiencies of integration have been present, recognized, and realized in firm structures for some time, while in the case of merger the efficiencies are either just becoming possible or are just being recognized, and firms are seeking to realize them through structural change.

Vertical integration is often believed somehow to cause or permit a firm to behave differently than it would in the absence of integration. Aside from the efficiency effect, however, it is clear that vertical integration does not affect the firm's pricing and output policies. If, for example, a firm operates at both the manufacturing and retailing levels of an industry, it maximizes overall profit by setting the output at each level as though the units were independent of one another. (One exception to this will be mentioned below.) The firm will not, as is frequently suggested, sell to its own retail subsidiary for less than it sells to outsiders, unless the efficiencies of integration lower the cost of selling to its own retail unit.

The reasons for this are obvious. It is impossible for a firm actually to sell to itself for less than it sells to outside firms because the real cost of any transfer from the manufacturing unit to the retailing unit includes the return that could have been made on a sale to an outsider. No matter what the bookkeeper writes down as the transfer price, the real cost is always the opportunity forgone. (If a garment manufacturer spends $50 to make a dress, could sell it for $100, but chooses to give it to his wife, the cost to him is $100, not $50, and the fact cannot be altered by any number he chooses to put in his books.) Nor would there be any point in the firm's subsidizing its retail level by transfers at artificially low prices. Such a policy would merely entail the sacrifice of return at the manufacturing level, and the self-deception as to true costs would cause the retailing subsidiary to operate at an uneconomical rate. If the marginal costs of retailing are rising—as they certainly are, unless the retailer is a natural monopolist—the artificially low price would result in an increased output at higher costs. The integrated firm would be paying more for the performance of the retailing function than it would if it recognized real costs and operated at a smaller scale on the retail level.

These principles may usefully be applied to varying industry structures. Where the firm is competitive at both levels, it maximizes by equating marginal cost and price at each level, and each level makes a competitive rate of return. Should the firm enjoy a monopoly at the manufacturing level but face competition in retailing, it will of course exact a monopoly profit in manufacturing; but, for the reasons discussed, it will sell to the retail level at the same monopoly price it asks of independent retailers.

If the integrated firm has monopoly positions in both manufacturing and retailing, however, the levels will not maximize independently. This is true because vertically related monopolies can take only one monopoly profit. If each level tries to maximize by restricting output, the result will be a price higher than the monopoly price and an output smaller, the result being less than a full monopoly return. The reason for this is easily seen. Suppose the firm starts as a manufacturing monopoly selling to a competitive retail level. The manufacturer would set his output and price so that the appropriate monopoly price would be charged consumers after retailers had added their costs, including a competitive return. The monopolist must allow the retailers a competitive return, and he will not want to allow them more than that. If he allowed them less, the level of investment and operation in retailing would decline to the manufacturer's detriment. If he allowed them more, the level of investment and operation would rise above the optimal, and the manufacturer would be paying for retailing services he did not want.

We may suppose that the manufacturer purchases all of the retailers, converting that level of the industry to a second monopoly held by him. This will not change his price and output decisions at all. Though he now holds both manufacturing and retailing, the monopolist is still facing the same consumer demand and the same costs at both levels. The maximizing price to consumers, therefore, remains the same. The new retail subsidiary will not be permitted to act independently and restrict output further than the manufacturing level had already restricted it, since that would result in an output lower and a price higher than the maximizing level.

This reasoning, where it applies, shows that a monopolist has no incentive to gain a second monopoly that is vertically related to the first, because there is no additional monopoly profit to be taken. The qualification is important, however, for John McGee and Lowell Bassett [8] have shown that my argument applies only in fixed proportion cases, i.e., when the monopolist sells an input that his customers must use in a fixed proportion with other inputs in making their products. Variable proportion cases are quite common, however. If it is possible to produce widgets with different proportions of X and Y, and if X comes to be held by a monopolist, widget manufacturers will begin to use more of Y and less of X. This has the effect both of making production of widgets more costly (not only because of the monopoly price charged for X, but because the new proportions of X and Y used are presumably less efficient than the old) and of giving the monopolist of X an incentive to gain a monopoly of either Y or widgets to prevent substitution of

Y for X from diminishing his monopoly profits. (Acquisition of a second monopoly of either Y or widgets is, properly speaking, a horizontal acquisition because the purpose and effect in each case is to eliminate the competition of a substitute, Y, that diminishes the market share of X. Thus, the acquisition of a widget monopoly, though vertical in form, does not actually raise a question about the vertical effects of the merger.)

No matter whether the monopolist of X chooses to gain a monopoly of Y of of widgets, the correct response of the law is simple if the monopoly of X was illegally gained. That monopoly should be dissolved, and so should the further monopoly in Y or widgets. Monopolistic restriction of output is thereby eliminated, and widget manufacturing returns to the most efficient combination of inputs X and Y.

The matter is not so clear, however, if the monopoly of X was acquired legally (is based, for example, on superior efficiency demonstrated through internal growth or upon a patent). Then, the monopoly of X is legally invulnerable, and it is not clear that prohibiting the acquisition of a monopoly of either Y or widgets would increase consumer welfare. Allowing the second monopoly would permit the monopolist of X to stop the substitution of Y, which would be detrimental because greater restriction of output would result, but it would also result in the most efficient proportions of X and Y being used to produce widgets, which is a gain in productive efficiency. When the outcome for consumer welfare is unclear, the tie-breaker considerations discussed in Chapter 6 indicate that the law should not intervene.

The case under discussion, is, in any event, a very rare one: the acquisition by a monopolist of a second vertically-related monopoly. Much of the theoretical case against vertical integration begins by trying to establish some possibility of competitive harm from the joining of two vertically related monopolies, and then proceeds on the unstated assumption that a case has been made which is applicable to all vertical mergers. The point here is that no case has been made against the vertical acquisition by a monopolist of a second monopoly; * moreover, even if such a case could be made, it would be largely an academic exercise and

* A further interesting sidelight on vertically related monopolies is that it may be better from the consumers' point of view for such monopolies to be integrated rather than in separate hands. That averts the danger that separate monopolists, unable to agree, would arrive at a final price above the one an integrated firm would have chosen. If there are two lawful, vertically related monopolies, therefore, integration or collusion is to be desired rather than attacked. This analysis demonstrates that the theory of countervailing power is wholly mistaken.

would have no force in the broader context of the vertical mergers the law is actually preventing.

The argument so far holds, of course, whether vertical integration is created by growth or merger. Vertical merger does not create or increase the firm's power to restrict output. The ability to restrict output depends upon the share of the market occupied by the firm. Horizontal mergers increase market share, but vertical mergers do not.

These observations indicate that vertical mergers are merely one means of creating a valuable form of integration and that there is no reason for the law to oppose such mergers. Adherence to an economic fallacy almost as old as antitrust policy, however, has caused the law to take an entirely different course.

"FORECLOSURE": THE LAW'S OBJECTION TO VERTICAL MERGER

The law developed under amended Section 7 of the Clayton Act assumes that vertical mergers may sometimes be beneficial or neutral but that their dominant effect is so heavily deleterious as to merit the prohibition of almost all such integrations. The law's current theory of the way in which vertical mergers injure competition is contained in the concept of "foreclosure." It is supposed that, for instance, a manufacturer may acquire a retailer, force the retail subsidiary to sell the manufacturer parent's products, and thus "foreclose" rival manufacturers from the market represented by the captive retailer. This is thought to be a means by which the competitive process may be injured.

In analyzing the *Brown Shoe* case we have seen the extremes to which this theory can be carried, but once an erroneous idea is let loose in antitrust it tends to run riot. Even before *Brown Shoe* the Federal Trade Commission had ingeniously devised what was, apparently, a doctrine of reciprocal foreclosure. This theory, whose sole merit is that it establishes a new high in preposterousness, is illustrated by the Commission's refusal to permit the acquisition by A. G. Spalding & Bros. of another full-line sporting goods company, Rawling Manufacturing Co.[9] The case was decided primarily as a horizontal merger, but the Commission objected to possible vertical foreclosure as well.

A fair sample of the *Spalding* opinion's foreclosure reasoning runs this way: before the merger Spalding did not manufacture baseball gloves but bought its requirements from others. Rawlings, on the other hand, made gloves and sold them to others. The merger might therefore wreak havoc on competition at both manufacturing and selling levels, for as the Commission saw it, "by acquiring Rawlings, Spalding can not only prevent competitors from purchasing [baseball gloves] from Rawlings but can also foreclose manufacturers of [gloves] from access to Spalding as a purchaser thereof."

A two-edged sword indeed! The Commission's opinion does not inform us why the people who formerly made gloves for Spalding could not sell them to the people who formerly bought gloves from Rawlings. Instead, we are left to imagine eager suppliers and hungry customers, unable to find each other, forever foreclosed and left to languish. It would appear the Commission could have cured this aspect of the situation by throwing an industry social mixer.*

The theory of foreclosure is, of course, a subcategory of the general theory of exclusionary practices which we examined in Chapter 7, in that it supposes rivals may be excluded by means other than efficiency. The older law, under the Sherman Act, supposed that the foreclosure might be deliberate or predatory. The law under amended Clayton 7 does not search for indicia of wrongful intent but applies automatically an inference of anticompetitive foreclosure. Predation through vertical merger is extremely unlikely. The Clayton 7 theory of automatic foreclosure is here, as in all contexts, completely improper. An example may help make the point.

Uniform Oil of South Dakota, we shall assume, refines 10 percent of the nation's gasoline. Neither Uniform nor any other refiner is integrated by ownership or contract into gasoline retailing. Uniform purchases all the share capital of Zeck Stations, a nationwide gasoline retail chain that makes 10 percent of sales to motorists. Prior to the acquisition Zeck had purchased gasoline from three other refiners, but not from Uniform.

The question is whether it will pay Uniform to require Zeck to retail Uniform's brand now. We must assume that there are no efficiencies that indicate this course of action, since we are testing whether a vertical merger of this sort is an appropriate implement for predation. It is plain

---

* A very similar holding by a district court was summarily affirmed by the Supreme Court. *Kennecott Copper Corp.* v. *United States,* 381 U.S. 414 (1965), affirming 231 F. Supp. 95, 103–104 (S.D.N.Y. 1964).

that it is not. In fact, this vertical merger is, if anything, a less appropriate tactic for predation than price cutting would be.

Let us assume, however, that Uniform, misled by the economic reasoning of the courts, decides to up its market share by forcing its new subsidiary, Zeck, to sell Uniform gasoline to the public. By continuing to sell to other retailers as it has in the past, Uniform expects to have 20 percent of the gasoline market instead of 10. It will discover that it has miscalculated. It must pay for the extra market share with losses. In the first place, prior to the acquisition Uniform must have been operating at a rate of output where price most closely approximated marginal cost. For Uniform, doubling that output without a price increase (and there is no way it can get one) means operating its refineries at a point where marginal and average variable costs are well above price. And price will in fact have dropped, since refiners who used to sell through Zeck will be competing for other outlets. This will further increase the spread between Uniform's costs and market price. Note that other refiners need not be taking losses: they may cut back to equate marginal cost with the new price. Uniform, given its imperialistic ambitions, cannot. It is caught in the trap that awaits all predators who must increase output to take over the market.

Worse still, Zeck will be in competitive difficulties. As a retailer Zeck preferred the pattern of brand distribution in existence prior to its acquisition by Uniform; that is the reason it did not then buy gasoline from Uniform. Forced to take that brand now, Zeck will bear the cost of an inappropriate distribution pattern. To sell as much gasoline as before—10 percent of the national market—Zeck will have to cut price. Since price and marginal cost were equated before, Zeck too is now operating at a loss. Predation has succeeded in turning two profitable operations into two loss operations.

Yet other costs have not been mentioned. If vertical integration was dictated by predatory ambition rather than efficiency, it is highly unlikely that the costs of integration are the same as those of nonintegration, which means it is very probable that these costs have also gone up. Management costs for the larger unit are among those that will probably rise.

Uniform, at this stage, has accomplished nothing more than to require its accountants to switch from black to red ink. In order to gain a monopoly it will have to acquire substantially all retail service stations. That merely means that the price war will consist of bidding for stations with high prices rather than bidding for motorists' patronage with low prices. There is no reason to think Uniform would be the successful bidder in most cases or, if it were, that it would find this course of action profitable. A monopoly is not worth much if you have to bid competitively for the right to own it.

We have not even considered the problem of entrants at the retail level—entrants who would arrive in sky-darkening swarms for the profitable alternatives of either selling popular gasoline brands that needed outlets or selling new service stations at inflated prices to Uniform. Even without the problem of entry, it is apparent that this vertical merger does not provide a means of gaining monopoly. As a predatory tactic it is a washout. This is obvious on theoretical grounds, but it should also be obvious on empirical grounds. Has anyone ever seen a company gain a monopoly by vertical merger? We have built up an extraordinarily severe law on the basis of speculation alone, and demonstrably empty speculation at that.

When the general theory of deliberate predation by vertical merger falls, so of course does the Clayton 7 theory that such mergers may improperly exclude rivals even without a wrongful intent by the acquiring company. The intent of Uniform in buying Zeck must be to make profits by driving out rivals unfairly or by creating greater efficiencies. We have seen that predation is most improbable,* and so we are left with the efficiency hypothesis. The law against vertical mergers is merely a law against the creation of efficiency.

This may be seen in the Supreme Court's decision in *Ford Motor Co.* v. *United States* [10] holding unlawful Ford's acquisition from Electric Autolite Co. of the name Autolite and certain spark plug manufacturing assets. One of the two grounds of the ruling was vertical, the district court's finding that the acquisition caused "the foreclosure of Ford as a purchaser of about ten percent of the total industry output."

Spark plug manufacturers sell in two related markets: to automobile manufacturers for installation in original equipment (the OE market), and to service stations for replacement of defective or worn plugs (the aftermarket). For many years prior to the merger, three manufacturers supplied the OE market. General Motors made the AC brand for installation in its own cars; and two independents, Champion and Autolite, supplied Ford and Chrysler, respectively, and between them also supplied American Motors.

These three manufacturers were also prominent in the aftermarket

---

* There seems to be only one restricted situation in which predation by vertical merger is even theoretically conceivable. The analysis, and the low level of probability, are the same as that given in Chapter 7, using exclusive dealing contracts as an example.

because of the "OE tie"—the tendency of mechanics to install replacement plugs of the same brand as the automobile's original plugs. Since plugs are designed for specific makes and models of cars, there is some objective reason for that tendency. The OE tie was by no means determinative of shares in the aftermarket, however. Although General Motors was producing roughly half of all American-made automobiles, AC's share of all plug output was only 30 percent. Champion had 50 percent of total output, even though Ford had made only about 30 percent of the cars in service. Autolite had 15 percent of output. The remainder of the industry's output was produced by several firms selling only in the aftermarket. The advantage of the OE tie was said to be sufficient, however, to permit sales in the OE market at well below cost, the loss apparently being viewed as a promotional expenditure for the aftermarket.

Wishing to enter spark plug manufacture, Ford determined that from five to eight years would be needed to develop an effective plug division of its own and that such a course would be more expensive than the acquisition of an existing manufacturer. At about that time, Autolite, apprehensive about the tenuousness of its position with Chrysler, approached Ford to sell plugs. Instead, in 1961, Ford purchased Autolite's spark plug assets, as well as a battery plant. Champion, Ford's former supplier, successfully sought the Chrysler account; however, since Champion was now supplying a smaller automobile manufacturer, its market share declined over seven years to 33 percent. The former Autolite management, located in a new corporate framework, began making plugs under the Prestolite name and obtained 1.2 percent of the market. Several other brands had strong backing. Sears, Roebuck's brand, Allstate, had 1.2 percent; Atlas plugs, sponsored by Standard Oil of New Jersey, 1.4 percent; and Riverside, sponsored by Montgomery Ward, 0.6 percent.

The Supreme Court quoted the district court on foreclosure:

It will also be noted that the number of competitors in the spark plug industry closely parallels the number of competitors in the automobile manufacturing industry and the barriers to entry into the auto industry are virtually insurmountable at present and will remain so for the foreseeable future. Ford's acquisition of the Autolite assets, particularly when viewed in the context of the original equipment (OE) tie and of GM's ownership of AC, has the result of transmitting the rigidity of the oligopolistic structure of the automobile industry to the spark plug industry, thus reducing the chances of future deconcentration of the spark plug market by forces at work within that market.

The Court's argument rests upon the assumption that an industry with three leading manufacturers cannot be fully competitive. There is, as we have seen, no sufficient basis for that idea. But in this chapter we shall examine the vertical foreclosure argument.

In *Brown Shoe* the merger was thought to foreclose the acquired firm as a market for rivals of the acquiring firm, but here the acquiring firm was said to have foreclosed itself as a market. There is a world of difference between the two formulations. If foreclosure were in fact a means of injuring competition, it would be understandable for a firm to wish to lessen the competition of rivals. But it is not understandable why Ford should wish to lessen competition among its suppliers. We are, in fact, safe in assuming that Ford will do nothing that reduces the overall efficiency of those who supply it with spark plugs. To that extent, Ford's interests coincide with the interests of ultimate consumers. The foreclosure, therefore, cannot have worked harm in the OE market.

The point may be put another way. The structure of an industry supplying the automotive industry will be whatever is most efficient for the automotive industry. Nor can there be anything wrong in the automobile manufacturers acquiring all of their own suppliers. The decision to make oneself or to buy from others is always made on the basis of difference in cost and effectiveness, criteria the law should permit the manufacturer to apply without interference.

The passage quoted by the Supreme Court mentioned the OE tie, however, and perhaps part of the evil of the Autolite acquisition was expected to occur in the aftermarket. The reference to forces at work for deconcentration almost certainly referred to some speculative testimony by one witness to the effect that private brand plugs sponsored by mass merchandisers might have considerably more success in the future. Once more, the Court cited no evidence that the aftermarket was performing poorly; it simply relied on an unarticulated inference from the fact of "concentration." Be that as it may, there was no showing that Ford's acquisition of Autolite would deflect the forces of deconcentration through the incursions of mass marketers. There was no reason to believe that the acquisition would affect, one way or the other, the tendency, never absolute in any case, of mechanics to replace plugs with the brand originally installed in the car. *

---

* The Court did suggest that Ford, as the owner of Autolite, would have an incentive to prevent the weakening of the OE tie, but nobody suggested how Ford might do that any more effectively than Champion or Autolite as independent corporate entities. Moreover, the suggestion overlooks the fact that Ford had a

The *Ford-Autolite* opinion fails to establish a valid theory of vertical foreclosure. It is almost certainly merely another example of efficient integration destroyed through reliance on an incorrect economic theory.*

But foreclosure theory is not merely wrong, it is irrelevant. Let us suppose, for the sake of argument, that it is possible for a firm to lever its way to larger market shares by foreclosing rivals with vertical acquisitions. Even so, there is nothing to fear unless a market share is gained that is large enough to permit profitable restriction of output. And there can be no possibility of that *if correct horizontal merger rules are applied.*

Let us assume, to return to the hypothetical case, that the refiner, Uniform Oil, can somehow purchase all the service stations in the country without paying too high a price; that for some reason (say, zoning regulations) entry at the retail level is utterly impossible; and that Uniform is able to establish a refining monopoly (the original purpose behind this complicated carom shot) by foreclosing its rivals from sales to service stations. Surely this would be a detrimental effect of foreclosure. But as a matter of fact, it would not. Foreclosure theory is like a conjuring trick: it causes you to look at the wrong level of the industry, in this case the refining level. The problem just stated is not vertical but horizontal; the evil is not the foreclosure of rival refiners but the establishment of a retail monopoly. Once the retail monopoly is secure, Uniform has no conceivable reason to foreclose rival refiners and, since the existing size distribution of refiners reflects cost conditions at that level, every reason not to. The retail monopoly confers the power to take all the monopoly profit possible out of the industry. We have already seen that in vertically related processes only one monopoly profit can be captured. (The problem of variable input proportions does not arise where the monopoly is at the retail level.)

To be clear about the conclusion that the evil is the horizontal merging of all the retailers rather than the vertical merger between Uniform and

---

stake in the preservation of the OE tie before the acquisition. The six-cent price to OE manufacturers was about a third of manufacturing cost and was justified only because of the OE tie. If that tie had disappeared or weakened significantly, the spark plug companies would no longer have had a reason to give the lower price to the automobile companies. There is thus no showing that the acquisition changed anything.

* The Court also rested on the horizontal theory of potential competition. Ford, it said, might have deconcentrated the market by entering without acquisition or might have controlled Champion just by the possibility of its entering. This notion, which often arises in conglomerate merger cases as well, is discussed in the next chapter.

the retail level, ask yourself whether the situation would be any different if a complete stranger to the industry—say, an insurance company—bought up all the gasoline retailers. The answer, clearly, is no: a horizontal monopoly would be created and output would be restricted just as much, even though there was no foreclosure of any refiner.

Another way of showing that verticality is not the problem is this: if Uniform Oil bought up every gasoline station in the United States, would the problem be solved by a decree requiring Uniform to dispose of its refining business so that it would not foreclose other refiners? Of course not. Verticality is destroyed, but monopoly remains.

Whether or not one believes in the law's foreclosure theory, therefore, *all so-called vertical merger cases should be handled through the application of horizontal merger standards.* * A pair of examples may make the implications of this rule clear.

(1) Uniform Oil, not already integrated into retailing, could acquire any one retailer, regardless of either Uniform's or the retailer's market share. Suppose the retailer had 50 percent of sales to motorists. The merger would not add to the retailer's market share, and so would not increase any ability to restrict output anyone might think it had.

(2) Uniform Oil, whatever its market share, could acquire any number of retailers until the share created at the retail level met horizontal merger limits or until it equaled Uniform's share in refining, whichever is greater. Correct horizontal merger standards would balance welfare considerations at the retail level; the reason for allowing Uniform, or a stranger to the industry, to make such acquisitions was argued in the previous chapter. Letting Uniform, but not a stranger to the industry, put together a larger share of retailing (where Uniform holds an equal share of refining already) follows from the principle that vertically related market shares permit a firm to restrict output only once. If Uniform had 80 percent of refining and acquired 80 percent of retailing, it would gain no increased power to restrict output. The reason for the acquisitions, then, must be the expectation of enhanced efficiency. In practice this would be a rare case, and the main thrust of the argument is that horizontal merger standards should be applied.

We may turn next to some specific objections that may be raised to the thesis so far developed.

---

* If there is any realism in the theoretical case of predation made out in Chapter 7, that may be handled by a rule making vertical mergers unlawful under Section 2 of the Sherman Act when the acquiring company has at least a market share of, say, 80 percent *and* specific intent to monopolize can be proved.

OTHER POSSIBLE OBJECTIONS
TO VERTICAL MERGERS

Most commentators who have suggested that the law concern itself with vertical mergers have not defended the law as it now stands but have argued for the possibility of harm in extreme cases. Thus, although the law now strikes at vertical mergers in which a company representing 1 percent of a market is acquired, most commentators discuss cases in which 100 percent of a market is acquired. But I think it can be shown that not even these extreme cases pose any danger to consumer welfare.

Phillip Areeda posits the case of a monopolist ingot manufacturer who creates a monopoly in fabrication by vertical acquisition.[11] Areeda agrees that the addition of the second monopoly does not increase prices or monopoly profit, and then continues:

But neither the monopolist nor the law should be indifferent to monopoly at the second level.

(1) The monopolist may have to operate at the second level in order to facilitate price discrimination between classes of customers.

(2) A vertically integrated monopolist selling to "consumers" might suppose that he would have fewer antitrust problems than if he were "exploiting" highly vocal processors.

(3) The monopolist may properly fear that his monopoly will not last. To monopolize both levels will make his position more impregnable to challenge. A new entrant into ingot production would also have to enter the fabrication business if there were no independent fabricators to sell to. The additional capital, expertness, and facilities required to enter simultaneously on both levels will obviously increase the difficulties of entering.

(4) With monopoly there may be less innovation at the second level.

We may agree with Areeda that the monopolist should not be indifferent to these factors (except the third, because the effort to block entry in this manner will surely prove both costly and fruitless), but it nevertheless seems clear that the law should be indifferent to them. The explanation of why antitrust should not concern itself with these matters even where vertical merger extends a monopoly from one level to another may further clarify why it is pointless to worry about mergers involving smaller market shares.

PRICE DISCRIMINATION

A monopolist may have two groups of customers with very different demand schedules but be unable to charge them different prices because those charged the lower price would find it profitable to resell to those charged the higher price. The monopolist can prevent cross-selling by acquiring one set of customers. The law should be indifferent to this possible use of vertical integration for several reasons. The primary reason is that the discrimination is at least as likely to increase the monopolist's output as to decrease it, thus bringing it closer to the competitive level and mitigating the misallocation of resources inherent in the monopoly. Indeed, the example of discrimination given by Areeda in a footnote results in an expansion of output, which he correctly characterizes as "socially desirable." It may well be that discrimination increases output more often that it decreases it. Given the rarity of this case in any event, the difficulty of detecting discrimination, and the costs of invoking the legal process, it seems clear that the law should be indifferent to a practice that is, in general, at worst neutral and perhaps beneficial. The more extended discussion of price discrimination in Chapter 20 is applicable here.

SILENT CONSUMERS VS. VOCAL PROCESSORS

Areeda's suggestion is not clear here. There is no way a monopolist can exploit processors more than ultimate consumers, so the suggestion must be that the articulateness of the former will call attention more rapidly to monopolies that should be attacked by antitrust. If one accepts the argument of this book about monopoly, the only such case would be where the enforcement agencies have overlooked monopoly created by predation or horizontal merger. Predation must be against firms that are as vocal as the processors, and the idea that a horizontal merger creating real monopoly power will be overlooked is so extremely improbable that it cannot be taken seriously as a reason for the law to attack vertical mergers. If the enforcement authorities observe a vertical acquisition by a monopolist, they need only ask whether the monopoly is lawful to satisfy this concern of Areeda's.

ENTRY BLOCKING

The suggestion that a monopolist can deter entry by integrating vertically has been carried by the law and by commentators other than

Areeda to the extent of supposing that even competitors may integrate in order to discourage newcomers. This notion is sometimes dignified with the name of "collective foreclosure." Clearly, however, if Areeda's more restricted case of the monopolist who seeks to block entry in this fashion proves untenable, the entire theory should be abandoned.

The idea that vertical integration may be carried out for the purpose of blocking entry requires the validity of two more general theories, each of which is invalid. By buying up the fabrication level, Areeda's ingot monopolist is relying upon adding to a potential entrant's problems a need for additional capital, facilities, and expertness. To suppose that this need will deter entry when higher-than-competitive profits will reward entry is to rely upon the theory of artificial barriers to entry. This theory is the subject of Chapter 16, which concludes that no such barriers exist in the economic world.

While there is no need to repeat the argument of that chapter here, an outline of the requirements of Areeda's suggestion may serve to show its implausibility. To the extent that the ingot monopolist integrates vertically for the purpose of blocking entry, he will incur diseconomies. Had there been economies, he would already have integrated vertically for that reason. The diseconomies may be of two kinds: higher costs due to the joining of ingot production and fabrication, and diseconomies of scale at the fabricating level. If more than one fabricator was active in that market, the marginal costs of fabrication are rising. When the ingot manufacturer takes over all fabrication, he will necessarily operate that level of the industry at significantly higher costs than the separate fabricators had incurred.

It is at once apparent that the vertical integration of the ingot manufacturer has had an effect opposite to that intended; it has provided an incentive to entry. If the only diseconomies he has incurred are in the scale of operation at the fabrication level, a new entrant can enter ingot manufacture and fabrication at the optimal size and beat him on costs. Since extranormal profits are to be had (the effort to protect such profits is the point of the exercise), there is no reason why the additional capital to enter at the fabricating level should not be obtainable by the entrant at the ingot level. Capital seeks its most profitable employment, even though more of it is required than for less remunerative investments. The need for facilities is simply an aspect of the capital problem, and the need for expertness in fabrication may be overcome in many ways, including the common tactic of hiring away some of the personnel already engaged in fabrication.

Worse then this, the monopolist cannot even impose the requirement that the entrant perform both ingot manufacturing and fabrication. Since greater-than-competitive profits are to be had, the entrant at the ingot level can find an entrant for the fabricating level, and this will be the preferred technique if there are diseconomies in vertical integration itself. Neither of the entrants will have a capital cost greater than if the manufacturer had not integrated, and they will have a significant cost advantage over the monopolist. The tactic supposed, therefore, appears to have the net effect of smoothing the path for entry.*

THREATS TO INNOVATION

Areeda's argument assumes that the second level of the industry would be more innovative when competitive than when monopolized; for purposes of this discussion, we will assume that to be a possible result. The difficulty with Areeda's position is that the loss of innovativeness is as much a cost to the vertically integrating monopolist as it is to society. Any ingot monopolist selling to competitive fabricators will want his customers to be as vigorous, imaginative, and active as possible, because their success will enable him to sell them more ingot at a monopoly price. If acquiring his customers would make them less efficient in any way, including a decline in the level of innovation, that is a

---

* I have conceded a possible, though unlikely, use of vertical merger for purposes of predation in a previous footnote and in Chapter 7. It seems even more improbable that the same tactic could be employed in order to create an artificial barrer to entry. The theoretical case for predation involved distorting distribution patterns to make them more costly. The case, as before, would apply only to a firm that expected, even after entry had taken place, to have at least 80 percent of the market. Moreover, vertical merger as an entry-barring device would be more costly than as a predatory device, for the firm would have to bear the extra costs of vertical integration permanently and not just as a temporary manuever. Entrants might be attracted at any time. Thus, the would-be entry barrer would have to incur a stream of sacrifices of current income in order to guard perpetually against possible future losses of greater size. The factors of uncertainty and the interest rate would very likely suggest that the company take present profits instead of losses and let entry in the future occur as it may. This is particularly true since the monopolist can have no way of knowing that potential entrants will not have sufficient market share, efficiencies, or reserves to permit them to enter regardless. An entrant that appeared able to stay the course would make the existing firm drop vertical integration in short order, for the latter would then be incurring costs to no purpose. All in all, the idea of deterring entry by accepting an unfavorable distribution pattern, like the idea of imposing capital costs, appears a most unpromising technique for guarding monopoly profits.

diseconomy in the vertical integration—a diseconomy the monopolist in ingot would have to weigh against any economies the merger would create. The ingot monopolist's decision, then, consists of weighing expected efficiency gains against expected efficiency losses, including any possible decline in innovation. If he thinks the benefits outweigh the costs, there is no reason for antitrust to second-guess him.

PRICE SQUEEZES

Areeda uses the example of *M*, a monopolist in ingot who is integrated into pipe fabrication, to illustrate the idea that vertical integration makes price squeezes possible: "By varying his ingot and pipe prices, *M* can squeeze independent fabricators' profit margins down (1) to perfectly competitive levels or (2) to unremunerative levels. The latter course will ultimately give *M* a monopoly of fabrication, but merely limiting excess fabrication profits is, generally speaking, socially desirable." Areeda is clearly correct about that. Vertical integration is a way the ingot monopolist can make sure a cartel among pipe fabricators does not create a second restriction of output, to both his and the public's detriment. If the monopoly in ingot is illegal, antitrust should attack that and not the vertical integration. If the monopoly is legal, the vertical integration supplies a measure of protection for consumers.

Areeda does not discuss his second possibility—that fabricators' margins would be squeezed to unremunerative levels. Since the ingot monopolist must have fabrication done by someone, he has no incentive to drive fabricators' margins below the competitive level and thus cause a decline in the performance of a necessary function. Nor will he be interested in a second monopoly as such. Only two possibilities come to mind. The first, which will be rare, is the necessity of control of fabrication to make price discrimination possible, and we have already dealt with that. The second possibility is not really a "squeeze" in any deliberate sense. The integration may cut costs, or the fabricating subsidiary of the ingot monopolists may simply be more efficient than other fabricating units. Any "squeeze" resulting from these causes is desirable, involving a shift in buiness from less to more efficient operations.

No matter what the reason for the "squeeze"—the elimination of cartel profits at the fabricating level, superior efficiency, or (rarely) the desire to discriminate—fabricating rivals will be heard to complain of ill treatment, the unfairness of "dual distribution," and predatory squeezing. There is no reason to pay any attention to such complaints, and every reason not to. Perhaps we should count integration that replaces "vocal processors" with silent consumers a clear gain.

FEAR OF FORECLOSURE

It is sometimes alleged that the danger of foreclosure is proved by the "undeniable" fact that firms fear it and engage in defensive vertical integration to avert it. This assertion (not made by Areeda) is worth discussion. Foreclosure may occasionally be a threat to individual firms. It is never a threat to competition. This proposition is illustrated in the series of vertical mergers that spurred the Federal Trade Commission to intervene in the cement industry.[12] Cement manufacturers sold in regional markets, and among their customers were ready-mix concrete companies operating in local markets. In a regional market there might of course be scores or hundreds of ready-mix firms, but in any particular local market there might be, to construct an example, only three with, say, five cement manufacturers vying for their trade. The acquisition of a ready-mix firm by a cement manufacturer in that market might reasonably arouse apprehension in the other four. Their possible customers have been reduced by a third, and if two more acquisitions should occur, at least two of the cement suppliers might be foreclosed from that market. A wave of vertical mergers is not at all unlikely, nor is a great deal of talk among manufacturers about the possibility of being "shut out" of lucrative markets. There is also the probability, amounting to a certainty, that one of the antitrust enforcement agencies will ride, superfluously, to the rescue.

Foreclosure may be of concern to the cement manufacturers, but for reasons we have discussed, it will not affect consumers. If three cement manufacturers acquire the only three ready-mix companies in town, market concentration will not have increased. If there was any restriction of output, due either to collusion or to noncollusive oligopolistic behavior, it is no more likely now than before the merger. Indeed, the prospects for collusion may be less when large firms subject to greater scrutiny by the Antitrust Division take over in the local markets. Neither is there any reason to fear the disappearance of the other two cement manufacturers, since they can respond by integrating vertically, either through merger or contract, in other local markets. If there are efficiencies in the integration, well and good. If there is no effect upon costs, there is no reason to worry. We need not worry about the possibility of diseconomies, for that would merely give some ready-mix firms an additional reason to remain independent and take advantage of their rivals' new handicap, and might lead as well to new entry at the ready-mix level.

* * * *

The analysis set out in this chapter suggests that, in the absence of a most unlikely proved predatory power and purpose, antitrust should never object to the verticality of any merger; much less should it adopt the stance of virtual per se illegality reflected in *Brown Shoe* and other cases. Properly drawn and applied horizontal rules are all that we need. Judge Taft's position on vertical arrangements in *Addyston Pipe & Steel*, discussed in Chapters 1 and 14, appears to have been correct. Today's law concerning vertical integration through merger is clearly destroying a valuable source of efficiency for no reason.

12

Conglomerate Mergers

PERHAPS no more disheartening evidence of antitrust's intellectual decline can be cited than the government's demonstrated ability to win conglomerate merger cases without ever advancing a plausible economic argument. Basic analysis shows that there is no threat to competition in any conglomerate merger, and it is good that the campaign against conglomerates has abated.

A conglomerate merger is usually defined as any merger that is not horizontal or vertical. An example would be the purchase of a New York garment manufacturer by a California wine producer. Mergers are conventionally categorized according to the relationship of the markets of the two firms. The merger of the garment maker and the wine producer is conglomerate because the firms do not sell in the same market and do not stand in the relation of supplier and customer. Classification is not always simple, however. When CBS acquired the Yankees, for example, the merger could have been classified as horizontal (by viewing the two firms as rivals in the entertainment market) or vertical (since the Yankees are a supplier of programs to television) or conglomerate (since baseball and television may be viewed as selling in somewhat discrete markets). To some extent, each of these views is defensible, so that market definition alone appears to be a slippery criterion.

It is probably more useful to classify mergers according to theories of injury to competition, recognizing that more than one may be advanced with respect to a single merger. Theory is horizontal, of course, if the merger is questioned because it is said to remove actual or potential competition between the firms involved. Vertical theory points to the supposed danger of foreclosure. Any other theory of injury to competition is conglomerate. The CBS-Yankee merger could have been challenged on any of these theories, but the major objection aired (no case was brought) was conglomerate: the speculation that CBS, being considerably wealthier than most other owners of baseball franchises, would pour so much money into the Yankees that they would become, or rather remain, unbeatable. That speculation about the sinister effect of riches has won other cases for the government. Its predictive power is eloquently testified to by the subsequent history of the Yankees and the ultimate decision of CBS to sell the club. (The later rise of the Yankees as the club's owners spent money more freely was accomplished without corporate merger.)

Until quite recently we got along beautifully without worrying about conglomerate mergers. There was no Sherman Act law on the subject, and few people, other than Corwin Edwards,[1] supposed there was a problem until a cryptic reference in the legislative history of the 1950 amendment to Section 7 of the Clayton Act suggested that conglomerate mergers were covered by the statute.[2] The theory by which such mergers could be charged with injuring competition was not immediately apparent, but given the ingenuity and flexibility of antitrust economics, that problem was not so great as it seemed at first sight.

Though there was no law about conglomerate mergers, there was (albeit not named or generally recognized as such) an antitrust law about conglomerate structures and their behavior. The *Griffith* decision, which we have analyzed in Chapter 7, is a case in point. The federal courts have always been suspicious of multimarket operations. They, or many of them, have believed that power somehow flows from one market position to another, giving the firm an unfair advantage in the second market. In *Griffith* the Supreme Court was willing to hold that power could flow even if the firm did not intend that it should. This theory has never been adequately explained by anyone, but it continues to operate in the law.

In *Brown Shoe* the Supreme Court was prepared to believe, without any explanation of the supposed phenomenon, that a chain of retail shoe stores could somehow "insulate" selected outlets from competition. Indeed, the entire law of vertical mergers and vertical contracts can be viewed as merely a subcategory of conglomerate theory, since it supposes that the joining of two markets, vertically related, causes power to flow from one to the other. But there is no valid theory to support such a supposition, and the attack upon conglomerate mergers is equally baseless.

Perhaps because we did not use the word "conglomerate" prior to the amendment of Clayton 7, we did not fully perceive the groundwork being laid in cases such as *Griffith,* and so did not see clearly enough what the law was building toward. Perhaps we still do not see the direction of movement clearly enough. From law about the behavior, or alleged behavior, of conglomerate firms and arrangements we have come to law about conglomerate mergers. The next step may be an attack on the mere existence of large diversified firms created by internal growth. This movement would parallel the current attempt to move from severe horizontal merger law to law challenging the existence of great companies created by internal growth in single markets. Such a development is not at all unlikely, particularly in view of the recent effusion of hate literature—it cannot be called anything else—directed toward corporations and business in general. In any event, antitrust is a hungry policy, always seeking new terrain to conquer as soon as it has won its victories and imposed rigid rules in older areas.

There exists a vast literature about conglomerate mergers. Much of it has to do with their effect on the overall concentration of the American economy, the tax incentives that propel them, the conglomerateur's propensity to issue weird and perhaps misleading securities, the difficulties of applying accounting principles to determine a conglomerate's real profitability, and many other matters. Of these issues I will have little or, more accurately, nothing to say. They all raise interesting and important questions, and on some of them the evidence is not yet in. But they have one thing in common. They are not *antitrust* issues. Antitrust is concerned with the effects of market behavior and structure upon consumer welfare. Other matters, if they raise problems, must be taken care of by other laws.

It seems quite clear that antitrust should never interfere with any conglomerate merger. Like the vertical merger, the conglomerate merger does not put together rivals, and so does not create or increase the ability to restrict output through an increase in market share. Whatever their other virtues or sins, conglomerates do not threaten competition, and they may contribute valuable efficiencies.

It is necessary to be quite clear on the point of efficiencies. The legality of such mergers under the antitrust laws should in no way depend upon a showing that any particular merger will create new efficiencies or that conglomerates as a class create efficiencies. It is enough that they do not create the power to restrict output. But some conglomerate mergers surely do create efficiencies, and a successful legal attack would deny us, in such cases, the benefits they can confer: revitalization of sluggish companies and industries; improvement of management efficiency, either through the replacement of mediocre executives or the reinforcement of good ones with aids such as superior data retrieval or more effective financial-control systems; transfer of technical and marketing know-how across traditional industry lines; meshing of research or distribution; increase in ability to ride out fluctuations; and the provision to owner-managers of successful small and middle-sized companies of a market for selling the enterprises they have created, thus encouraging other people to go into business on their own. Conglomerate mergers, moreover, often provide large amounts of capital to firms in need of additional financing. Such mergers thus provide one of the means by which the capital market overcomes its alleged "imperfections."

There is no need here to review the evidence of the relation between conglomerate mergers and efficiency; nor is it necessary to dispute those who think there may be little efficiency from conglomeration other than in the handling of money. Making the internal flow of funds more efficient is, of course, socially valuable, but it will be assumed, solely for the sake of argument, that conglomerate mergers create far fewer efficiencies than their proponents claim for them. It is realistic to assume that some conglomerate mergers create efficiencies, some do not, and some are outright business disasters. But antitrust does not exist as a means for federal courts to review and revise management judgments about efficiency. The initial question for the law is whether conglomerate mergers create the ability to restrict output. A negative answer should be the end of antitrust inquiry.

The enforcement agencies have had some difficulty thinking up ways in which conglomerate mergers could injure competition. The idea is an implausible one, and despite considerable ingenuity lavished upon a solid base of bad economic theory, they have been able to devise only a few theories whose thinness emphasizes the desperate nature of the task.

Among the most common charges leveled against conglomerate mergers are that they may: (1) create a "deep pocket" that enables a firm to devastate its less affluent rivals; (2) lower costs; (3) raise barriers to entry; (4) frighten smaller companies into less vigorous rivalry; (5) create the opportunity to engage in reciprocal dealing; and (6) eliminate potential competition. Of these alleged dangers, only the sixth, which is really a horizontal and not a conglomerate merger theory, has any possible validity, and that one will rarely be significant. There is, finally, an emerging "toehold" theory which would require in many cases that a conglomerate entering a new industry pick up one of the smaller firms rather than a leader.

THE THEORY OF THE DEEP POCKET

The theory of the deep pocket as it applies to conglomerate mergers is illustrated by the *Reynolds Metals* case.[3] As noted earlier, Reynolds, an integrated producer of primary aluminum and fabricated aluminum products, in 1956 acquired Arrow Brands, a firm engaged in decorating aluminum foil for resale to the florist trade. The foil was designed to improve the appearance of flower pots. The relative sizes of the two firms are indicated by net sales figures: Reynolds' net sales in 1957 were $446 million, while Arrow's, though it was the largest firm in its market, totaled just under $500,000. The Federal Trade Commission did not employ a vertical theory of foreclosure (an allegation that firms such as Alcoa and Kaiser were injured by the acquisition of one embellisher of flower pot wrappings would have appeared merely witty) but adopted a conglomerate theory.

The acquisition was found illegal simply because it gave Arrow financial strength it had not had before. As indicated in Chapter 9, Arrow kept its prices low from October 1957 to mid-1958 and built a new plant valued at $500,000. Arrow was not charged with deliberate predation, however. The record did not show who had started the price cutting, and the Commission said that was irrelevant anyway. The important thing was that through the merger Arrow had gained new power to "lower its prices and maintain them at low levels for an extended period." In a word, financial strength was illegal, whether or not it had been misused.

That the Commission was less concerned with competition in the florist foil-ornamentation industry than in safeguarding small firms from the discomforts of vigorous rivalry is shown by its refusal to reopen the record to consider the entry of Kaiser Aluminum into the field and the expansion by R. J. Reynolds Tobacco Co. of its activities there: "A new entry comparable in strength to Reynolds Metals Company could no doubt offer competition to the respondent; it could not restore the kind of competition which has been reduced and eliminated." The Commission referred to prior competition between small firms of roughly equal financial backing.

Surprisingly, the Court of Appeals for the District of Columbia affirmed the Commission and adopted its reasoning:

Arrow's assimilation into Reynolds' enormous capital structure and resources gave Arrow an immediate advantage over its competitors who were contending for a share of the market for florist foil. The power of the "deep pocket" or "rich parent" for one of the florist foil suppliers in a competitive group where previously no company was very large and all were relatively small opened the possibility and power to sell at prices approximating cost or below and thus to undercut and ravage the less affluent competition. The Commission is not required to establish that the Reynolds' acquisition of Arrow did in fact have anti-competitive consequences. It is sufficient if the Commission shows the acquisition had the capacity or potentiality to lessen competition. That such a potential emerged from the combination of Reynolds and Arrow was enough to bring it within Sec. 7.

The appellate court even said that the Commission had gone further than necessary, since actual rather than probable or potential anticompetitive effect was shown by the fact that because of Arrow's retroactive price reductions five of its seven competitors had lost from 14 to 47 percent of their sales and Arrow's sales had increased 18.9 percent. This equates business gains and losses, the ordinary consequences of competition, with the destruction of competition. The court did not explain why price cutting and shifts in market shares were anticompetitive here, nor why the behavior of the two firms that had not lost business, one of which had initiated at least some of the price cutting, was not to be deemed equally anticompetitive. Perhaps the answer to the latter question is simply that the other two firms had not been implicated in a merger and so were granted greater freedom to compete.

Fear of the deep pocket is wholly inadequate to support a law against conglomerate mergers for two reasons. The first we have already canvassed in Chapter 7. Predation by price cutting makes little sense in any antitrust context, and the law certainly cannot sensibly apply a presumption that the mere possession of capital will probably lead to such predation. Yet that appears to be the rule of the conglomerate merger cases. Second, any intelligible merger doctrine must state a danger to competition peculiar to mergers. We have seen that very great horizontal size is properly dealt with more severely when created by merger than by growth, because the implications for consumer welfare differ. But the possession of capital is the same whether achieved by merger or any other route.

If the theory of *Reynolds Metals* made sense, we would have to ask further questions. Should not the "assets" whose acquisition is made questionable by Clayton 7 be read broadly to include money or credit, so that it would be illegal for Arrow to borrow enough to build a new plant and survive a price-cutting campaign? Should there not in fact be a new statute making unlawful the possession of superior financial resources, no matter how gained? If the answer to these questions is no, it is difficult to justify *Reynolds Metals* or other decisions that strike at the acquisition of capital through conglomerate merger. And the answer must be no, since the possession of useful capital is an efficiency just as surely as is the possession of useful machinery, knowledge, or management skills.

LOWERING COSTS

The doctrine of *Reynolds Metals* has, in fact, been generalized as an objection to all efficiencies created through merger by certain Commission and judicial decisions. We have seen that the Supreme Court took this position with respect to vertical mergers in *Brown Shoe,* and we will see that it took essentially the same position with respect to conglomerate mergers in *Procter & Gamble.*

The Federal Trade Commission is notoriously hostile to efficiency. In *Foremost Dairies,*[4] where some of the mergers challenged were conglomerate, the Commission said Section 7 is violated if a firm's "over-all organization gives it a decisive advantage in efficiency over its smaller rivals." And in the *Scott Paper Co.* decision[5] the Commission held illegal the acquisition by Scott of three corporations engaged in the production of raw materials for finished paper products of the type Scott made and sold. Though the acquisitions were vertical, the Commission's theory was not one of vertical foreclosure but rather an anti-efficiency rationale that applies to any type of merger. Scott, the argument ran, acquired valuable sites upon which it built new plants, sites adjacent to raw material supplies, and full corporate establishments in being. By exchanging stock, Scott had avoided a prohibitively large cash outlay. "In our view, the critical fact is that the cumulative effect of respondent's acquisitions was to expand its production capacity and competitive resources in a manner which would have been impossible had it relied entirely on internal growth, and which was absolutely essential if respondent was to preserve its position of market power." Again: "Here, respondent used the technique of mergers to achieve what it could not achieve by 'natural,' internal growth, that is, the entrenchment of its market control to the detriment of competition."

Scott's share of major lines of paper products ran between 33 and 52 percent. The Commission was evidently not prepared to hold such market shares illegal. The Commission's decision, however, is exactly the same as if Scott were prohibited from giving stock in exchange for better machinery or offering stock as an inducement to talented management personnel, if those steps would enable it to achieve enough efficiency to hold its relative market position.

The impact of Scott's acquisitions upon consumers was precisely the same as if the efficiencies had been achieved by internal growth. The Commission's argument says no more than that a large company should not be permitted to attain efficiency if the Commission has a statutory pretext for stopping it.

RAISING BARRIERS TO ENTRY

The theory that a conglomerate merger could injure competition by raising "barriers to entry" entered the law in the 1967 *Procter & Gamble* decision.[6] But at no time in the progress of that case from the Federal Trade Commission to the Supreme Court did any tribunal or party explain how the entry barriers discerned differed from superior efficiency.

In *Procter & Gamble* the Supreme Court ultimately declared illegal Procter's ten-year-old acquisition of the Clorox Chemical Co. Clorox, the only nationally distributed brand of household liquid bleach, was the best-selling brand by far, and its market share had been growing in each of the five years prior to the merger. The company made no other product. Its principal shareholders were reaching retirement age; wishing to convert their stock for that of a flourishing corporation with a marketable security, they initiated negotiations with Procter. Though it made and sold a wide spectrum of related cleaning products, Procter had no entry in the household liquid bleach market. The merger appeared to promise major efficiencies in marketing and distribution.

The Federal Trade Commission's opinion focused upon the advantages in advertising and promotion that Procter would bring to Clorox, viewing these as barriers to entry. Rather untypically, the Commission's opinion attempted to justify the practice of viewing economies of scale as anticompetitive:

In stressing as we have the importance of advantages of scale as a factor heightening the barriers to new entry into the liquid bleach industry, we reject, as specious in law and unfounded in fact, the argument that the Commission ought not, for the sake of protecting the "inefficient" small firms in the industry, proscribe a merger so productive of "efficiencies." The short answer to this argument is that, in a proceeding under Section 7, economic efficiency or any other social benefit resulting from a merger is pertinent only insofar as it may tend to promote or retard the vigor of competition.

But that resolution simply sharpens the paradox. The "short answer" makes sense only if "competition" is defined as a comfortable life for competitors. That redefinition preserves the internal coherence of the passage at the price of destroying the internal coherence of the policy.

For those not satisfied with the "short answer" the Commission provided a longer one as well, but that reappears in the Supreme Court's opinion and may be examined there. The Court upheld the Commission in a murky opinion by Justice Douglas. Justice Harlan, who concurred, was moved to complain that Justice Douglas's opinion "leaves the Commission, lawyers, and businessmen at large as to what is to be expected of them in future cases of this kind." It is a just comment.

Justice Douglas began by denying that efficiency is a justification in Section 7 cases. From there, the elements of his argument ran like this: Clorox, with 49 percent of national household liquid bleach sales (even more in some regional markets), was the "dominant firm" in a highly concentrated, oligopolistic industry. Clorox and its largest rival, Purex, together accounted for almost 65 percent of national sales, and the top six firms accounted for almost 80 percent. Since "all liquid bleach is chemically identical," Clorox's dominance must rest on heavy expenditures for advertising and promotion. Procter's acquisition of Clorox (which was of the product-extension variety) would probably injure competition because "the substitution of the powerful acquiring firm for the smaller, but already dominant, firm may substantially reduce the competitive structure of the industry by raising entry barriers and by dissuading the smaller firms from aggressively competing. . . ."

The opinion cited three factors that might raise entry barriers: (1) Procter's great capital resources could supplement Clorox's limited advertising budget; (2) Clorox would share in volume discounts on advertising rates granted Procter by television networks and magazines; and (3) Clorox would obtain, in advertising and promotion, the advantages of a multiproduct firm (e.g., featuring several products in a single mailing or on a single network television program, scale economies that would cut the cost of advertising each product). Because the Court implicitly accepted the definition of "competition" as the number and comfort of competitors, the illegality of the merger was a foregone conclusion. Had "competition" been viewed as a shorthand phrase for consumer welfare, the Court would have had to ask some additional questions. Why is it not a valuable efficiency to bring capital to a firm that can use it? Why is it not good for consumers that Clorox might share in advertising and promotional cost savings that accrue to a firm with more than one product? Why is it not socially valuable for Clorox to share in volume discounts offered large advertisers by national media? (So far as the television networks are concerned, by the way, it has since been shown that the discounts, which played a central role in this case, were wholly mythological. They did not even exist.[7]) But these questions were neither answered not even recognized by the Court.

The *Procter & Gamble* opinion makes sense only when antitrust is viewed as pro-small business—and even then it does not make much sense, because small business is protected from Clorox's cost advantages only when they happen to be achieved through merger. In a consumer-oriented jurisprudence, the talismanic words "oligopoly," "highly concentrated industry," "dominant firm," and "barriers to entry" lose their magical potency. The real issue is seen to be one of alternatives. Should Clorox be allowed to become more efficient, even though that enables it to grow larger? Or is it preferable that the company be denied efficiencies, in order to limit its market share? Growth after conglomerate merger is the same as internal growth; in both cases the growth tends to concentrate the industry, making the firm "dominant" (whatever that means), while the efficiencies that cause the growth make entry less attractive. All of which means that the effects the Court and the Commission attributed to the merger were manifestations of efficiency, and hence reasons to welcome the merger rather than condemn it.

FRIGHTENING SMALLER COMPANIES

Justice Douglas, it will be recalled, suggested that the substitution of
Procter for Clorox might also reduce competition "by dissuading the
smaller firms from aggressively competing." Donald Turner has set
forth the reasoning that shows the inconsistency of claiming, as the
Procter & Gamble decision did, that a merger both creates economic advantages and dissuades smaller firms from competing vigorously: "The
smaller competitors, whether fearful or not, will be under heavy pressures to improve, rather than worsen, their competitive performance.
They will be forced to cut costs, to improve their product, to lower their
price in order to survive." [8] In a word, if Clorox is increasing its market
share, it would be suicidal for other firms to choose that moment to
compete less vigorously.

Turner sees merit in the "dissuasion" argument

only [in] those instances in which there has been vigorous price competition
in an industry simply because the number of sellers, while small enough to
make identity of competitors noticeable, is too large to enable them to arrive
at stable noncompetitive prices. Here there seems good reason to surmise that
the small competitors will become more timid in initiating lower prices, in
some instances to the point that the conglomerate firm will become the sole
price leader. They may over-assess the likelihood of severe disciplinary price
cuts by the large firm. Even if they do not, the possibility of such retaliation
is a new risk that must be taken into account in deciding whether to reduce
prices; and at any rate, the small firms know that their financial staying power
is much less than that of the large firm, so that the risk of serious adverse
consequences from price-cutting is in another respect greater than it was before. Thus, while there is no way of assessing how substantial the effect is
likely to be, it seems highly probable in the situation described that the consequence of the large firm's entry through acquisition will be *some* reduction
of price competition—a somewhat more "disciplined" oligopoly.

This argument seems unpersuasive, however. In the first place, Turner
probably seriously overestimates the amount of noncompetitive pricing
due to oligopoly in the economy, a topic already explored in Chapter 8.
But beyond that, Turner is here positing the likelihood of a variant of
predatory pricing: The conglomerate, having resources that can be
brought up as reserves from other markets, can afford an unprofitable
price war, not to drive the smaller firms out of business, but to frighten
them into charging higher prices in the future. A number of observations can be made about this theory. First, Turner himself does not think

much of the theory of predatory pricing, for he says elsewhere in the same article that "predatory pricing seems so improbable a consequence of conglomerate acquisitions that it deserves little weight in formulating antimerger rules based on prospective effects." I quite agree. But if predatory pricing is not a rational monopolizing tactic, it is not clear why it should be a rational disciplining tactic. The discipliner incurs smaller losses than the all-out monopolizer, but for a smaller prospective gain. Moreover, the smaller firms, far from knowing that their financial staying power is less than that of the conglomerate, will know that they have enormous advantages over any predator—economic advantages that are also backed up by the prohibitions of the law—so that the smaller firms need not fear being driven from the market. The idea that the smaller firms will refrain from profitable behavior out of fear seems wholly unlikely, unless someone can rehabilitate the discredited theory of predatory pricing.

But the difficulty with Turner's theory goes deeper even than this. Even if we assume, arguendo, that it is profitable for the conglomerate to commit resources to a price war in order to dissuade rivals from competing vigorously, we must wonder why the opportunity for tightening the discipline in an oligopolistic market was not recognized before the conglomerate firm appeared there. All the theory requires is a firm able to find and willing to spend money in a limited price war. Any firm with access to money can accomplish the same result, and since the profitability of that course of conduct is a necessary postulate of the argument, it should not be difficult for some firm in the market to obtain the money. If Turner's fear were realistic, therefore, the threat would have been realized before the conglomerate acquisition occurred.

All in all, there seems no merit in the idea that a conglomerate merger in which a very large company acquires a firm in an industry composed of small companies will have any adverse impact upon competition by frightening the smaller companies into semiparalysis.

OPPORTUNITIES FOR RECIPROCAL DEALING

At the outset of the Department of Justice's campaign against conglomerate mergers in 1969, the Attorney General stated that the potential for reciprocal dealing would be a key argument in the legal attack. He

characterized the practice of reciprocity as "one of the most easily understandable dangers posed by the conglomerate merger." On the contrary, in economic terms the "danger" is not understandable at all, much
less "easily understandable." It is nothing more than the standard *Griffith*
or leverage fallacy in yet another context. This can be demonstrated
by a brief analysis of the *Consolidated Foods* decision,[9] in which the
Supreme Court outlawed a merger because of potential reciprocal
dealing.

Consolidated Foods, a large processor of foods and the owner of
wholesale and retail food stores, acquired Gentry, a manufacturer of
dehydrated onion and garlic. The Federal Trade Commission brought
a Clayton 7 case on the theory that Consolidated might successfully
pressure its food suppliers to buy from Gentry. Indeed, Consolidated
had attempted to get its suppliers to do just that, but without much
success, and the efforts had largely ceased. Gentry had only one significant competitor, Basic, and the two of them accounted for almost 90
percent of industry sales. The Commission's fear, shared by the Supreme Court, was that pressures for reciprocal dealing would give Gentry
an advantage not warranted by competitive merit and would further concentrate the industry. It is impossible, however, to understand the mechanism that was supposed to produce these dire results.

Let us start with the plausible assumption that Consolidated's management was no more intelligent or rapacious after the merger than before.
If, before the merger, Consolidated used all of its "buying power" to get
the lowest possible prices from its suppliers, it had no buying power left
to coerce any unwarranted favors for Gentry after the merger. The
theory of the Commission and the Court is another instance of the
Griffith fallacy of counting the same market power twice. If one assumes
that Consolidated had some bargaining power it had not previously
used, the question becomes: Why did Consolidated not use its unliqui-
dated power to get a lower price rather than to foist Gentry's unwanted
product on a supplier?

The most plausible answer is that Consolidated was, in fact, using
Gentry in an attempt to obtain the equivalent of a price cut that could
not be granted directly. The attempt seems not to have been very
successful, but whether the disguised price cut was designed to outwit
a cartel arrangement or the Robinson-Patman Act's pressure toward rigid,
noncompetitive prices, it is wholly proconsumer.

It is sufficient here to demonstrate that the official theory of the
dangers of reciprocity misunderstands its purpose and effects. Whatever
reciprocity is, it is not a means of misallocating resources. If the prac-

tice itself is not to be feared, it is doubly improper for the courts and the enforcement agencies to strike down conglomerate mergers because they create a mere opportunity for reciprocity.

LOSS OF POTENTIAL COMPETITION

We come at last to a theory of injury to competition that contains a kernel of truth, albeit a small and wrongly classified one. The theory is illustrated by *Procter & Gamble,* where Justice Douglas, following the Federal Trade Commission, advanced the argument that Procter's acquisition of Clorox injured competition by removing Procter as the most likely entrant into the household liquid bleach market.

Given the present state of judicial economics, this potential competition theory appears to cast a substantial Clayton 7 cloud over most product-extension or market-extension mergers. Justice Douglas did not spell out the contours of the theory, but the Court's ability to spot an incipient "oligopoly" in a 5 percent market share in *Brown Shoe* suggests that we may be in for considerable shock when we learn what industries the Court considers so concentrated that potential entrants may not acquire existing companies. It will be necessary to confine the potential entry doctrine to reasonable proportions to avoid a judicially imposed efficiency loss, such as that which was surely inflicted by the *Procter & Gamble* decision.

The potential competition theory had two branches: (1) Procter would probably have entered the household liquid bleach market by internal growth, and its acquisition of Clorox thus prevented the appearance of a new competitor in an oligopolistic market; and (2) even if Procter would not have entered the market on its own, the companies making liquid bleach could not be sure of that, and so behaved more competitively because of Procter's looming presence on their horizon.

Though there is a core of truth to the potential entry argument, neither branch seems to justify the result in *Procter & Gamble.* As Turner says, in order for this theory to apply, "the market concerned must be an oligopoly market: the number of actual sellers must be sufficiently small for them to be able collectively, though not necessarily collusively, to maintain prices above competitive levels." [10] If that is not true, neither independent entry nor the threat of it could make any difference in price and output. The household liquid bleach industry was not sufficiently concentrated to make noncollusive restriction of output even a remote possibility. Six producers shared 80 percent of the market, and there were 200 smaller producers. Had there been a restriction of output by Clorox, the growth of some of its hundreds of rivals would very shortly have cured it. The entry of Procter or the threat of its entry was surely entirely superfluous.

By now it should be apparent that the theory we are discussing is not properly a conglomerate merger theory at all. It is a horizontal merger theory, involving the elimination of competition between firms that would otherwise be rivals. It is appropriate, therefore, to apply reformed horizontal merger rules to claims of lost potential competition. Thus, the theory should not come into play unless there are only two significant firms in the market and the potential entrant acquires one of them. If there are three significant firms, an outside firm should be permitted to acquire any one of them. If there is one large firm plus a scattering of small firms, the outside firm should be allowed to acquire any of the smaller firms, or it should be allowed to acquire the largest firm unless that firm has, say, over 70 percent of the market.

Even these rules should limit mergers only when three other conditions are met: the outside firm is a probable entrant by internal growth if the merger is disallowed; there are no other equally probable entrants; and entry is sufficiently difficult that restriction of output is possible. Very few industry situations will meet these conditions, and so very few market-extension or product-extension mergers should be blocked on potential entry grounds.

THE TOEHOLD FALLACY

The Neal Task Force recommended passage of a statute that would prohibit any firm with sales of $500 million or assets of $250 million from acquiring a "leading firm" in another industry.[11] A "leading firm" was one whose market share exceeded 10 percent and which operated in a market where four or fewer firms had an aggregate share of more than 50 percent. The Task Force majority was not entirely agreed on the reasons for the proposal. Some feared conglomerate mergers on the theory that "mere size and superior financial resources will confer unwarranted advantages on an acquired firm." Nobody explained how an unwarranted advantage differs from a warranted advantage, or how either of them differs from efficiency.

More interesting, however, was a second line of reasoning. This held that conglomerate mergers might indeed create efficiency, that efficiency is fine, but that the law should divert it to smaller firms so that their growth would deconcentrate the industry. No one, fortunately, has shown much interest in this proposed law, but the Federal Trade Commission has interpreted amended Section 7 of the Clayton Act as if it were the Task Force's statute. In outlawing Bendix's acquisition of Fram, the third-largest manufacturer of automotive filters, with 12.4 percent of the market, the Commission relied largely upon a notion that Bendix should have acquired one of the much smaller firms in the industry.[12] The Commission similarly ruled against the acquisition of Peabody Coal, the largest coal producer in the country, by Kennecott Copper.[13] (The coal industry does not, of course, begin to approach the concentration levels specified by the Neal Task Force for the application of its proposals.) Kennecott, the Commission ruled, should have purchased a "toehold" company.

The rationales of the Commission's toehold theory and the Neal Task Force proposal are quite similar, and they are wrong for the same reason. As we have seen, there is no possibility that conglomerate mergers can create output restriction. The arguments of the Task Force and the Commission can only succeed, therefore, if it makes sense to divert acquisitions from larger to smaller firms. Those who contend that conglomerate mergers create no or few efficiencies cannot speak to this point, for if such mergers neither restrict output nor create efficiencies, there is no conceivable reason for antitrust law to concern itself with them. For antitrust purposes such mergers are blanks, voids. But if we assume, as the Task Force and the Commission must, that conglomerate mergers are undertaken for efficiency reasons, then the toehold idea is easily shown to be a prescription for decreasing consumer welfare.

If conglomerate mergers are motivated by efficiency, the acquiring firm's choice of one firm in the industry rather than another must be dictated by a judgment as to their differing efficiency potentials. The acquiring firm may be looking for a partner with troubles—one whose performance can be improved; or it may want to acquire a sound management and a record of success—a firm whose strengths it can supplement. The mere fact that it chooses one firm over the others indicates that the chosen partner offers the greatest potential. When the law inter-feres with this choice on some version of the toehold theory, it either shifts the acquisition to a less preferred firm, causing a decrease in the efficiencies realized, or causes the abandonment of any plan to acquire a firm in that industry, thus forcing a complete loss of expected efficiencies.

The toehold theory is necessarily based on the erroneous idea that it is better for consumers to have less efficiency rather than more, so long as the decreased efficiency goes to smaller rather than larger firms. That is a preference for industrial fragmentation at the expense of con-sumers. Whatever else it may be, it is not a valid antitrust theory.

* * * *

We have now examined all the major theories of the ways in which conglomerate mergers may injure competition and found that none of them (with a minor exception for a theory that is really horizontal) bears analysis. The conclusion must be, therefore, that conglomerate mergers should not be prohibited by judicial interpretation of Section 7 of the Clayton Act.

13

Horizontal Price Fixing and Market Division

THE subject of cartels lies at the center of antitrust policy. The law's oldest and, properly qualified, most valuable rule states that it is illegal per se for competitors to agree to limit rivalry among themselves. We have already discussed in Chapter 1 the great cases that established and elaborated this doctrine: *Trans-Missouri, Joint Traffic, Addyston Pipe & Steel,* and *Standard Oil,* to which may be added *Trenton Potteries,*[1] and *Socony-Vacuum.*[2] There are, of course, hundreds of other cases in which the doctrine of per se illegality for eliminations of rivalry (e.g., price fixing and market division) has been applied, and without doubt thousands of cartels have been made less effective and other thousands have never been broached because of the overhanging threat of this rule. Its contributions to consumer welfare over the decades have been enormous.

Yet it is also true that the rule has become somewhat skewed over time, and on occasion produces undesirable results. It can easily be shown that price fixing and market division are beneficial in certain circumstances. The rule should be restated so that it is illegal per se to fix prices or divide markets (or to eliminate rivalry in any other way) only when the restraint is "naked"—that is, only when the agreement is not ancillary to cooperative productive activity engaged in by the agreeing parties. Only then is the effect of the agreement clearly to restrict output. Many price-fixing and market-division agreements make cooperative productive activity more efficient, and these should be judged, according to the circumstances, by the standards applicable to internal growth of firms or by horizontal merger rules.

Both internal growth and horizontal merger eliminate rivalry, and they do so more permanently than do cartel agreements. Prices are fixed and markets allocated within firms. The reason we do not make these eliminations of rivalry illegal per se is that they involve integration of productive activities and therefore have the capacity to create efficiency. Contract integrations (including those integrations involving price-fixing and market-division agreements) are also capable of producing efficiency. The law of contract integration and of ownership integration should, therefore, be made symmetrical. There is no justification for suspending the per se rule in one area and not the other.

The legal doctrine necessary to the correct treatment of price-fixing and market-division cases is already at hand in the concept of ancillary restraints. This may most easily be expounded in the context of the partnership, one of the oldest examples in antitrust literature of lawful contract integration. Justice Peckham cited it as a valid elimination of rivalry in *Joint Traffic*.[3] Justice Holmes argued from its assumed legality, even though it eliminated rivalry, in *Northern Securities*.[4] Judge Taft, in *Addyston Pipe & Steel*,[5] went further and listed the explicit agreement of partners not to compete with the partnership as one of the five ancillary restraints legal at common law and, he strongly implied, also valid under the Sherman Act. Taft's opinion provides the best approach to the problem, as well as a respectable legal precedent for reforming the law in this area.

Taft held that naked agreements—those that do nothing more than eliminate competition—should be illegal per se, and he applied that conclusion to both the price-fixing and market-division aspects of *Addyston*. But he suggested a different rule when the elimination of competition was a means of creating efficiency. Thus, Taft argued that the elimination of competition inherent in the joining of men as partners was justified because "this effect was only an incident to the main purpose of a union of their capital, enterprise, and energy to carry on a successful business, and one useful to the community."

As Taft realized, the polar models in this area of law are the naked cartel and the partnership, one creating resource misallocation and the other efficiency. Yet both involve the agreed elimination of competition, frequently through price fixing and market division. The law must learn better how to assign the agreements of businessmen to the appropriate model. Currently, the courts too often assign arrangements that carry the economic benefits of partnerships to the category of per se illegality appropriate only for naked cartels.

Many people seem to think that the formation of a partnership or joint venture somehow does not involve an agreement on prices and markets. Yet many partnerships rely upon just such agreements, and we recognize their economic utility. The typical law partnership provides perhaps the most familiar example. A law firm is composed of lawyers who could compete with one another but who have instead eliminated rivalry and integrated their activities in the interest of more effective operation. Not only are partners and associates frequently forbidden to take legal business on their own (Taft's example of a valid ancillary restraint), but the law firm operates on the basis of both price-fixing and market-division agreements. The partners agree upon the fees to be charged for each member's and associate's services (which is price fixing) and usually operate on a tacit, if not explicit, understanding about fields of specialization and primary responsibility for particular clients (both of which are instances of market division).

Nobody supposes that a law firm in New York fixes its fees or controls specialization and client contacts for the purpose of restricting output. Each firm faces the rivalry of scores or hundreds of other firms, so that output restriction is not a tenable hypothesis. The alternative hypothesis is that the partners believe the agreements make the firm more efficient. We have, therefore, a very common situation in which agreements fixing prices and dividing markets contribute to efficiency and certainly should not be held illegal.*

Though it would be perfectly proper to rest the case once it has been shown that an agreement cannot have been made for the purpose of restricting output, it may be more persuasive to suggest the means by which the agreements under discussion here create efficiencies.

Judge Taft suggested the theory of efficiencies when he stated: "Restrictions in the articles of partnership upon the business activity of the members, with a view of securing their entire effort in the common enterprise, were, of course, only ancillary to the main end of the union,

---

* Curiously, it is with respect to the legal profession that the law has made precisely the correct distinction between partnerships and cartels. The propriety of fee schedules ancillary to a partnership is taken for granted, but the Supreme Court struck down as violative of Section 1 of the Sherman Act a minimum fee schedule applicable to the entire bar of a state. *Goldfarb* v. *Virginia State Bar*, 421 U.S. 773 (1975). The distinction between price fixing within an integrated economic unit and price fixing among competitors who have integrated none of their productive activities could not be clearer. If the courts can generalize that distinction, the law in this area can be made rational.

and were to be encouraged." By "ancillary" Taft meant that the agreement was subordinate to the main transaction, the partnership, and contributed to its efficiency. This definition requires that the agreement eliminating competition be no broader than the need it serves.

It may be desirable, however, to be somewhat more specific about the nature of the causal relationship between agreement and efficiency than Taft was. (The subject of the efficiencies that may flow from both horizontal and vertical agreements fixing prices or dividing markets is treated more extensively in the Appendix to Chapters 13 and 14.) One obvious function of an agreement not to compete is the prevention of what has been called the "free ride" problem. One or more of the partners must be prevented from appropriating for personal profit the contributions made by other partners. If such appropriation occurs, or is suspected to be occurring, the partners who view themselves as victimized will certainly decrease or stop altogether their contributions to the partnership activity. The result will be a less effective partnership because the efficiencies of integration will be less completely realized. This decay of efficiencies is prevented by requiring each partner to agree not to compete with the firm. Each then feels free to contribute without fear of being victimized by others, and the partnership is a more efficient economic unit.

Free riding may deteriorate the efficiency of a law partnership in a variety of ways. In order to further the prosperity of the firm, for example, the various members may specialize in different lines, and each may make known to clients and to the community the excellence of the others in their specialties. If business comes to one partner because of a reputation so gained, and he takes it for his individual profit, he has taken a free ride upon the efforts and sacrifices of the other partners. It would often be difficult or impossible to segregate business engendered by the firm from that engendered by the individual, and to the extent that other partners suspect that such parasitical behavior is occurring, they will be less willing to leave areas of specialization to each other, to put their own clients in touch with other partners, and to advertise each other's merits. Partners will also be less willing to share assets such as specialized knowledge and competence, unique methods of practice, client contacts, and the like.

For the Sherman Act to allow the partnership (with its inevitable replacement of rivalry by cooperation) in the interest of increased efficiency, but to disallow the ancillary agreement that makes the integration more stable and complete, and hence further increases its efficiency, would be a pointless contradiction in policy. It would be like allowing a horizontal merger where there was no danger of restriction of output, and yet insisting that half the firms' operations not be integrated.

Taft's basic insight—one that the modern law would do well to rediscover—is that the fundamental criterion for determining the legality of agreed eliminations of competition (including agreements on prices and markets) is not their explicitness or implicitness, not the number or aggregation of restraints involved, and not the severity or thoroughness with which they are enforced, but simply their capacity for contributing to the efficiency of a contract integration. His doctrine of ancillary restraints offers the Sherman Act a formula for preserving socially valuable transactions by defining an exception to an otherwise inflexible prohibition of agreements eliminating rivalry. It provides as well a measuring rod for confining the exception to the scope of its reason for existence.

None of this analysis in any way detracts from the merit of the per se rule. It simply argues that the rule can be made more beneficial by confining its scope to its rationale. Price-fixing and market-division agreements (and any other horizontal agreements eliminating competition) should be illegal per se when they do not accompany a contract integration or are not capable of contributing to its efficiency. This is not to suggest that every ancillary restraint should be lawful. A showing that a restraint is ancillary, in the sense just stated, merely lifts it out of the per se category and subjects it to the other tests of the rule of reason: market share and specific intent. A finding of ancillarity merely proclaims the presence of an economic integration that entitles the restraint to be judged on the same terms as horizontal mergers or internal growth, the reason being that the same need to weigh possible efficiencies against possible restriction of output is present. We would then be treating economically identical phenomena in the same way, which is surely desirable.

In order to anticipate attack from the other direction, however, perhaps a word should be said in defense of the per se rule when price fixing or market division is naked, i.e., does not contribute to the efficiency of economic integration. That rule properly governed such cases as *Trans-Missouri, Joint Traffic, Addyston Pipe & Steel, Trenton Potteries,* and more recently, the prosecutions for price fixing in the electrical equipment industry and the plumbing fixture industry. All of these were cases in which the parties had engaged in no significant productive integration: the sole purpose of the agreements was to raise prices by restricting output.

Yet the propriety of any true per se rule—one which finds illegality on the face of the agreement without examining questions of market power and intent—is occasionally questioned. The most common objections seem to be that (1) even without the integration of productive economic activities the agreement may create efficiencies; (2) there can scarcely be inferred either a wrongful intent or effect from a naked price-fixing or market-division agreement between parties who lack market power; and (3) it seems unfair to punish persons who may have had a wrongful intent but whose conduct cannot conceivably have succeeded in harming consumers.

The efficiencies arising from a naked price-fixing or market-division agreement, if any ever do arise, must be so minor that the law is justified in ignoring them. Conceivably an agreement on prices could enable some of the firms to spend less on gathering price information (though they might spend more conferring on proper price levels and policing prices to make sure the agreement was kept), but the possibilities of saving seem minuscule compared to the certainty of output restriction.

Occasionally, price fixing will be accompanied by integration whose purpose is to enforce the agreement, and this may have the side effect of some cost reduction. The agreement in *Joint Traffic* provided for the creation of joint freight and passenger soliciting and contracting agencies, and these may have reduced some of the railroads' costs. The agreement was properly held illegal per se, however, because such joint agencies did not require a rate agreement to make them efficient, and also because the agreement for the equitable division of business showed that the main object was the elimination of competition. On its face, the integration was subordinate to the price fixing, and not the other way around. The efficiencies arising from a naked agreement eliminating competition may safely be ignored as either nonexistent or de minimis, while those integrations that are merely means of implementing the price fixing will usually be obvious from the terms of the arrangement. Those few that are doubtful may survive the per se rule, but they are very unlikely to survive the test of market power or the test of intent.

The other two objections may be illustrated and answered by taking a pair of hypothetical situations. Suppose that two realtors in New York City make an agreement to fix commissions but do not coordinate their activities in any other way. Two other realtors in the city form a partnership and agree upon the commissions they will charge. In neither case does it appear conceivable that the agreement will have any effect upon the general level of commissions.

The version of the per se rule defended here would result in automatic illegality for the first agreement but not for the second. The second agreement, once the small market share is shown or conceded, should be completely lawful. This difference arises from economic presumptions and considerations of efficient law enforcement. The economic presumptions differ because there is a contract integration to which the commission agreement is ancillary in one case and not in the other. It may be objected that, given the trivial market shares assumed, there is no likelihood of consumer detriment in either case, and so no occasion to invoke the law in either. But considerations of law-enforcement efficiency support the invocation of the per se rule against the naked commission-fixing agreement. There being no possibility of efficiency, nothing is lost to society by outlawing the agreement. If these parties were allowed to prove lack of market power, all parties would have that right, thus introducing the enormous complexities of market definition into every price-fixing case. A cartel in the steel industry could not be declared unlawful without a trial on the cross-elasticities of demand between steel, aluminum, copper, cement, wood, and so on. There would be no net gain from such trials. In fact, the only result would be to make the prosecution of output-restricting cartels much more difficult, rendering the law less effective. Very few firms that lack power to affect market prices will be sufficiently foolish to enter into conspiracies to fix prices. Thus, the fact of agreement defines the market. There is no unfairness in applying the per se rule to parties whose agreement was useless, since their intent was wrongful. This consideration bears more properly on prosecutorial discretion in bringing such cases and on judicial discretion in imposing penalties. The per se rule against naked price-fixing and market-division agreements is thus justified not only on economic grounds but also because of the rule's clarity and ease of enforcement.

Justice Thurgood Marshall put the case for per se rules very well in his *Container Corp*. dissent: [6]

Per se rules always contain a degree of arbitrariness. They are justified on the assumption that the gains from imposition of the rule will far outweigh the losses and that significant administrative advantages will result. In other words, the potential competitive harm plus the administrative costs of determining in what particular situations the practice may be harmful must far outweigh the benefits that may result. If the potential benefits in the aggregate are outweighed to this degree, then they are simply not worth identifying in individual cases.

Interestingly enough, many courts seem to realize that the present rules of per se illegality for all price-fixing and market-division agreements are out of kilter, that something valuable may be lost. These signs of doctrinal malaise are encouraging, but so far the courts have not adopted the one distinction—that between ancillary and naked restraints—that can make this area internally coherent.

The Supreme Court's 1967 decision in *United States* v. *Sealy, Inc.*[7] illustrates both the law's uneasiness and the needless destruction of an efficiency-creating system of ancillary restraints. Sealy and its predecessors had for over forty years engaged in the business of licensing manufacturers of mattresses and bedding products to make and sell such products under the Sealy name and trademark. At the time of the trial there were about thirty Sealy licensees distributed across the nation. These manufacturer-licensees owned substantially all of Sealy's stock; according to Sealy's bylaws, each of its directors had to be a stockholder or a stockholder-licensee's nominee. This control of Sealy by its licensees caused the Supreme Court to decide, without doubt correctly, that the restraints could not be classified as vertically imposed but were horizontal restraints between the controlling manufacturer-licensees.

The Sealy licenses required the bedding-product manufacturers to follow promulgated standards and specifications in order to ensure the uniformity of the products appearing under the licensed name and marks. Both price fixing and market division were features of the arrangement. The manufacturers agreed, through Sealy, to impose resale price maintenance upon their outlets—a horizontal agreement between firms at the same level of the industry. They further agreed that each manufacturer should sell Sealy-brand mattresses and bedding products only within a designated territory, though each manufacturer remained free to make and sell other bedding products under other names anywhere it might choose. Funds for national advertising of the Sealy-brand products were contributed by the manufacturer-licensees.

The primary purpose of this cooperative effort by geographically dispersed bedding-product manufacturers seems to have been the national distribution of a uniform product in order to make possible the advantages of national advertising and promotion. Certainly, nothing about the plan resembled an attempt to eliminate competition in the bedding-product market. New licenses were issued only to manufacturers in territories not already served by an existing licensee or which were deemed inadequately served. Geographical coverage was the main concern, and there was no attempt to bring into the group any manufacturer competing with an existing licensee, as there would have been if the suppression of competition had been the object. There was no attempt to bring in all or even a substantial proportion of existing manufacturers. There was at least one national manufacturer and seller of such products, along with several other groups organized on principles similar to Sealy's. There were also many local manufacturers not involved in any group. It is thus impossible to see the Sealy group as organized for the purpose or with the effect of restricting output. But that basic observation seems to have played almost no part in the decision of the case.

The government's posture in the trial court reflected a devotion to semantic labels rather than to economic analysis. Government counsel insisted that price fixing and market division are always and everywhere illegal.[8] Rejecting the suggested application of Judge Taft's ancillarity concept (which was cited but not explored by defense counsel), the government urged upon the trial court the flat and unexplained proposition that "price fixing and territorialization are not and cannot be ancillary to anything." That bold assertion was not plausibly maintained. The district court recognized that something other than a mere cartel was before it,[9] but the resources of current doctrine were not adequate to cope with the situation. The court applied the standard doctrine of per se illegality to the price-fixing agreement, but rejected, rather inconsistently, the per se doctrine as applied to market division. On this branch of the case, the district court found there was no "central conspiratorial purpose," which was of course equally true of the resale price agreement. Relying entirely upon evidence introduced by the government, the court ruled:

Plaintiff's evidence, read as a whole, conclusively proves that the Sealy licensing arrangements were developed . . . for entirely legitimate business purposes, including royalty income . . . and the benefits to licensees of joint purchasing, research, engineering, advertising and merchandising.

Sealy did not appeal the adverse decision on the horizontal agreement to employ resale price maintenance, its counsel no doubt concluding, and with good reason, that such an appeal would have been fruitless (given the mood of the Supreme Court at that time) and could only prejudice its attempt to salvage from the wreck the district court's holding that the market division was reasonable and lawful.

Even that limited aspiration proved beyond reach, however, for the price-fixing scheme poisoned the market-division agreement, and the Supreme Court struck the latter down. And that is the interesting part of the case. The Court could easily have said, with perfect accuracy so far as precedent was concerned, that horizontal agreements allocating markets had been illegal per se for years and remained so in this case. But it took a different tack, apparently precisely to avoid holding that market division between competitors is invariably unlawful. Instead of relying upon the quick and easy (though economically inapposite) formula of per se illegality, the Court argued that the case presented an "aggregation of trade restraints," citing *Timken Roller Bearing* for the proposition that such aggregations are unlawful.[10] The aggregation in Sealy consisted of a string of agreements, all of which boiled down to an agreement that resale prices should be maintained and that the maintained prices should be advertised and enforced. The Court said these activities violated the Sherman Act. "Their anticompetitive nature and effect are so apparent and so serious that the courts will not pause to assess them in the light of the rule of reason." Which was really too bad, because no anticompetitive effect is visible at all in the price agreements. They were horizontal agreements to employ vertical price fixing. The horizontal agreements could not restrict output because the group engaged was not a sufficiently large segment of the market. And as we shall see in the next chapter, vertical price fixing can never restrict output and should never be illegal.

The Supreme Court, however, has a fixed aversion to all price fixing and condemned the market division because it was related. "The territorial restraints . . . gave to each licensee an enclave in which it could and did zealously and effectively maintain resale prices, free from the danger of outside incursions. It may be true, as appellee vigorously argues, that territorial exclusivity served many other purposes. But its connection with the unlawful price-fixing is enough to require that it be condemned as an unlawful restraint. . . ." The Court was thus able to avoid analyzing the economic consequences of either the price fixing or the market division. Which makes it especially difficult to know what may have been intended by the Court's deliberate mention that some forms of market division may be lawful:

It is urged upon us that we should condone this territorial limitation among manufacturers of Sealy products because of the absence of any showing that it is unreasonable. It is argued, for example, that a number of small grocers might allocate territory among themselves on an exclusive basis as incident to the use of a common name and advertisements, and that this sort of venture should be welcomed in the interests of competition, and should not be condemned as *per se* unlawful. But condemnation of appellee's territorial arrangements does not require us to go so far as to condemn that quite different situation, whatever might be the result if it were presented to us for decision. For here, the arrangements for territorial limitations are part of an "aggregation of trade restraints" including unlawful price fixing and policing. . . . Within settled doctrine, they are unlawful under § 1 of the Sherman Act without the necessity for an inquiry in each particular case as to their business or economic justification, their impact on the marketplace, or their reasonableness.

Quite obviously, the *Sealy* opinion will not wash. Why is the Sealy arrangement "quite different" from the hypothetical small grocers' case? No real answer is given because none exists. The "aggregation of trade restraints" distinction is meaningless. Suppose the small grocers want to advertise a sale and so agree on a discounted price to be offered through the newspapers. Would the addition of that price agreement so infect the market division that the court need "not pause to assess them in the light of the rule of reason"? Why? Suppose the small grocers offer to show that each restraint in the "aggregation" serves a different efficiency-creating function. Can the rule be that an "aggregation of efficiencies" is illegal? Even on its own terms the "aggregation" theory is nonsensical. If the price fixing was anticompetitive (though that was not shown or even discussed) and if it has been forbidden, why cannot the market division continue without the price fixing unless it is shown to be evil by itself?

The "aggregation of trade restraints" doctrine merely sidesteps the question of whether the restraints, singly or collectively, create efficiencies or restrict output. An aggregation of restraints that does not restrict output is simply a somewhat more complex system of restraints ancillary to a contract integration. In such a case, the more restraints, the more efficiency.

The *Sealy* case illustrates that principle. The case is in fact an exact parallel to the partnership situation we have discussed. The separate mattress manufacturers, as the record showed, found that national advertising was a distinct advantage but that it required a scale of operations which no one of them could achieve alone—hence the idea of a group distributed across the nation using identical brands, names, and product specifications. But why the market division and agreement to maintain resale prices? The problem of the "free ride" offers one obvious explanation. (Others are offered in the Appendix to Chapters 13 and 14.) The need for market division very likely arose from the fact that each member also engaged in considerable individual local sales and promotional effort. Such efforts may range from local advertising to the employment of salesmen, the provision of information to prospective customers, and so forth. Local sales and promotional efforts cost money that can be recaptured only in the price at which the products are sold. The firm that is large enough to distribute nationally under its own trademark will measure such local efforts and expenditures simply by their relation to expected sales and revenues.

The member of a contract-integrated group has a special problem, however. Because the Sealy licensees were selling identical products, it would have been possible for one member of the group to let his neighbor spend the money and time convincing prospective purchasers that the Sealy mattress was preferable to others, and then offer a lower price that did not have to recapture those necessary expenditures. The underselling firm would thus get a free ride, and this very fact might be what enabled it to undersell profitably. The objection to this behavior from the consumer's point of view is not that the practice is unfair but that, if it persists, manufacturers in the system will decrease the amount of local sales and promotional effort they are willing to do. To that extent, the group becomes a less efficient marketer than a single, fully integrated firm of the same size. The Sealy system, that is to say, would not contain the optimal amount of local effort and would be less efficient.

Market division solves the problem and leaves each member free to do the amount of local selling appropriate to his market. In *Sealy*, market division may not entirely have solved the problem because the manufacturers sold to retailers who might cross-sell, particularly since the agreement did not control the price the manufacturer charged his retailers. Perhaps the agreement to maintain resale prices was a means of reinforcing the market division by making sure that a reseller given a low price in order to meet the competition of manufacturers of other brands could not sell in the territory of another manufacturer. There are, as we shall see, other explanations for vertical price fixing that might have been operative in the Sealy system.

The *Sealy* case thus involved a contract integration whose challenged restraints were clearly capable of creating efficiency. The Supreme Court's best course would have been to remand the case for trial on the issue of market size. Since Sealy apparently did not have market control or even a very large share of the market, it should probably have received a favorable judgment. Instead, it and similar cooperative groups had efficiency-creating agreements dismantled by inappropriate legal doctrine.

The faint hint of the birth pangs of doctrinal reform contained in *Sealy*'s small grocer example was, most unfortunately, shown to be a false labor by the Court's subsequent decision in *United States* v. *Topco Associates, Inc.*[11] Topco was a cooperative association of twenty-five small and medium-sized regional supermarket chains operating stores in thirty-three states. Topco functioned as a purchasing agent for its members, ensured quality control on purchased products, developed specifications for certain types of products, and performed other tasks that gave members the efficiencies usually attainable only by large chains.

Topco's stock was owned by its members, and indeed its structure and method of governance was very like Sealy's. Members were geographically dispersed and had varying market shares in their respective areas. The range, the Court noted, was from 1.5 percent to 16 percent, with the average about 6 percent. Sales volume was exceeded by only the three largest chains, A&P, Safeway, and Kroger.

Topco's legal difficulties arose from its private-label program. The Court remarked that the founding members of Topco were experiencing difficulty in competing with larger chains and that this problem was to some degree attributable to the larger chains' ability to develop their own private labels. The opinion sets out some of the efficiencies of private labeling:

> It is obvious that by using private-label products a chain can achieve significant cost economies in purchasing, transportation, warehousing, promotion, and advertising. These economies may afford the chain opportunities for offering private-label products at lower prices than other brand-name products. This, in turn, provides many advantages of which some of the more important are: a store can offer national-brand products at the same price as other stores, while simultaneously offering a desirable, lower priced alternative. . . . Other advantages include: enabling a chain to bargain more favorably with national-brand manufacturers by creating a broader supply base of manufacturers, thereby decreasing dependence on a few, large national-brand manufacturers. . . .

The Court noted that Topco members were frequently in as strong a competitive position in their respective areas as any other chain and that this strength was due, in some measure, to the Topco-brand products the association supplied its members. This was true even though only about 10 percent of the total goods sold by members bore the Topco name.

The problem, in the eyes of the Antitrust Division, was that members could only sell Topco-brand products in designated territories, and these were usually exclusive. Member chains could expand into each other's territories, and did, but they could not sell the Topco brand if another member held the rights for that territory. This restraint had a very plausible connection with efficiency. As Topco's answer said, "Private label merchandising is a way of life in the food retailing industry, and exclusivity is the essence of a private label program; without exclusivity, a private label would not be private." Topco noted that each national and large regional chain had its own exclusive private-label products. "Each such chain relies upon the exclusivity of its own private label line to differentiate its private label products from those of its competitors and to attract and retain the repeat business and loyalty of consumers. Smaller retail grocery stores and chains are unable to compete effectively with the national and large regional chains without also offering their own exclusive private label products." The reason, probably, was very similar to that in *Sealy*: effective promotion of a particular product line can be had only when the firm asked to incur the expense also reaps the benefit of the promotion.

Despite considerable economic argumentation that had persuaded the district court to uphold the restraint, a majority of the Supreme Court held the agreement illegal in an uncritical application of the per se concept: "We think that it is clear that the restraint in this case is a horizontal one, and, therefore, a *per se* violation of § 1 [of the Sherman Act]." The case was governed by *Sealy,* the majority said, and the opinion went on in a footnote to iron out any wrinkles left in that case's doctrine: "It is true that in *Sealy* the Court dealt with price fixing as well as territorial restrictions. To the extent that *Sealy* casts doubt on whether horizontal territorial limitations, unaccompanied by price fixing, are *per se* violations of the Sherman Act, we remove that doubt today."

It is correct, of course, to treat price fixing and market division similarly, since they are simply different means of eliminating rivalry, but it is not correct to apply a per se rule to a case like *Topco.* The fashioning of a per se rule for such cases does not meet the criterion laid down by Justice Marshall in his *Container Corp.* opinion that the gains from the rule far outweigh the losses. The *Topco* majority seemed troubled by this, for the balance of the opinion is largely taken up with an argument that the Court cannot escape the per se rule when price fixing and market division are involved. It asserts that courts are of limited utility in examining difficult economic problems and that "without the *per se* rules, businessmen would be left with little to aid them in predicting in any particular case what courts will find to be legal and illegal under the Sherman Act. Should Congress ultimately determine that predictability is unimportant in this area of the law, it can, of course, make *per se* rules inapplicable in some or all cases and leave courts free to ramble through the wilds of economic theory in order to maintain a flexible approach."

In this view the Court majority was clearly misled by a misunderstanding of the alternatives open to the law. The choice was not between a per se rule and a "ramble through the wilds of economic theory," nor is the problem too difficult for courts. The entire attempt of this book is to demonstrate that correct antitrust rules require only basic economics and that they are capable of easy and precise application by courts. In this instance the Court had only to note the difference between partnerships and cartels (which is the difference between ancillary and naked restraints, which is in turn the difference between eliminations of rivalry essential to economic integration and efficiency, and eliminations of rivalry whose sole object must be the restriction of output). Since the Topco division of territories accompanies a joint effort to achieve the scale necessary to obtain the business efficiencies of a private-label program, the restraint was clearly ancillary. That being true, the *per se* concept, which makes sense only with respect to naked restraints, should not be applied. The restraint should have been tested on the other criteria of the rule of reason: market power and intent. These distinctions (which are already used in the law of mergers and elsewhere) are by no means too difficult for courts, and they provide the predictability that businessmen and their counsel desire.

Perhaps the Court majority was put off by a misperception of the task required if a per se rule were not applied:

Our inability to weigh, in any meaningful sense, destruction of competition in one sector of the economy against promotion of competition in another sector is one important reason we have formulated *per se* rules. . . . If a decision is to be made to sacrifice competition in one portion of the economy for greater competition in another portion, this too is a decision that must be made by Congress and not by private forces or by the courts. Private forces are too keenly aware of their own interests in making such decisions and courts are ill-equipped and ill-situated for such decision-making. To analyze, interpret, and evaluate the myriad of competing interests and the endless data that would surely be brought to bear on such decisions, and to make the delicate judgment on the relative values to society of competitive areas of the economy, the judgment of the elected representatives of the people is required.

When the problem before the Court is properly understood, however, no weighing of values or of the merits of competition in different sectors of the economy is required. The integration of Topco's members in the private-label program is exactly the same as the integration of persons in a corporation or partnership. These integrations create productive efficiencies. Courts do not have to engage in a delicate weighing of values when they decide that it is lawful under the Sherman Act that corporations and partnerships exist. They do not have to sift through endless data.

When it is seen that no power to restrict output is involved, the law allows the firm or partnership to decide how much rivalry shall be eliminated internally. Absent the power to restrict output, the decision to eliminate rivalry can only be made in order to achieve efficiency. The per se principle applied to Topco, if it were consistently invoked, would destroy all firms and economic integrations in the society. Surely a law capable of avoiding that disaster is capable of using the same principle of avoidance in cases of contract integration. All the court need do is decide that an economic integration capable of producing efficiencies is before it, determine whether the restraint (price fixing, market division, or other) is capable of adding to the efficiencies, and then decide the case on the basis of market power and intent rather than a per se proscription. That procedure would have upheld the restraints in both *Topco* and *Sealy*. It would have spared the Court the uncomfortable knowledge that it was destroying efficiencies, a form of discomfort that seems apparent in the majority opinion and becomes explicit in Justice Blackmun's concurrence and Chief Justice Burger's dissent. The Justices feel that this sort of case is different from the garden variety price-fixing ring, and they are right. The law should have the resources to make that felt difference explicit and operative.

It has been suggested here that contract integrations and ancillary price-fixing and market-division agreements should be treated, according to circumstances, either like single firms or like horizontal mergers. Since the legal results will be very different, this observation requires a word of explanation. When the parties are capable of operating alone, they should be permitted to join and employ ancillary restraints only if the share of the market they would then control would pass muster under rational horizontal merger standards. Thus, we should have no trouble with a group of small grocers, having only, say, 30 or 40 percent of a relevant market, who pool their advertising funds to advertise jointly using media they could not afford individually, and who agree upon prices that will be advertised and charged. Rational merger law would permit them to merge, and so they should be permitted an ancillary restraint that makes very limited merger of their activities effective.

On the other hand, some activities can only be carried out jointly. Perhaps the leading example is league sports. When a league of professional lacrosse teams is formed, it would be pointless to declare their cooperation illegal on the ground that there are no other professional lacrosse teams. In this case the league is best viewed as being the firm, and horizontal merger limitations are inappropriate. Such limitations may become appropriate, of course, when leagues seek to merge.

The upshot is that when the integration is essential if the activity is to be carried on at all, the integration and restraints that make it efficient should be completely lawful. But when the integration may be useful but is not essential (in the sense that cooperation is not the essence of the activity), then the joint venture and its ancillary restraints (including price fixing and market division) should be lawful when three conditions are met:

(1) The agreement fixing prices or dividing markets is ancillary to a contract integration; that is, the parties must be cooperating in an economic activity other than the elimination of rivalry, and the agreement must be capable of increasing the effectiveness of that cooperation and no broader than necessary for that purpose.

(2) The collective market share of the parties does not make the restriction of output a realistic danger (judged by rational horizontal merger standards).

(3) The parties must not have demonstrated a primary purpose or intent to restrict output.

Where any one of these conditions is not met, the horizontal agreement should be unlawful. Where there is no coordination of productive activities, the first condition is violated; such an agreement is naked rather than ancillary and should be illegal per se.

14

Resale Price Maintenance and Vertical Market Division

THE law of resale price mainte-
nance and vertical market division is not only at war with sound antitrust
policy but is decidedly peculiar even on its own terms. Vertical price
fixing (a phrase here used interchangeably with resale price maintenance) has been illegal per se since Justice Hughes's 1911 opinion in the
Dr. Miles case,[1] discussed in Chapter 1. Vertical market division has
the same economic impact as vertical price fixing, the same relation to
competition and consumer welfare, and yet the law does not treat it
with equal severity. The Supreme Court has recently widened this anomalous gap by easing, as it should have, the law's strictures on a manufacturer's division of its dealers' markets.

The law of resale price maintenance has become increasingly severe
through a long series of Supreme Court decisions. The *Colgate* doctrine[2] appeared to create an exception to *Dr. Miles* per se rule by
allowing a manufacturer or other supplier to control resale prices by announcing his wishes on the subject and simply refusing to sell to any
retailer who did not comply. The idea was that in such cases there was
lacking the agreement essential to a Sherman Act contract, combination,
or conspiracy. The *Colgate* rule was of quite limited commercial use,
however, since the fatal element of agreement might be created by any
manufacturer's discussion of his price condition with a retailer, by the
retailer's unsolicited assurance that he would abide by the condition,

or even by the reinstatement of an errant retailer after a period of disciplinary nondealing (since it would appear that at least a tacit agreement to comply existed). The only effective course clearly within the law was for the manufacturer to drop the best-known price cutters without warning or discussion and refuse to deal with them indefinitely. Though the example made of such retailers might persuade the rest to abide by the manufacturer's wishes, the best-known discounters were often also the manufacturer's biggest customers. That lessened enthusiasm for price maintenance under the *Colgate* doctrine.

Doubt was cast on the legality of even this course of action by the Supreme Court's opinion in *Parke, Davis*.[3] The majority opinion suggested that any method of securing compliance with announced resale prices that was as effective as an agreement would be an unlawful "combination" under Section 1 of the Sherman Act, even though no actual agreement was present. Alternative means of controlling outlets' prices have also been declared illegal. Control cannot lawfully be accomplished by use of agency contracts, nor (when a widespread marketing plan is involved) by the use of consignment contracts which leave legal title to the goods in the manufacturer.[4] It was true, prior to the repeal of the Miller-Tydings and McGuire acts, that a manufacturer could control resale prices with safety if he followed the path provided by a valid State Fair Trade Act, but this was not terribly helpful. Those laws commonly restricted the application of such contracts to goods bearing a trademark or name; moreover, the laws varied from state to state, some states did not have them, and many states did not have nonsigner provisions, which permit the manufacturer to bind all retailers by signing a contract with one. These and other difficulties prevented many manufacturers from using Fair Trade statutes at all and made them of quite limited usefulness for most manufacturers.

Finally, the Supreme Court has even gone so far as to declare per se illegal a manufacturer's attempt to fix *maximum* resale prices. In *Kiefer-Stewart*,[5] Seagram and Calvert, two commonly owned liquor manufacturers, agreed to sell only to those Indiana wholesalers who would not resell above stipulated maximum prices. The Supreme Court held legally insufficient their defense that they were attempting to counteract a wholesaler price-fixing ring. In *Albrecht* v. *Herald Co.*[6] the Court held that the publisher of a newspaper, the St. Louis *Globe-Democrat,* could not enforce maximum prices at which independent carriers could sell to home subscribers. There could, of course, be no anticonsumer effect from such price fixing, and one suspects that the paper has a legitimate interest in keeping subscriber prices down in order to increase circulation and maximize revenues from advertising. The rule against vertical price fixing is so inflexible, however, that the Court will not pause for such considerations.

As a matter of logic, one would expect the law about vertical market division to be equally harsh. Horizontal price fixing and horizontal market division are the same phenomenon in the contemplation of the law. Both have been illegal per se for decades. Justice Hughes laid down the axiom that since horizontal price fixing is per se unlawful, it follows that vertical price fixing should be unlawful as well, and the law has adhered to that dubious equation. Clearly, then, since horizontal market division is illegal per se, vertical market division should be also. Yet that is not the case.

In *White Motor* [7] the government mounted a Sherman 1 attack on a truck manufacturer's distribution system, which involved closed marketing territories for its retail outlets (no outlet could sell to a customer with an address outside its assigned territory) and reservation of certain types of customers for direct sale by the manufacturer. Relying upon the logic set forth above, the government won a summary judgment in the district court, but the Supreme Court refused to fashion a per se rule for vertical market division, saying it knew too little of the practice's economic impact. Justice Douglas's opinion did suggest that vertical territorial limitations might be "allowable protections against aggressive competitors or the only practicable means a small company has for breaking into or staying in business," and hence within the rule of reason. This seems akin to the suggestion in *Brown Shoe*, which Justice Douglas cited, that any efficiencies which might be created were allowable only in certain classes of cases, and such classes are primarily instances of small firms struggling with giants. The efficiency is apparently not available to large or successful firms. The contours of these suggested defenses were not explored upon remand, however, for the case was settled below and did not clarify the law further.

THE *SCHWINN* CASE

Clarification seemed to be at hand when the *Schwinn* case [8] reached the Supreme Court in 1967, but once more we learned little more than that the Court is uneasy about the conclusion inherent in its prior reasoning, i.e., that vertical market division is illegal per se. Schwinn was a family-owned corporation engaged in the manufacture of bicycles. In 1951 it had 22.5 percent of the United States market and was the largest manufacturer. Ten years later Schwinn's market share had fallen to 12.8 percent, despite a considerable increase in volume. In the ten-year period, in fact, Schwinn had exchanged market positions, almost to the percentage point, with a rival, Murray Ohio Manufacturing Company. Schwinn sold primarily through twenty-two wholesale distributors, sales to the public being made by a large number of retailers. Slightly over a tenth of its output was sold to B. F. Goodrich for resale through Goodrich retail or franchised stores.

The government charged, among other things, that Schwinn had violated Sherman 1 by requiring outlets to adhere to prices it established for Schwinn products and by allocating exclusive marketing territories to its wholesalers. There were thus charges of both vertical retail price fixing and vertical wholesaler market division. The district court found that Schwinn had not set retail prices except where there were valid Fair Trade laws in force. The government did not appeal this finding, but it was clear that the district court and the Supreme Court continued to view resale price maintenance as a per se violation.

The market-division issue was more complex. Schwinn had three principal marketing techniques: (1) sales to wholesalers, B. F. Goodrich, and hardware jobbers for resale to cycle retailers; (2) sales to retailers by consignment or agency arrangements with wholesalers; and (3) sales to retailers under the "Schwinn Plan," by which Schwinn shipped direct to the retailer and paid a commission to the wholesaler taking the order. Whichever way the defendant sold, it was clear, the Supreme Court said, that Schwinn had been "firm and resolute" in requiring that the wholesalers sell only within their assigned territories and only to retailers franchised by Schwinn, and that the retailers sell only to consumers. This "firmness" was "grounded upon the communicated danger of termination."

The Court recognized that Schwinn's purpose was to improve the efficacy of its distribution system, but thought that was not enough in itself to save the whole arrangement. Justice Fortas's opinion made no effort to explain why efficiency in distribution should be regarded as less worthy than efficiency in manufacturing. Yet, once more, the Court was unwilling to opt for per se illegality, and instead chose a curious method of sawing the baby in half:

We conclude that the proper application of § 1 of the Sherman Act to this problem requires differentiation between the situation where the manufac-

turer parts with title, dominion, or risk with respect to the article, and where
he completely retains ownership and risk of loss. . . . Where a manufacturer
sells products to his distributor subject to territorial restrictions upon resale,
a *per se* violation of the Sherman Act results. And, as we have held, the same
principle applies to restrictions of outlets with which the distributors may
deal and to restraints upon retailers to whom goods are sold. Under the
Sherman Act, it is unreasonable without more for a manufacturer to seek to
restrict and confine areas or persons with whom an article may be traded
after the manufacturer has parted with dominion over it. [Citing *White
Motor* and *Dr. Miles.*] Such restraints are so obviously destructive of competition that their mere existence is enough.

Neither here nor in any other vertical restraint case did the Court
ever explain why such restraints are destructive of competition. They are
only "obviously" so if the Court is defining competition as the complete
freedom of the outlet. But that is a definition of competition not keyed
to consumer welfare. Indeed, the definition's only criterion—the freedom of the dealer—seems designed simply to destroy contractual obligations. The Court's reasoning is unsatisfactory because the meaning
of "competition" has not been thought through. Justice Fortas
continued:

On the other hand, . . . we are not prepared to introduce the inflexibility
which a *per se* rule might bring if it were applied to prohibit all vertical
restrictions on territory and all franchising, in the sense of designating specified distributors and retailers as the chosen instruments through which the
manufacturer, retaining ownership of the goods, will distribute them to the
public. Such a rule might severely hamper smaller enterprises resorting to
reasonable methods of meeting the competition of giants and of merchandising through independent dealers, and it might sharply accelerate the trend
towards vertical integration of the distribution process.

Once more the Court displayed concern for efficiency only when a
small firm acquires it in order to do battle with the "giants," and the
Court assumed that vertical integration was a condition to be avoided.
And if there are benefits to be gained by permitting vertical restraints,
why should it make any difference whether the manufacturer or the retailer has title to the goods at the time they are sold to the consumer?

But to allow this freedom where the manufacturer has parted with dominion
over goods—the usual marketing situation—would violate the ancient rule
against restraints on alienation and open the door to exclusivity of outlets
and limitation of territory further than prudence permits.

That is all too typical of the antitrust analysis offered by the Supreme
Court during the late 1950's and the 1960's. We are not told why pru-

dence does not permit complete freedom to choose exclusivity of outlets and limitation of territory. Indeed, the only "reason" offered is the "ancient rule against restraints or alienation." After years of unexplained antitrust policy, we are at last offered this distillation of the subtle interactions between law and economics: equitable servitudes do not run with chattels personal. It is hardly reassuring to learn that the sole basis for antitrust's answer to a modern business problem is the solution given three or four hundred years ago by an English judge who was talking about something else.

But *Schwinn* maintained even more profound distinctions—that, for example, between vertical price fixing and vertical market division. The reason this distinction is so profound is that it does not exist. Each is a method by which a manufacturer limits rivalry among his resellers. Why is vertical price fixing uniformly held per se illegal? Because, though it may benefit the manufacturer, it eliminates rivalry among resellers. Why is vertical market division sometimes lawful? Because, though it eliminates rivalry among resellers, it may benefit the manufacturer.

Antitrust is capable of sustaining meaningless distinctions and sterile paradoxes, but those of *Schwinn* were too many and too obvious to persist for long. The precedent suffered a timely and a deserved demise shortly after its tenth anniversary.

THE *SYLVANIA* CASE

The litigation in *Continental T.V., Inc.* v. *GTE Sylvania Inc.*[9] brought the Supreme Court face to face with yet another luminous inconsistency in the law of vertical restraints. Though a manufacturer was only sometimes allowed to divide the territories of his outlets in the sense of dictating that they not sell to customers outside a defined region, he had always been able without interference from the law to follow an announced policy of having only one dealer in any particular area. Franchise agreements often specify the business address of the franchisee, and though it may not be a formal promise, each franchisee usually understands that if all goes well the manufacturer will not locate a second franchisee in the first one's market area. This is, of course, a form of vertical market division. It relies on the costs of doing business at a distance rather than on an agreement to keep the dealers from competing with each other. The only difference between such a franchise policy and closed dealer territories, as exemplified by the arrangements in *Schwinn,* is the sharpness with which the edges of the territories are defined. It was inconsistent of the law to allow one and disallow the other. The inconsistency could not easily be cured by disallowing franchise systems, for this would mean that manufacturers must either accept as outlets any "qualified" retailers who apply or permit dealers to choose their own locations (results which would wreak havoc with many distribution systems); alternatively, the law must specify the minimum number of outlets every manufacturer must have in every territory (an enormous task for which the litigation process is unsuited). The remaining course—freely allowing all vertical market division—would bring consistency to the law and would also be the proper decision for consumers. This, to the delight and astonishment of much of the business world, was the result the Supreme Court seems to have approximated in its 1977 *Sylvania* decision. Moreover, *Sylvania* accomplished these improvements by adopting a mode of reasoning that will prove enormously beneficial if employed throughout antitrust.

Before 1962, Sylvania, a manufacturer of color television sets, sold to wholesalers who resold to a large and diverse group of retailers. In an effort to reverse a decline in its market share to 1 or 2 percent, Sylvania then adopted a franchise system under which it sold directly to a smaller number of selected retailers. The number of franchises in each area was limited, and each agreement specified one or more locations from which sales could be made. Although Sylvania retained discretion to add franchisees in any market, the intent and effect of the system clearly were to decrease rivalry among resellers of Sylvania products. Whether because the system induced greater dealer effort or for other reasons, Sylvania's share of the national market rose to 5 percent by 1965.

The dispute with Continental, a franchised San Francisco television retailer, had complex origins, but centered in its Supreme Court phase on Sylvania's refusal under the location clause to permit Continental to sell Sylvania sets from a new location in Sacramento. Proceeding on the not unreasonable theory that the location clause was invalidated by *Schwinn,* Continental won a judgment in the district court, lost in the en banc court of appeals, and brought the case to the Supreme Court.

The Supreme Court majority, in an opinion by Mr. Justice Powell, overruled *Schwinn,* held vertical market division not properly subject to a per se rule, and upheld Sylvania's location clause. *Schwinn,* Justice

Powell said, was impossible to distinguish. (The court of appeals, unhappy with the precedent but lacking the authority to overrule it, had purported to distinguish the case.) Title to the television sets passed upon sale from Sylvania to the retailer, and in both cases the retailer's freedom to sell as he might wish was limited. Rather than apply the much-criticized *Schwinn* per se rule, the Court reexamined it and found it unjustified.

Justice Powell began the reexamination with the observation that "the market impact of vertical restrictions is complex because of their potential for a simultaneous reduction of intrabrand competition [rivalry between sellers of the same brand] and stimulation of interbrand competition [rivalry with sellers of other brands]." He went on to cite ways in which "vertical restrictions promote interbrand competition by allowing the manufacturer to achieve certain efficiencies in the distribution of his products." A variety of likely efficiencies were mentioned. Since there had been no showing that vertical restrictions have a pernicious effect on competition, a rule of per se illegality was inappropriate, *Schwinn* was overruled, and Sylvania's location clause upheld.

The opinion carefully reserved the possibility that some (unspecified) applications of vertical restrictions might justify per se prohibition and that others (also unspecified) might fall under a case-by-case examination of competitive effects. These reservations may be viewed either as unfortunate wafflings or as judicious concessions necessary either to put together a majority or to guard against unforeseen situations. Whichever, we must be grateful for the main thrust of the opinion, which is surely one of the best in the modern career of antitrust.

The great virtue of *Sylvania* is not so much that it preserves a method of distribution valuable to consumers, though that is certainly a welcome development, but that it displays a far higher degree of economic sophistication than we have become accustomed to, and introduces an approach that, generally applied, is capable of making antitrust a rational, proconsumer policy once more. Both Justice Powell for the majority and Justice White in concurrence gave weight to business efficiency in framing their respective rules. The majority opinion specified some of the efficiencies involved, including the "free ride" effect, which will be discussed subsequently. For years the Court has denigrated business efficiency either as irrelevant to antitrust analysis or as a factor weighing on the side of illegality. I have argued in this book—to the verge of harping on the subject, and perhaps beyond—that this has been the cardinal sin of the policy as the modern Court has elaborated it. *Sylvania* may presage a general reformation of a policy gone astray. I will indicate next the full implications of this approach for the law of vertical restraints.

THE POLICY

Analysis shows that every vertical restraint should be completely lawful. The majority opinion in *Sylvania* was careful in a footnote to state that its reasoning did not apply to the rule of per se illegality for vertical price fixing. The supporting argument consisted of Justice Brennan's observation in a concurring opinion in *White Motor* that resale price maintenance is not designed to, but in fact almost invariably does, reduce price competition not only among sellers of the product directly affected but also between that product and competing brands; the claim that "industry-wide resale price maintenance might facilitate cartelizing"; and the suggestion that Congress approved of the per se illegality of vertical price restrictions by repealing those provisions of the Miller-Tydings and McGuire acts that permitted resale price maintenance pursuant to state Fair Trade statutes.

These considerations are not adequate to support different rules for vertical price and territorial restraints. Justice Brennan's observation runs counter to theory and experience. The cartelization objection is insubstantial, as we shall see. The repeal of Miller-Tydings and McGuire leaves Section 1 of the Sherman Act in place as a delegation to the courts of the power to create rules forwarding consumer welfare. There is no reason for the Court to interpret the repeal as freezing in place forever the mistaken economics of Justice Hughes in the *Dr. Miles* case. As Chief Justice White said in *Standard Oil*, the Court should continue to reinterpret the Sherman Act under the rule of reason as its economic understanding evolves.

A restraint—whether on price, territory, or any other term—is vertical, according to the usage employed here, when a firm operating at one level of an industry places restraints upon rivalry at another level for its own benefit. (This definition excludes restraints, vertical in form only, that are actually imposed by horizontal cartels at any level of the industry, e.g., resale price maintenance that is compelled not by the manufacturer but by the pressure of organized retailers.)

Vertical restraint law has reached its present unhappy state because the Supreme Court is struggling with the logical results of an incorrect premise laid down sixty years ago by Justice Hughes in the *Dr. Miles* opinion. That premise, as we have seen, holds that there is no more reason to permit a manufacturer to eliminate rivalry among his retailers than there is to permit the retailers to eliminate rivalry by agreement among themselves. The premise is wrong. Retailers who agree to a horizontal restraint that the manufacturer does not desire are almost certainly attempting to restrict output for the sake of monopoly gains. If such a restraint would increase efficiency, the manufacturer would not only favor it but would impose it himself. When a manufacturer wishes to impose resale price maintenance or vertical division of reseller markets, or any other restraint upon the rivalry of resellers, his motive cannot be the restriction of output and, therefore, can only be the creation of distributive efficiency. That motive should be respected by the law.

Judge Taft saw this in *Addyston Pipe & Steel* [10] when he justified "a case in which a railroad company made a contract with a sleeping-car company by which the latter agreed to do the sleeping-car business of the railway company on a number of conditions, one of which was that no other company should be allowed to engage in the sleeping-car business on the same line." This is a vertical elimination of rivalry. Taft argued:

The railroad company may discharge this duty [of furnishing sleeping-car facilities] itself to the public, and allow no one else to do it, or it may hire someone to do it, and, to secure the necessary investment of capital in the discharge of the duty, may secure to the sleeping-car company the same freedom from competition that it would have itself in discharging the duty.

Taft saw that since the railroad company could furnish the sleeping-car facilities itself without competition, nothing is lost if it grants to its hired sleeping-car company the same freedom from competition. In fact, something must be gained. The railroad company will choose between offering the services itself and getting some other firm to offer them on the basis of comparative cost. The decisions to bring in a sleeping-car company means a judgment that that is the less costly method. The vertical restraint results in no increase in output restriction but effects some decrease in costs, a net benefit to consumers. And this is true regardless of the market share of the railroad company.

Precisely the same analysis may be applied to all vertical restraints. The *Schwinn* case may be used for illustration. Schwinn's vertical price fixing (in states that permitted Fair Trade contracts) and vertical market division did not eliminate the rivalry of any other bicycle manufacturer with itself. These vertical restraints could not, therefore, create any additional power in Schwinn to restrict output. This would be true whether Schwinn had 1 or 100 percent of the bicycle market. If it had any power to restrict output, it would exercise that power directly and take the monopoly profits itself. There is no need for vertical restraints on retailers or wholesalers. The vertical restraints could not be anticompetitive for any effect they might have on the manufacturer's level of the industry.

But by maintaining its retailers' prices and dividing its wholesalers' markets, did Schwinn simply give retailers and wholesalers the power to restrict output? That is so unlikely as not to be worth consideration. No manufacturer or supplier will ever use either resale price maintenance or reseller market division for the purpose of giving the resellers a greater-than-competitive return. The extra return would be money out of his pocket for no good reason, and we may safely assume that manufacturers are not moved to engage in that peculiar form of philanthropy. The manufacturer shares with the consumer the desire to have distribution done at the lowest possible cost consistent with effectiveness. That is why courts need never weigh the opposing forces of lessened intrabrand and heightened interbrand competition. When the manufacturer chooses, he chooses on critieria that also control consumer welfare. No court is likely to make a more accurate assessment than does a businessman with both superior information and the depth of insight that only self-interest can supply.

Since vertical restraints are not means of creating restriction of output, we must assume that they are means of creating efficiencies, and it is perfectly clear that they are. The Court in *Schwinn* admitted as much. The most obvious efficiency is the purchase of increased sales and service efforts by the reseller. A retailer whose price is controlled will have to vie for business by sales and service effort. In the absence of resale price maintenance, the problem of the free ride may arise, just as it does in horizontal systems like that displayed in *Sealy*. Customers will be able to go to the retailer who offers a display of the full line, explanation of the product, and so forth, and then purchase from the retailer who offers none of these things but gives a lower price. The result will be a diminution in the amount of sales and service effort by all retailers. When this is to the manufacturer's disadvantage, he may wish to employ either resale price maintenance or vertical division of territories to get the performance he wants. This technique is preferable to direct payment for such effort. Direct payments may be accepted and competed away in lower prices, again destroying the incentive of other outlets to provide the desired efforts. The manufacturer would have to engage in extensive policing activities to catch such actions, and would have to argue the question of whether the efforts being made were the correct amount. A vertical restraint, however, will be policed for the manufacturer in large measure by other outlets, which will quickly feel and report any price cutting or crossing of territorial lines. When the restraints are complied with, arguments about the amount of effort being made are minimized, since each outlet has the same incentive as the manufacturer to provide such efforts at the proper level. (Other efficiencies attainable by vertical restraints are discussed in the Appendix to Chapters 13 and 14.)

OBJECTIONS TO VERTICAL RESTRAINT

The argument thus far has attempted to show that a manufacturer imposing a vertical restraint, such as resale price maintenance or closed dealer territories, will be attempting to create distributive efficiency and not to restrict output. To this thesis and to the policy conclusion that vertical restraints should always be lawful a variety of objections may be raised, and we shall attempt to deal briefly with them.

William Comanor has objected to my conclusion on the ground that the efficiencies cited are largely in sales and promotion and that these create product differentiation, which enhances market power.[11] He opts for a rule of per se illegality. This is a thoroughly inadequate argument, for it implies that all sales effort, including promotion and advertising, should be illegal per se—an impossible position. That being so, it seems curiously inconsistent to pick out for prohibition only that sales effort which is enhanced by vertical restrictions. In any case, we shall see in Chapter 16 that the objection is meaningless, since it says no more than that success in selling products makes a firm successful, and a successful firm may achieve market power. Comanor's objection reduces to an attack upon efficiency that leads to growth.

Here I shall deal with four objections, which may be characterized as (1) the dealer cartel objection, (2) the manufacturer cartel objection, (3) the price discrimination objection, (4) the restriction of output objection.

THE DEALER CARTEL OBJECTION

The dealer cartel objection arises from the observation that some seemingly vertical restraints may actually have been forced upon manufacturers by a reseller cartel. This constitutes a serious objection to the proposed legality of all vertical restraints only if (1) reseller coercion or inducement is more common than manufacturer origination of vertical restraints, *and* (2) there is little likelihood that the antitrust enforcement agencies can tell the two apart. It seems highly doubtful that the first condition obtains, and the second certainly would not.

Market division seemingly imposed by the manufacturer would be a poor instrument for reseller cartels, since it would not eliminate the rivalry of resellers of other manufacturers' products. Where the outlets are exclusive and the products somewhat different, resale price maintenance would be relatively ineffective as the instrument of a dealer cartel because of the difficulty of negotiating agreeable price differentials among all the retailers and manufacturers. The problem is complicated for all dealer cartels by the modern development of new high-volume, low-price methods of retailing, which create so much diversity among retailers that cartelization is more difficult than ever. It seems unlikely, therefore, that vertical restraints are usually disguised horizontal restraints imposed by a reseller conspiracies.

Moreover, the enforcement authorities should have no difficulty in detecting those restraints that are really horizontal. First, if manufacturer-imposed restraints were lawful, any disguised agreement could be presumed horizontal and unlawful. Second, attention could be directed to those industries in which almost all of the output was subject to seemingly vertical restraints. A manufacturer-imposed restraint would make economic sense even if no other manufacturer employed the same method, but a reseller cartel must control at least a large majority of industry sales in order to restrict output. This fact would considerably narrow the range of restraints the enforcement agencies must scrutinize. Third, coerced manufacturers will often complain to the enforcement agencies. Fourth, reseller cartels are very easy to detect because the large numbers and disparate interests involved make such cartels notoriously difficult to organize, administer, and police. Observation of some such cartels shows the necessity for open meetings, fight talks, advertisements and stories in trade papers, complaints by dissident resellers, and so forth. Reseller cartels tend to be so visible that they are hard for an enforcement agency to miss. The large numbers involved also mean that an investigation will usually turn up a paper record of the conspiracy and will always locate some persons willing to describe it. Conspiracies are very difficult to run and impossible to administer without leaving a trail. Once an investigation begins, fear of the law ensures cooperative witnesses.

The proposed legality of vertical restraints need not be questioned on the theory that it would enable successful and undetectable horizontal reseller cartels.

THE MANUFACTURER CARTEL OBJECTION

It has been suggested that manufacturers may agree to use resale price maintenance as a means of discovering defections from their own horizontal cartel.[12] Where the manufacturers' prices to their retailers are not visible, the theory runs, price cutting by a manufacturer may be hard for other cartel members to detect; but if the manufacturers agree to use resale price maintenance, any defection could be seen at the retail level. There would, moreover, be no incentive to cheat on the cartel price if a manufacturer's price cut could not be passed on to consumers. Of course, this theory does not apply to vertical market division, which would not provide any means of policing a manufacturer cartel.

But even the theory that a manufacturer cartel might use resale price maintenance to police compliance with the agreement does not seem a substantial one. Resale price maintenance is totally unnecessary to enforcement of a manufacturer's cartel where the manufacturers sell through common outlets, because the outlets themselves would instantly report any price cut by one to the others in an effort to get matching price reductions. Resellers continually play one supplier off against another in an attempt to get better terms. The device would be of limited utility even where outlets were specialized by brand, for price cheating on the agreement would show up in manufacturer rivalry for new or better outlets. Again the outlets would report to other manufacturers the bids made.

When outlets are specialized by brand, moreover, there exists a good deal of product differentiation. Two things are true of such cases. First, cartelization is more difficult because the products are not easily compared, resulting in difficulties in agreeing on price and other terms. Second, resale price maintenance would not completely eliminate the incentive for a manufacturer to offer a price cut as a means of cheating on the cartel. The price cut would be used by the outlets to offer consumers other terms, services, and sales and promotional effort. The diversion of competition to these forms may reduce the incentive for a manufacturer price cut, but a substantial incentive will still exist. Policing the agreement will actually be made more difficult, since the signs of cheating will not be lowered retail prices, which are easy to detect, but heightened retail sales effort, which is far more difficult to prove and trace to a lowered manufacturer's price.

These considerations suggest that it will be unusual for resale price maintenance to give the manufacturer cartel a means of internal policing it would not otherwise possess, and that the imposition of resale price maintenance will still leave intact a major portion of the incentive to cheat through price cuts to retailers.

But there is still another disadvantage to resale price maintenance as a tool of a manufacturer cartel—its cost. Since the outlets will have differing costs of operation, resale price maintenance will present serious inefficiencies. The agreement on resale prices will have to take account of the differing efficiencies of the various outlets, the differences in products, and constantly changing marketing conditions. The costs to the manufacturers will arise not only from the time and effort devoted to the constant operation of the machinery of this detecting device but also from the loss of reseller efficiency, since the outlets are, by hypothesis, subjected to artificial price constraints that the manufacturers would not individually have chosen as means to distributive efficiency.

Finally, if some cases of manufacturer agreement to use resale price maintenance as a policing device for a manufacturer cartel do arise, they should not be difficult for antitrust enforcement agencies to detect. In fact, the presence of an industry-wide pattern of resale price maintenance should, as in the case of the dealer cartel, attract government attention and make easier the discovery of the basic manufacturer cartel. The need to coordinate the various manufacturers' policies with respect to resale prices will produce additional evidence of cartelization. Another telltale sign would be any manufacturer's attempt to discourage competition on terms other than price, since the legitimate use of resale price maintenance is to obtain just such reseller efforts.

In sum, the manufacturer cartel objection to the legality of vertical restraints appears insubstantial. It applies only to resale price maintenance, would at best provide only a marginal advantage as a means of detecting defections, would encourage other forms of retail competition, would not remove most of the incentive to cheat on the agreement, would incur substantial costs, and would increase the likelihood of detection by the antitrust enforcement agencies. It is not certain that resale price maintenance is never actually used for the purpose of policing a manufacturer cartel, but it appears reasonably certain that such use will be so rare and the ease of detection so great that this objection should not stand in the way of the legality of truly vertical restraints.

THE PRICE DISCRIMINATION OBJECTION

Some vertical restraints can be used to separate markets in order to make price discrimination possible. Resale price maintenance cannot be used in this fashion, since reselling among customers would destroy the market separation. Vertical geographic market division will not be employed when the presence of rivals in one market but not another indicates different revenue-maximizing prices. The restriction on dealers is unnecessary if the markets are separated by transportation costs. If they are not, the restriction is pointless, since rival sellers in the lower-price market, not being bound by the restraint, can sell in the higher-price market. But vertical customer allocation might be used to separate purchasers with different elasticities of demand if rival sellers did not have a product appropriate to the low-elasticity, high-price market.

Such cases are probably not very common, but the conclusion that the law should not worry about them rests on three other grounds. First, the identification of discrimination, particularly in a litigation context, is probably impossible, so that a law against discrimination might easily compel more discrimination than it stopped. Second, any attempt to enforce a law against discrimination imposes costs which, if fully measurable, might be considered prohibitive. Third, even if price discrimination could be readily identified and costlessly prohibited, it is unclear whether, on balance, discrimination benefits or injures consumers, and there is some indication that its net effect is beneficial. These considerations, which are taken up at greater length in Chapter 20, seem overwhelmingly to support the conclusion that the law simply should not concern itself with price discrimination in any context.

THE RESTRICTION OF OUTPUT OBJECTION

This chapter has argued that a manufacturer will never institute resale price maintenance or closed dealer territories for the purpose of restricting output: the practice does not eliminate any rivalry he faces, and he has no reason to restrict the output of his resellers—quite the contrary. A more sophisticated version of the restriction of output objection has been advanced by J. R. Gould and B. S. Yamey.[13] They have suggested that resale price maintenance, by obtaining successful promotional efforts from dealers, would shift the final demand curve and the marginal revenue curve upward and to the right while adding to dealer costs, thus shifting the marginal cost curve upward and to the left. This raises the possibility that the new intersection of the marginal revenue and marginal cost curves will be to the left of the old, signifying a higher price and a reduced output.

I think this suggestion incorrect for two reasons. First, and perhaps less fundamental, the general effect of promotional activity, as of advertising, is to increase the sales of the product promoted. This is a widely known result of advertising and promotion. The mere possibility of drawing curves that give a different result should not overcome the almost universal testimony of business experience. The new intersection of the cost and revenue curves will almost surely lie to the right of the old.

The second and more basic objection to the observation advanced by Gould and Yamey takes account of even the theoretical possibility that the new intersection lies to the left of the old. Their argument leaves out of account a fundamental change that resale price maintenance has introduced into the situation: a change in the composition of the product offered. Thus, even though it is theoretically conceivable that, in some rare case, resale price maintenance, like advertising, would lead to fewer sales of the physical product and to increased expenditures by consumers, it does *not* follow that output is lower or price higher. The error consists in failing to count the efforts of the reseller, purchased through resale price maintenance, as an economic output. The consumer is no longer offered merely a physical product but a composite product, part of which is the same physical product and part of which consists of the information, display, services, conveniences, etc., that the reseller now provides. These things must be counted as part of the product, as economic outputs, for we know that consumers willingly pay for them even when they are offered the alternative of the physical product without them. Stores charge for décor in the price of the clothing, restaurants charge for atmosphere and service in the price of the food, gasoline stations charge for rest rooms, window washing, and air pumps in the price of the gasoline. It would be completely wrong to say that these additions are not part of the product, or that consumers are paying more for less when they patronize such establishments instead of those that offer merely the physical product.

Such changes in product composition are a general means of economic progress. When a truck manufacturer, such as White Motor, switches from selling trucks to selling trucks plus reseller-provided information and service, it is changing product composition just as certainly as if it had switched from offering a stripped-down model to a model with a variety of extra features. This, in turn, is no different from the change-over in the razor blade industry from carbon steel to stainless steel blades. Perhaps these changes might conceivably have led to the sale of fewer trucks and fewer razor blades, but it would be fallacious to contend that output had been restricted. The measure of output is really the utility offered, and the mere number of physical items sold, considered by itself, tells one nothing about that. The only safe guide is whether consumers respond to the change in product composition, and we measure that by whether the manufacturer finds it profitable to continue offering the new product. That analysis holds true for the addition of dealer services through resale price maintenance just as for the change in truck models or razor blade types. And it is as improper for the law to forbid the addition of those services and efforts by banning vertical price fixing and market division as it would be for the law to require the truck manufacturer to switch back to the stripped-down model or the razor blade maker to return to carbon steel.

*   *   *   *

We have seen that vertical price fixing (resale price maintenance), vertical market division (closed dealer territories), and, indeed, all vertical restraints are beneficial to consumers and should for that reason be completely lawful. Basic economic theory tells us that the manufacturer who imposes such restraints cannot intend to restrict output and must (except in the rare case of price discimination, which the law should regard as neutral) intend to create efficiency. The most common efficiency is the inducement or purchase by the manufacturer of extra reseller sales, service, or promotional effort.

The proposal to legalize all truly vertical restraints is so much at variance with conventional thought on the topic that it will doubtless strike many readers as troublesome, if not bizarre. But I have never seen any economic analysis that shows how manufacturer-imposed resale price maintenance, closed dealer territories, customer allocation clauses, or the like can have the net effect of restricting output. We have too quickly assumed something that appears untrue.

Perhaps the ambiguity of the word "restraint" accounts for some of our confusion on this topic. When the Supreme Court speaks of a restraint it often, or even usually, refers merely to the manufacturer's control of certain activities of his resellers or to the elimination by the manufacturer of some forms of rivalry among his resellers. There is, of course, nothing sinister or unusual about "restraint" in that sense. It is merely a form of vertical integration by contract, a less complete integration than that which would obtain if the manufacturer owned his outlets and directed their activities. It is merely one instance of the coordination of economic activities which is ubiquitous in the economic world and upon which our wealth depends. The important point is that such vertical control never creates "restraint" in that other common meaning, restriction of output. Perhaps, if we are more careful about the ambiguity of the word and make clear in which sense we use it, our reasoning about antitrust problems, including the problem of vertical restraints, will improve.

The perception that the vertical elimination of rivalry does not always injure competition has long troubled the courts, producing the tortured reasoning of cases like *Schwinn*. Even that is infinitely preferable to the dogmatic error of cases like *Kiefer-Stewart*. *Sylvania* represents at last a long stride in the right direction. This field of law can be made clear, internally consistent, and congruent with reality only when we face the fact that the premise laid down in *Dr. Miles*—that the vertical elimination of dealer rivalry has the same effect as a horizontal cartel —is incorrect and must be rejected. That premise was adopted by the Supreme Court, and it may properly be abandoned by the Court.

15

Exclusive Dealing
and Requirements Contracts

$\mathbb{A}$N exclusive dealing contract
exists when one firm agrees to buy only from another, most commonly
when a dealer agrees to handle only the goods of a particular manufacturer. Requirements contracts come to much the same thing, except that
the seller agrees to supply all of the buyer's requirements for a specified
product. Sometimes the same result is achieved by a contract promising
to supply a stated amount of the product during a time period, the
amount being calculated to approximate the buyer's requirements.

Quite obviously, exclusive dealing and requirements contracts are
forms of vertical integration. The law deals with such contracts under
Section 3 of the Clayton Act, which is an incipiency statute, and Section 1
of the Sherman Act, which is not, nominally, but has come to apply doctrine distinguishable from the doctrine of Clayton 3 only by a metaphysi-
cian. Not too surprisingly, the law has come to treat these forms of vertical integration by contract as severely as it treats vertical merger.

The beginning of the law's march to its present excessively harsh view
of exclusive dealing may probably be located in Justice Frankfurter's
opinion for the Supreme Court majority in the 1949 *Standard Stations*
case.[1] Standard Oil Company of California sold petroleum products in
five states the Court referred to as the "Western area." Standard was the
largest seller of gasoline in the region, accounting for 23 percent of the
taxable gallonage, of which 6.8 percent was sold through company-

owned service stations and 6.7 percent through independent service stations operating under exclusive dealing contracts. The rest was sold to industrial users. Standard's six leading competitors sold 42.5 percent of the total gallonage through service stations, and they also used exclusive dealing contracts. Standard had such contracts with 16 percent of the retail outlets in the area. The government challenged Standard's contracts, and the district court held them illegal.

The case came to the Supreme Court for decision under Clayton 3. Justice Frankfurter stated the question:

The issue before us, therefore, is whether the requirement of showing that the effect of the agreements "may be substantially to lessen competition" may be met simply by proof that a substantial proportion of commerce is affected or whether it must also be demonstrated that competitive activity has actually diminished or probably will diminish.

Anybody who has read this book to this point will guess instantly, and correctly, that the former showing sufficed for illegality. The reasoning by which Frankfurter reached this result sheds a good deal of light on the way the Court has performed as an economic forum.

Justice Frankfurter noted that previous exclusive dealing decisions did not control the disposition of this case, but, sounding an ominous note, he noted the similarity of exclusive supply and tying contracts. (A typical tying contract might require the lessee of a machine also to purchase the supplies used in the machine from the lessor. A requirements contract may be seen, if one is so disposed, as a tie-in because, for example, to buy any Standard gasoline one must buy only from Standard.) The question was whether the per se rule against tying contracts laid down in *International Salt* [2] should be applied to exclusive dealing.

Justice Frankfurter remarked that there were important economic differences between the two varieties of contracts. "Tying agreements," he said, in one of the most quoted and least justifiable dicta in antitrust, "serve hardly any purpose beyond the suppression of competition." On the other hand, "requirements contracts . . . may well be of economic advantage to buyers as well as to sellers, and thus indirectly of advantage to consumers." Frankfurther recited some of the advantages he perceived and concluded the case could not be disposed of with a mere reference to *International Salt*. He outlined some of the tests a court might use to determine the legality of any particular contract, and then suddenly veered away from economic argument. There would, he said, be serious difficulties in applying such tests, and besides, "When it is remembered that all of the major suppliers have also been using requirements contracts, and when it is noted that the relative share of the business which fell to each has remained about the same during the period of their use, it would not be farfetched to infer that their effect has been to enable the established suppliers individually to maintain their own standing and at the same time collectively, even though not collusively, to prevent a late arrival from wresting away more than an insignificant share of the market." That supposition might not be farfetched if Justice Frankfurter had offered any economic reasoning to support it, but he offered only this raw correlation between requirements contracts and relative stability of the major refiners. Not a word was expended upon any theory of a causal relation between those two facts.

Justice Frankfurter went further, seeking to justify the exclusion of evidence relevant to the inference of causal relationship:

[T]o demand that bare inference be supported by evidence as to what would have happened but for the adoption of the practice that was in fact adopted or to require firm prediction of an increase of competition as a probable result of ordering abandonment of the practice, would be a standard of proof if not virtually impossible to meet, at least most ill-suited for ascertainment by courts.

The case ultimately rests, therefore, not upon economic analysis, not upon any factual demonstration, but entirely, and astoundingly, upon the asserted inability of courts to deal with economic issues. For that reason, the requirement of Clayton 3 that the contracts be shown likely to injure competition or create monopoly was effectively read out of the statute. Yet the reason given—the helplessness of courts before economic controversies—would equally have supported the opposite holding, that such contracts are almost always lawful because courts cannot be sure they are bad. And so, for reasons of judicial administration rather than economic wisdom, requirements contracts were treated very like tying contracts, and an industry's distribution practices were outlawed.

The criteria governing the legality of exclusive dealing and requirement contracts remained somewhat vague until the *Tampa Electric* decision in 1961.[3] The law then moved from the obvious inadequacy of the *Standard Stations* reasoning to an analysis parallel to the law of vertical mergers, thereby gaining more complex inadequacy. In *Tampa* the Supreme Court upheld a twenty-year requirements contract, but did so in circumstances unlikely to arise very often. After Tampa Electric, a public utility, decided to try coal rather than oil as boiler fuel in two new generating units, it entered into a requirements contract for twenty years with Nashville Coal Co. Both parties had expended substantial sums

—Tampa in construction of the new facilities, Nashville in preparing to carry out the contract—when Nashville announced that the contract violated the antitrust laws and that it would not honor its obligation.

The Supreme Court computed that the contract might preempt 0.77 percent of the market for twenty years. It did not say that such a trivial foreclosure was too small to violate the law, but pointed out that there was no seller with a dominant position in the market, nor any industry-wide practice of exclusive contracts; the Court also noted that public utilities require a steady and ample supply of fuel. Overhanging the decision, moreover, was the feeling that Nashville had used the antitrust law as an excuse to escape a bargain which it had repented. The suspicion remained that in a less appealing case even this small amount of foreclosure might be illegal.

It remained for the Brown Shoe Co., which had previously had the unsought honor of giving direction to merger law under amended Clayton 7, to confirm that suspicion. Brown, we may assume, still made and sold perhaps 5 percent of the shoes sold in the United States. In dollar volume it was the second-largest manufacturer; in number of shoes sold it was third. The Federal Trade Commission proceeded against Brown under Clayton 3 and also under Section 5 of the Federal Trade Commission Act, on the theory that its "Brown Franchise Stores' Program" constituted an "unfair practice." Approximately 650 retail stores were considered franchised, although only 259 had actually executed agreements. Under the program Brown supplied the franchised dealer, but not other customers, with certain valuable services, including architectural plans, merchandising records, services of a Brown field representative, and a right to participate in group insurance at lower rates than the dealer could obtain individually. The participating dealers agreed to "concentrate" on Brown shoes and not to carry conflicting lines. The franchised stores purchased about 75 percent of their shoes from Brown; the remainder were mostly in lines not conflicting with Brown's. The franchised stores amounted to about 1 percent of the nation's shoe stores, and the Commission predictably concluded that the program would foreclase rival manufacturers.[4] It relied upon the prior *Brown Shoe* merger decision, involving an almost identical percentage, to show competitive effect.

After the court of appeals had reversed the Commission, the Supreme Court reversed the court of appeals [5] and reinstated the Commission's decision. The brief opinion, written by Justice Black, engaged in no economic analysis whatever. The Court said that under Section 5 the Commission has power to declare trade practices unfair which conflict with the basic policies of the Sherman and Clayton acts, even though the practices do not violate those statutes. Brown's "program obviously conflicts with the central policy of both §1 of the Sherman Act and §3 of the Clayton Act against contracts which take away freedom of purchasers to buy in an open market." Justice Black did not deal with the problem that Brown's program did not, in fact, "take away freedom" from anybody. The dealers agreed to certain conditions in return for benefits that seemed sufficient to them, and remained free to leave the program whenever they wished. The opinion might more accurately have stated that the Court was imposing a policy against vertical integration by contract, however temporary and however satisfactory to both parties.

There was, of course, no conceivable way in which Brown's franchise program could harm competition, and it obviously provided efficiencies for both Brown and the dealers. Yet that had been just as obvious in the merger case Brown lost four years previously. Here the Court brushed aside the question of injury to competition because the government was proceeding under Section 5 rather than Clayton 3 and "the Commission has power under §5 to arrest trade restraints in their incipiency without proof that they amount to an outright violation of §3 of the Clayton Act or other provisions of the antitrust laws."

This doctrinal gambit merely shows how far the Court will go to strike down an exclusive dealing contract. Clayton 3 itself is an incipiency statute, designed to arrest restraints in their earliest stages. Section 5 of the Federal Trade Commission Act is on a par with Clayton 3 in this respect. It is both improper statutory construction and mind-boggling economics to read Section 5 as outlawing an incipient incipient restraint of trade. Nobody can have the slightest idea what an incipient incipiency is. Be that as it may, there is the law of exclusive dealing and requirements contracts. In its ferocity, as in its lack of reason, it rivals the law of vertical mergers.

The law of exclusive dealing and requirements contracts, whether applied through Sherman 1, Clayton 3, or Federal Trade Commission Act 5, operates on the theory that competition may be injured through foreclosure of rivals when a firm integrates vertically by contract. This is precisely the same foreclosure theory that supports the law of vertical mergers under Clayton 7, Sherman 1, and Federal Trade Commission Act 5. It is fallacious in this context for the same reasons it is fallacious there. Exclusive dealing, being a form of vertical integration, creates efficiencies and does not create restriction of output. It should, therefore, generally be lawful.

Many commentators appear to think that though exclusive dealing

creates some efficiencies, it also threatens some loss to consumers. Thus
Phillip Areeda: [6]

Exclusive dealing arrangements might foreclose the market opportunities of
the seller's competitors, especially where the buyer is not a dealer but uses the
product himself. If all food canners, for example, agree to buy exclusively
from giant can maker Alpha, there would be no customers left for Alpha's
rivals. This example invites two further points. First, while all buyers might
conceivably choose to make each purchase from Alpha in any event, that
possibility does not dissolve our concern with the contractual limitation on
their future freedom of choice. Second, if only a portion of the buyers were
covered, it would not have the same obvious impact on Alpha's rivals, but it
might limit their opportunities to some degree. Whether the resultant "clog
on competition" is socially serious is another question. It certainly would be
when Alpha's arrangements deprive rivals of the business that would otherwise permit them to operate at an efficient scale and in sufficient numbers to
guarantee workable competition.

Whether any of this is "socially serious" is, of course, the only question for antitrust policy. I think it is clear that there will be no danger
in the situation Areeda posits. The statement that if all canners agreed
to buy exclusively from Alpha, there would be no customers left for
Alpha's rivals, is not a theory of injury to competition but a tautology.
It is equivalent to the statement that, if Alpha made all the sales in
the market, nobody else would make any sales. We must look further to
find a causal relation between exclusive dealing and monopoly.

Let us begin by examining the case in which Alpha has, say, 30 percent of the can market. Is there a possibility that it may be able, as
Areeda suggests, to sign up 100 percent of the canners? Why do not
some of them sign requirements contracts with Alpha's various rivals
or, if there are no particular efficiencies in such contracts, simply continue to buy from Alpha's rivals? Because Alpha makes a better can? But
then Alpha would get all the customers for that reason, and the requirements contracts would have nothing to do with it. Because Alpha offers
some extra inducement, such as a lower price? But that sounds like competition, and surely Alpha's rivals can be relied upon to meet competition. If they cannot, the market is destined for monopoly anyway, because of Alpha's superior efficiency.

It is important to see that Alpha must offer something to the food
canners to get them to sign requirements contracts, and it must offer that
something for the life of the contract, which means that, in terms of
cutting out rivals, the contract offers Alpha no advantages it would not
have had without the contract. The advantage of the contract must be the

creation of efficiency, and Areeda cites a variety of efficiencies that such contracts may create. In this situation, efficiencies are the reality, and the fear of foreclosure is chimerical.

Harlan Blake and William Jones [7] offered the *Standard Fashion* [8] case as an illustration of the harm done by exclusive dealing contracts. The supposed example is worth examination. Standard, a manufacturer of dress patterns, contracted with Magrane-Houston Co., a Boston dry goods store, to supply patterns on condition that Magrane not sell the patterns of any other manufacturer. Magrane violated the condition, and Standard sued to enforce it. Holding that the agreement was unenforceable because it violated Section 3 of the Clayton Act, the Supreme Court noted that Standard and its affiliates controlled 40 percent of the 52,000 pattern agencies in the country and quoted the reasoning of the court of appeals:

The restriction of each merchant to one pattern manufacturer must in hundreds, perhaps in thousands, of small communities amount to giving such single pattern manufacturer a monopoly of the business in such community. Even in larger cities, to limit to a single pattern maker the pattern business of dealers most resorted to by customers whose purchases tend to give fashions their vogue, may tend to facilitate further combinations; so that plaintiff, or some other aggressive concern, instead of controlling two-fifths, will shortly have almost, if not quite, all the pattern business.

Blake and Jones concede that "the record disclosed no evidence of such a tendency to monopoly." And it is apparent on theoretical grounds that Standard could not gain a monopoly through these contracts. The analysis we have just applied to the Alpha case is fully applicable here. But Blake and Jones argue that the industry was highly concentrated, since Standard and three other concerns controlled about 90 percent of the pattern agencies, most of them under exclusive dealing arrangements, so that smaller pattern manufacturers and new entrants would be hampered. The argument they offer for this conclusion runs:

The most desirable sites for pattern agencies—dry goods and department stores—were limited in number, and the major companies, by reason of their popularity and long lines of styles, could preempt the best outlets, relegating to inferior locations newer and smaller manufacturers with shorter and less well-known lines. In communities where suitable outlets were scarce, all but one or a few pattern manufacturers would have been excluded. While the *Standard Fashion* decision might not have been necessary to ward off monopoly, it was clearly helpful in facilitating entry into a concentrated industry and making possible the wider distribution of competitive lines.

This argument is not valid for at least three reasons. In the first place, it incorrectly assumes the desirability of having more firms in the industry. With four major firms and a number of minor ones, the industry was competitively structured. There is no need to worry about barriers to entry.

Second, we ought to take a closer look at those fierce, entry-barring contracts. The Magrane contract had a term of two years. If Standard's other contracts with approximately 20,800 outlets had similar terms, this means that an average of 10,400 outlets were relieved of contractual obligations to Standard every year. In other words, 20 percent of the outlets of the entire industry were released from Standard alone every year. If other pattern manufacturers had similar arrangements, 50 percent of the outlets became available every year. But the situation was even more fluid than that, for some outlets had not signed any exclusive dealing contracts. This does not even take into account the increase and turnover of retail establishments, which would provide additional outlets for smaller manufacturers and new entrants. Some degree of realism is necessary in assessing commercial practices, and as barriers to entry these contracts had about the solidity of a sieve and the tensile strength of wet tissue paper.

Finally, the idea that Standard could use such contracts for the purpose of barring entry rests upon the fallacious theory of predation we have already examined in the case of the can manufacturer Alpha. An argument might be constructed to the effect that Standard's case is different, lending itself more readily to predation. We may assume that Standard had the longest and best line of dress patterns in the industry and that retail outlets require a complete line. Standard, the argument might run, could therefore present a store with an ultimatum: either take our line exclusively or not at all. Perceiving the greater cost of assembling a complete line from the offerings of several other manufacturers, the store agrees, though it would prefer to continue to carry other lines as well. The uniqueness of Standard's line of patterns thus gives it market power which it can use to demand exclusivity and injure rivals or new entrants.

That argument merely repeats the fallacy of the *Griffith* case (see Chapter 7) in a new context. Standard can extract in the prices it charges retailers all that the uniqueness of its line is worth. It cannot charge the retailer that full worth in money and then charge it again in exclusivity the retailer does not wish to grant. To suppose that it can is to commit the error of double counting. If Standard must forgo the higher prices it could have demanded in order to get exclusivity, then exclusivity is not an imposition, it is a purchase. We have seen that a supplier cannot purchase its way to monopoly through exclusive dealing contracts, and there is no point in purchasing a market position short of monopoly, for that is to buy a less profitable market share. If Standard finds it worthwhile to purchase exclusivity from some retailers, the reason is not the barring of entry but some more sensible goal, such as obtaining the special selling effort of the outlet. That is one of the efficiencies arising from exclusivity noted by Areeda.

This analysis throws new light on the supposition of Blake and Jones that Standard could get the most desirable outlets or the only outlet in a town. If that occurred, consumers would be benefited. We will discuss the one-store town (the store with the most desirable location in a larger city is merely an example of lesser market power). The only store in town has a monopoly and will charge accordingly. Moreover, it, not Standard, is in the better position to bargain. The retailer has alternative suppliers. Standard has no alternative outlet with which to reach customers in that town. The store's monopoly is not made more oppressive if it carries only Standard's patterns. Exclusivity has necessarily been purchased from it, which means that the store has balanced the inducement offered by Standard, presumably in the form of lower prices, against the disadvantage of handling only Standard's patterns and found the inducement greater. The advantage to the store is also an advantage to consumers because monopolists, as we have seen, sell more at lower prices when their costs are lowered. If consumers would prefer more pattern lines at higher prices, the store would not accept Standard's offer. The store's decision, made entirely in its own interest, necessarily reflects the balance of competing considerations that determine consumer welfare.

Put the matter another way. If no manufacturer used exclusive dealing contracts, and if a local retail monopolist decided unilaterally to carry only Standard's patterns because the loss in variety was more than made up in the cost saving, we would recognize that that decision was in the consumer interest. We do not want a variety that costs more than it is worth. All that has happened when Standard purchases exclusivity from such a store is that it has offered terms which make variety of pattern offerings cost more than they are worth in comparison with Standard's terms.

It is quite clear, therefore, that the contracts in *Standard Fashion* could not, as a factual matter, have blocked entry or retarded the growth of smaller manufacturers. The same conclusion follows from economic analysis. Once more, all the case did was dismantle an efficient distribution system because of a false fear of monopoly.

Blake and Jones offer one other case—*F.T.C.* v. *Motion Picture Advertising Service Co.*[9]—that deserves analysis. In *MPAS* the four largest producers and distributors of advertising films had separately made contracts with theater owners for the display of their films. Most of the contracts were for one or two years (some ran up to five years), and a "substantial number" contained a provision that the exhibitor would show only the advertising films of the particular producer-distributor. Though they were not acting in collaboration, the four leading producer-distributors had "exclusive arrangements for advertising films with approximately three-fourths of the total number of theatres in the United States which display advertising films for compensation." The Federal Trade Commission, despite evidence that theaters often preferred the longer terms, ordered the contracts limited to one year, and the Supreme Court affirmed. Blake and Jones, attacking an argument I had made previously to the effect that vertical integration can never improperly impede entry, say of the *MPAS* case:

The weakness of Professor Bork's argument that entry can always be effectuated by seeking a collaborator to enter at the blocked level is particularly apparent in a case like this, where the size of the firm in the business into which entry is sought (here, the production of advertising films) is small by comparison with the capital investment in the vertical channel which is blocked (motion picture theaters). One can hardly be expected to bring into existence numerous motion picture theaters to provide outlets for advertising films.

Blake and Jones appear, however, to have the case and the argument the wrong way round. Under what theory can small firms take a monopoly profit and actually use the difficulty of entry at the large firms' level as the factor that preserves their ability to exploit the large firms? The large firms, here the theaters, would not stand for such nonsense for a moment. They would support new entrants in the production and distribution of advertising films or enter that activity themselves. They would certainly not use their own market strength to give a monopoly to their suppliers. That is true whether the monopoly returns are taken directly from the theaters or indirectly from the advertisers. In either case the theaters would receive less than they should. And, of course, the facts refute any suggestion that a monopoly position was being protected. There were already twenty-four other film distributors in the market. There was no problem with entry. The larger distributors were merely more successful. The facts that the exclusive contracts were preferred by the theater owners is additional proof that those contracts were not the means of creating a monopoly for the film distributors.

Justice Frankfurter's dissent pointed out that more than half of MPAS's exclusive contracts ran for only one year, so "that part of respondent's hold on the market found unreasonable by the Commission boils down to exclusion of other competitors from something like 1,250 theaters, or about 6%, of the some 20,000 theaters in the country. The hold is on about 10% of the theaters that accept advertising." It is clear that neither the facts nor the theory of the *MPAS* case support the idea that the exclusive contracts hurt competition.

The truth appears to be that there has never been a case in which exclusive dealing or requirements contracts were shown to injure competition. A seller who wants exclusivity must give the buyer something for it. If he gives a lower price, the reason must be that the seller expects the arrangement to create efficiencies that justify the lower price. If he were to give the lower price simply to harm his rivals, he would be engaging in deliberate predation by price cutting, and that, as we have seen in Chapter 7, would be foolish and self-defeating behavior on his part.

Bidding for exclusive dealing or requirements contracts would be a particularly foolish form of predation, for the seller must commit himself to the unprofitable low prices for years in advance, thus locking himself into a losing predatory campaign. If he merely offered lower prices, he could either maintain them or abandon them as he learned whether the campaign was succeeding or failing.

The seller may not offer lower prices, however. Instead, he may offer new efficiencies to the purchaser, such as an assured source of supply and the elimination of selling and buying costs. Increased efficiency, of course, cannot be classified as improperly exclusionary, and there is every reason to believe that exclusive dealing and requirements contracts have no purpose or effect other than the creation of efficiency.

16

"Barriers to Entry"

THE concept of barriers to entry is crucial to antitrust debate. Those who advocate extensive and increasing legal intervention in market processes cite the existence of entry barriers as a reason to believe that unassisted market forces very often fail to produce adequate results. We have seen, for example, that belief in the existence of barriers to entry was crucial to the reasoning of the oligopolyphobes of the Neal Task Force, to William Comanor's objection to vertical division of dealer territories, to Judge Wyzanski's condemnation of United Shoe Machinery's leasing system, and to the Supreme Court's prohibition of Procter & Gamble's acquisition of Clorox. The ubiquity and potency of the concept are undeniable.

Yet it is demonstrable that barriers of the sort these commentators and jurists believe they see do not exist. They are ghosts that inhabit antitrust theory. Until the concept of barriers to entry is thoroughly revised, it will remain impossible to make antitrust law more rational or, indeed, to restrain the growth of its powerful irrational elements.

We may begin by asking what a "barrier to entry" is. There appears to be no precise definition, and in current usage a "barrier" often seems to be anything that makes the entry of new firms into an industry more difficult. It is at once apparent that an ambiguity lurks in the concept, and it is this ambiguity that causes the trouble. When existing firms are efficient and possess valuable plants, equipment, knowledge, skill, and reputation, potential entrants will find it correspondingly more difficult to enter the industry, since they must acquire those things. It is harder to enter the steel industry than the business of retailing shoes or pizzas, and it is harder to enter either of these fields than to become a suburban handyman. But these difficulties are natural; they inhere in the nature of the tasks to be performed. There can be no objection to barriers of this sort. Their existence means only that when market power is achieved by means other than efficiency, entry will not dissipate the objectionable power instantaneously, and law may therefore have a role to play. If entry were instantaneous, market forces would break up cartels before a typist in the Antitrust Division could rap out a form complaint. Antitrust is valuable because in some cases it can achieve results more rapidly than can market forces. We need not suffer losses while waiting for the market to erode cartels and monopolistic mergers.

The question for antitrust is whether there exist artificial entry barriers. These must be barriers that are not forms of superior efficiency and which yet prevent the forces of the market—entry or the growth of smaller firms already within the industry—from operating to erode market positions not based on efficiency. Care must be taken to distinguish between forms of efficiency and artificial barriers. Otherwise, the law will find itself—indeed, it has found itself—attacking efficiency in the name of market freedom. Joe Bain, whose work has done much to popularize the concept, lists among entry barriers such things as economies of scale, capital requirements, and product differentiation.[1] There may be disagreement about two of these barriers, but it is clear that at least one of them, economies of scale, is a form of efficiency. Uncritical adapters of Bain's work have not sufficiently inquired whether the others may not also be efficiencies.

Before examining some claimed entry barriers to determine whether they are efficiencies or artificial clogs upon competition, it should be noted that we have already discussed this general subject under another name. An artificial barrier to entry is, of course, an exclusionary practice. The argument of Chapter 7 indicates that no barrier is unintended. Every barrier will be either a form of efficiency deliberately created or an instance of deliberate predation. There is no "intermediate case" of nonefficient and unintended exclusion. Failure to bear that in mind leads to serious policy mistakes.

The claimed entry barriers to be discussed are physical product differentiation, advertising and promotion, capital requirements, and vertical arrangements such as dealerships, leases, and deferred rebates.

PHYSICAL PRODUCT DIFFERENTIATION

Bain mentions physical product differentiation as a barrier to entry, but I am unable to understand, from his writings or from anybody else's, why it is not clearly a form of efficiency.

Sellers differentiate their products physically in order to increase their appeal to customers. The differentiation may be strictly functional in a mechanical sense, or it may be decorative. In any case, the differentiation is profitable only if consumers respond to it favorably. For this reason, physical product differentiation must, when it succeeds, be classified as a form of efficiency. But can it bar entry? Of course it can. The entrant is free, however, to form his product as he wishes, and the incumbent's differentiation can make his path more difficult only if consumers prefer the incumbent's version of the product. There is nothing remotely objectionable in that.

But differentiation may also provide routes for entry. Again and again, new firms enter markets by offering something different from the products of established firms. The survival of American Motors in the automobile industry and the deconcentration of that industry by the entry of foreign firms, particularly German and Japanese manufacturers, has been due to the opportunities afforded by product differentiation.

Failure to understand the role and nature of product differentiation can lead to preposterous policy conclusions. It has been argued, for example, that the automobile industry's annual model change, which is a form of product differentiation, requires firms of such large size that the industry necessarily has too few rivals.[2] The suggestion was made, therefore, that the Federal Trade Commission order an end to model changes, at least by the larger firms, in order to reduce the size of automobile manufacturers. This argument fails to deal with the obtrusive fact that model changes are important in the industry because many consumers like them. If that were not so, the firm that practiced model changing would merely incur useless costs, acquire a competitive handicap, and lose market share to firms that changed models less often or not at all. If large firms are needed to provide model changes, we are faced with an economy of scale. The proposal to ban changes is nothing more than a suggestion that consumers be denied products they prefer so that economies of scale will be less important. That incoherent argument ought not to masquerade as an antitrust proposal.

Yet another argument against product differentiation claims that it raises internal barriers to competition.[3] It is said that the movement in a market from standardized products to differentiated products replaces a competitive market with a series of fragmented markets in which each seller has a small monopoly. A seller with a slightly different product that some consumers prefer has to some degree a sloping rather than a nearly horizontal demand curve. Product differentiation thus creates a divergence between price and marginal cost, and hence a restriction of output. The realism of this analysis is open to some question. The degree of market power will be slight; so, correspondingly, will be the power to restrict output. Besides, where a significant fraction of consumers is indifferent to the differentiation, the seller may have to forgo output restriction and a higher price to those who do prefer his product in order to capture the sales of the others. Where other sellers are free to approximate each other's differentiating features (should they wish to do so), product differentiation represents no more than different amounts of the same product, and that, rather than market power, accounts for the different prices.

But there are more basic answers. In the first place, the presence of a variety of sellers offering differentiated products necessarily means that the market is more accurately reflecting the diversity of consumer tastes than would the provision of a standardized product. Second, even if the charge of output restriction were completely true, it would not support an antitrust objection to the practice. When consumers prefer the differentiated product and hence make output restriction possible, they have shown that they prefer the higher price for that product to a lower price for a standardized product. To deny them the opportunity to get the differentiated product is to lessen their satisfaction.

Much of the objection to physical product differentiation rests, at bottom, on an unadmitted bluenoscism. In discussions one is aware constantly of the unspoken premise that, for example, automobile buyers should not be willing to pay for chrome, fins, styling, exotic colors, fast pickup. This premise is easily converted into the assertion that consumers "really" do not want them. From there it is but a short step to the authoritarian conclusion that consumers would be better off if law kept them from having things they are willing to pay for but "really" do not want. Consumers—other consumers, of course, never oneself—are dazzled, manipulated, and captured by product differentiation. Apparently they lose their faculties and surrender their wills. So addictive is the narcotic of differentiation that they are powerless to choose the plain product we know they prefer, even when it is placed before them. This frame of mind was nicely illustrated in a conversation some years ago with a leading antitrust scholar. He urged that antitrust break up the major automobile companies because (odd notion) that would lead to less fancy cars, and consumers really want only "basic transportation." It was pointed out that if that was what they wanted, they could get it. Somebody would offer a product that would sweep the market. Even then there were available such options as Volkswagens and the sedans made by Checker. His answer was, "But most people don't buy those."

The objection to physical product differentiation is essentially sumptuary. It rests upon the conviction that people ought not to be allowed to buy what they prefer. That is undoubtedly true as to some classes of harmful products, but in such cases the argument ought candidly to be put in just those terms, and the law to be enacted will not be antitrust law. The sumptuary impulse has no legitimate place in the interpretation of antitrust laws that are necessarily premised on the ideal of the maximum satisfaction of consumer wants as they exist.

ADVERTISING AND PROMOTION

Advertising and promotion are particular obsessions of antitrust zealots. The Federal Trade Commission wages an ill-conceived campaign directly against advertising, but our topic here is the way in which hostility to advertising impinges upon antitrust decisions in a variety of fields.

Current antitrust objections to advertising and promotion are incomprehensible, for if there is one charge that cannot with justice be laid against these activities, it is the allegation that they impair competition. They are, on the contrary, essential to vigorous market rivalry.

We may first take up the allegation that advertising and promotion create artificial barriers to entry. Suppose that the sole firm in an industry is taking monopoly profits and wishes to deter the entry of potential rivals who would share and ultimately erode those returns. Advertising will not bar the door. There is no monopoly of access to advertising. The entrant can find an advertising agency just as easily as the monopolist. Indeed, he will have agencies clamoring for the account. Since the incumbent has, by hypothesis, been taking a monopoly profit, the available profits more than cover the costs of advertising. With respect to advertising expenditures in any given time period, the entrant and the established firm start even. It is often objected, however, that advertising has a long-run effect, that the established firm enjoys the benefits of past advertising. If true, the proposition does not demonstrate an artificial entry barrier. It means only that advertising and the reputation it creates are capital assets. The established firm has only the advantage of having already paid for its capital asset, just as it has already paid for a factory. If the above-normal profits are there, the entrant will be willing to pay for both the advertising and the factory. It is impossible to see how advertising and promotion can artificially keep other firms out of lucrative markets.

Someone is certain to suggest, however, that the established firm might be willing to use excessive advertising as a predatory tactic, squandering all the incumbent's profits until the entrant collapsed. The established firm would not, of course, make such expenditures until an entrant had appeared. A policy of continuous, anticipatory predatory advertising would dissipate the profits the monopolist was trying to protect. The question, then, is whether the threat of massive advertising upon the appearance of an entrant could bar entry. The answer is negative because the threat is not credible. Predatory advertising is very similar to predatory price cutting and is not, therefore, a feasible tactic.

Predatory advertising is, by definition, advertising that does not pay for itself in current revenues and will not pay for itself even in the long run, unless the victim is driven from the market. As the warfare proceeds, the predator must advertise enough to expand sales and take away the victim's market share. But advertising, like all other economic behavior, is subject to the law of diminishing returns, and the effectiveness of advertising driven beyond the point of profitability would certainly diminish, probably very rapidly. In this situation, every increase in sales is accomplished at a rising marginal cost of advertising, and that marginal cost is increasingly above marginal revenue. The predator and the victim are thus in very different positions. The predator must take away all of the victim's market share, and satisfy all of the additional demand provoked by the extraordinary advertising campaign, while the victim need not take away any of the predator's share. In fact, the victim, perceiving that the predator is using up his reserves at a much faster rate, need not even attempt to hold all of his own share. The analysis is precisely the same as that already given in Chapter 7 with respect to predatory price cutting. In fact, it may be that advertising is even a more suicidal weapon for the would-be predator, since advertising has a spillover effect and the predator's advertising may in some part redound to the benefit of his victim.

Theoretical considerations indicate, therefore, that advertising and promotion cannot create artificial barriers to entry. The argument is so clear that it should come as no surprise whatever to learn that empirical work indicates the same conclusion. Lester Telser, for example, concludes from factual studies: "Increased advertising, far from signifying an obstacle to entry, is very often symptomatic of the reverse. It is the high turnover of brands and sometimes of firms that accounts for the large advertising outlays on some products." [4] James Ferguson tested Joe Bain's assertion that barriers to entry based on advertising were especially high in the liquor industry and discovered that the evidence points the other way.[5] Among other things, Ferguson found subsequent entry by at least ten successful firms, a decreasing share of the market held by the four largest distillers (despite a decrease in the number of distillers and an increase in the ratio of advertising to sales), falling and lower rates of returns for the top four distillers compared to smaller distillers, and rapid turnover among top brands. Yale Brozen, taking into account these and other studies, concludes that advertising is a means of entry, not a barrier to it.[6] New products are advertised more intensively than old; there is less customer loyalty in markets with intensive advertising than in those with less; and the firm with the largest market share usually does not advertise so intensively as those seeking to gain market share. This, together with the other evidence, indicates that advertising is a means of providing information. The provision of information about alternatives tends to break down established market positions, and no amount of information provided by the firm with an established position can drown out the news of an alternative.

Indeed, the proposition that advertising is not a barrier to entry can be supported by an example often advanced to show that it is. For many years, four cigarette manufacturers were dominant in the industry; their aggregate share of the market remained high, although it fluctuated widely. Since cigarettes were a heavily advertised product, the dominance of the four was attributed to the entry-barring effect of advertising. But the crucial aspect of cigarette advertising is that the companies advertise brands rather than company names. Few smokers can tell you which firms make which brands, and even fewer care. Moreover, the industry has been characterized by the introduction of new brands accompanied by heavy advertising, as well as by the decline and disappearance of old brands. Advertising was a route of entry for new brands, and it did not save older ones. Yet consumers did not identify the new brands with particular manufacturers and purchase them because of that identification. Where advertising was important, with respect to brands, entry was rapid and continuous. Where advertising was unimportant, with respect to the corporate identity of manufacturers, entry was slow and sporadic. Entry of new brands of cigarettes has declined markedly since the 1970 ban of cigarette advertisements on television. The dominance of the four largest cigarette manufacturers will have to be explained on some ground other than the entrenching effect of advertising.

Advertising and promotion can be better understood if they are viewed as products or outputs in themselves. The contempt for advertising which is *de rigueur* in certain strata of our society is based on invincible ignorance of the functions it serves and the reasons it is presented to the public as it is. The chief function of advertising and promotion, of course, is the provision of information. Even the least informative advertising tells consumers of the existence of particular products, what functions they perform, what kinds of outlets sell them, and (usually) the general range of prices. Many forms of advertising provide much more detail. Often advertising is rather general, its object being to get consumers interested, so that they will come to outlets where additional information can be more economically provided. Thus, colorful advertising with a minimum of facts draws the prospective purchaser into the store, where a salesman offers more details. The division of function between broadly phrased and widely circulated advertising messages and more detailed information available only through the dealer or salesman is surely based on the costs of providing information. Information is expensive to transmit, and more of it can be transmitted once the prospective purchaser has identified himself in response to the general message.

Advertising is often repetitive and fairly simple for very good reasons, not because it appeals to the irrational side of consumers. Messages must be repeated because each message reaches only a fraction of the possibly interested population, because people forget, because consumers are constantly entering and leaving the market. Messages must be relatively simple because most consumers are relatively inattentive and can retain only a few points, and because the costs of longer messages are higher. Everyone who attempts to instruct a mass audience learns to keep the message simple and to repeat it: politicians, preachers, teachers, boot camp drill instructors. There is no reason to belabor the advertisers for recognizing, as everyone else does, the limitations of the audience.

Advertising has other functions, of course. Advertisers often attempt to wrap their product in an aura, a daydream. With a bottle of Pabst beer you get nostalgia for an older and allegedly simpler time. With a certain cigarillo you capture the feeling of an aggressive young man on the way up. Charisma and charm come with cigarettes; a humorous attitude about certain ills of the flesh is packaged with Alka-Seltzer. Prestige or a dashing attitude surrounds certain makes of cars, not usually the same makes. Charles Revson, of Revlon, said of his cosmetics business simply "We sell hope." Much of human happiness depends on the fleeting fantasies and comforting attitudes with which we bolster our morale in the face of the "objective" truth of our lives and prospects. Only a modern Puritan can object to these evanescent satisfactions which advertisers provide us. For those who do not want them, there are usually lower-priced commodities that provide the same purely physical characteristics.

Advertising and promotion are peculiar products only in the sense that entrepreneurs have so far devised few ways to sell them and their benefits separately from the physical products. The firm that sells information must recover its costs, and the most effective way of doing that is in the price the consumer pays for the product. Product differentiation is a way of wrapping the information and the physical product together, so that the two are paid for at once. Without the differentiation, the firm that incurred the costs of the information would not be paid for it and would cease providing it. If consumers do not want the information or the aura provided, some firms can make a great deal of money by supplying only the physical product at a lower price. Indeed, in most markets firms will be found that do just that, catering to a segment of the market that responds to price rather than information and service.

It is conventional to speak of advertising and promotion as pushing the demand curve for a product up and to the right, increasing the demand. But that usage may be misleading. Demand may increase, but it may not be useful to think of it as being a demand for the same product. When advertising and promotion provide information, pleasure, or what have you, the composition of the original product is changed. The original product, after all, is usefully thought of not merely as a physical object, but rather as a bundle of services or gratifications to be derived from the object. The provision of information or aura adds another group of services or gratifications. This change in the composition of the product offered the consumer will require that resources be bid away from other employments. But if the new product proves more profitable, this means that consumers prefer the new allocation of resources—and that efficiency has been increased.

Such changes in product composition are a general means of economic progress. And when products are seen as bundles of services or gratifications, the product differentiation created by advertising and promotion becomes indistinguishable from the physical differentiation of products. (This is the same point made in Chapter 14 about the effects of resale price maintenance and vertical market division, but it is so generally overlooked that it is worth restressing in this context.) Thus, when White Motor chose not to sell trucks alone but to sell trucks plus reseller-provided information, that was precisely the same as a decision not to sell a stripped-down truck model but to sell models with a variety of extra features. Consumers dictate the composition of the product in both cases. There is no infringement of their choice. When a detergent manufacturer adds bleach crystals to his product, those consumers who preferred his detergent without bleach have had their choice restricted. But if the change proves profitable to the manufacturer, we may confidently assume that consumers as a group are better satisfied. A law prohibiting the sale of trucks with extra features or forbidding the addition of bleach crystals to detergent would not widen the range of consumer choice but would restrict it. Precisely the same analysis applies to all antitrust efforts to interfere with the means—merger, resale price maintenance, vertical division of territories—by which the contributions of advertising and the promotion are made more effective.

This analysis, I believe, undercuts both of the points against advertising and promotion made by Donald Turner: [7]

Economies in production, research, distribution, and the like will inevitably lower average costs and will tend to lower prices—thus easily qualifying as procompetitive consequences. Economies in promotional expenditures, on the other hand, present less impressive qualifications. They may not lower average costs at all, since total promotional efforts may increase; and if promotional efforts are intensified, they will raise barriers to entry whenever they increase the durability of consumer preferences for established brands. In short, promotional economies, generally speaking, are not as procompetitive as other kinds of economies. . . .

The fallacy of viewing advertising as a barrier to entry has already been explained. The remainder of the argument rests on what I believe to be a misconception of efficiency. Efficiency does not arise solely from cutting costs. It also arises from offering products that people want more, even if those products cost more to produce. It is wrong to say that the Mustang is produced more efficiently than the Lincoln Continental because it costs less. Raising average costs through promotional and informational expenditures is no different from raising average costs through expenditures on larger engines. Both are efficient and procompetitive if consumers like them.

The usual effects of advertising, however, are probably to lower prices. Yale Brozen examined the average price of prescription drugs in California, the state with the most restrictive laws on advertising and retailing of pharmaceuticals, with the average price in states with the least restrictive laws.[8] In 1970 the averages were $4.95 and $3.52, respectively. Also important are the findings of Lee Benham concerning the marketing of eyeglasses.[9] The estimates of eyeglass prices suggested that advertising increased the price paid by 25 percent to more than 100 percent. Advertising generates the volume low price sellers require and, by lowering the costs of consumer search, makes markets more competitive.

There is, then, no general case against advertising, and certainly no reason to level an antitrust attack upon mergers or other business arrangements that are likely to produce economies in advertising. Such economies are efficiencies like any other, and just as procompetitive.

CAPITAL REQUIREMENTS

Capital requirements exist and certainly inhibit entry—just as talent requirements for playing professional football exist and inhibit entry. Neither barrier is an any sense artificial or the proper subject of special concern for antitrust policy.

Though much has been made of so-called capital barriers in antitrust literature, the topic is actually embarrassingly empty. Consider first what a capital barrier of interest to antitrust policy would have to involve. I can think of two types of assertions. The first is that a monopolist may impose excessive capital requirements on potential rivals in order to prevent their entry into his market. This is a theory of the predatory use of capital requirements. The second is that capital requirements themselves prevent entry, even though the established firm has done nothing artificial to enlarge the requirements. We may take these theories one at a time.

The predatory theory of capital requirements supposes that an established firm, or a group of established firms acting together, may find it profitable to behave as they otherwise would not, in order to require entrants to come in with much larger amounts of capital. It is difficult to think of situations in which that might appear even superficially plausible. A firm cannot raise barriers to entry by making itself larger horizontally than it should optimally be. That would merely raise its own costs, and an entrant would be given the advantage of coming in at a more efficient size.

The case usually cited is that of a monopolist who integrates vertically in order to require entrants to come in at both levels at once, the theory being that the additional capital required is a deterrent. The notion has been extended by some commentators, including Harlan Blake and William Jones, to include industries with a "few" firms enjoying oligopolistic profits.[10] Thus, in attempting to support a theory of capital barriers that would justify a law against vertical integration, they begin with "the extreme case of a fully integrated industry—where one or a few manufacturers own the key sources of supply and the existing channels of distribution" and conclude that in such an industry "no entry is feasible at any level without entry at all levels," and, therefore, that entry requires "vast amounts of capital." The implication is that "vast amounts of capital" will be unavailable, so that the incumbent firm or firms will continue to enjoy undisturbed above-normal profits through restriction of output.

Because "extreme cases" have a way of becoming "general cases" without notice in antitrust debate, it is important to note that this capital barrier theory would, if it were correct, apply *only* to the extreme case and not to most vertical integration. Wherever the industry is not "fully integrated"—that is, wherever there is at least one firm that is willing to buy from or sell to other firms—entry at one level is possible. Moreover, wherever there are more than one or two firms in the industry, noncollusive restriction of output is not likely to be a problem of any significance. Thus, the "extreme case" is just that, a case that rarely exists. Argument from it does not begin to support the present severe law against vertical integration. But let us examine the proffered extreme case to see whether even that situation would present a capital barrier.

Since we are dealing with a theory of intentional blockage of entry, of the predatory imposition of capital costs, it is relevant to discuss both the costs of the action to the established firm and the impact upon the entrant. The costs to the established firm are too often overlooked. Assume a monopolist in manufacturing who, fearing entry, considers buying up all existing channels of distribution in order to discourage possible entrants. If vertical integration were a more efficient way of doing business,

he would have purchased the outlets anyway. To object to such integration is to object to superior efficiency. Then the entrant would be required to come in at both levels in order to be as efficient as the monopolist. But we are asked to assume that the vertical integration occurs for
other reasons. In that case, the fact that the industry was not vertically
integrated and that there was more than one distributor indicates that
our hypothetical monopolist must incur two kinds of inefficiency. He
not only incurs the higher costs of vertical integration, but by putting
together distributors he also operates the distribution level inefficiently.
The fact that there was more than one distributor shows that distribution
is, as you would expect, an operation in which marginal costs are rising.
Putting a number of firms into one will raise the costs of distribution.

This means that the supposed barrier imposes additional costs on the
monopolist; he is sacrificing part of his monopoly profit continually in
order to preserve the rest. But will the tactic preserve the rest? It is impossible to see how it could. In the first place, it is not true that the
entrant would be required to come in on both levels at once. If the industry is attractive—and if it is not, there will be no entry anyway—
the prospective entrant in manufacturing should have no difficulty in
finding someone else to enter distribution. He will have two incentives to
offer: a greater-than-competitive profit is being made in the industry
(that is why the monopolist is interested in barring entry), and the
established firm has saddled itself with higher costs through integration
than the separate entrants in manufacturing and distribution need incur.
What could be more enticing? The capital required of the manufacturing
entrant, therefore, is no greater than it would have been if the monopolist had not integrated vertically, and the prospects of success are greater.

But assuming, for the sake of argument, that the entrant decides (or
is required for some unknown reason) to come in at both levels at once,
what is the case for supposing that the necessary capital will be unavailable? Capital suppliers, like all other suppliers, are interested in maximizing their returns, and an industry where greater-than-competitive returns
are available should be particularly attractive. To this observation Blake
and Jones merely reply:

Traditional capital analysis assumes perfect foresight. Yet capital markets, unlike commodity markets, are inherently incapable of operating "perfectly" because uncertainty is always present with respect to the outcome of arrangements currently undertaken. It is hard to conceive of a use of capital more
fraught with uncertainty than an attempt to break into an industry occupied
by vertically integrated firms enjoying the fruits of their fewness of number.
And the stakes will often be high. It is elementary "game theory"—or what

is the same thing, known to any poker-player—that one does not knowingly enter into a "two-person, zero-sum" game or a poker game without having resources equal to the opponent's, or at least knowledge of their dimension.

These remarks fail to resuscitate the expiring theory of capital barriers to entry. The argument advanced here does not require perfect foresight or anything like it. It merely requires the assumption, hardly improbable, that capital suppliers prefer higher returns to lower ones. That capital suppliers sometimes make mistakes is not to be denied, but why should one suppose that the mistakes are always on the side of not investing where greater returns are to be made? As John McGee puts it, "since the capital markets often finance firms that do badly or go broke, it should be obvious that the mistakes are not all of one kind." [11] Capital suppliers take risks when the stakes are high.

It is hard to follow the assertion that there is a particularly high degree of uncertainty when an industry is "occupied by vertically integrated firms enjoying the fruits of their fewness." It is precisely the presence of those fruits that makes entry attractive and less uncertain. The reference to a poker game is wholly misplaced, since the responses of firms to a new entrant are controlled by cost and demand conditions. The only response I can think of that would resemble a poker game would be a predatory price war, and we have already seen why the established firms would not engage in that self-defeating tactic.

There being nothing to the notion that an established firm might integrate vertically in order deliberately to raise the capital requirements of entry, we may turn to the second type of assertion—that capital may itself be a barrier, even though the requirement of large capital is not imposed artificially by existing firms. It is at once apparent that such a barrier is not artificial; the scale of operation requires the capital. One should not, of course, interfere with the industry structure in order to reduce capital requirements, since that is merely to sacrifice economic performance to ease of entry. And, once more, if there are greater-than-competitive returns being taken in the industry, the requisite capital for entry should be forthcoming.

It has been urged that there may be a rising cost in acquiring capital, since the borrower must deal with progressively less informed lenders. But this does not mean that capital requirements are artificial barriers. It means only that there are costs involved in raising capital, as there are costs involved in every activity, and that the potential entrant must overcome this cost as well as others. In this sense, the possession of capital is an important efficiency because the firm need not expend money to provide information to persons with capital. Thus, the possession of capital by an established firm gives it an advantage over potential entrants without capital precisely like its advantage in having a functioning management team, knowledge, commercial contacts, and so on. In fact, capital, being fungible and easily transferred, may be much less of an obstacle than the requisite specialized assets.

In sum, capital does not constitute an artificial barrier to entry, capital requirements cannot be arbitrarily imposed upon potential entrants, and the possession of capital is merely a socially valuable efficiency.

DEALERSHIPS, LEASES, AND DEFERRED REBATES

There are so many versions of barrier-to-entry theory loose in the literature that it seems well, before moving on, to discuss a few other phenomena that are often viewed as creating such barriers. In this subsection I will deal with three other varieties of vertical integration—this time by contract—that may be thought to inhibit entry improperly. We shall see that they do not.

In discussing the automobile industry, Joe Bain, whose work has heavily influenced thought on the entire subject of barriers to entry, cites the dealership system as perhaps the leading barrier.[12] It is important to understand what Bain actually says because many antitrust lawyers and economists appear to have read normative implications into his description that do not belong there. That is to say, they think that Bain's work supports proposals to lower barriers either by legal modification of the dealership system or by dissolution of the leading firms. This leap from the descriptive to the normative is wholly improper, as may be seen from a summary of what Bain actually says.

He begins with the factual assertion that all car manufacturers generally use exclusive franchise policies to restrict their dealers to their brands. This is not the case and has not been for a long time; many dealers do take on the cars of rival manufacturers. But that does not seem central to Bain's point. He goes on at some length to say that the dealer not only promotes sales but also provides maintenance, repairs, and parts. The geographical density of dealers of a particular manufacturer varies with that manufacturer's sales volume. Dealers are important in maintaining product preferences for two reasons. There is, first, the loyalty of buyers to individual dealers because of "their reputations for fair dealing and for provision of satisfactory service" and on the basis of relative probability of their remaining in business. Second, for ease of obtaining parts and service, buyers like to purchase a brand offered by many dealers nationwide. These factors give the larger automobile makers significant advantages because, having larger volumes, they are able to attract more and better dealers, and dealers who, because of their own or the manufacturer's financial strength, are generally better able to ride out depressed business conditions.

One finishes reading Bain's much-cited argument with astonishment. Is that it? It is. He has said no more than that manufacturers who sell more, attract more and better retail outlets, and it is an advantage to have more and better retail outlets. Not only is this analysis trite, but it also fails to raise any discernible problem of concern to antitrust. We already knew that more successful firms are harder to compete against.

To give the argument policy implications one would have to say that a new manufacturer with a good product would be unable to find dealers. There is no theoretical reason why this should be true. If it can be established that a manufacturer with a product the consuming public would like to buy cannot find dealers willing to make a profit, a revolutionary discovery about human motivation will have been made. Worse for the argument, it has been refuted by subsequent events. Volkswagen, Toyota, Datsun, and Volvo have all been able to establish dealership networks in the United States, and some of them have succeeded spectacularly. The theory of dealership systems as barriers to entry must be regarded as an empty notion.

It is sometimes argued, however, that a manufacturer can create barriers to entry by the conditions he imposes in his contracts with customers. The leases employed by United Shoe Machinery are widely regarded as a case in point. Judge Wyzanski believed the same thing, and pointed out that "when a lessee desires to replace a United machine, United gives him more favorable terms [particularly on the charges associated with machine returns] if the replacement is by another United machine than if it is by a competitive machine." [13] It seems obvious to most people that such a practice would have the effect of artificially barring the entry of rival shoe manufacturers. It is in fact *not* obvious, and I think it easily demonstrable that entry is not barred.

Even after United gives more favorable terms to a lessee who takes another United machine, it must still be making a monopoly profit; otherwise there is simply no point to the tactic. This means that the entrant could nevertheless price below United and still make at least a competitive return—perhaps more. The need of the monopolist to retain for himself a greater-than-competitive return is the flaw in almost all theories of artificial barriers to entry. When that is seen, United's lease terms take on a new appearance. If no cost reasons prompted the differential enforcement of the lease terms, they are probably best seen as a competitive bid to induce a lessee to remain a customer. It is usual to view the enforcement pattern as a penalty for switching, but it is no more a penalty for switching than an incentive for staying.

If the differential enforcement is known to lessees, the United leases closely resemble deferred rebate contracts. These have often been viewed as improperly exclusionary, but analysis demonstrates that they cannot impede entry so as to preserve a monopoly position. Suppose that a monopolist in widget manufacture has 1,000 customers, each of whom buys 100 widgets a year. In order to hold them against potential entrants, he sells on deferred rebate contracts which call for the payment of $100 per year. If the customer purchases that amount in each of ten successive years, he receives a $100 rebate at the end of the tenth year, which means (ignoring interest for the sake of simplicity) that the real (monopoly) price is $90 per year, or 90 cents per widget. We must assume, of course, that the competitive price would be less, say $80 per year or 80 cents per widget.

After the widget maker has been in business for some time, a new widget manufacturer appears. He can, of course, compete for the custom of those purchasers whose contracts end each year, a tenth of the population, or 100 customers annually. And if the monopolist sticks to his contract system, the entrant can get all such customers for a price of $89.99 per year. That observation alone is sufficient to destroy the realism of the notion that the contracts prevent entry. But let us assume the entrant would like to expand more rapidly than that. He therefore analyzes the prospects of getting customers who have not completed the ten-year term to switch to him and forgo their rebates. He will conclude that he can take half the market at prices above the competitive price and leave the monopolist selling at a loss to the remainder.

Table 2 makes this clear. Remember that at the end of each contract year the customer can look forward to getting 100 widgets times the number of years left under the contract, at a price of $100 times the number of years left minus $100 (the rebate at the end). I assume that at each stage both the supplier and the customer regard bygones as bygones, so that both are interested in the benefits and costs of future

TABLE 2
Effective Prices Under a Deferred Rebate Contract

End of Year No.	Total Price for Widgets	Effective Price (Price per Widget)
0	1000 W for $1,000−100 = $900	90¢
1	900 W for 900−100 = 800	88.9
2	800 W for 800−100 = 700	87.5
3	700 W for 700−100 = 600	85.7
4	600 W for 600−100 = 500	83.3
5	500 W for 500−100 = 400	80
6	400 W for 400−100 = 300	75
7	300 W for 300−100 = 200	66.7
8	200 W for 200−100 = 100	50
9	100 W for 100−100 = 0	0

rather than past transactions. Thus, the price for widgets grows smaller and smaller as the end of the term approaches, and the rebate becomes larger in proportion to the price the purchaser must pay.

Since the competitive price is 80¢ per widget, it is quite clear that the entrant can bid low enough (and still make more than a competitive profit) to get any customers who are ending year 0 (customers who have finished their contracts with the monopolist and are considering whether to sign a new one) and any customers who are finishing years 1, 2, 3, or 4 of their ten-year terms. Thus, he can get half the customers at prices above the competitive price, and if he wants to cut to competitive levels, he has an even shot at customers ending year 5.

Let us assume for simplicity that the entrant must charge the same price to all customers and that he would just as soon make a profit above the competitive level. If he chooses to charge 82.9¢ per widget, he can take half the customers (500) and leave the monopolist in a most unhappy position. The monopolist winds up with 100 customers who are paying a competitive price of 80¢ per widget (those ending year 5); 100 customers to whom he will sell 400 widgets each at a loss of 5¢ per widget (those ending year 6); 100 customers to whom he will sell 300 widgets each at a loss of 13.3¢ per widget (those ending year 7); 100 customers to whom he will sell 200 widgets each at a loss of 30¢ per widget (those ending year 8); and—his prize collection— 100 customers to each of whom he will give 100 widgets absolutely without charge, a loss of 80¢ per widget (customers ending year 9). These customers will not leave him, though he wishes to heaven they would, until their contract terms run out. The only thing that the deferred rebate contract has accomplished is to put the monopolist in a loss position for five years while the entrant takes the cream from the market. Even if he tries to bid back the customers who went to the entrant, thus driving those prices to the competitive level, he can only get part of them, and he must still bear losses on the customers who stayed with him.

The situation is that the entrant will be able to bid away the customers in the early years of the contract, precisely the customers the monopolist would like to keep; and the entrant will not be able to take away customers in the later years of their contracts, precisely the customers the monopolist would love to relinquish.* He will be left only with those customers to whom he sells at a loss.

In other words, the deferred rebate contract encourages entry at those points where the monopolist least wants it, and bars entry at those points where the monopolist would welcome it. The contract is no more than a binding promise to engage in a predatory price war under circumstances where it cannot succeed.

We may conclude that deferred rebate contracts, which operate like United Shoe Machinery's leases (as they are conventionally understood), do not provide a means of barring entry, and nobody would enter one for that purpose. That being the case, it appears that the law has incorrectly analyzed such contracts and the United leasing system.

*   *   *   *

The concept of barriers to entry is badly misunderstood. We have seen that the confusion of natural barriers with artificial barriers has led to a number of mistaken decisions. It leads economists to suppose that ordinary market forces do not control the structure of industries, and hence to recommend governmental intervention or investigation. A final example—dozens could be chosen—is Mark Schupack's application of the ideas of Bain: [14]

Consider what a potential entrant to the automobile industry would have to face in order to successfully overcome the product differentiation barrier. It would have to undertake heavy advertising expenditures to woo consumers

---

* If the future series of payments for widgets and the rebate of $100 at the end were subjected to a discount at the interest rate, customers would be willing to switch to the entrant in years after year 5, making matters still worse for the monopolist.

away from other firms where they have already established some brand loyalty. It would have to spend money to differentiate its product successfully from closely related automobiles. It would have to undertake annual model changes. And perhaps most important, it would have to build a large nation-wide network of dealers who are pretty much committed to the new manufacturer's products.

This catalogue is intended to suggest that competition would not necessarily shape the structure of the automobile industry, that something artificial, something other than the efficiency of existing firms, keeps potential entrants out. Schupack might just as well have said: the new entrant would have to make an automobile with appealing features, change models to keep up with competition, spend money to inform consumers of what it had to sell, and find people who thought the car would sell well enough to make it profitable to retail and service the product. He might, with equal pertinence, have added that the entrant would also have to build a plant, hire engineers, sales experts, designers, accountants, lawyers, and managers, buy steel and fabric and paint, and so on. He actually says nothing more than that a new entrant would have to do the things other companies have found essential to please consumers. In that respect, there is no difference whatever between advertising or finding dealers and building a plant.

This is true of any and all industries. Where the product and its service are complex and expensive, it is natural that the entrant will have to do many complex and expensive things, and do them well, in order to succeed. These are natural barriers or costs of entry. To identify them is merely to make a descriptive statement, one that does not imply the propriety of invoking law to alter the size or behavior of firms already in the market.

The argument of this chapter in no way suggests that there are no artificial barriers to entry. It does suggest that the only artificial barriers of interest to antitrust are those capable of creation by private parties, and that such barriers are always instances of deliberate predation. The next two chapters deal with types of predation that may be employed either to block entry or to injure existing rivals. Unlike the faulty theory of entry barriers now in vogue, however, the possibility of predation does not require or justify such steps as prohibiting mergers or outlawing the vertical division of dealer territories. Prophylactic rules for predation are not justified, as we have seen, and the law should concern itself with entry blocking only in those instances where a deliberate attempt to block entry by means other than efficiency is proved.

17

Boycotts and Individual Refusals to Deal

$\mathbb{A}$NTITRUST has long attempted to deal with boycotts and with individual refusals to deal, but it has developed no satisfactory theory with respect to either. We shall examine each of these phenomena in turn, in an effort to discern the criteria upon which useful theory can be built.

BOYCOTTS

According to conventional wisdom, boycotts (or agreements among competitors to refuse to deal) are illegal per se. But that proposition is easily shown to be false. Many agreements not to deal with others are perfectly lawful, and will certainly remain so, because they are indispensable to the conduct of the businesses involved. The categories of lawful and unlawful boycotts have never been defined, however, so that the law makes many mistakes and does much harm.

The belief that all boycotts are illegal per se rests upon an uncritical acceptance of repeated Supreme Court pronouncements to that effect. A case often cited as the final victory of the per se rule in this area is

Klor's, Inc. v. *Broadway-Hale Stores, Inc.,*[1] but as we shall see, the case cannot be read as holding that all agreements not to deal are illegal. No matter how sweeping its language, *Klor's* will not be applied that way in the future.

According to the Klor's complaint, the defendant Broadway-Hale operated a chain of department stores, one of which was located next door to Klor's. The two stores competed in the sales of various household appliances. Klor's alleged that Broadway-Hale demanded that manufacturers and distributors of such well-known brands as General Electric, RCA, Admiral, Zenith, and Emerson either not sell to Klor's or sell to it on unfavorable terms. The manufacturers and distributors were alleged to have agreed with one another and with Broadway-Hale to comply with these demands. Affidavits showed that there were "hundreds of other household appliance retailers, some within a few blocks of Klor's, who sold many competing brands of appliances, including those the defendants refused to sell to Klor's." The district court thought these facts made out no violation of the law and granted defendants' motion for summary judgment.[2] The court reasoned that there was no injury to the public, the dispute being a "purely private quarrel." The Court of Appeals for the Ninth Circuit affirmed, stating that "a violation of the Sherman Act requires conduct of defendants by which the public is or conceivably may be ultimately injured."[3]

The Supreme Court reversed. Justice Black's opinion discussed the category of restraints illegal per se and said, "Group boycotts, or concerted refusals by traders to deal with other traders, have long been held to be in the forbidden category." Turning to the pleadings, the opinion continued:

Plainly the allegations of this complaint disclose such a boycott. . . . This combination takes from Klor's its freedom to buy appliances in an open competitive market and drives it out of business as a dealer in defendants' products. It deprives the manufacturers and distributors of their freedom to sell to Klor's at the same prices and conditions made available to Broadway-Hale and in some instances forbids them from selling to it on any terms whatsoever. It interferes with the natural flow of interstate commerce. It clearly has, by its "nature" and "character," a "monopolistic tendency." As such it is not to be tolerated merely because the victim is just one merchant whose business is so small that his destruction makes little difference to the economy. Monopoly can as surely thrive by the elimination of such small businessmen, one at a time, as it can by driving them out in large groups.

This argument is not, of course, strong enough to carry the case. The statement that Klor's was driven from the sale of certain appliances is one of fact, and does not indicate the significance of that fact for a policy about market competition. That the suppliers were deprived of freedom is also a truism; that was the purpose of their agreement, as it is the purpose of all agreements. And one cannot take seriously the suggestion that the boycott of Klor's was the first step in a march to retail monopoly. Not only was the action taken too trivial for any such interpretation, and the prospects of success infinitesimal, but the manufacturers and distributors would certainly not acquiesce in any scheme which would replace a set of competitive customers with a monopsonist. If the decision is to find justification in antitrust terms, it must be because the boycott contained, so far as we can tell, no possibility of efficiency and did deprive consumers of an outlet they had shown they wanted. To remove Klor's artificially was to move the distribution pattern further from the optimal. The decision can thus perhaps be defended on consumer welfare grounds.*

But one would not be justified in concluding from the unqualified language of *Klor's* that all boycotts are really unlawful. They are not, and it is certain that they never will be. The reason is easily seen.

Agreements to refuse to deal are essential to the effectiveness and sometimes to the existence of many wholly beneficial economic activities. All league sports from the Ivy League to the National Football League, an increasingly wider spectrum, rest entirely upon the right to boycott. Members of the league agree not to play with nonmembers or to limit the number of games with nonmembers. Were leagues denied the power to enforce such agreements, they would have to admit any and all applicants, regardless of qualifications or the manageable size of the league. No court is likely to hold that every sandlot team in America is given a right by the Sherman Act to play baseball in the American League. The league would be destroyed. For the same reason, a court of appeals held in *Deesen* v. *Professional Golfers' Assn.*[4] that a player with rather poor scores could lawfully be deprived of his status as an approved tournament player and thus excluded from further tournament participation. And *Molinas* v. *National Basketball Assn.*[5] held that a league could adopt and enforce a rule prohibiting any of its teams from employing a player suspended for gambling.

Examples from sports make the point most clearly, but boycotts are essential elsewhere as well. When a group of lawyers, conventionally

---

* An alternative explanation which would cast doubt on the decision is that the case involved the "free rider" problem, i.e., Broadway-Hale may have been providing advertising, promotion, and information, while Klor's provided none but, being next door, used lower prices to capture the customers Broadway-Hale had attracted.

known as a firm or partnership, refuses to hire an applicant or turns down a prospective client, there is an agreement to refuse to deal by persons perfectly capable of acting individually. An agreement by screw manufacturers to standardize sizes is an agreement to refuse to deal except upon stated terms. Neither of these is likely to be held unlawful per se.

The explanation for the legality of these group refusals to deal is that they benefit consumers by enhancing the efficiency of the organizations adopting them. Unless, therefore, we redefine "boycott" and "concerted refusal to deal" to mean only those agreements that harm consumers, it must be true, as James Rahl has said, that "any comprehensible per se rule for boycotts is . . . out of the question." [6]

Unfortunately, antitrust courts have failed to generalize the principle that necessarily underlies cases like *Deesen* and *Molinas*. Only the most obvious efficiencies are recognized as justifications for boycotts; other efficiencies are ignored and hence destroyed by law. This inconsistency in the law is illustrated by the decision in *United States* v. *Nationwide Trailer Rental System*.[7] NTRS was an organization of trailer rental operators created to facilitate the movement of trailers rented for one-way trips between cities. Membership was limited to one operator per city, and members exchanged trailers only with each other. The district court held it unlawful per se for NTRS to refuse admission to competitors of members. The Supreme Court affirmed summarily,[8] despite the argument that "when persons who build up, by advertising and sales effort, a valuable organization must share that property with every newcomer who applies, it must be obvious that there will be no incentive for further membership or investment in such an organization." [9] It was thus unlawful to achieve an important business efficiency by refusing to deal with more than one operator per city.

The district court also held illegal per se the general power conferred upon NTRS's board of directors by its bylaws to expel members when "necessary to keep this System out of legal entanglements or to preserve the good name and business of the System." The court applied the rule of per se illegality because this provision constituted the power to order a boycott.

The paradox of the case is that the court, apparently without perceiving any contradiction, then provided the power to order boycotts by its own decree. The decree stated that membership could be conditioned upon the applicant's agreement to meet its financial obligations and to maintain safety standards. The expulsion of members who failed to keep those agreements was approved. The court's decree thus belied the court's insistence that boycotts are illegal per se. Boycotts were permissi-

ble when the court approved their purposes. The approved purposes—
maintenance of financial integrity and safety standards—related to the
efficient functioning of the NTRS system. The difficulty is that the court
gave no explanation of why one system efficiency is more worthy than
another. Once more, this time in the context of boycott law, a court was
unable fully to exclude the demands of efficiency but equally unwilling
to achieve consistency by giving efficiency full weight.

A comparison of *Klor's* and *NTRS* suggests that boycotts are likely
to be predatory when the parties are engaged in no other joint economic
activity, and may be efficiency-creating when they are. Which is to
suggest further that the dichotomy between naked and ancillary restraints
has application here, too. To draw once more on the insights of Judge
Taft in *Addyston Pipe & Steel* (and to parallel the argument already
offered with respect to horizontal price fixing and market division),
analysis indicates that per se illegality should be reserved for naked boycotts, those not accompanying a lawful joint economic endeavor. When
a boycott is found in the context of lawful joint behavior, it is not
automatically lawful, for the law must still be satisfied that the restraint
is aimed at creating efficiency rather than destroying or coercing rivals
by means that do not benefit consumers. Boycotts that enhance efficiency
may be called ancillary, while those that accompany a joint endeavor
but are actually predatory may be called disguised naked boycotts.

NAKED BOYCOTTS

Since the naked boycott is a form of predatory behavior, there is little
doubt that it should be a per se violation of the Sherman Act. But it may
be useful to indicate why the naked boycott may be a successful form of
predation. The sine qua non of predation, as we have seen, is the ability
to impose greater costs upon one's victim than upon oneself—greater,
that is, in proportion to the parties' respective reserves. An illustration
of how that may be possible in a boycott context is provided by the
reported facts of *Eastern States Retail Lumber Dealers' Assn.* v. *United
States.*[10]

The members of the association in *Eastern States* circulated lists of
lumber wholesalers who sold directly to consumers. The purpose of the
circulation, the trial court found, was to induce retailers to refuse to
deal with such wholesalers, and so coerce them to leave the consumer
market to retailers. Under certain circumstances this might conceivably
be a successful tactic. Suppose that in a particular geographic market
there are ten wholesalers and a hundred retailers. The wholesalers do not

find it economical to integrate fully into retailing, but one wholesaler finds it profitable to sell directly to a few large, lucrative consumer accounts. To see the effect of a retailer boycott of that wholesaler, we may assume, for simplicity's sake, that previously each wholesaler sold in equal proportions to each retailer. This pattern of distribution is presumably optimal. Though the wholesaler may very probably induce ten retailers to continue to deal with him, the disruption of his optimal distribution pattern may inflict costs equal to those borne by the boycotting retailers as a group. The outcome will depend, among other things, on the size of the additional costs and the reserves available to the parties. The retailers, collectively, having a larger market share, may have larger reserves than the single wholesaler. The predatory retailers have not had to increase output or cut prices to achieve their result. The wholesaler cannot raise prices to cover the added costs because his retailers would switch to other wholesalers. Under such conditions, the victimized wholesaler may decide to give up selling directly to consumers.

This analysis suggests only that some boycotts may be successful. Obviously, many will not. Success will depend on a number of factors, including the alternatives open to the boycotted party, the cohesiveness and fighting spirit of the boycotting group, and the significance of the cost increase.

I expect that most predatory boycotts of this type are utterly ineffective because too many participants will find it in their interest to break ranks. The analysis of Chapter 7 reinforces that belief. The boycotting group would have to control 80 or 90 percent of the market to have any chance of success, and the losses the group accepts as well as inflicts through disruption of the distribution pattern must not only be substantial but must be proportionally larger for the victim than for the group if the victim's reserves are to be exhausted before the group begins to suffer defections. These preconditions for successful predation by naked boycott seem very unlikely to exist. Probably most such boycotts reflect trade association politics and evanescent bravado more than they do serious threats to competition. But since such behavior carries no possible benefit to consumers, the law is probably correct in outlawing all naked boycotts, regardless of their prospects for success.

DISGUISED NAKED BOYCOTTS

The fact that a boycott appears as a regulation of a cooperative group, such as an exchange or board of trade, is not, as already noted, any guarantee that it is ancillary to the legitimate economic efforts of that group. Where a boycott or other restraint is employed by such a group, the law should investigate to determine its relationship to efficiency. We have seen, in Chapter 7, that the restraint enforced by boycott in *Chicago Board of Trade* was very likely a predatory attempt to destroy the superior efficiency of certain traders. At least that is a tenable hypothesis, while the claims of efficiency arising from the restraint itself advanced by Justice Brandeis do not withstand analysis.

The threat of boycott is likely to be particularly effective in the case of cooperating groups because a group often creates an economy of scale to which any firm must have access in order to be profitable. A trader excluded from the Chicago Board of Trade, a broker excluded from the stock exchange, or a professional football team turned out of its league is likely to have a very hard time of it. The alternatives are far fewer than those available to the victim of a naked boycott, such as the wholesale lumber dealer in *Eastern States*.

But the law need not experience any great difficulty in penetrating the disguise of predatory boycotts in group effort contexts. Once the issue is put in efficiency terms by the courts, the probing of counsel will disclose the purpose and effect of most restraints. Examples of the proper handling of the problem are found in *United States* v. *Southwestern Greyhound Lines, Inc.*,[11] and *Gamco Inc.* v. *Providence Fruit and Produce Building, Inc.*[12] Each involved the predatory use of an economy of scale.

In *Southwestern Greyhound* the defendant interstate bus companies jointly operated a bus terminal in Tulsa, Oklahoma. One of their tenants, a local bus operator, entered into arrangements with another line that converted the tenant into a through interstate carrier offering greater competition to the defendants. Defendants applied several restrictions to this tenant and ultimately evicted it from the terminal. Because it had to use separate and poorer facilities, the evicted company was hurt financially and might have been forced from business. There was no general obligation upon defendants to accept any bus company as a tenant in their terminal, but the court had no difficulty in perceiving the connection between the evicted tenant's increased competition and the eviction. Violations of both Section 1 and Section 2 of the Sherman Act were found.

Gamco presented a similar situation. Plaintiff Gamco purchased fruit and vegetables in truck and freight-car lots from interstate dealers for sale to the bulk jobbers and retailers of Providence, Rhode Island. It leased space in the Produce Building, where the wholesalers of the city operated. (Alternative facilities close to the railroad track did not exist but might have been developed at considerable expense.) The building was owned by a corporation whose stock was held by other wholesalers. Gamco ran into financial difficulties and was refused renewal of its lease. Though Gamco shortly thereafter became affiliated with a Boston whole-sale dealer, the board of directors of the building corporation continued to refuse renewal of the lease; ultimately, they instituted suit in the state courts to have Gamco ejected. Plaintiff lost its antitrust suit in the district court but won a reversal in the Court of Appeals for the First Circuit. That court handled the issue in a manner suitable to disguised naked boycott cases:

Admittedly the finite limitations of the building itself thrust monopoly power upon the defendants, and they are not required to do the impossible in accepting indiscriminately all who would apply. Reasonable criteria of selection, therefore, such as lack of available space, financial unsoundness, or possibly low business or ethical standards, would not violate the standards of the Sherman Antitrust Act. But the latent monopolist must justify the exclusion of a competitor from a market which he controls. Where, as here, a business group understandably susceptible to the temptations of exploiting its natural advantage against competitors prohibits one previously acceptable from hawking his wares beside them any longer at the very moment of his affiliation with a potentially lower priced outsider, they may be called upon for a necessary explanation. . . . Defendants thus had the duty to come forward and justify Gamco's ouster. This they failed to do save by a suggestion of financial unsoundness obviously hollow in view of the fact that the latter's affiliation with Sawyer & Co. put it in a far more secure credit position than it had enjoyed even during its legal tenancy.

As *Southwestern Greyhound* and *Gamco* illustrate, predatory boycotts engaged in by members of a joint venture are relatively easy to spot. There will usually be a precipitating event whose temporal relation to the boycott will shift the burden of persuasion to the group. Even where there is no such event, the terms of the boycott, to whom it is applied and to whom not, will demonstrate its purposes. There is little reason to fear, therefore, that any significant number of disguised naked boycotts will manage to pass muster as truly ancillary boycotts.

ANCILLARY BOYCOTTS

An ancillary boycott, of course, is a concerted refusal to deal that contributes to the efficiency of a cooperative economic activity. As already suggested, certain boycotts are essential to the conduct of league sports, tournaments, and similar activities. The law must develop doctrine to accommodate such boycotts. The need for such doctrine is, however, by no means confined to sports. We have seen that cooperating groups like NTRS require the right to boycott and that the court partially recognized that need, albeit without doctrinal justification.

There is no need here to discuss at length the efficiencies of ancillary boycotts, for the subject is very similar to ancillary price fixing and market division. Boycotts are the means used to enforce such other efficiency-producing restraints. Thus, the group of bedding manufacturers in *Sealy* [13] could be viewed as having agreed to boycott (by not licensing) applicants in the territories already assigned to members of the group. The same observation may be made of the retail grocery chains in *Topco*.[14] In such cases one must look to the underlying restraint in order to learn the efficiency potential of the boycott. The only point to be insisted upon here is that some boycotts are obviously indispensable (just as some price fixing or market division is indispensable). That being the case, there is no reason for the law not to recognize the entire principle involved, and to accept as lawful as well all boycotts that are merely beneficial.

THREE DOUBTFUL CASES

Present law prevents courts from making the examination required to learn whether a boycott is predatory or efficient. With respect to some of the most celebrated cases, therefore, we simply do not know whether the law has done more harm than good. Three examples may suffice. These are the Supreme Court's decisions in *Fashion Originators' Guild of America* v. *Federal Trade Commission*,[15] *Associated Press* v. *United States*,[16] and *Silver* v. *New York Stock Exchange*.[17] It is impossible to tell from the opinions of the Court whether these cases reached the right result.

Fashion Originators' Guild involved a trade organization whose member firms performed various functions related to women's garments. Some were engaged in design, manufacture, sale, or distribution of the garments, while others made, dyed, or converted the textiles from which the garments were constructed. The garment manufacturers claimed to be creators of original and distinctive dress designs, and the textile manufacturers claimed to create similarly original fabric designs. Other manufacturers, not members of the Guild, systematically copied these designs and sold their copied dresses at lower prices. The Guild members agreed to boycott retail stores that sold such dresses.

The Supreme Court viewed the boycott as an attempt to suppress the competition offered by the copyists, and it is quite possible that the purpose of the Guild was predatory in this sense. There is, however, an alternative possibility that might have been explored. It is conceivable that the Guild members were seeking to obtain the advertising and promotional advantages that exclusive dealing confers, and such an object ought not to be illegal.

A single garment manufacturer may advertise and may also wish his retailers to engage in in-store sales and promotional effort. Such activities are likely to prove ineffective if his retailers also sell lower-priced copies. Many retailers may, in fact, use the manufacturer's higher-priced garments as little more than displays in order to sell the other garments. A problem like that of the "free ride" arises. Thus, the manufacturer may turn to an exclusive dealing policy to ensure that his advertising inures to his own benefit and that retailers will be motivated to provide the in-store sales effort he desires.

There may, however, be disparities in the optimal scales of operation in manufacturing and retailing, so that no one manufacturer can offer a sufficiently complete line of garments to enable retailers to deal exclusively with him. One solution may be to aggregate manufacturers of garments of the same general type and price range, to provide retailers with the necessary variety of products. The insistence of the group that copies not be sold by their retailers may look like predation directed at the copyists, but it may be nothing more than an attempt to gain the efficiencies of advertising and promotion that lead to exclusive dealing in many industries. Whether or not this was the explanation of the boycott in *Fashion Originators' Guild* I do not know, but the possibility of explanations such as this ought not to be overlooked in future cases that bear a similar aspect.

The Supreme Court's disposition of the *Associated Press* case was more clearly mistaken, for the factual investigation required by the issues pleaded was never carried out. Associated Press, a cooperative association engaged in the collection, assembly, and distribution of news, had as members at the time of the government's action against it the publishers of more than 1,200 newspapers. AP's bylaws, the focus of the government's displeasure, prohibited members from supplying news to non-members and granted each member the power to block its rivals from obtaining membership. The bylaws thus gave each member the ability to invoke a boycott of its rivals by other AP members.

The Supreme Court's affirmance of the trial court's grant of summary judgment for the government remains incomprehensible to this day. The defendants had denied every material allegation of the complaint, including the allegations of wrongful intent, market power, and anti-competitive effect. They would seem, therefore, to have been entitled to a trial. Though the rhetorical force of Justice Black's opinion for the majority is considerable, that force is ultimately illegitimate, because it is gained by assuming intentions, powers, and effects that were not proved and were controverted. Justice Robert's analytical dissent demonstrates these points conclusively.

The issues raised by the *Associated Press* opinion are too many for review here, but two themes merit notice. These are the majority's confusion over the meaning of "competition" and its hostility to efficiency.

Justice Black's opinion rests in large measure on his insistence that, as the district court had found, AP's bylaws were "plainly designed in the interest of preventing competition." He appeared to think that sufficient to make the bylaws illegal on their face. But the observation advances the argument not at all. What the bylaws showed on their face was a design to prevent competition in the offering of AP news, which is not at all the same as a design to prevent general competition in the distribution of news. Perhaps AP's power was so great that a denial of access to AP news had the effect of suppressing competition generally, but that was the precise issue defendants wanted to try and Justice Black said need not be tried. Yet without proof of market control, the AP bylaws could not be distinguished from any other exclusive dealing arrangement, including arrangements whose legality Justice Black conceded—the exclusive contract of a reporter with a newspaper, and the exclusive interchange of news between two newspapers. The *Associated Press* decision rests largely, then, on a confusion between two meanings of "competition." Justice Black improperly equated the word with access to a particular source of supply rather than with effectiveness of rivalry in the general marketplace. Justice Roberts's dissent attempted unsuccessfully to shift the discussion back to the correct view of the problem:

Are the members of AP acting together with the *purpose* of destroying competition? I have not discovered any allegation in the complaint to that effect. The court below has not made any such finding. They deny any such purpose or intent. . . . [Emphasis in the original.]

The majority opinion is no more satisfactory on the topic of efficiency. Expressing hostility to efficiency as the result of cooperation between legally separate firms, a hostility that continues in the law to the present, Justice Black argued:

The Sherman Act was specifically intended to prohibit independent businesses from becoming "associates" in a common plan which is bound to reduce their competitors' opportunity to buy or sell the things in which the groups compete. Victory of a member of such a combination over its business rivals achieved by such collective means cannot consistently with the Sherman Act or with practical, everyday knowledge be attributed to *individual* "enterprise and sagacity"; such hampering of business rivals can only be attributed to that which really makes it possible—the collective power of an unlawful combination. [Emphasis in the original.]

The passage opens with an assertion that is simply wrong. There is nothing, specific or otherwise, in the text or the legislative history of the Sherman Act that prohibits cooperation by separate economic entities in the production of a commodity or service and a subsequent refusal to sell it to persons or firms outside the group. If there were, partnerships, exclusive dealing arrangements, and league sports would be per se illegal. If there were, Justice Black could not have conceded the legality of an exclusive exchange of news between two newspapers or between a reporter and a newspaper.

The Justice was objecting to superiority gained through economic cooperation, a principle that, applied consistently, would make the existence of any firm or corporation a sin against the law. In the end, Justice Black was forced to assume the conclusion he sought to prove, for he said victory of such a group in the marketplace was due to "the collective power of an unlawful combination." But the unlawfulness of the combination was the point to be established. The real question—and the *Associated Press* opinion never addresses it, or even recognizes it— was whether the exclusivity of membership tended to make possible efficiencies of operation * or merely injured rivals for the purpose of establishing local monopolies.

Perhaps the reason that question was not addressed is that the opinion displays hostility to the very concept of efficiency. Defendants may have lost the case when they admitted that membership in AP gave a "competitive advantage." One would suppose that to be self-evident. Why would any firm pay for any exclusive right unless it derived an advantage related to business and hence to competition? A confession of "competitive advantage" did not necessarily admit more than that, and yet Justice Black, who claimed not to be erecting a rule of per se il-

---

* Exclusivity may have been designed to encourage local papers to put stories on the AP wire promptly, without fear that a local competitor, also an AP member, would obtain a free ride by being able to print the news as rapidly as the paper that developed it.

legality for exclusive arrangements, made this the crux of the bylaws' illegality:

> It is apparent that the exclusive right to publish news in a given field, furnished by AP and all of its members, gives many newspapers a competitive advantage over their rivals. Conversely, a newspaper without AP service is more than likely to be at a competitive disadvantage.

This particular word magic has become more familiar today in the context of merger litigation under amended Section 7 of the Clayton Act. *Associated Press* demonstrates that the Court's aversion to efficiency is older than amended Clayton 7 and transcends statutory bounds.

The Court did not destroy AP. It required that membership be open to competitors of existing members. Perhaps the decision stands for the proposition that efficiency is lawful so long as there is a means by which the law can require that it be shared. Where it cannot be shared, as in merger cases, the cause of the efficiency must be destroyed. Both propositions suggest that one of the first principles of Court-made antitrust is not consumer welfare but producer egalitarianism.

The Court's *Silver* decision is troublesome for the same reasons as *Fashion Originators' Guild* and *Associated Press* but manages to incorporate some additional grounds for unease. Silver's firms were dealers in municipal bonds and corporate over-the-counter securities. They were not members of the New York Stock Exchange, but Silver arranged private direct telephone wire connections with a number of member and nonmember firms. Pursuant to NYSE rules, all but one of the member firms applied for Exchange approval of these connections. "Temporary approval" was granted for them, and also for a direct teletype connection to a member firm and stock ticker service from the floor of the Exchange. Some months later, however, the Exchange disapproved these arrangements, directed its members to discontinue the wire connections, and notified Silver of termination of the stock ticker service. The Exchange refused to disclose its reasons, and Silver resorted to the Sherman Act.

The Court's opinion, by Justice Goldberg, began with the formula recited in the prior cases:

> It is plain, to begin with, that removal of the wires by collective action of the Exchange and its members would, had it occurred in a context free from other federal regulation [the Securities Exchange Act of 1934], constitute a *per se* violation of § 1 of the Sherman Act. The concerted action of the Exchange and its members here was, in simple terms, a group boycott depriving petitioners of a valuable business service which they needed in order to compete effectively as broker-dealers in the over-the-counter securities market.

This formulation of the law is, as we have seen, impossibly severe. The NYSE is a joint economic endeavor, and there must be *some* circumstances under which it can order its members to refuse to deal, even without the justification of other federal regulation. The Court can hardly mean, for example, that an exchange must award seats to all who wish them, no matter what. If it did entertain any such rule, the Court should not have refused review of *Deesen* but should have granted certiorari and summarily reversed the Ninth Circuit's judgment in favor of the PGA.

But in *Silver* the Court permitted the NYSE's obligation to pursue the goals of federal securities regulation to play the role that I have suggested the presence of a lawful joint venture should play. If the restraint was ancillary (the Court did not use that terminology) to the obligation, it might be lawful. Yet the NYSE lost the case—not because its boycott was not ancillary (that was not discussed), but because Silver had not been given the equivalent of a due process hearing by the Exchange.

Given the principle that exchange self-regulation is to be regarded as justified in response to antitrust charges only to the extent necessary to protect the achievement of the aims of the Securities Exchange Act, it is clear that no justification can be offered for self-regulation conducted without provision for some method of telling a protesting non-member why a rule is being invoked so as to harm him and allowing him to reply in explanation of his position.

The question arises whether the *Silver* requirement of a due process hearing is applicable to those cases where courts in fact permit boycotts by members of joint ventures. The further question arises of who bears the burden of persuasion in such hearings. The idea of a due process hearing is always attractive to many people, a fact which accounts for the judicialization of an increasing number of relationships in our society, but it seems misplaced in the context of joint ventures and business organizations. The member or nonmember who suspects that he has been improperly dealt with can always get his hearing by a court action. If the group must give him one before the action is brought, a great many normal business judgments will be defeated simply because of the added costs of making decisions. It is particularly important, if hearings are required, that the complainant bear the burden of persuasion, since refusals to deal are often based on intuitions and judgments of degree that are difficult to prove. The absence of a proved illegal motive should suffice for exoneration.

Perhaps the *Silver* case, limited to a regulatory context, is not too serious, though one wonders why the Exchange was held liable for damages for not complying with an antitrust requirement that was yet to be formulated. But the logical extension of the doctrine to all group refusals to deal—or, indeed, to individual refusals to deal—would impose serious efficiency costs. The refusal of a joint venture to explain the grounds for a boycott to the injured party may properly be considered as evidence of intent in doubtful cases, but the courts certainly ought not to make a due process hearing within all joint ventures the sine qua non of all lawful refusals to deal.

INDIVIDUAL REFUSALS TO DEAL

In some ways, individual refusals to deal are more difficult to analyze than boycotts. Present law leaves the individual firm free to refuse to deal with others, unless the refusal is intended to support another illegal restraint or constitutes an attempt to monopolize. The presumption of freedom seems appropriate to a free market economy. Indeed, that presumption should be broader than it is, since, as already argued, many practices the law now bans should be lawful.

Problems arise primarily with respect to monopolization by refusal to deal, since it is often hard to distinguish such cases from lawful demands for exclusive dealing arrangements. Two cases that may usefully be contrasted are *Lorain Journal Co.* v. *United States* [18] and *Packard Motor Car Co.* v. *Webster Motor Car Co.*[19] They reach opposite results, both seem clearly correct, and yet it is rather difficult to articulate the distinction between them.

The *Journal*, a newspaper published in Lorain, Ohio, "enjoyed a substantial monopoly in Lorain of the mass dissemination of news and advertising, both of a local and national character." It had a 99 percent coverage of Lorain families. "Those factors," the Supreme Court said, "made the *Journal* an indispensable medium of advertising for many Lorain concerns." In 1948 the beginnings of a challenge to the *Journal*'s monopoly arose with the establishment of radio station WEOL in Elyria, Ohio, eight miles south of Lorain. The publisher responded by refusing to accept local advertisements in the *Journal* from any Lorain County advertiser who advertised over WEOL. The Supreme Court had no difficulty in perceiving an attempt to monopolize, illegal under Section 2 of the Sherman Act, in this refusal to deal. The decision seems entirely correct. The situation resembles that in the *Griffith* case, discussed in Chapter 7, but the decision does not involve the fallacy of double counting which flawed that decision. Here the *Journal* had an overwhelming market share and a clearly displayed predatory intent. There was no apparent efficiency justification for its conduct. To say that the predation might have succeeded does not mean that the extra concession extorted from its advertisers cost the *Journal* nothing. It must have, but the form of predation used did not require the expansion of output, and the *Journal,* with presumably larger reserves, could probably outlast WEOL. Moreover, the radio license, which the *Journal* had earlier unsuccessfully applied for, constituted a monopoly granted and protected by the government. If the *Journal* could bankrupt WEOL and gain the license, it would, as Ralph Winter has pointed out to me, have much better reason than most predators to hope to be secure from further entry into its market.

But compare the *Packard* case. There were three Packard dealers in Baltimore, of which Webster was one. In 1953 the largest of the three, Zell Motor Car Company, told Packard it was losing money and would quit unless Packard gave it an exclusive contract. Packard agreed, gave the other two dealers notice their contracts would not be renewed, and was sued by Webster both for monopolization and for conspiracy in restraint of trade. The jury returned a verdict for Webster, but on appeal the Court of Appeals for the District of Columbia Circuit reversed. The Sherman 2 monopolization charge was dismissed because there were other cars like Packard sold in Baltimore, so that an exclusive contract for selling Packards did not create a monopoly. That is troublesome, for it assumes the answer. If Zell acted with a wrongful intent, it must have thought there was a sufficiently separate demand for Packards in the area to make a monopoly of the market for that particular car worthwhile. We do not know whether that was the case or not, but we cannot safely dispose of the issue by asserting without evidence that there was no distinctive demand for Packards.

The court also reversed the finding of conspiracy in restraint of trade on grounds that seem uneasily metaphysical:

The fact that any other dealers in the same product of the same manufacturer are eliminated does not make an exclusive dealership illegal; it is the essential nature of the arrangement. The fact that Zell asked for the arrangement does not make it illegal. Since the immediate object of an exclusive dealership is to protect the dealer from competition in the manufacturer's product, it is likely to be the dealer who asks for it.

But how does the case differ from *Lorain Journal* or, for that matter, from *Klor's*? The instinct of the courts in all three cases seems correct (though not clearly so in *Klor's*), but the doctrinal justifications for the differences in outcome appear weak. The use of phrases like "exclusive dealing arrangement" or "attempt to monopolize" expresses a conclusion rather than an argument.

The distinction between the cases probably lies in the fact that the court was offered what was essentially an efficiency defense in *Packard* but not in the other two cases. Zell claimed it was losing money and would go out of business unless it was the sole outlet for Packards in Baltimore. Offered a choice, Packard preferred Zell alone to the other two dealers. Zell's explanation of its motivation was not successfully challenged, and the appeals court, on that state of the record, quite properly accepted it. *Klor's* displayed an attack on a particular store rather than a demand for exclusive dealing, and if there was an efficiency explanation for the behavior, apparently it was not given. *Lorain Journal* could be characterized as a demand for exclusive dealing, but again no efficiency defense was offered, and such a defense would have seemed implausible.

Probably this sort of rough separation is the best that can be done in cases of individual refusals to deal. Boycott cases are easier to deal with because the purposes of the group and the terms of the exclusion give greater guidance to the efficiency potential of the refusal to deal. Where an efficiency potential appears in a case involving an individual refusal to deal, and there is no clear evidence that the purpose of the refusal was predatory, courts should generally find the refusal lawful, both because of tie-breaker considerations and because predation by an individual refusal to deal will be very uncommon.

18

Predation Through Governmental Processes

PREDATION by abuse of governmental procedures, including administrative and judicial processes, presents an increasingly dangerous threat to competition. Antitrust law is beginning to catch up with it, but the criteria that are to govern this field are not yet fully formulated.

In the early years of antitrust policy there were fewer opportunities for monopolization through misuse of government because governmental regulation was not so pervasive as it is today. The last several decades have witnessed an enormous proliferation of regulatory and licensing authorities at every level of government, federal, state, and local. In order to enter the market and vie for consumers' favor, businesses of all types must gain various types of approval from governmental agencies, departments, and officials. Licensing authorities, planning boards, zoning commissions, health departments, building inspectors, public utilities commissions, and many other bodies and officials control and qualify the would-be competitor's access to the marketplace.

The modern profusion of such governmental authorities offers almost limitless possibilities for abuse. They range from outright bribery to much subtler forms of improper influence upon officials. We will focus here, however, primarily upon oppositions to market entry before administrative and judicial institutions. As a technique for predation, sham litigation is theoretically one of the most promising. Litigation, whether before an agency or a court, can often be framed so that the expenses to each party will be about the same. Indeed, if, as is usual, the party seeking to enter the market bears the burden of going forward with evidence, litigation expenses may be much heavier for him. Expenses in complex business litigation can be enormous, not merely in direct legal fees and costs but in the diversion of executive time and effort and in the disruption of the organization's regular activities. Thus, the firm resisting market entry through sham litigation can impose equal or greater costs upon the entrant and, if it has greater or even equal reserves, may be able to outlast the potential rival. This tactic is likely to find unqualified success only against smaller firms, since the costs of litigation must loom large relative to reserves if the firm is to be driven out. The tactic may be successful against larger firms if the costs are large relative to expected profits in a small market.

The predator need not expect to defeat entry altogether. He may hope only to delay it. Sham litigation then becomes a useful tactic against any size firm, regardless of relative reserves, for it may be worth the price of litigation to purchase a delay of a year or several years in a rival's entry into a lucrative market. In such cases, successful predation does not require that the predator be able to impose larger costs on the victim, that the predator have greater reserves than the victim, or that the predator have better access to capital than the victim. No other technique of predation is able to escape all of these requirements, and that fact indicates both the danger and the probability of predation by misuse of governmental processes.

This mode of predation is particularly insidious because of its relatively low antitrust visibility. The enforcement agencies have been preoccupied with the mythical dangers of mergers, vertical restraints, and price cutting. The fact that many battles fought before agencies like local zoning boards are designed to preclude market entry does not come to their attention. Since much of this predation occurs at local levels through misuse of state and municipal procedures, the victims are often small businessmen with no, or very little, idea of the possible protection afforded by the antitrust laws.

There is, of course, no way of estimating precisely how much competition is crippled or stifled each year through the abuse of governmental processes. However, the number of cases beginning to arise in this relatively new field of litigation (as well as some practical experience with local businessmen) leads one to believe that this form of predation may be common and that the aggregate annual loss to consumers may be very large. The antitrust laws can make a major con-

tribution both to free competition and to the integrity of administrativ
and judicial processes by catching up with this means of monopolization

The primary difficulty in the way of antitrust enforcement is the claim
by predators that they are merely exercising their First Amendment
rights to petition and to influence government. It is clear, moreover,
that some forms of predation are constitutionally protected on just such
grounds. But it is equally clear that many forms of such predation are
and must be reachable by law. We will first examine the Supreme Court
decisions that frame the issues.

THE CASE LAW

A zone of immunity from Sherman Act liability, or indeed from any
legal liability, is created by two cases, *Eastern Railroad Presidents Conference* v. *Noerr* [1] and *United Mine Workers* v. *Pennington*.[2] An area
of Sherman Act liability for the misuse of governmental processes is
created by three other cases, *Walker Process Equipment, Inc.* v. *Food
Machinery & Chemical Corp.*,[3] *California Motor Transport Co.* v. *Trucking Unlimited*,[4] and *Otter Tail Power Co.* v. *United States*.[5] The Supreme Court's opinions in these cases by no means completely clarify
the law and its criteria, but these decisions, each of which seems entirely
correct, provide the benchmarks for the law that is yet to be made.

Noerr involved a Sherman Act claim by forty-one Pennsylvania truck
operators and their trade association against twenty-four Eastern railroads, an association of the presidents of those roads, and a public relations firm. The complaint alleged that the railroads had hired the
public relations firm, as the opinion put it, "to conduct a publicity
campaign against the truckers designed to foster the adoption and re-
tention of laws and law enforcement practices destructive of the trucking business, to create an atmosphere of distaste for the truckers among
the general public, and to impair the relationships existing between the
truckers and their customers." The campaign involved both propa-
gandizing the general public and lobbying the Pennsylvania legislature.

The complaint alleged that the campaign was motivated solely by the
railroads' desire to injure the truckers and destroy them as competitors
in the long-distance freight business, and, further, that the publicity

matter was made to appear as the views of independent persons and civic groups, although it was produced by the public relations firm and paid for by the railroads. The truckers won a judgment from the trial court; the Court of Appeals for the Third Circuit affirmed, one judge dissenting.

A unanimous Supreme Court reversed. Justice Black's opinion for the Court began from the premise, established in *United States* v. *Rock Royal Co-op* [6] and *Parker* v. *Brown*,[7] that "where a restraint upon trade or monopolization is the result of a valid governmental action, as opposed to a private action, no violation of the Act can be made out." That premise is unassailable.* As Justice Black put it, "These decisions rest upon the fact that under our form of government the question whether a law of that kind should pass, or if passed be enforced, is the responsibility of the appropriate legislative or executive branches of government so long as the law itself does not violate some provisions of the Constitution."

From this premise it follows ineluctably, given our system of representative government, that attempts to persuade legislatures to adopt or retain particular laws or to persuade executive officers to adopt or retain particular enforcement policies cannot be punished. Of what use is democratic government if the people may not freely make known their desires to their representatives? Thus, Justice Black's opinion noted the "essential dissimilarity" between agreements jointly to seek legislation and law enforcement and agreements traditionally condemned by Section 1 of the Sherman Act. The application of the statute was conclusively barred when this element was considered along with two other factors. The first of these was that the application of the Sherman Act would "substantially impair the power of government to take actions

---

* It still seems so, despite the plurality opinion in *Cantor* v. *Detroit Edison Co.,* 428 U.S. 579 (1976), which appears to say that the exemption of private conduct permitted or even compelled by state regulation depends on a judicial determination that the exemption is necessary to make the regulations work. The Court was badly split over the appropriate rationale, offering at least four. The position taken in a concurring opinion by the Chief Justice, which may seem congenial because it is like the one I urged for the United States as amicus curiae, seems most useful for the law: the *Parker* exemption did not apply because the state was neutral with respect to the behavior in question and would "command" it or not as the regulated party chose. This approach preserves the power of the state to regulate, which the Sherman Act most certainly was not intended to deny; relieves federal judges of the inappropriate task of deciding whether the state needed to regulate particular conduct; prevents private parties from tucking anticompetitive behavior into regulatory schemes and gaining an exemption, though the state has no particular desire to compel the behavior; and tends to make regulatory agencies focus on what it is they are trying to achieve.

through its legislature and executive that operate to restrain trade." Representative government, the opinion noted, depends upon the ability of the people freely to inform their representatives of their wishes. Second, such an application of the statute would raise important constitutional issues, particularly the right to petition protected by the First Amendment.

It did not matter, therefore, that the political campaign operated by the railroads employed deception and misrepresentation, or that it had the effect of inflicting direct injury on the truckers. To hold that either of these factors removed the immunity demanded by the theory of representative government would be to cut too deeply into the political process and to chill the right of petition.

The *Noerr* case, however, did not say or imply that any attempt to get any governmental official to do anything was beyond the reach of the Sherman Act or other legal sanctions. The opinion stated:

> There may be situations in which a publicity campaign, ostensibly directed toward influencing governmental action, is a mere sham to cover what is actually nothing more than an attempt to interfere directly with the business relationships of a competitor and the application of the Sherman Act would be justified.

By speaking only of "valid" action by "appropriate" branches of government, Justice Black further qualified the immunity created. Those qualifications were built into his premise. And it was essential that they be built in. A realistic appreciation of the needs of government demands both that citizens have great latitude in making their views known and that governmental bodies not be misused to accomplish ends for which they were not designed and over which they have no legitimate authority.

Pennington held that antitrust liability does not attach to those who persuade an executive officer of government to take an action clearly within his lawful discretion. The conspirators persuaded the Secretary of Labor to establish a minimum wage for employees of contractors selling coal to the TVA. They also urged TVA officials to curtail spot market purchases, a substantial portion of which were exempt from the minimum wage order. The conspirators were UMW officials and certain large coal producers, and their purpose was to injure smaller coal operators. *Pennington* did not create a blanket immunity for all attempts to influence government officials. The case did not involve an official who acted outside the area of discretion confided to him. Justice White's opinion suggested another important qualification of the immunity created: "The conduct of the union and the operators did not violate the [Sherman] Act, the action taken to set a minimum wage for government purchases of coal was the act of *a public official who is not claimed to be a coconspirator.* . . . [Emphasis added]"

Noerr and *Pennington* were frequently represented, particularly by antitrust defendants, as establishing a rule of complete immunity for attempts to influence government. That, of course, was not and could not have been the case. These decisions did not address the question of what predation through governmental processes could be reached by law. Subsequent decisions have shed some, but not sufficient, light on this question.

In *Walker Process Equipment* the original plaintiff, Food Machinery, filed suit against Walker for infringement of a patent covering knee-action swing diffusers used in aeration equipment for sewage treatment systems. After pretrial discovery, Food Machinery moved to dismiss its own complaint because its patent had expired, but Walker amended its counterclaim for a declaratory judgment that the patent was invalid to state instead a claim under Section 2 of the Sherman Act. The amended counterclaim alleged that Food Machinery had illegally monopolized commerce by maintaining and enforcing a patent obtained by fraud on the Patent Office. Upon Food Machinery's motion to dismiss, both lower courts held that the counterclaim failed to state a claim upon which relief could be granted. The Supreme Court reversed, holding that "the enforcement of a patent procured by fraud on the Patent Office may be violative of §2 of the Sherman Act provided the other elements necessary to a §2 case are present." The crux of the case, therefore, was the knowing assertion of a baseless claim in court for the purpose of injuring a competitor.

Some commentators appear to suppose that *Walker* merely held that a fraud on the Patent Office is illegal, but that is a misreading of the decision. The significance of the fraud on the Patent Office was quite different. Food Machinery attempted to argue that the counterclaim was based on the wrongful procurement of the patent and, therefore, that Walker was attempting to have the patent canceled, something only the United States may accomplish by a lawsuit. Justice Clark's opinion for the Court rebutted that argument by showing that the fraud was significant only because it took the case outside the exception to Section 2 liability for those who enforce patents, valid or not, in good faith. Antitrust sanctions can hardly be applied to one who litigates his patent in good faith, even though the patent is ultimately held to be invalid. That would chill legitimate patent litigation.

The antitrust significance of the fraud, therefore, is simply that it showed Food Machinery to be litigating in bad faith. *Walker* is thus not a mere patent decision but an antitrust precedent of general applicability. It stands for the proposition that pressing claims known to be without foundation for the purpose of stifling competition is a violation of Section 2 of the Sherman Act.

This much was confirmed, though the law was not particularly clarified, by the Supreme Court's decision in *Trucking Unlimited*. Plaintiffs were fifteen trucking firms operating in California. Defendants were nineteen of the largest trucking firms in the state. The complaint alleged that defendants, discomfited by the increasing competition of smaller truckers, entered into a conspiracy to inhibit and deter that competition. They banded together to create a joint trust fund to be used in opposing all applications for operating rights by smaller trucking firms. Such opposition was to be pursued before all available courts, as well as before the California Public Utilities Commission and the Interstate Commerce Commission. Defendants, it was alleged, agreed to pursue their oppositions regardless of the merit of any application and regardless of the absence of any basis for opposition. To complete the intended terroristic effect of their scheme, defendants warned the smaller truckers that they had put the plan into operation and that the smaller truckers could avoid the costs that would be inflicted upon them only by refraining from asking for new operating rights.

The case came to the Supreme Court on the pleadings because the trial court had dismissed the complaint on the authority of *Noerr,* and the Ninth Circuit had reversed. Justice Douglas's opinion for the Court majority agreed that *Noerr* controlled, but not that it shielded the conspirators:

The same philosophy governs the approach of citizens or groups of them to administrative agencies (which are both creatures of the legislature, and arms of the executive) and to courts, the third branch of Government. Certainly the right to petition extends to all departments of the Government. The right of access to the courts is indeed but one aspect of the right of petition.

Remarking that *Noerr* had reserved the possibility of attaching liability to sham petitions or campaigns, however, Justice Douglas noted particularly the complaint's allegations that defendants harassed and deterred plaintiffs in their use of administrative and judicial proceedings. He made it plain that misrepresentation and unethical conduct are less allowable in adjudicatory than in legislative processes, and concluded:

First Amendment rights may not be used as the means or the pretext for achieving "substantive evils" . . . which the legislature has the power to control. . . . A combination of entrepreneurs to harass and deter their competitors from having "free and unlimited access" to the agencies and courts, to defeat that right by massive, concerted and purposeful activities of the group are ways of building up one empire and destroying another. . . . If these facts are proved, a violation of the antitrust laws has been established. If the end result is unlawful, it matters not that the means used in violation may be lawful.

Justice Douglas stated that the allegations in the case came within the "sham" exception of *Noerr,* as adapted to the adjudicatory process. The complaint upheld, the case was remanded for trial.

A concurring opinion by Justice Stewart found some of Justice Douglas's dicta overbroad, but favored remand for trial because

the [plaintiffs] are entitled to prove that the real *intent* of the conspirators was not to invoke the processes of the administrative agencies and courts, but to discourage and ultimately to prevent the [plaintiffs] from invoking those processes. Such an intent would make the conspiracy "an attempt to interfere directly with the business relationships of a competitor and the application of the Sherman Act would be justified."

The distinction between the majority and concurring opinions is not entirely clear, unless perhaps Justice Stewart was claiming that the *only* intent that would justify application of the Sherman Act to predatory litigation is an intent to keep the victims from employing administrative and judicial processes. Yet that seems unlikely. Certainly, in a proper case, a proved intent not to bar competitors from the courtroom but, by the litigation of baseless claims, to bar them from a market or to delay their entry should suffice for violation of the Sherman Act. The *Walker* decision holds as much, and there is no indication that *Trucking Unlimited* represents a retreat from *Walker.* On the contrary, the concurring Justices seemed to feel that the *Trucking Unlimited* majority was opening up broad new areas of liability.

The *Otter Tail Power* litigation indicates that the broad view of *Walker* is correct and that the argument of *Trucking Unlimited* did not portend a narrowed rationale. Otter Tail was an investor-owned electric utility that served small towns in Minnesota and the Dakotas. Occasionally, some of the towns would attempt to replace Otter Tail with municipal systems, and Otter Tail responded with a variety of tactics held to be monopolizations violative of Section 2 of the Sherman Act. Among these was the institution or sponsorship and financial support of litigation in order to frustrate the sale of revenue bonds to finance the municipal systems. The pendency of litigation prevented the marketing of the bonds because their successful sale depended upon "no litigation certificates." All of the litigation failed on the merits, except for one case in which it was held that Otter Tail lacked even standing to sue. The district court found that the delay occasioned by the litigation halted or appreciably slowed efforts for municipal ownership.

Otter Tail claimed the *Noerr* exemption, but the district court held that the exemption applied only to efforts to influence the legislative and executive branches and not to litigation in the courts. On direct appeal the Supreme Court remanded this aspect of the order for consideration in light of its intervening decision in *Trucking Unlimited.* Without taking further evidence, the district court found that "the repetitive use of litigation by *Otter Tail* was timed and designed principally to prevent the establishment of municipal electric systems," and that it therefore came "within the sham exception to the *Noerr* doctrine" as defined in *Trucking Unlimited.* This time the Supreme Court summarily affirmed the judgment. The significance of this is that there was no requirement that the municipalities must have been discouraged from using judicial processes, merely that the suits must have been filed "principally" to delay or halt competition.

CRITERIA FOR ANTITRUST ENFORCEMENT

The Court has not yet been required to provide this field of developing litigation with an overall structure, and it may be useful here to outline the criteria that seem relevant to the subject. Cases involving attempts to invoke governmental processes necessarily implicate profound values of a democratic system of government. But those values do not, as many commentators appear to believe, all press in one direction. There is the need, as *Noerr* fully recognized, that citizens have the widest latitude in bringing their views, information, and desires to the attention of their representatives. That need, of course, finds recognition and protection in the First Amendment to the Constitution. But there is also the correlative need that government be able to protect the integrity of its processes, that it be able to punish those who would abuse them. The power of government to do that is inherent and has never been doubted. It finds recognition not merely in cases such as *Walker*, decisions finding federal power to protect federal agents and functions,[8] but also in countless other ways, such as the power of governmental agencies to punish perjury and false affidavits, to summon witnesses, and so on.

Because there is a degree of tension between these constitutional values, the cases involving attempts to use governmental processes for private gain will lie along a spectrum from the completely punishable to the completely immune. To lump all cases under either category would deny the needs of government and the values protected by our Constitution. A number of considerations seem proper in placing various situations on the spectrum and determining the liability or immunity of those who misuse governmental procedures. I can offer no single bright line that disposes easily of all cases, dropping them neatly into one category or the other. Reflection suggests that no such line exists. But the factors that do control are sufficient to offer the degree of certainty and predictability the field requires.

The opinion by the Court of Appeals for the Ninth Circuit in *Trucking Unlimited* suggests that in considering attempts improperly to influence governmental bodies, a line should be drawn between those whose functions are essentially legislative or representational (in which latter category the court includes law enforcement officers) and those whose functions are essentially adjudicative. The appeals court decided that the need for uninhibited communication which *Noerr* perceived with respect to representational bodies or officials does not exist to the same extent with respect to adjudicative bodies. It noted that "there is a marked difference between the processes by which they arrive at decisions, the materials upon which they may properly rely, and the atmosphere consistent with the effective performance of their respective functions." [9]

There is much to this insight, though, as the Supreme Court held, not enough to remove the *Noerr* protection from litigation altogether. But perhaps the distinction may be refined and taken further. The nature of the governmental body is not alone the decisive factor—which is perhaps just as well, since there are many governmental bodies whose "nature" on the representative-adjudicative continuum it would be difficult to state with confidence.

We have a moderately well-defined law about misuse of courts to harm competition, but so far little that is authoritative about the misuse of other governmental bodies and processes for that purpose. It may be useful to speculate about the considerations which should govern the application of *Noerr* in a variety of governmental contexts, since, for the reasons given at the beginning of this chapter, it is desirable that antitrust should attack the predatory use of governmental processes with increased vigor.

The following five factors would appear to be prominent among those which should determine the liability of persons charged with improper attempts to employ the coercive powers of government for wrongful ends: (1) the intent of the parties; (2) the means employed; (3) the character of the governmental process involved; (4) the character of the decision to be made; and (5) the degree to which the process focuses upon the formulation of general rules or upon the specific rights or liabilities of particular parties. These five factors should usually be decisive. Obviously, not all of these factors need point to liability for that to be the proper result in a particular case. The attempt to bribe a legislator to vote for a general rule of law, for example, is clearly constitutionally punishable under an appropriate statute, even though the setting is legislative and the rights of a specific person are not directly involved.

THE INTENT OF THE PARTIES

Liability will usually attach only if the parties attempting to use government for their own ends have a specific intent which would render their behavior unlawful had they chosen other means of accomplishing their ends. When the sanctions invoked against such persons arise from the antitrust laws, there must be an intent to suppress competition by the destruction or harassment of business rivals. But a specific intent, in the sense of an ultimate purpose which is wrongful, will not be essential in all types of cases. Sometimes the employment of wrongful means, the factor to be discussed next, will suffice. Thus, one who commits perjury or attempts to bribe an official may be punished even though his ultimate purpose, the result he seeks, may be described as laudable. For antitrust cases, however, it is difficult to imagine a situation in which a specific intent to monopolize or restrain trade would not be an essential element of the case.

Though I have argued in Chapter 7 that a rule against predatory price cutting is too vague and, when applied, will suppress competitive pricing, an analogous danger does not attach to rules against predatory litigation. Analysis and experience indicate, for one thing, that very little (if any) predation is accomplished through pricing, while a good deal is achieved through litigation. Thus, the benefits of a rule are far greater in the latter case. Judges, moreover, have far more experience with and understanding of litigation than of economics and business behavior. They are far less likely to make mistakes about the former.

In any event, the distinction between legitimate and predatory litigation is not that difficult to make. The *Trucking Unlimited* defendants, for example, attempted to wrap the cloak of the First Amendment about their agreement to advance baseless claims before courts and administrative tribunals. It was a very poor fit. It is necessarily incongruous when commercial predators attempt to rely on such cases as *NAACP* v. *Button*,[10] *Brotherhood of Railroad Trainmen* v. *Virginia*,[11] *United Mine Workers* v. *Illinois State Bar Association*,[12] and *United Transportation Union* v. *State Bar of Michigan*.[13] If *Button* had been interpreted as broad enough to control *Trucking Unlimited*, every abuse of the procedures of courts and administrative tribunals would be "political expression" and sanctified.

In *Button* the NAACP had organized in order to advance the constitutional rights of Negroes in the federal courts, as well as to see that Negroes' legal rights were protected in practice. That purpose was held essentially "political," and the state was unable to interfere with it through laws about the relationship of lawyers and their clients. *Button* fell within the area protected by the First and Fourteenth amendments to the Constitution.

There was no way the *Trucking Unlimited* defendants could make their alleged conduct look like the conduct of the NAACP in *Button*. They were not organized to advance legitimate constitutional claims, nor was their purpose to protect the procedural rights of large truckers to fair trials. To make *Button* resemble that case, one would have to change its facts completely and imagine that the NAACP had decided to advance the welfare of Negroes by threatening the white employers in an area with continual lawsuits, whether there was a valid claim or not, until, from sheer economic coercion, the employers agreed to practice reverse job discrimination and to pay blacks more than whites. That abuse of judicial processes, involving the advancing of baseless claims in order to destroy and coerce people economically, would certainly not have merited or received the constitutional protection that was in fact accorded to the legitimate use of litigation in *NAACP* v. *Button*.

Reliance upon the labor union cases was equally misplaced. The Court had held only that workers had a right to band together to obtain competent legal counsel to press their claims. There was not a breath of a suggestion in those cases that they had a First Amendment right to band together to press baseless claims for the ulterior purpose of making employers give way on wage bargaining.

Access to judicial and administrative processes may be a constitutional right, but there is no constitutional right to make deliberate misrepresentations to such tribunals or to press baseless claims for the ulterior purpose of wreaking economic injury upon a competitor. *Button* and the labor union cases would have come out differently if that had been what they involved.

THE MEANS EMPLOYED

Regardless of intent, parties can be held liable only if they employ means of influencing governmental action that are in themselves illegal or reprehensible. The *Trucking Unlimited* defendants were alleged deliberately to have agreed to press baseless oppositions to applications for operating rights before courts and before administrative tribunals, and they were alleged to have done what they agreed to do. Had they employed other means (e.g., individually opposing applicants only where the defendant in opposition had reasonable cause for his position), there could have been no Sherman Act liability. Similarly, the knowing use of perjured testimony or the bribery of an executive officer would subject the party engaging in such conduct to liability.

The use of illegal or reprehensible means of influencing government is perhaps a necessary condition for liability, but it is not a sufficient one. *Noerr* demonstrates the truth of that proposition. The railroads there employed tactics that were certainly unethical, including the formation of sham citizens groups which put out as their own product the statements and material that had actually been prepared by the railroads and their public relations agency. These misrepresentations were immunized, however, because they occurred in an explicitly political context. Thus, the character of the process in which the use of reprehensible tactics occurs affects the question of liability. We turn to this factor next.

THE CHARACTER OF THE GOVERNMENTAL PROCESS

The more open, informal, and explicitly political is the governmental process the conspirators use, the greater is the scope of their immunity for reprehensible tactics intended to injure or destroy rivals. The *Noerr* case dealt with the employment of a completely political process, and the conspirators' immunity was therefore complete. Even the use of misrepresentations was held not to destroy immunity, and that decision was clearly demanded by the philosophy of the First Amendment, in order to allow free play to the rough-and-tumble political struggles characteristic of democracy.

As the governmental process of information gathering and decision making becomes more formalized (i.e., moves more toward the model of judicial decision making), the immunity of the conspirators correspondingly begins to narrow. If, in the context of the dispute disclosed in *Noerr,* the Pennsylvania legislature had decided to get at the merits of the controversy by establishing a legislative investigating committee, the scope of the conspirators' immunity would have been considerably reduced. Constitutional considerations would not have prevented the punishment of any industry representative who, testifying under oath before the committee, made misrepresentations of the sort contained in the publicity campaign. When the legislature creates a fact-finding process fashioned after the judicial model—with witnesses, oaths, cross-examination, a written record, and the like—it becomes correspondingly able to punish deliberate falsehoods and other abuses of its process that would be immune in the regular political arena. It hardly requires saying, of course, that the creation of a fact-finding committee does not displace the general political arena: the immunity the conspirators enjoy there continues.

We have seen that law may punish those who knowingly advance baseless claims in court, and it is undisputed that the legislature may punish those who lie to its investigative committees. What these situations have in common is a formalized process by which judicial or legislative tribunals attempt to find facts. Both courts and legislative committees may have the lawful power to make policy judgments, but that does not make everything that is said to them, no matter how groundless or false, immune. The distinction is essential. Our society requires a wide-open political process, robust and free. It also requires that there be more formal, constrained procedures for the establishment of certain types of facts and the application of particular policies. Processes of the latter type must be guarded from abuse if they are to be effective. To say that everything that is said to any kind of tribunal is "political expression" and therefore unregulable is to "politicalize" the courts, legislative fact-finding committees, and administrative tribunals so that they lose much of their present value and may become unmanageable. This is why the character of the governmental decision-making process affects the scope of conspirators' immunity from liability.

THE CHARACTER OF THE GOVERNMENTAL DECISION

The character of the decision that government must make will, of course, greatly influence the character of the process that is employed. But this relationship is not neat and invariable. Sometimes, for example, an executive officer is entrusted with what amounts to legislative discretion, as was the Secretary of Labor whose discretion to impose minimum wage standards was involved in *Pennington*. In such cases, no particular form of process may be specified, and the official is properly free to arrive at his conclusions in the manner he finds most expeditious. If he acts within the area of his lawful discretion, no court will interfere, and no court will impose liability, under the Sherman Act or any other statute, upon those who attempt by lawful means to persuade him to take one decision rather than another.

But when the official, agency, or tribunal has circumscribed powers of decision, courts may invalidate actions that are outside the area of discretion and may impose liability upon those who knowingly and wrongfully induce action that is beyond the power of the agency involved. The classic example, of course, is the bribery of an official to take unlawful actions, but many other situations allow no immunity for attempts wrongfully to influence governmental action.

This topic appears to be closely related to the "political question" problem so frequently raised in constitutional law. Indeed, it appears that the two problems are rooted in the same policy grounds and should find similar solutions. When Chief Justice John Marshall laid the foundations of the "political question" doctrine in *Marbury* v. *Madison*,[14] he made a distinction that is fully applicable to many issues of liability for attempts to influence governmental action. "It is not by the office of the person to whom the writ is directed, but the nature of the thing to be done that the propriety or impropriety of issuing a mandamus is to be determined." So here, it is not by the "nature" of the arm of government that decides, but by the character of the decision to be made, that the decision of liability for those who seek to invoke the action of any agency of government is to be determined.

If the agency of government in question has no authority to do what it is used for, then those who procure such action, knowing the limits of authority and with wrongful intent, may properly be held liable. Two illustrations come to mind. First, we may hypothesize a combination of automobile dealers in a city who are upset by the aggressive competition of one dealer. That dealer makes a practice of acquiring and reselling to the public makes and models of automobiles for which he is not franchised. Under the Sherman Act (whether rightly or wrongly is of no consequence here) the manufacturer who does franchise him may not penalize him for this practice. His rivals, however, induce an employee of the state's Department of Motor Vehicles to harass this dealer until he stops selling makes for which he is not franchised, and this is done even though the department has been given no authority over such questions whatever. Here a government official is acting in an area where he has no power to act, deciding issues of competition that he has no authority to decide. Courts may properly restrain him and, provided the requisite knowledge and intent are proved, may hold liable under the Sherman Act those who induced the action.

The second illustration is of a slightly different nature, but its outcome should be the same. Suppose that a large chain of motion picture theaters decides to block the access of rivals to towns where it has the only theater. To that end, the chain adopts the tactic of opposing the construction of any additional theaters before the local zoning boards and of pursuing such opposition through all state courts. The zoning boards, under state law, have no authority to consider the desirability of competition but may only consider effects upon surrounding residential property, the capacity of the streets to handle increased traffic flow, and like matters. The motion picture chain, though it has absolutely no interest in such issues and no legal right to raise them, nevertheless battles through the zoning board and all state courts, striving for as much delay and expense at each stage as possible. Here no governmental agency is induced to take action that is outside its discretion, but the procedures of the zoning boards and the courts are invoked merely to create expense and delay in order to postpone or prevent the appearance of competition. If a would-be entrant could prove that it had been delayed by the invocation of the board procedures, that it had suffered heavy expense, that the opposition was sham and without merit and put up in bad faith for the sole purpose of monopolizing, then there can hardly be a doubt the entrant would have a valid claim under Section 2 of the Sherman Act. *Walker* holds as much. The character of the decision the tribunal is empowered to make is quite different from the effect the predator seeks by misusing the tribunal.

The *Noerr* opinion suggested that even an approach to a legislative body might subject predators to liability if the apparent effort to influence the legislators was a clear sham and engaged in only to inflict harm upon business rivals. That is a possibility the Court was wise to keep in reserve. It is far clearer that sham approaches to judicial and administrative tribunals, with the intention only of inflicting competitive injury, should constitute offenses under the Sherman Act.

THE GENERALITY OR SPECIFICITY OF THE PROCESS

Immunity is properly broader when the framing of general rules is the object of a governmental process than when the force of government is to be brought to bear on the specific rights of particular parties. This factor overlaps and complements the others, but it has weight of its own.

In part, this consideration parallels the distinction between legislative and judicial functions, but it also applies in other contexts where persons attempt to influence official action. Citizens groups, for instance, frequently meet with police officials to make known their desires with respect to law enforcement policy, and it would be unthinkable for an individual citizen to be held liable for the motives which underlay his urging of a general policy or even for misrepresentations about the seriousness of the situation. But when the discussion narrows and begins to focus on action to be taken against an individual, the immunity of the person who urges the police to act begins correspondingly to narrow. If one person tells what he knows or thinks he knows about another, he is surely safe. But no one would urge that a person be immune from prosecution who improperly, whether by falsely representing facts or by bribery or by other reprehensible means, induces the police to arrest and imprison his personal enemies or business rivals.

Perhaps one reason this factor is important is that processes which focus on the individual party have a far greater capacity to hurt than do processes aimed at the formulation of general rules. Even when there is nothing to the claim, the person or firm forced to fight a baseless assertion is required to expend time and money. In many cases the cost may keep the party out of the market altogether. In others, the price of buying delay is worthwhile to the predator, who reaps noncompetitive profits in the meantime. Such results are less likely when the governmental process aims at general rule making. Thus, the predator in *Walker* was able to force its victim to defend an expensive patent litigation. The same result could not have been achieved had the predator attempted to obtain from Congress a favorable change in the patent laws. The very generality of the proposal would have attracted the interested participation of many persons, in and out of Congress, so that the burden of fighting the issue would not have fallen upon a single victim.

It is true that courts and administrative tribunals often formulate general rules in the course of deciding particular controversies and the rights and liabilities of individuals. Predators will rely upon that truism in an effort to convert their harassment of rivals into a large-spirited effort to alter public policy. However, there comes a time when, after repeated unsuccessful attempts to get a judicial or administrative tribunal to adopt a policy one wants, it must be admitted that the law is otherwise. Courts, particularly in their function of interpreting and applying the Constitution, formulate broad policies. It is legitimate for persons dissatisfied with a particular formulation to hope that the courts will alter their view and overrule it. That possibility has led many persons, and even state and local governments, to resist the law of the Constitution as announced by the Supreme Court. The problem has been acute in issues of racial segregation in public schools. But there comes a time when, at last, one must accept the fact that the law is otherwise than one would wish, and cease resistance to it. As Herbert Wechsler has said, "When that chance [of a change in policy] has been exploited and has run its course with reaffirmation rather than reversal of decision, has not the time arrived when its acceptance is demanded, without insisting upon repeated litigation? The answer here, it seems to me, must be affirmative, both as the necessary implication of our constitutional tradition and to avoid the greater evils that will otherwise ensue." [15]

On a more mundane level, a person bothered by the noise a neighbor's children made when playing in their backyard could not endlessly sue the neighbor on the ground that while the facts had not changed, one was entitled perpetually to hope for a judicial alteration of tort law. At some point the pretense of using the individual case as a vehicle for seeking new general rules must be recognized for what it is, the deliberate harassment of a private party. At that point the neighbor can secure an injunction against further harassing litigation on the same issue, and damages for the tort of malicious litigation.

The matter is even clearer, however, when the business predator makes no effort to have agencies or courts change their general rules. Then reliance upon a claim obviously baseless can be motivated only by anticompetitive intent.

* * * *

Predation through the misuse of governmental processes appears to be a common but little-noticed phenomenon. Some of it is unreachable by law because the attempt would interfere with explicitly political processes that must be left free, but much predation of this type can be halted. In this area, antitrust can not only perform a valuable service to consumers but, as a by-product, can also contribute to the integrity and efficiency of administrative and judicial processes.

19

Tying Arrangements and Reciprocal Dealing

ANTITRUST cases on the topic of tie-in sales and reciprocal dealing are at once instructive and disheartening. A review of these cases reveals the sterile circularity of the law's reasoning, the untenability of its premises, and the error of its most assured pronouncements. These matters have been repeatedly and conclusively demonstrated by a number of commentators,[1] yet the law remains majestically impervious to any critical analysis.

Tying arrangements and reciprocal dealing are the same economic phenomenon. Antitrust treats them both as utterly pernicious, despite the increasingly obtrusive fact that it has found no adequate grounds for objecting to them at all. Tying exists when a seller of product A requires his purchasers to take product B as well. Reciprocity exists when firm X purchases from firm Y only upon the condition that Y purchase another product from X. There are many variations on these patterns, but tying arrangements and reciprocal dealing are alike in conditioning a transaction with respect to one product upon a transaction with respect to another product.

The Supreme Court has seen in this tying together of transactions nothing but the suppression of competition. Yet, though we are far from a full understanding of the functions of tying and reciprocity, it is safe to say that suppression of competition is the one function not accomplished by the arrangements the Court has struck down. The Court's theory of tying and reciprocity is that they are means of extending power from one market to another. When a seller of product *A*, the tying product, requires that purchasers also take product *B*, the tied product, the Court assumes that some market power inhering in *A* is extended or transferred to *B*, so that the seller now has two monopolies or positions of strength in place of one. This is the same fallacious transfer-of-power theory that underlies so many fields of antitrust law. We have repeatedly analyzed it, but the fallacy's career is worth following in this context.

THE CASE LAW

The theory appeared as early as 1912 in Chief Justice White's dissent from the *A. B. Dick* decision,[2] and it became the basis for the law five years later in the *Motion Picture Patents* case.[3] The first of these cases involved a machine that fastened buttons on shoes; the seller of this machine required that the purchaser also take from the seller the required wire. In the second case, patented motion picture projectors were sold on the condition that purchasers use them to show only films covered by other patents of the seller. Although these cases were decided under the law of patent misuse, they became precedent for antitrust decisions. The antitrust cases are rested on Section 1 of the Sherman Act or Section 3 of the Clayton Act. Owing to the migration of the Clayton Act's supposedly more stringent tests into the Sherman Act, the standards of those two statutes have become so similar that any differences remaining between them are of interest only to antitrust theologians.

The main antitrust story begins with the 1947 *International Salt* decision.[4] The Supreme Court upheld a grant of summary judgment against a defendant which had leased patented salt-dispensing machines on condition that the lessees purchase the necessary salt from the lessor. Justice Jackson, writing for the Court majority, cited a boycott case for the proposition that "it is unreasonable, per se, to foreclose competitors from any substantial market," and then disposed of the major issue before him with this simple statement: "The volume of business affected by these contracts cannot be said to be insignificant or insubstantial and the tendency of the arrangement to accomplishment of monopoly seems obvious." He cited no evidence and disclosed no line of reasoning to support that conclusion. If there is anything about Justice Jackson's conclusion that escapes the reader, it is the claimed quality of obviousness. The tie-in tended to the accomplishment of *what* monopoly? In the machines? Requiring a purchaser to take salt does not build a monopoly in the machines; it would tend to have the opposite effect. In salt? It is inconceivable that anybody could hope to get a monopoly, or anything remotely resembling a monopoly, in a product like salt by foreclosing the utterly insignificant fraction of the market represented by the salt passing through these leased machines. Whatever International Salt thought it was accomplishing with these tying requirements, it was not monopoly. Not only do the circumstances make the notion implausible, but we shall see that analysis renders it impossible.

Yet by 1949, when the requirements contracts involved in *Standard Stations* [5] were before the Court, Justice Frankfurter, without further demonstration, felt able to report in his majority opinion that there were "important economic differences" between the contracts then under scrutiny and those deplored in *International Salt,* since "tying arrangements serve hardly any purpose beyond the suppression of competition." This remarkable assertion has never been supported either theoretically or empirically, and it has become increasingly evident, outside the world of judicial economics, that if there is one purpose a tie-in does not serve it is the suppression of competition.

By the time *Northern Pacific* [6] reached the Supreme Court in 1958, the law's theory of tying arrangements had begun to collapse of its own intellectual weightlessness. It was increasingly obvious that most tying arrangements appeared in situations where the tying product had no monopoly power that could conceivably be transferred. This was true in *Northern Pacific* itself, where the defendant railroad had sold land along its right of way upon the condition that the purchasing companies ship over the seller's line unless a competing carrier offered lower rates. Northern Pacific did not, of course, have a monopoly on land suitable for factory sites, and it could not have been extending power from the land market to the transportation market.

No matter, the Supreme Court found an illegal tying arrangement without difficulty. Justice Black's opinion for the majority made the customary assertion that tying arrangements serve hardly any purpose, etc. In tying cases this formula has become as ritualized as the last rites, and even more surely foretells the outcome. In avoiding the objection that the defendant had no power in the market for land, Justice Black argued, moreover, that market power in the tying product is not an important element of the offense. It is sufficient if the tying product has sufficient power to command the arrangement, which is to say that a tie-in is illegal if it exists. In stressing this, Justice Black merely emphasized the degree to which the entire development of the law of tying arrangements rested upon an intuition that is held above the ordinary processes of disproof. Rejecting the railroad's contention that market power had always before been essential and had been presumed in *International Salt* because the machines were patented, Justice Black noted that patents often do not confer real monopolies and may give only slight economic power. "As a matter of fact," he continued, "the defendant in *International Salt* offered to prove that competitive salt machines were readily available which were satisfactory substitutes for its machines (a fact the Government did not controvert), but the Court regarded such proof as irrelevant." This fact, not mentioned in the *International Salt* opinion, is startling. How could the defendant suppress competition when not only the salt but even the machines were competitive? If there was no monopoly power to transfer, what was the case about?

The importance of this removal of the requirement of market power is not that it makes the law irrational—the entire theory of tying arrangements as menaces to competition is completely irrational in any case—but rather that it makes the irrationality of the law unconfinable. It becomes impossible, on any terms but those which the law is currently unwilling to accept, to distinguish illegal tie-in sales from any other sales.

The Court gave a partial demonstration of that in its 1969 decision *Fortner Enterprises, Inc.* v. *United States Steel Corporation,*[7] a case that illustrates antitrust's tendency to pursue premises, good or bad, to their extremes. United States Steel, through its Home Division, made prefabricated houses and sold house components to real estate builders and developers. It offered credit to purchasers through a wholly owned credit corporation. Real estate developers, however, commonly needed financing for the purchase of the land as well as the houses, and the credit corporation gave loans for that purpose also, on the not unreasonable condition that United States Steel houses be used. The corporation dealt with Fortner on this basis, but he demanded larger loans than were usual, and these were granted reluctantly. A dispute broke out over the quality of the houses supplied, and Fortner, instead of bringing a warranty action, proceeded under Sections 1 and 2 of the Sherman Act, alleging an illegal tying arrangement. The credit corporation, he said, would only lend money if the borrower purchased houses at artificially high prices from United States Steel.

Fortner had the matter backward. United States Steel was not in the general lending business. It was trying to sell houses, and to facilitate that enterprise aided developers, who are chronically low on cash, with loans. In any case, a five-member majority of the Supreme Court agreed that summary judgment should not have been entered against Fortner and sent the case back for trial. Justice Black's opinion for the majority did not quite say that economic power in the tying product, cash, was irrelevant, but it might as well have. Economic power became the ability to offer loans on better terms: ". . . uniquely and unusually advantageous terms can reflect a creditor's unique economic advantages over his competitors. . . . They could well mean that U.S. Steel's subsidiary Credit Corporation had a unique ability to provide 100 per cent financing at cheap rates." That argument is breathtaking for two reasons. It was Fortner who demanded the 100 percent financing, and the credit corporation that resisted. The reason the cheap rates were available, moreover, was precisely because of the tying arrangement. The effective holding of the case is that Fortner was getting credit terms more favorable than he could get elsewhere and was entitled to prove it in order to recover triple damages. Reason totters.

Justice Black was then faced with one form of the problem of distinguishing tie-ins from legitimate sales. He did not achieve a very satisfactory solution:

All of the respondents' arguments amount essentially to the same claim—namely, that this opinion will somehow prevent those who manufacture goods from ever selling them on credit. But our holding in this case will have no such effect. There is, at the outset of every tie-in case, including the familiar cases involving physical goods, the problem of determining whether two separate products are in fact involved. In the usual sale on credit the seller, a single individual or corporation, simply makes an agreement determining when and how much he will be paid for his product. In such a sale the credit may constitute such an inseparable part of the purchase price for the item that the entire transaction could be considered to involve only a single product.

That passage gives no hint of the criteria by which one is to judge whether the credit is an "inseparable part of the purchase price." In fact, there is no way it could be inseparable. Sellers could be required to have one price for those who pay cash and a higher one for those who take credit. The reason no such requirement has yet been imposed is that it would force higher costs upon sellers that would be reflected in prices to consumers. But that raises antitrust's forbidden topic, efficiency. Almost as if recognizing the danger that efficiency might be tolerated, Justice Black added the threatening statement: "It will be time enough to pass on the issue of credit sales when a case involving it actually arises."

Upon remand, the district court found that the credit offered to Fortner was unique because it covered all of Fortner's costs and carried a relatively low interest rate. This it thought—and the court of appeals agreed—made the tie-in illegal. The Supreme Court reversed,[8] not by reforming the sorry, metaphysical doctrine of the field (which, in any event, it was precluded from doing because *Fortner I* was the law of the case), but by holding that the evidence of uniqueness was insufficient.

Quite clearly, if the evidence merely shows that credit terms are unique because the seller is willing to accept a lesser profit—or to incur greater risks— than its competitors, that kind of uniqueness will not give rise to any inference of economic power in the credit market. Yet this is, in substance, all that the record in this case indicates.

To be guilty, U.S. Steel would have had to have "some cost advantage" or the ability to "offer a form of financing that was significantly differentiated from that which other lenders could offer if they so elected." This addition to the doctrinal wrinkles of tie-in lore has the merit (and it is a considerable one) of averting a wretched miscarriage of justice in the particular case. That, given the binding force of *Fortner I,* may have been the best the Court could do, and perhaps the refusal to find uniqueness in the tying product, credit, without proof that the offerer had an absolute advantage over rivals (proof that will often be extremely difficult) raises the hope that many future tying arrangements will be found lawful. Perhaps, to be more optimistic, *Fortner II* signals a realization that something quite profound is wrong with tying doctrine. But, at least for the time being, the general theory of tie-in law remains intact, capable of working new mischief and suppressing all manner of socially beneficial transactions.

In *Fortner II* the Court necessarily accepted the holding of *Fortner I* that two separate products were tied together. Yet so long as the notion persists that there is some point in distinguishing one-product sales from two-product sales, so long will the law find itself face to face with the problem of how a tie-in sale can be distinguished from any sale. Any product or service can be broken down into smaller components, and the seller who refuses to do so is insisting upon tying the components together. Automobile dealers refuse to sell the chassis without the rest of the car; coal dealers may refuse to deliver amounts of less than a ton; shoe retailers may charge the same price for one left shoe as for the pair; liquor wholesalers may refuse to sell less than a case. Most lawyers would probably say that these arrangements do not constitute tying arrangements, but they would probably not articulate the basis for that conclusion, and they would be even less likely to generalize their rationale. The reason for not calling these arrangements tie-ins is that requiring the seller to deal in smaller quantities (and there is no limit to the smallness of the quantity one could demand) would introduce obvious diseconomies. It would be inefficient and, therefore, anticonsumer.

There is no doubt that this sense of efficiency is what lies behind the law's attempt to decide whether a tying arrangement exists by determining whether one product or two are being sold. The apparently metaphysical test is actually a vague economic intuition. But the intuition ought to be made explicit. Otherwise, courts find themselves determining the efficient way to run a business, a subject in which they have little expertise.

This process is illustrated by the district court's opinion in *United States* v. *Jerrold Electronics Corporation*.[9] Jerrold made community antenna systems for towns remote from television transmitting stations. These systems were quite complex. As the court said, "Such systems may include antenna construction quite remote from the town served, amplification of the received signal, conversion to a channel different from that received, and transmission by cable directly to subscribers' homes." Jerrold would not sell separate parts but only whole systems, and then only on the condition that Jerrold install and service the systems. Many of its contracts required the exclusive use of Jerrold equipment whenever extra capacity was added, and forbade the installation of any additional equipment without Jerrold's approval. The government attacked these arrangements as illegal tie-ins.

In judging the tie of the service contract to the sale of the system, the court considered the economic arguments for the practice—primarily the unsatisfactory performance of systems installed and serviced by persons without the requisite knowledge and skill—and concluded the tie had been reasonable when the industry was new but was no longer so. This was a direct judgment of the efficiency of a tie-in, and it is doubtful that the court was in position to judge. (To be fair, it is doubtful also that applicable Supreme Court precedent left the court free to be as thoughtful as in fact it was.) Turning to the refusal to sell components separately, the court said:

The difficult question raised by the defendants is whether this should be treated as a case of tying the sale of one product to another or merely as the sale of a single product. [Jerrold contended the system was the product.] It is apparent that, as a general rule, a manufacturer cannot be forced to deal in the minimum product that could be sold or is usually sold. On the other hand, it is equally clear that one cannot circumvent the anti-trust laws simply by claiming that he is selling a single product. *The facts must be examined to ascertain whether or not there are legitimate reasons for selling normally separate items in a combined form to dispel any inferences that it is really a disguised tie-in.* [Emphasis added.]

The court then engaged in what was necessarily an unsatisfactory review of the arguments about efficiencies, and finally cut the knot by concluding that the policy of full system sales was an adjunct to the policy of compulsory service. Since it had decided there was no longer a compelling need for compulsory service, the economic reasons for selling systems rather than components disappeared. "Absent these economic reasons, the court feels that a full system was not an appropriate sales unit." Thus, the issue of tie-in versus single-product sale was decided in terms of economic efficiency, and necessarily, as we shall see, decided wrongly.

Jerrold Electronics and the other tie-in cases discussed were decided incorrectly because there is no viable theory of a means by which tying arrangements injure competition, and there are several obvious ways in which they benefit both seller and consumer. Since reciprocal dealing is a form of tying arrangement, the following discussion of tying arrangements is fully applicable to reciprocal dealing.

OBJECTIONS TO TYING ARRANGEMENTS

We will first examine the objections to tying arrangements to show that they are erroneous, and then discuss the real functions that such arrangements (and reciprocal dealing) may serve. What will be said here is by no means new. The law's theory of tying arrangements is merely another example of the discredited transfer-of-power theory, and perhaps no other variety of that theory has been so thoroughly and repeatedly demolished in the legal and economic literature. That the law's course remained utterly undeflected for so long casts an illuminating and, if you are of a sardonic turn of mind, amusing sidelight upon the relation of scholarship to judicial lawmaking.

The fallacy of the cases on tying arrangements may be shown through a hypothetical example based on the facts of *International Salt*. Suppose that a food canner is just willing to pay $100 for a one-year lease of a salt-dispensing machine. How is it possible for the lessor of the machine to make him pay $100 and, in addition, require him to take all his salt from the lessor. If the requirement is necessary, the lessee is giving up something he values. If the lessor has charged the full value of the machine, he cannot then charge still more in the form of coercion to take what amounts to a requirements contract for salt. That is double counting of monopoly power. The tying arrangement, whatever else it may accomplish, is obviously not a means of gaining two monopoly profits from a single monopoly.

The argument is identical with respect to reciprocity. In *Consolidated Foods* [10] the Supreme Court struck down Consolidated's acquisition of Gentry, a small manufacturer of dehydrated onion and garlic, on the theory that Consolidated, a large food processor, might condition its purchases from food suppliers upon their willingness to purchase from Gentry. There is, however, no way in which that practice could be anticompetitive. Suppose that both Consolidated and Gentry buy and sell in fully competitive markets. Consolidated will then have no market power with which to force its suppliers to purchase from Gentry. The suppliers can turn to other customers. Suppose, however, that all markets involved display large elements of market power. Consolidated, before its acquisition of Gentry, may be presumed to have negotiated the best price it could from its suppliers. The acquisition of Gentry does not alter Consolidated's purchasing power, but the attempt after the acquisition to force Gentry's onions and garlic on suppliers as a condition of continued purchases by Consolidated is merely a way of demanding a still lower price from the suppliers. If the tactic works, Consolidated merely learns that it was paying too high a price to begin with: it would be better off renegotiating prices than cramming unwanted onions and garlic down its suppliers' throats. Nor is the theory improved by assuming that Consolidated understands all this and agrees to pay suppliers more in return for purchases from Gentry as a tactic of monopolizing the onion and garlic market. Rival sellers in Gentry's market can respond in a variety of ways, the most obvious being a price cut that just matches the price increase laid out by Consolidated. In that kind of price war, Consolidated has no advantages.

But perhaps the most concise devastation of the law's tie-in theory was provoked by the Supreme Court's 1962 *Loew's* decision. [11] Distributors of pre-1948 copyrighted motion-picture feature films for television exhibition engaged in the practice of block booking their films to television stations. The stations had to take entire groups of films and could not pick and choose particular films from the proffered packages. The Court majority held, of course, that the practice violated Section 1 of the Sherman Act. The opinion's economic analysis of block booking was confined to a recitation of Justice Frankfurter's by then clearly indefensible dictum on the purpose of tying arrangements.

The inadequacy of the Supreme Court's theory of tying was well stated by George Stigler in a critique of the *Loew's* opinion: [12]

Consider the following simple example. One film, Justice Goldberg cited 'Gone With the Wind', is worth $10,000 to the buyer, while a second film, the Justice cited 'Getting Gertie's Garter', is worthless to him. The seller could sell the one for $10,000 and throw away the second, for no matter what its cost, bygones are forever bygones. Instead the seller compels the buyer to take both. But surely he can obtain no more than $10,000, since by hypothesis this is the value of both films to the buyer. Why not, in short, use his monoply power directly on the desirable film? It seems no more sensible, on this logic, to blockbook the two films than it would be to compel the exhibitor to buy 'Gone With the Wind' and seven Ouija boards, again for $10,000.

To these queries the law has no answers. Indeed, it has so far successfully managed to ignore the existence of the queries.

Attempts have been made to rehabilitate the rule against tying arrangements, but they have not been notably successful. Carl Kaysen and Donald Turner proposed a per se ban: [13]

A tie-in always operates to raise the barriers to entry in the market of the tied good to the level of those in the market for the tying good: the seller who would supply the one, can do so only if he can also supply the other, since he must be able to displace the whole package which the tying seller offers. Developing a substitute for the tying product may be very difficult, if not impossible. Thus tying tends to spread market power into markets where it would not otherwise exist: for example, few firms are prepared to supply machines like those of IBM, whereas many may be prepared to supply punch cards.

The reference to barriers to entry, currently one of the law's most potent empty concepts, may make the argument appear new, but it is in fact nothing more than a rehearsal of the mistaken theory of the law. Entry into the market for punch cards to be used with IBM's machines * is

* Kaysen and Turner alluded to the facts underlying *International Business Machines Corp.* v. *United States,* 293 U.S. 131 (1936). IBM leased machines that did mechanical tabulations and computations by using punched cards. IBM required lessees to purchase the cards from it.

unimportant unless a monopoly profit is being taken there. We have seen that IBM cannot get a monopoly profit on both machines and cards; if there is a higher payment for the cards, it is actually part of the payment for the machine. There is no effect upon any card market broader than that of cards used in IBM's machines. If the machine monopoly is lawful, there is no reason to worry about the tie-in of the cards. If the machine monopoly is unlawful, that monopoly should be attacked by the law. Severing the tie in either case is likely only to make matters worse for consumers.

Merton Burstein and James Ferguson, writing independently, think the per se ban on tying arrangements justified because it limits the potential gains from monopoly power.[14] Indeed it does, but that is to apply the wrong criterion to the problem. The objection to monopoly is not that it makes some people too rich but that it leaves consumers poorer than they need be. The question to be answered, then, is whether consumers are better or worse off if tying arrangements are allowed. Often, permitting a monopolist to maximize his gains will be better for consumers. Monopoly misallocates resources because the monopolist must restrict output to maximize net revenues—but that proposition holds only if the monopolist is confined to charging a single price. If he could charge the monopoly price to all who would pay it, and a series of lower prices to others, he would produce the same amount as a competitive industry. Under such circumstances, there would be no misallocation of resources. As we shall see in this and the next chapter, tying arrangements are often methods of approximating this result. When they are, they are both promonopolist and proconsumer, and it makes no particular sense to object to the promonopolist effect and overlook the proconsumer effect. Striking the tie-in such cases merely makes everybody worse off.

FUNCTIONS OF TYING ARRANGEMENTS

If the law's theories of tying arrangements and reciprocal dealing are inadequate, as they demonstrably are, it is important to ask why such arrangements are used. A number of theoretical answers have been devised,[15] and it seems clear that at least some of them are useful explanations of observed tie-ins. Of the many possible explanations I shall rehearse only a few that seem most realistic. Tying arrangements and, in some cases, reciprocal dealing have among their explanations: (1) evasion of price regulation, (2) price discrimination, (3) nondiscriminatory measurement of use, (4) economies of scale, and (5) technological interdependence or the "protection of goodwill."

EVASION OF PRICE REGULATION

Where the price of product X is regulated, it may be possible to evade the regulation and obtain a higher price by requiring the purchaser to take unregulated product Y as well, and at a higher price than Y would command by itself. If the regulated price of X is below the free market price, purchasers will be willing to play the game. A tie-in may also be used to cut prices. The facts of *Northern Pacific* strongly suggest this was the purpose of the tie there. In order to avoid ICC rate regulation, the railroad may have offered rate reductions to potential shippers through bargain land prices. The requirement of shipments over the railroad vendor's line (so long as it offered at least equal rates and services) would be necessary to make sure the road got the business it paid for.

Price cutting may also be the explanation for some instances of reciprocal dealing. A manufacturer's pricing freedom may be curtailed by the Robinson-Patman Act or by a cartel agreement. Reciprocal purchasing offers a means of giving or obtaining a price cut not readily detectable by Robinson-Patman enforcers or other cartel members. This may conceivably have been the reason for the attempts to coerce reciprocity in *Consolidated Foods*. Justice Stewart's concurring opinion noted that Consolidated had been more successful in getting smaller processors without brand names to buy from Gentry than it had been with the large, name-brand processors. Perhaps Consolidated thought it should be getting a better price from the smaller processors but was prevented by the Robinson-Patman Act from demanding it. Reciprocal dealing would be a way of getting the lower price in a disguised form.

PRICE DISCRIMINATION

Tie-ins may also be used to accomplish price discrimination. This can be done when the tying and tied products are sold in either varying or fixed proportions to one another.

The variable proportion case may be illustrated with a hypothetical example similar to the facts of the old *IBM* case. The manufacturer of business machines using punch cards may perceive that his customers differ considerably in the amount of use they give the machines; he may also observe that the heavy users are generally willing to pay more than those whose use is less intensive. The heavy users have a lower elasticity of demand. Being of sound mind, the manufacturer would like to take advantage of this fact. If he sets a single price, some heavy users will pay less than they would be willing to, and some light users will be priced out of the market. The manufacturer would like to raise the price to heavy users and lower it to light users, ideally charging each customer the top price it would pay. But if he adopted such a policy, the manufacturer would shortly discover that all his sales were to light users at low prices, for the customers, being also of sound mind, would find that it paid to have the light users purchase machines and resell to the heavy users. It is essential to the manufacturer's plan that this cross-selling be stopped.

The solution is simple. First, the machines should be leased only, so that cross-selling is made impossible. The leases could be at different rentals, but this would require rather crude guesses as to the elasticity of each customer's demand and would entail the risk of significant changes in elasticity during the term of the lease. The second step, therefore, is to require each customer to purchase the punch cards from him. The direct rental charge for the machine will be less than otherwise, and a price above normal will be charged for cards. Each customer will now pay a price for the machine in direct proportion to his use of it, just as if the machine were metered. The machine manufacturer now receives different returns from each customer and, through price discrimination, has maximized his returns.

The price discrimination hypothesis fits the facts of the *IBM* case. The Supreme Court's opinion, which struck the tying arrangement down as restricting competition in the sale of cards (which was not at all the point of the arrangement), noted that the government as lessee of the machines had bargained for the right to make its own cards and had paid a 15 percent increase in rental for the privilege. This indicates that lessees were paying for the machines in the price of the cards.

Price discrimination in a fixed proportion case may be illustrated, as Stigler and others have noted, by the practice of block booking motion picture films. We may assume that a film distributor sees that Channels 2 and 4 have different demands for the two films he has to offer at the moment. The prices they are willing to pay are as follows:

	Channel 2	Channel 4
Gone with the Wind	$1,000	$600
Getting Gertie's Garter	400	500

The distributor will see that if he offers the same price to each station, he will do best by charging $600 for *GWTW* and $400 for *GGG*. By selling each film to each station, he receives a total revenue of $2,000. Had he charged the higher price either station would pay for each film, he would have sold one film to each and received a total of only $1,500. But he can achieve a solution better than either of these. If he charges each station the maximum it is willing to pay for each film, practicing perfect price discrimination, the distributor will get $2,500. But that may not always be possible or wise. Blatant price discrimination might cause resentment, might arouse the interest of the Antitrust Division or the Federal Trade Commission (whose inattention is worth money), or might be difficult to accomplish when the distributor is not sure of the precise maximums of many stations. He may, therefore, choose to block book the films, refusing to sell except in one package at a single price. By setting a package price of $1,100 for *GWTW* and *GGG* together, he can sell both channels and receive a total revenue of $2,200, a $200 improvement over selling the films separately.

NONDISCRIMINATORY MEASUREMENT OF USE

Price discrimination exists, in the situations just described, because the seller receives different rates of return from sales to different customers. However, it is also possible that the seller's costs will vary with the use his machine receives. If, for instance, the seller finds it most efficient to offer a package of machine and repair service rather than selling each separately, he may find that a single price for the package undercharges heavy users (which have a correspondingly heavy demand for repair service) and overcharges light users. A tie-in—say, of punch cards with business machines—may provide a way of recovering the costs of service, and there would be no price discrimination in such a case.

ECONOMIES OF SCALE

Every person who sells anything imposes a tying arrangement. This is true because every product or service could be broken down into smaller components capable of being sold separately, and every seller either refuses at some point to break the product down any further or, what comes to the same thing, charges a proportionally higher price for the smaller unit. The automobile dealer who refuses to sell only the chassis or the grocer who declines to subdivide a can of pears are engaged in tying. The law, as we have seen, attempts to avoid this ridiculous conclusion by distinguishing between packages that are inherently one product and those that are inherently more than one. But the distinction makes no sense. There is no way to state the "inherent" scope of a product. The judge who attempts it either decides according to product dimensions that seem to him natural because he is accustomed to them, or explicitly decides on grounds of efficiency. An automobile and a can of pears are perceived as single products because it would be too expensive to require the seller to subdivide them further. Economies of scale determine the definition of the product.

Economies of scale may account for many arrangements that the law now regards as sinister. The tying of a machine lease and a service contract, as was the practice of United Shoe Machinery and IBM, may be less expensive than selling the two separately. The practice may cut selling costs or internal administrative costs, or it may be less expensive to combine service calls and calls on customers for other purposes. Similarly, the tying of salt to a salt-dispensing machine may be the equivalent of a requirements contract, and so lower both selling and manufacturing costs. The elimination of selling costs may also explain some reciprocal dealing.

TECHNOLOGICAL INTERDEPENDENCE OR THE "PROTECTION OF GOODWILL"

As Ward Bowman points out, "The usefulness of a particular product or device may depend not only upon its own adaptability but equally upon the adaptability of some essential component. If the essential component did not conform to exact specifications, it might impair the operation or usefulness of the principal product." [16] This defense, he notes, was invoked by IBM to justify its practice of tying cards to business machines, and "in the early shoe machinery cases, the United Company stressed the very close technological interdependence of a wide variety of machines each of which, although doing a separate task, was only efficient if properly coordinated with the others." Perhaps a similar explanation accounts for United's practice of tying its repair service to its machine leases, and for IBM's practice, since abandoned but cited by the government in its monopolization case, of tying software and supporting services to its computers.

One wonders whether this justification for tying is not worthy of more respect than it has been accorded. The only ground for skepticism about this defense is the argument that the tie is unnecessary to the accomplishment of the purpose. Since the lessor and lessee of a machine have identical interests in its proper operation, the argument runs, the lessor need not tie the related product. His statement that his own make of the related product is preferable, if based on fact, will be believed by the lessee; or the lessor can write a set of careful specifications for the related product, letting his lessee purchase from anyone who can meet the specifications. These observations are true so far as they go, but they do not go far enough to settle the matter. There is no showing that these alternative routes will be as effective as the tie-in of the related product, or that they will accomplish the result as inexpensively. The problem is one of information and policing. The manufacturer is likely to understand the technical problems of his machines much better than the lessees. Despite the law's easy assumption that the lessor can persuade the lessees to take his related product, that may not be easy. The provision of information to numerous lessees will be expensive, and some of them may be skeptical of the lessor's arguments. Moreover, they may experiment with other products and impair the functioning of the machine. The writing of specifications and the continual policing required to make sure they are complied with is also certain to be more expensive than supplying the related good oneself. The courts have assumed too facilely that technological interdependence does not justify tying arrangements.

The functions of tying arrangements and reciprocal dealing discussed are by no means the only ones advanced in the literature or the only ones that may fit business reality. What we have seen in this chapter, however, is that there is no validity to the law's explanation of tying arrangements and reciprocal dealing. They simply do not threaten competition, as the courts have supposed for so long. We have seen also that in the effort to distinguish tie-ins from ordinary sales, the law has been driven to a de facto recognition of the desirability of economies of scale. If this principle and its necessary implications were explicitly accepted, the law of tying arrangements and reciprocal dealing would be transformed. Economies of scale are, after all, no more valuable to consumers than other efficiencies, and a logically consistent law would have to accept the legality of all tying arrangements and reciprocal dealings that create efficiencies.

In our present state of knowledge, this means the law would accept the legality of all tying arrangements and all reciprocal dealing. The reason is that we have no acceptable theory of harm done by these phenomena, but a number of plausible theories of the good they may do. It seems plain enough that tying arrangements used to achieve economies of scale, nondiscriminatory measurement of use, and efficient technological interdependence are valuable not merely to the firm but to consumers. Price discrimination, as we shall see in the next chapter, should also be classified as an efficiency valuable to consumers. The evasion of price regulation is beneficial in some cases, and neutral for antitrust purposes in the remainder. When the regulation is that of cartelists, evasion is clearly desirable. When the regulation is that imposed by a separate field of law, such as ICC minimum rate regulation, its evasion is probably beneficial to consumers, but courts cannot countenance violation of law on that account. Such use of tie-ins is not, however, a concern of antitrust, and courts ought not to strike them down under the antitrust laws. Each body of law has its own purposes and its own scale of remedies and punishments. It is important to the integrity of law that the wrongdoer not be convicted under any law that just happens to be handy, when his conduct does not in any way contravene the goals and rationale of that law. When the Department of Justice came across the tie of land to railroad service, it should have placed a telephone call to the Interstate Commerce Commission instead of proceeding with the *Northern Pacific* case.

A review of the cases and the economics of tying and reciprocity, then, leads inescapably to the conclusion that the law in this field is unjustified and is itself inflicting harm upon consumers.

20

Price Discrimination

THE attempt to counter the supposed threat to competition posed by price discrimination constitutes what is surely antitrust's least glorious hour. The instrument fashioned for the task was the Robinson-Patman Act, the misshapen progeny of intolerable draftsmanship coupled to wholly mistaken economic theory. One often hears of the baseball player who, although a weak hitter, was also a poor fielder. Robinson-Patman is a little like that. Although it does not prevent much price discrimination, at least it has stifled a great deal of competition.

Revision of the statute is not the answer, however, for price discrimination is not a proper target for antitrust and, in any event, the phenomenon seems beyond the effective reach of law.

THE ROBINSON-PATMAN ACT

The genesis of the Robinson-Patman Act is an oft-told tale.[1] Enacted in 1936, the statute was a child of the depression, as was so much pernicious economic regulation. Robinson-Patman shared with much of that other regulation (notably, the National Industrial Recovery Act) the premise that free markets were rife with unfair and anticompetitive practices which threatened competition, small business, and consumers. Price discrimination was thought to be such a practice, in large measure because of the chain store movement, of which A&P was the prime example in the popular mind. The chains purchased in volume and often took over certain distributive functions from suppliers, thus creating cost savings that were reflected in an ability to buy for less. Superior efficiency is not popular with those who must compete against it, and it never seems well understood by lawmakers. In any case, the cry went up that the chains were prospering unfairly as recipients of discriminatorily low prices; anti-chain store legislation in various forms was adopted in many states, and at the national level the result was a statute drafted by counsel for a wholesale grocers association, the Robinson-Patman Act.

STRUCTURE OF THE ACT

Robinson-Patman was in form an amendment to Section 2 of the Clayton Act, which had dealt half-heartedly and ineffectually with price differences. There is no need here to delineate Robinson-Patman's seemingly endless complexities and perversities,* and I shall merely summarize the statute's main structural features in order to give a general idea of its thrust and ambitions. Section 2(a) makes it "unlawful for any person . . . to discriminate in price between different purchasers . . . where the effect of such discrimination may be substantially to lessen competition or tend to create a monopoly . . . or to injure, destroy, or prevent competition with any person who . . . knowingly receives the benefit of such discrimination, or with customers of either of them."

Though the statute speaks of price discrimination, it is settled that the act merely means price difference.[2] The distinction is important. Price discrimination in the economic sense occurs when a seller realizes different rates of return on sales of the same product to different purchasers. (Another way of saying the same thing is that a seller who discriminates charges different purchasers prices that are proportionally unequal to his marginal costs.) It is thus clear that price difference does not necessarily involve price discrimination, and price identity does not rule out discrimination. Since the triggering event for Section 2(a) is a price difference, the statute simply ignores economic discrimination when prices are the same.

Robinson-Patman attempts to deal with economic discrimination rather than mere price difference by providing in 2(a) that the law does

* That has been accomplished once and for all by Frederick M. Rowe in his authoritative work *Price Discrimination Under the Robinson-Patman Act* (Boston: Little, Brown, 1962).

not "prevent differentials which make only due allowance for differences in the cost of manufacture, sale, or delivery resulting from the differing methods or quantities" in which commodities are "sold or delivered." Cost justification is an affirmative defense, so the burden of proof is on the accused seller.

Section 2(b) provides that a seller may rebut a prima facie case "by showing that his lower price or the furnishing of services or facilities to any purchaser or purchasers was made in good faith to meet an equally low price of a competitor, or the services or facilities furnished by a competitor."

These are the main features of the statute which we will consider in analyzing its impact upon markets and competition. However, other features of the act are, within their compass, equally or more objectionable. Section 2(c), for example, an attempt to prevent unearned brokerage payments that were actually camouflaged discounts, has made dangerous and often impossible certain discounts given for the actual performance of brokerage functions by purchasers. For present purposes, however, we may confine our analysis to Sections 2(a) and 2(b) and omit 2(c), (d), (e), and (f), which are, in any event, essentially ancillary to 2(a).

PERNICIOUS INFLUENCE OF THE ACT

A word should be said at the outset about the pervasiveness of Robinson-Patman's influence in the economy. The following theoretical discussion does not indicate what every antitrust practitioner knows, that tens of thousands, probably hundreds of thousands, of pricing decisions every year are altered through fear of Robinson-Patman. Quantity discounts, promotional discounts, discounts to recognize the purchaser's assumptions of tasks that would otherwise fall on the seller, discounts because of the purchaser's stage in the distribution chain, promotional allowances, advertising allowances—all these and many more are forgone or changed by the law. If that law is mistaken in its assumptions and further deformed in its application, as almost all respectable scholarship finds it to be, the needless deformation of market processes and the destruction of national wealth is enormous.*

* Some examples are given in Richard Posner, *The Robinson-Patman Act: Federal Regulation of Price Differences* (Washington, D.C.: American Enterprise Institute, 1976). According to Yale Brozen's foreword, the old Federal Energy Administration estimated that one ruling by the FTC relating to departures from "delivered pricing" systems makes it uneconomic for purchasers with trucks to

The fact is that no other antitrust statute has been subjected to so steady a barrage of hostile commentary as the Robinson-Patman Act. Indeed, the scholarly and professional literature on the statute resembles a cascade of vituperation.[3] There is no space here to rehearse all the charges that have been made and substantiated against this unhappy law, but it is important to understand the ways in which anticompetitiveness and business inefficiency are built into it.

The statute proceeds from the idea that price discrimination is a means of injuring competitors, usually small ones, and that injury to competitors results in injury to competition. The act purports to be about real economic discriminations. Although it is triggered by mere price differences, it provides, as noted above, the cost justification defense, which is intended to let the seller rebut a prima facie case by showing that a price difference is not actually an instance of discrimination.

It may clarify discussion if we begin by assuming that the cost justification defense is fully adequate, so that the act can identify and prohibit all real economic discriminations that are reflected in price differences. The object of this initial discussion is to show that Robinson-Patman's premise is faulty. Price discrimination should not be expected to injure competitors in any improper way. Thus, even if the act accomplished its purpose, it would accomplish little of value to the health of competitors.

Next, we will introduce a modicum of legal realism by showing that the statute does not come close to accomplishing its stated purposes, and in a real sense does not even address them, because two essential safeguards—the cost justification and the meeting competition defenses—do not work. This means that the law's results in action bear almost no resemblance to its stated objectives.

This chapter concludes with a general discussion of the problem of price discrimination, including the question of its impact on consumers and the feasibility of any law that attempts to prohibit discrimination.

ROBINSON-PATMAN'S THEORY OF INJURY TO COMPETITORS

Section 2(a) is read to protect competition between the discriminating seller and his rivals, between his customers, and occasionally between

---

pick up goods from their suppliers rather than return from trips empty, because they may not receive a "discriminatory" discount for providing the transportation. The result is an estimated annual waste of 100 million gallons of truck fuel and a national cost of $300 million. The literature of Robinson-Patman abounds with such horror stories, and the total wealth loss due to this one statute must be staggering.

the customers of his customers (that is, as the cognoscenti are apt to put it, competition at the primary, secondary, and tertiary levels). It will suffice to discuss the impact of discrimination on the seller's rivals and on his customers.

The theory that price discrimination may injure competition at the seller's level is merely the theory of predation by price cutting that we have already examined and found wanting. But Section 2(a) adds a curious twist to the theory, for price cutting is questionable here only if the seller charges two different prices. The reason for that curious requirement may be reliance on the ancient fallacy of recoupment. The discriminating seller is sometimes thought to be able to finance his predatory price cuts by raising his prices in other markets. But the seller would undoubtedly have been charging the profit-maximizing price in other markets already, so he would have no ability to raise prices there and recoup losses in the low-price market. Price discrimination confers no peculiar ability to conduct predatory price war. Alternatively, some legislators may have thought that a ban on price differences would make predation in local markets too expensive by requiring the predator to lower prices everywhere. The ban would have that effect if locally lower prices usually meant predation rather than different demand and cost conditions.

In any event, this aspect of Robinson-Patman is an unwelcome addition to existing law. Cases of deliberate predation by price cutting, if they exist, are taken care of by Section 2 of the Sherman Act. The argument of Chapter 7, that rules against predatory price cutting are probably useless and will certainly do more harm than good, is fully applicable here. Robinson-Patman is particularly unfitted for the task of stopping predation because it is an incipiency statute. This means that courts and the Federal Trade Commission may find a seller in violation of the law without finding either that he intended to injure competition or that his lower prices in one market did injure competition. They are empowered to guess, and often do guess, that the loss of sales by a rival in and of itself constitutes a threat to competition. For this reason, Robinson-Patman is unable to distinguish between vigorous competition and predation at the seller's level. Those who would avoid embroilment with the law must often refrain from competing.

The Supreme Court's decision in *Utah Pie Company* v. *Continental Baking Company* [4] is one of many illustrations of the statute's effects.*

* The definitive dissection of this decision is to be found in Bowman, "Restraint of Trade by the Supreme Court: The Utah Pie Case," 77 *Yale L.J.* 70 (1967).

Plantiff Utah Pie alleged that the three defendants—Pet Milk Company, Carnation Milk Company, and Continental—had injured competition by selling frozen fruit pies at discriminatorily low prices in the Salt Lake City market. A local jury found that defendants had not acted in collusion but that each had violated the statute, so that Utah Pie was entitled to treble damages. The court of appeals reversed, but the Supreme Court reinstated the jury's verdict. The facts of the case were these. Before Utah Pie entered the market in 1957 and built a new plant the following year, the Salt Lake City frozen-pie market was supplied by branches of national companies with plants elsewhere. Utah Pie entered aggressively and, with no or small transportation costs, undercut the national companies' prices. In its first full year of business it acquired 66.5 percent of the Salt Lake City market. Defendants countered by lowering their prices, and at times one or another of the defendants was selling for higher prices outside Utah, despite lower transportation costs in those markets. By 1961, Utah Pie's market share stood at 45.3 percent. The competition of the defendants had reduced it from a market share that Judge Learned Hand's *Alcoa* opinion thought possibly an illegal monopoly to a status as merely the largest seller in the market.

During the period of price discrimination the frozen-pie market in Salt Lake City expanded greatly, rising from 57,000 dozen pies in 1958 to almost 267,000 dozen pies in 1961. The supposed victim of the price discrimination, Utah Pie, not only retained its leading market position but greatly expanded its absolute sales volume and made profits throughout the period. Moreover, Utah Pie had initiated the price cuts. The predatory strategies of the defendants must have been of unbelievable subtlety. There is no economic theory worthy of the name that could find an injury to competition on the facts of the case. Defendants were convicted not of injuring competition but, quite simply, of competing. The Supreme Court's opinion finds a violation of Section 2(a) of Robinson-Patman solely because the market price for frozen pies went down in Salt Lake City. There could be no clearer demonstration than the *Utah Pie* decision that the statute is essentially anticompetitive and anticonsumer.

Matters are no better when the measure is applied to competition among the customers of a discriminating seller. There is little possibility that price discrimination can injure consumers by injuring competition between such customers. Yet the law is rigidly applied to stop price differentials to competing customers, and the only result is to prohibit more efficient modes of doing business.

Two general cases deserve examination: where the seller faces active rivals, and where he possesses monopoly power. Economic price discrimination in the former case will be only fleeting, transitory, a means of creating competition rather than of injuring it. Persistent price differentials between customers in this case are not price discriminations at all. Yet the law typically finds discrimination and punishes it in markets characterized by active rivalry.

Transitory discriminations occur in all active markets. "With ever-changing supply-demand conditions," Morris Adelman states, "new profit discrepancies are constantly being created and destroyed. The transitory discriminations are incentives for better resource use, because they occur as part of a competitive process which eventually liquidates them." [5]

Both general price rises and reductions in competitive markets—or, often, in other markets—are likely to begin with a seller altering a price here and there, testing responses, feeling for a better alignment with the powerful but only partially discernible forces to which he must conform. The evanescent discriminations of competitive markets are the sellers' antennae. This adjustment to shifting costs and demand is socially desirable, and it is best that appropriate responses be made as quickly and sure-footedly as possible. The cost justification defense is of no help in these situations because none exists. Sellers' inability to raise or lower prices selectively, to feel for the balance of market forces, makes prices more rigid and markets less sensitive to changing demands and costs. The ability to make transitory discriminations is thus a valuable element in the continuing process of adjustment, and it is unfortunate that the law should interfere with such discriminations.

Where there are rivals in a market and also persistent price differences to particular customers or classes of customers, those price differences are not price discriminations. The reason is clear. Every seller prefers a higher to a lower rate of return. Where there are rivals, no seller will be able to discriminate persistently, because his rivals will take away his disfavored customers (who pay a higher rate of return) with offers of slightly better prices. This process will continue until the rates of return to be had from selling to all customers are equal.

Persistent price differences in markets with rivals, therefore, are not price discriminations. They necessarily reflect differences in the cost of doing business with different customers. Such differences arise from a variety of factors, including the amounts customers purchase, selling costs, service costs, the performance of distributive functions by the customer, and so on. This fact means that the law should never attack price differentials of this sort. Not only is enormous pressure put on the cost justification defense—which, if it worked perfectly, would succeed in all such cases—but the mere threat of litigation and the expense of establishing the defense, which can be considerable, will inhibit sellers from giving full recognition to cost differences. This handicaps more efficient modes of doing business and reduces or removes incentives for creating them.

Persistent price differentials also occur in markets where a seller possesses monopoly power, perhaps because of a patent or economies of scale. These may be true discriminations, since there are no rivals able to undersell him to the disfavored customers. Such discriminations, it will be argued later, are likely to be better for consumers than the alternative of a single monopoly price. And, given monopoly upstream, we are unlikely to care about monopoly at the next stage (see Chapter 11).

It may be said that the discriminating monopolist seeks to exploit his customers' differing demands for his own profit. Nevertheless, he does not wish to destroy any customer or class of customers, for he would then lose profitable accounts. The discriminating monopolist can hardly be supposed, even for the sake of argument, to be suffused with a motiveless and self-destructive malignity. The destruction of any acceptably efficient customer will raise the cost of reaching ultimate consumers, to the monopolist seller's detriment. Note that competitive customer firms are necessarily operating where marginal costs are rising. To destroy some and transfer their business to others, who would expand output, is to raise the marginal cost of performing the customers' productive or distributive function. That increase in costs of getting goods to the ultimate consumer lowers the monopolist's profits.

This analysis also disposes of the theory, underlying the entire statute and explicitly embodied in Section 2(f), that a powerful customer may injure competition by extorting unjustified discounts from sellers. It may be worthwhile to discuss this theory, since it is widely held. Where sellers are competitive, there is no way for a large buyer to extract any discount that is not cost-justified. Sellers are making competitive returns, and any cut of that return would merely drive them from the market or reduce the amount they are willing to supply. When sellers are making returns above competitive levels, perhaps because of collusion, there is room for a powerful customer to negotiate a special discount. We tend, rather too loosely, to describe this situation as one in which the customer has "bargaining power," a term that becomes confused with absolute size and so is applied to situations (e.g., that of the employer agreeing to a wage contract with a nonunion employee) where it has no meaning. A large customer dealing with a cartelist does have bargaining power, however. He can make an all-or-nothing offer and have little to lose, since he can always buy elsewhere for the price the cartelist is asking. The cartelist has a definable amount of profit to lose and may make price concessions. It is difficult to see why we should do anything but rejoice when a seller in such a situation is forced to give a discriminatory discount. This may be the beginning of retaliatory discounts that move the price lower for all customers, in which case the discount and the price instability it causes represent a clear social gain. But let us assume, arguendo, that only one customer gets the discount, and prices otherwise remain high. This, too, is a result preferable to uniform high prices. The favored customer's output increases, driving down prices to ultimate consumers. The situation more closely approaches the price and output that would prevail under competition. Only sympathy for other business units that overrides sympathy for consumers could lead one to object to this result, for the ability to obtain such price concessions is clearly a socially valuable efficiency.

But may the customer not gain a monopoly? Impossible. In the first place, other large units will appear to gain the bargaining advantages that accrue to such units, or smaller customers will band together to gain the negotiating advantages of relative size. In the second place, sellers who saw a monopoly developing at the customer level would offer the lower prices to other customers to prevent that outcome. A monopsonist would squeeze all the extracompetitive profit from the cartelists by playing them off against each other and would also restrict output. The sellers would be better off producing at competitive rates and prices. There is, therefore, no reason why price discrimination should ever injure competition between the customers of the seller. Because the Robinson-Patman Act comes into operation only when such an injury is found to be possible, the statute is rendered incoherent at the outset: there is and can be no congruence between its major operative concept and reality.

The enforcement agencies and the courts are saved from knowledge of what they are actually doing by another feature of the statute. Robinson-Patman, as the use of the word "may" in the injury-to-competition clause warns, is an incipiency statute. This means that a court or the Federal Trade Commission need not believe it sees any actual injury to competition before applying the law, but must strike down price differences it thinks may inflict such injury. As we have seen repeatedly in other statutory contexts, the incipiency idea is an open invitation to outlaw any firm's behavior that costs another firm money, especially since any price differential is viewed as costing the less favored customer the amount of the differential. It follows, on incipiency logic, that any price differential threatens an injury to competition. The law has adopted this view from time to time, perhaps most notoriously in the Supreme Court's *Morton Salt* decision: [6] "In a case involving competitive injury between a seller's customers the Commission need only prove that a seller charged one purchaser a higher price for like goods than he had charged one or more of the purchaser's competitors." The law has at other times retreated somewhat from this position, but never far enough. The law will never find a sensible and comfortable resting place, however, because it is purporting to find something that does not exist. That is one reason why courts, which have a built-in tropism toward standards, are constantly tempted to settle on the only firm, if nonsensical, standard available: proof that a customer paid more is proof that he was hurt, and that, in turn, is proof that competition was, at least incipiently, injured.

TWO DEFENSES: COST JUSTIFICATION AND MEETING COMPETITION

Robinson-Patman equates price discrimination with price difference. This, as we have seen, is a false equation. The drafters of the law attempted to compensate partially for this problem by providing a cost justification defense. Section 2(a) states that price discriminations (by which it means price differences) are lawful if they "make only due allowance for differences in the cost of manufacture, sale, or delivery resulting from the differing methods or quantities in which such commodities are to such purchasers sold or delivered." Thus, price discrimination that exists when prices are equal is not covered by the statute, but a seller is entitled to try to show that price differences are not price discriminations because they are fully accounted for by cost differences.

This cost justification defense is less useful than it may appear. In the first place, it goes only to the issue of whether a discrimination exists, not whether the discrimination is desirable or undesirable. Nothing in Robinson-Patman permits proof that real economic discrimination is beneficial. That is unfortunate because the inhibition of discrimination in rivalrous markets makes them less sensitive and responsive. Even the inhibition of persistent discrimination probably harms consumers on balance.

But the situation is worse than this, for the cost justification defense does not even save price differences that do reflect only differences in cost. Thus, the statute cuts into economic efficiency. The inadequacy of the defense is due to its limited scope, the nature of costs, and the hostility of the Federal Trade Commission. Adelman explains one point about the inadequacy of the cost justification defense: [7]

> The burden of proof of a cost differential is on the seller. Any cost differential is presumed to be "unjustified" unless and until the Commission finds to the contrary. The procedural requirements are such that a cost differential must be disregarded unless it is certain and precise. But, since cost differentials are inherently uncertain and imprecise, most of them cannot exist in the contemplation of law.

There are, however, other reasons why the Robinson-Patman Act cannot give full weight to costs. In the first place, real costs are opportunity or alternative costs: "the cost of any productive service to use A is the maximum amount it could produce elsewhere. The forgone alternative is the cost." [8] Accounting records are not kept this way and could not well be, since forgone alternatives are only partly known and are constantly shifting in value. This means that when different services or amounts of service are used in producing and selling to different customers, cost differentials will rarely, if ever, be subject to even reasonably accurate measurement.

There are many other cost enigmas sufficient to make cost justification, and hence any rational price discrimination law, impossible. There is, for example, the common and insoluble problem of allocating segments of joint or common costs to one product or activity rather than another. The division is always arbitrary over very large ranges and consists, as Corwin Edwards has said, of "policy decisions which masquerade as mere accounting procedures." [9] Moreover, there is the awkward fact that economics is still engaged in identifying all of the factors that influence costs, and the law has not caught up even with the work that has been done. For example, we have been proceeding in this book on the assumption that marginal costs are determined by the firm's rate of output. For purposes of sketching the broad difference between competitive and monopolistic output decisions, that assumption is good enough. But when we turn to finer problems of the variations in an individual firm's costs, it simply will not do. Armen Alchian has shown that costs are also importantly affected by the volume or total amount of the good to be produced and the date the output is to be completed. [10] This may, incidentally, explain quantity discounts based on aggregate purchases over time, which the law and most commentators have regarded as not susceptible to cost justification. The seller can offer such a discount schedule with reasonable confidence that certain identifiable large buyers will take advantage of it, and this enables the seller to plan the volume of his output, giving him the possibility of the most efficient method of production for that volume. The effect is something like that of a requirements contract or vertical integration. The law has not even recognized these factors in cost justification, much less essayed the rather hopeless task of measuring them with any precision.

The situation is made worse than it need be by the Federal Trade Commission's hostility to cost justification, with the result that even costs that are reasonably estimable often fail to be taken into account. Any lawyer who has advised in this field has seen business judgments and pricing policies warped by the impossibility of pinning down costs he knows exist, by the expense of assembling data, and by the high probability that the law will reject whatever data he can put together. The good businessman differs from the mere bookkeeper in the extra qualities he brings to decisions—judgment and intuition based on knowledge of the processes involved (judgments and intuitions whose degree of accuracy will be tested by the forces of the market)—and these are precisely the qualities that the Robinson-Patman Act says he must put aside when making pricing decisions. Cost justification is thus an illusory defense. Adelman, as usual, puts the implications of that fact succinctly: [11]

To say that the cost-justification section of the Act might just as well not be there would be only a negligible exaggeration. It follows that taking all transactions as a group, the lower-cost buyers must be discriminated against, in that the sum of price differentials in their favor must fall very far short of the sum of cost differentials.

Nor is this the worst, for important sections of the Robinson-Patman Act—2(c), 2(d), and 2(e), dealing with payment of brokerage and payment for or furnishing of services and facilities—do not permit cost justification and thus prohibit the recognition of cost differences in practices closely analogous to price differentiation.

The result of the law's inability and, in part, refusal to recognize cost differences is the destruction of efficiency and wealth. When sellers are not permitted to recognize cost differences in price differences, purchasers lose an incentive to take over distributive functions they can perform more efficiently.

The other major defense to a charge of price difference is also inadequate to prevent the statute from suppressing competition. Section 2(b) provides that a seller may rebut a prima facie case made against him under Section 2(a), which is usually no more than a showing that he charged two different prices, "by showing that his lower price . . . to any purchaser or purchasers was made in good faith to meet an equally low price of a competitor. . . ." This defense, too, ignores the possible desirability of price discrimination. More to the present point, the defense is quite limited. It permits a seller only to meet the lower price of his competitor and not to beat it, a grudging concession to the right of commercial self-defense, not to the ideal of vigorous competition. The defense's limited value has been further narrowed by restrictive interpretations.

The Robinson-Patman Act, then, is billed as a law designed to protect competition from price discrimination. It is, in fact, a law that attacks a nonexistent threat and hinders the free movement of prices in markets needlessly. The policy of Robinson-Patman is directly contrary to the Sherman Act rule against price fixing.* They cannot both be considered sound antitrust policy.

THE PROBLEM OF PRICE DISCRIMINATION

If the Robinson-Patman Act must be considered a failure, the question remains whether antitrust should attempt to deal with price discrimination in some other fashion. This is a more difficult question, but the better guess, it seems to me, is that antitrust policy would do well to ignore price discrimination. That estimate is based upon the judgment that price discrimination is, on balance, probably better for consumers than any rule enforcing nondiscrimination, and upon the belief that law cannot satisfactorily deal with the phenomenon in any event.

THE IMPACT OF PRICE DISCRIMINATION ON CONSUMERS

We have seen that the fleeting discriminations characteristic of active markets are favorable to consumer welfare because they are part of the mechanism by which markets are enabled more rapidly to respond to and

* The policies conflict not only philosophically but in quite practical terms. The meeting-competition defense forces rivals into a knowledge of each other's prices and a pattern of matching rather than beating prices that closely resembles price fixing. Among thousands of examples of the collision of the opposed policies of the Sherman and Robinson-Patman acts: the recent exoneration from criminal collusion charges of wallboard suppliers whose defense was that they "verified" each other's prices to comply with Robinson-Patman requirements for the "good faith" meeting of competition.

balance the forces of supply and demand. We have also seen that persistent price differentials in rivalrous markets are not discriminations but recognitions of cost differences that ought to be allowed for the good of consumers. Price discrimination poses a consumer welfare problem only when it is relatively stable, and that will occur only when the seller has monopoly power. It is this variety of discrimination to which hostility is usually directed, though many people wrongly perceive it in cases where it does not exist.

Persistent or stable price discrimination in favor of specific customers is often said to require as preconditions: a seller possessing both a substantial degree of market power or monopoly (so that rival sellers will not take away customers who pay higher rates of return); a means of segregating customers into separate markets (so that those paying lower prices cannot resell to those whom the seller wishes to charge more); and customers with differing elasticities of demand (so that the maximizing prices will be different). Two of these preconditions are actually not required in all cases, for it is discriminatory to charge customers the same price when costs of serving them differ, and in such cases the customers need not be segregated and need not have differing elasticities of demand. All three preconditions are essential, however, in any case where the discrimination also involves charging different prices.

The monopolist discriminates in price in order to make a greater return from his monopoly position. That proposition by itself tells us nothing of the desirability of price discrimination. For present purposes, we must assume that the monopoly is lawful and unassailable, based perhaps on a patent or on economies of scale. The evil of monopoly is restriction of output and consequent misallocation of resources. The question, therefore, is whether the misallocation will be greater under a rule permitting discrimination or under a rule requiring a single price to all customers. That question, in turn, translates into the question of whether discrimination expands or further restricts the monopolist's output. If discrimination increases output, it tends to move resource allocation and value of marginal product toward that which would obtain in a competitive industry. A decrease in output has the opposite effect. The impact of discrimination on output, therefore, may be taken as a proxy for its effect on consumer welfare.*

* It is no objection to this criterion that, regardless of its effect on total output, discrimination will cause some customers to pay more and others less. Antitrust has available no criteria for comparing the respective income effects on the two groups or for weighing the alterations in their levels of satisfaction (see Chapter 3). The total output test, on the other hand, views consumers as a collectivity and avoids interpersonal comparisons.

An objection to the use of output effect as the sole basis for judging the results of price discrimination on consumer welfare has been raised by Richard Posner.[12] His point is that since price discrimination makes monopoly more profitable, firms will spend additional sums in an effort to gain monopoly, and such expenditures of resources may be largely or entirely social wastes. This point was touched on in Chapter 5. Posner's observation seems less an objection to permitting a monopolist to maximize his revenues through price discrimination than an additional reason to object to the achievement of monopoly through certain means. Thus, the resources expended in forming and maintaining a cartel are social wastes as much as is the dead-weight loss due to output restriction discussed in Chapter 5. Posner's point also shows that price regulation will lead firms to compete for market share by nonprice means, and so convert monopoly profits to costs. These points do not seem objections, however, when the monopoly is obtained in ways of which antitrust approves. The observation shows that there will be extra innovative effort to gain patent monopolies; such efforts should increase if the monopolist is permitted to discriminate, but it is impossible to say that the innovative efforts of those who fail to gain a patent, or who gain one only to discover that it does not confer real market power, are social wastes. A great deal of increased efficiency may be produced without the necessity of paying for it in monopolistic restriction of output. To come more directly to purely antitrust concerns, the only monopoly the law should countenance, according to the argument of this book, is that based upon superior efficiency. It cannot be said that the extra resources committed to the effort to achieve superior efficiency in anticipation of the ability to discriminate in price are wasted. It is theoretically possible that, for example, more resources will be devoted to cutting costs than would be profitable but for the anticipation of expanded monopoly profits, but it is dubious that much of the expenditure can be said to be wasted.

The basic theory of price discrimination is quite simple. A monopolist faces a sloping demand curve. The market demand, however, is likely to be a composite of widely differing demands of individual customers. Such demands are said to be relatively elastic if price changes result in relatively large changes in the amount of the product demanded, and relatively inelastic if price changes produce smaller effects on amounts demanded. A monopolist who is moderately thoughtful about his self-interest will realize that he could increase net revenues if he could segregate his customers according to the elasticities of their demands. The reason is obvious. When the demand elasticities of customers are different, no single price can extract the maximum return from each. If they can be segregated so one class of customers cannot resell to the other, the monopolist can charge them different prices and so extract the maximum return from each class.

The movement from a single price to a two-price system clearly benefits the seller; the question for antitrust policy is what it does to output. There is no easy answer in this simple two-market case, though Joan Robinson, whose analysis seems as complete as any that has appeared since, thought it more probable on the whole that output would be greater under discrimination than nondiscrimination.[13] She based this conclusion on a demonstration that output will increase when the demand curve in the lower-priced market is more concave than the demand curve in the higher-priced market, plus the belief that this will more commonly be the case.

There are, perhaps, some additional reasons for suspecting that Robinson's estimate of probable output effect is correct. We tend to discuss the theory as though the seller were instituting discrimination between two classes of customers he already serves, but discrimination may be a way of adding an entire category of customers he would not otherwise approach because the lower price would have spoiled his existing market. It is possible, also, that there are situations in which a product or service would not be produced at all without discrimination.[14] Moreover, where there is a relation between the two markets such that each demand curve depends in some degree on the price set in the other market, the effect will be to hold prices down somewhat in the higher-priced market as the lower-priced market expands.* This leakage between markets means that the conventional view of price discrimination overstates the output restriction caused by discrimination in the higher-priced market.

Finally, since we are comparing the results of a policy of permissiveness with an alternative of legally required nondiscrimination, it may be useful to suggest that the short run and long run effects of a rule pro-

---

* "Often there is some direct movement of consumers between markets: if first run movies get more expensive relative to second runs, some people will shift from the former to the latter. Often the movement is indirect. For example, if a railroad has no competition at *A* but other transportation rivals at point *B*, we should expect demand for railroad transportation to be less elastic at the former point. Yet if the firms at *A* and *B* are in the same industry and selling in the same markets, in the long run the branch of the industry at *A* will decline if high rates are charged." (Stigler, *The Theory of Price*, 3d ed. [New York: Macmillan, 1966], p. 211.) And, it appears, the branch of the industry at *B* will expand.

hibiting discrimination will not invariably be identical. If the seller has some costs that he cannot discontinue at once, he may find it profitable, when freedom to discriminate is initially denied, to charge in both markets a single compromise price. This may give him the greatest net revenues over his temporarily unalterable costs. But over time the seller may fail to replace equipment, facilities, and personnel, thereby rearranging his cost structure so that he is finally able to sell in the higher-priced market alone. He will then abandon the lower-priced market and make a greater return on investment. The long-run effect of prohibiting discrimination will have been to decrease output. These considerations, some of them admittedly minor, taken together appear to increase the likelihood that two-market discrimination will have an output-expanding effect.

If the better guess is that two-price systems usually increase output over legally compelled uniform pricing, the general policy of antitrust should prefer such discrimination to nondiscrimination. If, as seems very probable, the relative output effects of two-market discrimination and nondiscrimination are at worst indeterminate, there is no affirmative case for legal interference with the seller's choice.

There is more to the argument than this, however. The case for allowing discrimination freely is strengthened by the observation that the more a monopolist is able to discriminate, the more likely becomes the favorable result of an increase in output. In the limiting case, the perfectly discriminating monopolist will produce the same output as would a competitive industry. The limiting case is that in which the monopolist is able to treat each customer as a separate market. In other words, when the monopoly involved is lawful, the more the monopolist is permitted to discriminate, the better are the results in terms of resource allocation.

There appears, then, to be no general case against price discrimination on consumer welfare grounds, and the better guess seems to be that, in general, price discrimination benefits consumers. There remains the question of whether law can single out and ban only anticonsumer discriminations.

THE FEASIBILITY OF ANY LAW AGAINST PRICE DISCRIMINATION

We have seen that it is impossible to say that price discrimination in general is bad. In fact, in general it seems to be desirable. And we have seen that the Robinson-Patman Act bears precious little relationship to real discrimination, except that, by its inability to recognize cost differences, it creates discrimination. Moreover, if Robinson-Patman could recognize discrimination, the law's tests are not addressed to output effects, the sole issue discrimination presents.

The question remains of whether it would be wise to substitute a law that makes persistent price discrimination unlawful when its effect is to decrease the seller's rate of production. The answer is yes, it would be desirable if we could (1) identify the existence of price discrimination with some precision, (2) predict accurately the long-run effect upon the seller's rate of output of a prohibition on discrimination, and (3) do these things at a cost in enforcement resources lower than the benefits derived. It seems clear that none of these conditions can be met, and therefore that the proposed law, while less disastrous than Robinson-Patman, would be a thoroughly bad idea.

That there now exist no reliable means, and certainly no means suitable for use in litigation, to identify price discrimination is in itself a conclusive argument against adopting a law dealing with the practice. Robinson-Patman's tendency to equate price differentials with price discrimination is, as we have seen, wholly erroneous. In order to deal with real discrimination, the law must replace direct observation of prices, which are visible, with a comparison of returns, which are not visible. This means that in every case in which price discrimination is suspected, a process must be undertaken similar in general purpose to Robinson-Patman's cost justification. Our previous consideration of that process and the nature of costs applies here. The problems are, given present and foreseeable techniques, insurmountable. And it must be remembered that failure to identify discrimination and measure its size is not costless. Every time the law makes a mistake and wrongly decides the presence or degree of price discrimination, it necessarily makes judgments about output effects that have no relation to reality. Every time, on the basis of such error, the law orders "discrimination" ended, it is not merely forcing real discrimination upon the seller but ordering a misallocation of resources. The difficulty, amounting usually to the impossibility, of the enterprise ensures that mistakes will be a frequent, if not the invariable, outcome. Fear of the law and its inaccuracies, moreover, will chill highly desirable freedom of pricing behavior, even as today Robinson-Patman induces sellers to make pricing decisions that would be irrational but for the utility of avoiding legal entanglement. These are heavy costs inflicted by the law itself.

If discrimination could be identified and measured accurately, the law would then face the necessity of predicting whether a ban on the practice would increase or decrease output. Accurate estimation is impossible, however, because it requires empirical data concerning the demand schedules of the customers. Nobody will have that data. The demand and cost curves we draw on graphs are purely for the purpose of illustrating reactions as firms feel their way toward a profit-maximizing position. The executive who thinks about the matter in these terms—and it is not necessary that he do so in order to arrive at the best position—may be rather confident that he has approximated an equation of marginal revenue and marginal cost, but he will have no way of describing the shape of either curve any distance from their intersection. The prospects of a tribunal's being able to predict the output effect of a ban on what it thinks is discrimination are therefore bleak, to say the least.

It might be thought that the relative sizes of the markets would give some indication of the seller's conduct after the prohibition of discrimination. If the lower-priced market is much the larger, perhaps requiring a single price would lead the seller to keep both by adopting uniformly the price there. This would expand his sales to the formerly higher-priced market. But this prediction is far from sure. Once the two markets are joined by law, the seller's maximizing solution may be a price anywhere between the former prices, and the effect upon total output is once again uncertain. Ordering him to adopt the lower prices would require perpetual regulation to see that all future prices were actually those that would have obtained in the lower-priced market alone. Besides, as we have seen, the long-run and short-run effects may differ, the seller opting for an increased output until he can discontinue some costs and adjust so that he can serve the higher-priced market alone. Where multimarket discrimination is at issue, predictions of output effect are, of course, even less likely to be accurate.

In making these two points—about the identification of price discrimination and the prediction of output effect—we have not so far mentioned a further complication. These judgments depend, respectively, upon knowledge of costs and of demand elasticities. I have sufficiently labored the point that they are unknowable. But, to make the impossible worse, they are also subject to continual change. Thus, a decision about price discrimination and its effects is subject to very rapid obsolescence. We can hardly expect, or want, either courts or commissions to sit as permanent regulatory bodies over all American business.

Finally, it is also necessary, when deciding whether to adopt a new legal policy or to continue an old one, to count the direct costs of enforcement. Resources expended in law enforcement and compliance are as effectively lost to consumers as resources misallocated by cartels. Unnecessary antitrust law occupies the time and energy of an enormously able body of persons—judges, lawyers in and out of government, economists, and businessmen—who could otherwise be contributing something worthwhile. Such costs ought to weigh decisively against the adoption of any policy that cannot rather persuasively be shown to be likely to do more good than harm. That showing, it appears, cannot be made with respect to any proposal to restrict price discrimination. Therefore, the law ought not to attempt to deal with the subject.

PART III

SUMMATION

21

Recommendations

To the degree that this book's analysis of the fundamental concepts and major doctrines of antitrust is correct, the law requires reform. As matters stand, the law pulls in opposite directions, producing a pattern of results without policy coherence. This situation is not inevitable; it flows from a small number of intellectual errors that can be corrected. The only cure for bad theory is better theory.

The lines along which the law should be reformed are clear. I will not rehearse the argument or its implications in detail, but will merely set out the major conclusions that follow from it.

(1) The only goal that should guide interpretation of the antitrust laws is the welfare of consumers. Departures from that standard destroy the consistency and predictability of the law; run counter to the legislative intent, as that intent is conventionally derived; and damage the integrity of the judicial process by involving the courts in grossly political choices for which neither the statutes nor any other acceptable source provide any guidance.

(2) In judging consumer welfare, productive efficiency, the single most important factor contributing to that welfare, must be given due weight along with allocative efficiency. Failure to consider productive efficiency—or, worse, the tendency to view it as pernicious by calling it a "barrier to entry" or a "competitive advantage"—is probably the major reason for the deformation of antitrust's doctrines.

(3) The law should be reformed so that it strikes at three classes of behavior:

(a)   The suppression of competition by horizontal agreement, such as the nonancillary agreements of rivals or potential rivals to fix prices or divide markets.

(b)   Horizontal mergers creating very large market shares (those that leave fewer than three significant rivals in any market).

(c)   Deliberate predation engaged in to drive rivals from a market, prevent or delay the entry of rivals, or discipline existing rivals. The kinds of predation that are likely to occur have been discussed, and care must be taken not to confuse hard competition with predation.

(4) The law should permit agreements on prices, territories, refusals to deal, and other suppressions of rivalry that are ancillary, in the sense discussed, to an integration of productive economic activity. It should abandon its concern with such beneficial practices as small horizontal mergers, all vertical and conglomerate mergers, vertical price maintenance and market division, tying arrangements, exclusive dealing and requirements contracts, "predatory" price cutting, price "discrimination," and the like. Antitrust should have no concern with any firm size or industry structure created by internal growth or by a merger more than ten years old.

These are not prescriptions for the nonenforcement of the antitrust laws, but rather for their enforcement in a way that advances rather than retards competition and consumer welfare.

Two of the three classes of behavior at which antitrust should be directed appear presently to have too few resources devoted to them. Experience with antitrust suggests that there is far more price fixing in the economy than the enforcement authorities detect. The major reason for the poor detection record is the paucity of Antitrust Division field offices. Field offices are located in a few major cities, and their staffs tend not to work at any distance from their bases. One way to compensate for this deficiency is to give antitrust enforcement authority to states' attorneys general, but this may be a dubious solution. The attorneys general of many states may prove more willing to attack large out-of-state corporations than to punish price fixing by politically important local businesses. The better solution would be to create more Antitrust Division field offices by dispersing the personnel now concentrated in Washington. Price-fixing cases deliver more consumer welfare for the enforcement dollar than any other kind of prosecution.

Dispersal of antitrust personnel across the nation would also make possible more attention to the predatory misuse of courts—federal, state, and local—administrative agencies and regulatory bodies, and private, quasi-governmental groups like organized exchanges. Predation through such institutions appears to be more frequent than has been supposed.

Finally, there is the extremely important task of bringing the original and still valid antitrust philosophy of free entry, open markets, and vigorous competition to those areas where anticompetitive behavior now occurs with governmental blessing. This can be done in two ways. The first is intervention in federal, state, and local regulatory processes to extend the competitive ethic as broadly as possible. There are many regulatory schemes that leave room for antitrust in their interstices. Much regulation does not, for example, assume the suppression of all competition in the industry; but through inattention or worse, regulated industries have been permitted to cartelize in ways not necessary to the success of the regulation. Antitrust enforcement can challenge such developments and make clear the limits of regulation as well as the claims of competition.

More than this may be done, however. The Antitrust Division is not merely a litigating agency; it has important responsibilities in the formulation of new legislation. It should expand its portfolio to encompass testimony on the merits of new legislation that has implications for competition. The Division may often be unable to litigate once regulation is in place, but it is able to testify and to publicize its opposition to anticompetitive measures and to seek the repeal of legislation that has needlessly suppressed free market forces.

Positive programs such as these would be enormously beneficial to the wealth of our nation and to the competitive ideal. Such programs would, moreover, elicit enough opposition from affected industries to dispel any notion that a policy of free markets is in any sense narrowly pro-business.

Final Thoughts

$\mathbb{T}$O claim, as I have, that antitrust is a subcategory of ideology is necessarily to assert that it connects with the central political and social concerns of our time. The claim is not grandiose; it could as well be made for any major field of law. Antitrust law, however, is a particularly instructive microcosm because its issues are framed with clarity by price theory and because the law is so largely judge-made, which means that every decision requires a written explanation.

Antitrust connects to the political issues of our time in a variety of ways. Though these do not break down neatly, since they are interwoven, for convenience I have divided them into two parts: first, the capacity of the American lawmaking process to create and apply complex social policy; and, second, the relationship of the struggle of ideas within antitrust to ideological progressions in the larger social order.

SOCIAL POLICY AND
THE LAWMAKING PROCESS

The paths by which antitrust law has come to its modern condition—exhibiting the paradox of great popularity and vigorous enforcement coupled with internal contradiction and intellectual decadence—are worth examining. That the lawmaking process has performed inadequately, viewed in the light of the results, seems both self-evident and an understatement. Given the great number of very good minds that have labored to produce the policy, an examination of the reasons for the failure of the process may induce a degree of modesty about the abilities of government, and modesty is a condition essential to freedom and democracy.

The reasons for the inadequate performance of the legal institutions that shape antitrust is a complex topic. No single institution is wholly responsible, but perhaps it can be said that the factor common to the performance of all of them was, and is, the absence of a rudimentary understanding of market economics. Few of the actors in the process, however, seemed to display any lack of self-confidence in economic argument.

The central institution in making antitrust law has been the Supreme Court.* That is true because the antitrust laws are so open-textured, leave so much to be filled in by the judiciary, that the Court plays in antitrust almost as unconstrained a role as it does in constitutional law. As Judge Wyzanski put it: [1] "In the anti-trust field the courts have been accorded, by common consent, an authority they have in no other branch of enacted law." To stress the latitude given courts by the antitrust statutes is not, of course, to concede that it is unlimited, but it remains true that even if courts accept consumer welfare as their sole guideline, they have been granted an exceptionally broad mandate to make law.

The Supreme Court labors under important and perhaps decisive institutional handicaps in its effort to make sensible law. It may sound perverse to describe the Court's obligation to respond to the will of Congress as an institutional handicap, but in a very real sense it is. That obligation poses a jurisprudential problem because the will of Congress contains internal contradictions.

Certain of the antitrust statutes, the Clayton Act and the Robinson-Patman Act, direct the courts' attention to specific suspect business practices. Though these practices are almost entirely beneficial, Congress has indicated its belief that they may—not always, but under circumstances deliberately left undefined—injure competition. Is a court that understands the economic theory free, in the face of such a legislative declara-

---

* It may not remain so. Impatience with the time major cases take in court has led to proposals that Congress decree the restructuring of industries, either in general (on the erroneous supposition that conventional oligopoly theory provides a safe guide to policy) or sector by sector (as the fickle winds of public antipathy dictate).

tion, to reply that, for example, no vertical merger ever harms competition? The issue is not free from doubt, but I think the better answer is yes. The court is told to look for a condition it knows not to exist. It seems clearly improper for the court to "solve" the dilemma by striking down every instance of the behavior specified, and it seems hardly more proper for it to set up arbitrary criteria concerning the circumstances in which the behavior will be deemed to injure competition.*

An analogous case would be presented if a particularly benighted legislature declared that poltergeists were the cause of many automobile accidents and that apparent negligence should be excused if the court finds, upon a preponderance of the evidence, that poltergeists were responsible. Should a court frame rules about the criteria for showing infestation by spirits and deny recovery to victims even though it knows the legislature is wrong? Is the matter different if the court has good reason to think that the legislature really wanted to relax the rules about driving while drunk? One is an instance of plain mistake by the legislature, the other of a desire to accomplish surreptitiously that which it does not wish to be seen doing openly. In either case, the court should probably respond that it will do whatever the legislature commands, but that since poltergeists apparently do not cause automobile accidents, the court is incapable of framing rules on the subject. This is not a statement that the rules may not be made but that, if they are to be made, the legislature must do it. Thus, the legislature could respond by enacting a statute specifying that poltergeistism should be conclusively presumed in stated circumstances, or that drunken driving should not be evidence of negligence. The court, not having to invent criteria it knows to be nonsense, could enforce such laws. No court is constitutionally responsible for the legislature's intelligence, only for its own.

So it is with the specific antitrust laws. Courts that know better ought not accept delegations to make rules unrelated to reality and which, therefore, they know to be utterly arbitrary. They can accept arbitrary or even pernicious rules from the legislature. It would have been best, therefore, if the courts first confronted with the Clayton Act and later the Robinson-Patman Act had said something along these lines: We can discern no way in which tying arrangements, exclusive dealing contracts, vertical mergers, price differences, and the like injure competition or lead to monopoly. We certainly are unable to estimate the likelihood of such results in their incipiency. For these reasons, and since the statutes

---

* It does not seem a more legitimate strategy for a court to pretend to apply a statute but always to find that the law's criteria are not met.

in question leave the ultimate economic judgment to us, we hold that, with the sole exception of horizontal mergers, the practices mentioned in the statutes never injure competition and hence are not illegal under the laws as written. (There may be another exception in the predatory employment of such practices, but that is both highly improbable and already covered by Section 2 of the Sherman Act.) Congress may think our judgment wrong, or it may have other reasons to outlaw certain of the practices involved. Should it enact a law describing what is to be outlawed with some particularity, or enunciating criteria that we are capable of applying, we will of course enforce that law.

That would have begun a useful dialogue. It did not occur, probably because the courts lacked strong economic theory and hence found it impossible to resist the congressional suggestion that certain practices may be anticompetitive. A court without any particular economic sophistication will almost certainly respond to the congressional suggestion by finding that in some instances the practices designated do threaten competition. Having begun, it will find no principled stopping point precisely because the original idea was wrong and because there are no real criteria that distinguish one instance of such a practice from any other. For that reason, the law moves steadily toward a rule of per se illegality for practices that were never intended even by Congress to be per se illegal and which are, in fact, economically desirable.

The law's technique of reasoning by analogy, in general so essential, reinforces and speeds this tendency. Analogy is a dangerous mode of argument because one cannot possibly know whether situations are analogous unless one bears in mind the principle according to which they are to be compared. If one is fuzzy or inexplicit about the principle, superficial analogies may be made between things that are quite different in the respects that count; alternatively, real similarities may be missed. Where there is no valid principle, as in the case of these suspect practices, analogical reasoning produces mindless law.

We seem intent on making difficult matters worse by pressing upon our federal courts tasks of a number and complexity unequaled by those assigned the judiciary of any other nation. In courts, as in all other working units, there are problems of economies of scale, of optimal size and workload. By any standard, our courts are badly overloaded. That handicap is in part self-inflicted. The modern Supreme Court has reached out, usually through interpretations of the Constitution, to assume supervision of an ever-increasing span of activities. Simultaneously, however, Congress has thrust upon the courts a docket of increasing

size and complexity, as it continues to transform us into a highly regulated welfare state. Numbers of cases do not tell the story, though they
tell much. Not only are statutory programs more complex, but it is common for Congress to enact programs with many of the basic policy
choices unmade, leaving essentially legislative choices to the courts. The
upshot is that, for a variety of reasons, the federal courts, and ultimately
the Supreme Court, must address not merely conventional "legal" issues but broad and profound questions of economics, sociology, political philosophy, criminology, and the like. Moreover, through the accidents of litigation, these issues are presented to the Court in random
order. To make public policy really well under such conditions is probably beyond the capacities of any tribunal, however competent its
members.

Yet the performance of the courts would have been far better in antitrust, as in other fields of law, had they received the support they were
entitled to expect from the other participants in the policymaking enterprise. Courts are not supposed to be able to make law unaided, and our
courts have had too little assistance from Congress or from the practicing bar.

It was, perhaps, never to be expected that Congress would create
the details of a rational antitrust policy. As a body, it is capable of
deciding questions that require a yes or no, of adopting correct broad
general principles, or of writing codes reflecting detailed compromises;
but whatever the merits of individual members, Congress as a whole
is institutionally incapable of the sustained, rigorous, and consistent
thought that the fashioning of a rational antitrust policy requires. No
group of that size could accomplish the task. Large bodies simply do not
reason coherently together. Congress could, for example, adopt a useful
general goal in the Sherman Act. It proved unable to supply sensible
specifics in the Clayton and Robinson-Patman acts.

Congress is also a forum for interest-group politics, and antitrust
rules affect a number of very specific interests. The tax laws are a sufficient illustration of the effect of interest-group politics upon complex legislative efforts. While the results may be acceptable in the field of taxa-
tion, where multiple objectives compete and interest groups often have
good or at least plausible claims for different treatment, it is intolerable
in antitrust, where a single principle of competition in the public interest
is supposed to govern.

There is always in Congress, moreover, a strong element of anti-
corporate populist sentiment, a desire to punish business precisely be-

cause it is successful. Examples abound and need not be multiplied. A very prominent congressman endorsed President Carter's energy plan, which calls for public sacrifices, and added that both Wall Street and the petroleum companies must be made to hurt, too, the oil companies by being broken up. That it makes no sense whatever to inflict pain, and hence disincentives, on the businesses to which the public must look for energy seems to matter not at all. The populist strain runs strong in Congress, of course, because it runs strong in the electorate. The functions performed by markets are almost wholly unknown and unappreciated in this bastion of capitalism.

These are perhaps sufficient reasons why Congress has not aided the courts greatly in forming antitrust doctrine, and why any future congressional participation is likely to make matters worse. But the courts could nonetheless have done much better had it not been for the lapses and intermittent inadequacies of another and crucial legal institution, the practicing bar.

Because federal judges are busy generalists, it should be obvious that the lead in the theoretical analysis that underlies doctrine must come from outside the courts, from specialized practicing lawyers and from academic specialists in the law and in related social sciences. The theory is that skilled advocates not only bring to a court conflicting evidence but also explore the resources of legal doctrine and illuminate the policy considerations that guide the choice of doctrine and its reformulation while being applied. It is always open to an advocate to go back to first principles. Whether or not he does so depends on his tactical situation, for his first duty is to his client and not to an abstract conception of the public welfare. But tactics in the great cases, cases that set the direction of the law, invariably invite one side or the other to initiate a discussion of first principles. For this reason it has correctly been said that an advocate before the Supreme Court represents more than a client, he represents an idea that is contending for acceptance or dominance in the society. Both his client and the law are in jeopardy if he does not understand that idea and its relation to the great ideas that animate the society.

The adversary system assumes—in fact requires, if it is to work adequately—that in seminal cases the contending lawyers place before the courts the major alternative lines of argument, that advocates discuss the policy choices to be made and their consequences. In an adversary process where judges rely on what the lawyers bring before them, it is important that both sides discuss more than the application of existing doctrine to the facts; it is crucial that they debate the larger issues, the fitness of the rules. The system does not perform this function well in any complex field of law. That is due partially to the unspecialized nature of the American bar and partially to the fact that even among specialists there are widely varying degrees of competence. Cases of importance to the theoretical development of the law are almost, though not quite, distributed at random among members of the bar. It is commonplace for a case of the greatest significance to be argued in the Supreme Court by counsel who have little or no grasp of the significance of the issues that underlie the controversy. The lawyers are there not because of their own attainments but because they happened to be retained in a matter that turned out to have an issue worthy of the Court's attention. In such cases, the Court must itself find and explore the issues without real help from adversary presentations.

Though this is a general problem, and antitrust is by no means a unique instance, the particular problems that afflict antitrust litigation are worthy of remark. The dismaying fact is that the business community and its lawyers have not in general urged the basic ideas of the free market in the courts. They have tended to accept the government's antimarket premises and to proceed, necessarily defensively, from there. No doubt this was due in part to the fact that the Court was for a considerable period of time overtly hostile to the market economy and its institutions; but because that hostility went largely unchallenged, it was perhaps not seen for what it was, either by the Court itself or by the society. Dissents that could have been evoked and might have formed the basis for a rational law in the future went unwritten. Arguments that might have changed the terms of discourse not only in the courtroom but also in professional, business, and academic circles remained unspoken.

The causes of the defense bar's default are undoubtedly complex, but one is surely a lack of adequate economic sophistication. The great antitrust cases, those that set trends and establish principles, inevitably turn on inferences drawn from economic analysis. Many otherwise excellent lawyers have not grasped that microeconomics is now their province, and that they cannot discharge their responsibilities by employing an economist as an expert witness at trial. Economics informs the entire process, and the antitrust specialist should have as much command of basic price theory as specialists in other fields have of forensic medicine or tax accounting or chemistry. The bar's specialization and the bench's generalism are each necessary safeguards for the weaknesses inherent in the other. The evidence, unfortunately, is that part of the antitrust bar remains uninterested in the fundamentals of economics, preferring the relatively sterile function of weaving together old decisions in an attempt, usually futile, to design a legal fabric at once a little more appealing to their clients' needs and to the courts' tastes.

Another factor that has handicapped business defendants before the courts is the difference in the nature and structure of the contending interests. The government is represented by the Antitrust Division of the Department of Justice and by the Federal Trade Commission, permanent bodies with long-range interests and points of view. These agencies are organized to advance a single principle, and it is observable throughout government, as elsewhere, that men and women in organizations whose existence and success is defined by a single principle tend to push that principle well past the point at which a more balanced judgment would conclude, not merely that returns were diminishing, but that the principle itself had become deformed through the pressure required to extend it ever farther against equally valid competing principles.

Pressures of that sort have long been at work within the Antitrust Division and the Commission, producing many of the bizarre theories examined in this book. The government many years ago succeeded in establishing as law most of what can be regarded as sound policy: the per se rule against price fixing and similar naked eliminations of competition, the rule against large horizontal mergers, and the rule against predation. More recent extensions of law have been anticompetitive, and these have also been the growing area of the law, the subject of most litigation about rules. The sound, well-established rules are no longer under debate. Hence, in modern times, if not in earlier antitrust history, the government has, more often than not, represented the anti-free market position and the defendant the free market position. The Antitrust Division and the Commission have in a sense been frustrated by their own successes, and must continually press on to fresh territory, seeking theories that broaden the application of the law and make violations easier to establish. They enjoy great advantages in that effort. They are viewed by the public and to some extent by the courts as expert bodies representing the public interest. More than that, the enforcement agencies, having long-range objectives, are concerned less with immediate results than with ultimate doctrine; having a great many possible cases to choose from, they can wait and select the best vehicles for their purposes. That is a tactical advantage of no small importance.

The defense bar has none of these advantages. It is fragmented, without central direction, and without a cohesive philosophy. No individual lawyer or law firm has an incentive to plan for the future establishment of an important principle, largely because it is highly unlikely that any particular lawyer or firm will get a case where the principle is at stake. It is sheer chance which of several thousands of lawyers happens to find himself before a court in a case crucial to the direction of the law. Nor, since the government has chosen it, is the case likely to be attractive from the defense point of view.

The Antitrust Division and the Federal Trade Commission are, moreover, their own clients. They are advocates only for a position of their own devising; if they select the right case, they have little at stake other than their theory. Defense counsel represents a business client who, quite naturally, tends to regard a major antitrust case not as an opportunity to advance a principle but as a nonrecurring catastrophe, a situation to be gotten out of with as little damage as possible. That inclination is rational. Should the Antitrust Division succeed in establishing a new rule, the benefit will accrue to it and to the Commission. Should a corporation succeed, it will do so at great cost, and almost all of the benefit will accrue to other corporations that have borne none of the cost. The result is that defendants are often less interested in the broad rule than is the government. It may be this factor or merely lack of sophistication that leads to defenses disastrous to the intellectual integrity of the law. The government employs the stratagem of preempting the strongest defense available by calling business efficiency by names like "competitive advantage" or "barrier to entry." Socially beneficial efficiencies are thus made to sound like harmful market imperfections. Many lawyers and businessmen are at pains to deny anything that sounds bad, so they insist they have no competitive advantage, with the consequence that the government's semantic conversion is not challenged.

The deficiencies of our litigative process tend, therefore, to press in one direction and to deny the courts the full assistance they should obtain from counsel. Concepts of extremely dubious merit or even of undoubted pernicious tendency pass into law and become conventional wisdom without ever having been subjected to the rigorous testing that informed adversary debate provides.

Having said this much in defense of the Supreme Court over the lifespan of the antitrust laws, I must also observe that there remain reasons to be critical of its performance. The Court has not merely followed Congress and the enforcement agencies, it has upon occasion and in a significant sense led and educated all the institutions that deal with antitrust. Of the Warren Court it is possible to say, I think without injustice, that having been forced by the specifics of some of the antitrust statutes to go one mile along the wrong road, it willingly went two, and eyed the third with something suspiciously akin to enthusiasm.

Since the inadequacies of the adversary process and the intractability of the material with which it had to deal forced the Court to proceed in partial darkness, it would have done better to move more cautiously. The Court may not be expected to know much economic theory, particularly when the bar has done so little to inform it, but it can be expected to know that it does not know, and to walk softly as it learns. Antitrust, after all, is a massive introduction of public force into an area of private activity which is valuable both to the actors as an aspect of their freedom and to the society as the source of its wealth. It would seem preferable for judges who are uncertain about the conduct they must scrutinize to hold close at first to areas where the laws clearly bite and then to move outward only as their understanding increases, and not, as they have done time and again, to resolve doubts in favor of illegality.

The fact that the lawmaking process has not worked well in antitrust may have significance beyond the bounds of that field. There are obvious dangers in generalizing from the single body of law examined in this book, but if I may be permitted to draw upon experience with the process in other fields of law (even though that experience has not been related here), I would suggest that the outcome in antitrust is not untypical. We may, as a society, lack the resources, the skill, and the sophistication to carry into effect all of the policies we have adopted. When the desirability of a policy is debated, we tend not to weigh in the balance the distortions that will be introduced by the workings of institutions that must interpret and apply the policy. Law that seems preferable, in the abstract, to unregulated social and economic processes is all too likely, given our frequent inability to apply policy without deforming it, to produce results different from, if not opposed to, those we intended.

The defects in our lawmaking process are not given, of course. The institutions we have been discussing are capable of better performance and may provide it if we evaluate and criticize them with some sympathy and sophistication. But the process by which we translate policy into law will always produce some significant degree of deflection, and we must learn to allow for that. The defects inherent in our lawmaking process form part of the case for judicial caution and self-restraint, and that is, in turn, part of the more general case for simplified policies and limited government. Though our experience with antitrust certainly does not prove that case, it at least suggests it.

ANTITRUST AND POLITICAL TRENDS

The thesis of this book has been that modern antitrust has so decayed that the policy is no longer intellectually respectable. Some of it is not respectable as law; more of it is not respectable as economics; and now I wish to suggest that, because it pretends to one objective while frequently accomplishing its opposite, and because it too often forwards trends dangerous to our form of government and society, a great deal of antitrust is not even respectable as politics.

Antitrust was originally conceived as a limited intervention in free and private processes for the purpose of keeping those processes free. It tempered laissez faire in order to preserve a free market system. That view is not refuted by the fact that very early some fallacious economic theories entered the law and began to make it unnecessarily intrusive. The conception was one of free markets with minimal government involvement.

For that reason, antitrust became a symbol of resistance to collectivist, statist, interventionist, and ultimately authoritarian economic ideologies. Calls for socialist reform were deflected by counterproposals to enforce the antitrust laws more vigorously. Of course, that was not without cost, because the process tended to make antitrust more interventionist in order to show that other reforms were not needed, and so the ideas that propelled statist philosophies gradually edged into antitrust and lodged themselves there. The invasion of the law by ideologies foreign to its nature is what brings antitrust to a crisis. The capture of antitrust's potent symbolism and educative power by the ideologies of statism and interventionism would be a major loss to the ideology underpinning a liberal, democratic, and capitalist social order.

The trends observable in antitrust, I have suggested, are four: (1) a movement away from political decision by democratic processes toward political choice by courts; (2) a movement away from the ideal of free markets toward the ideal of regulated markets; (3) a tendency to be con-

cerned with group welfare rather than general welfare; and (4) a movement away from the ideal of liberty and reward according to merit
toward an ideal of equality of outcome and reward according to status.
Common to all of these movements is an anticapitalist and authoritarian ethos. It is that spirit which creates these tendencies, and it is their
success which reinforces that spirit.

Such trends do not proceed continuously and smoothly, without inter-
ruption or even temporary reversal, but there is good reason to think
them steady in the long term. From the inception of antitrust to the present day, the law has displayed a persistent shift in the directions described, a shift that has now become substantial. There have been pauses.
We appear to be in one at the moment. If the current Supreme Court
has not reformed much of the disfigured doctrine it inherited, at least it
has refused, albeit often by narrow margins, to carry old doctrine to its
logical conclusions.

The tendencies described are not, of course, inexorable, and any assessment must at least pause to note hopeful developments. The *Sylvania*
decision, discussed in Chapter 14, is important not only because it
reached a correct result by giving favorable consideration and dispositive weight to business efficiency and consumer welfare for the first time
in decades. It is also a hopeful development because the majority es-
chewed political and social argument, and ignored the themes of dealer
"bondage" and business egalitarianism that were so prominent in the
jurisprudence of preceding Courts. Whether we are witnessing the birth
of a countertrend in the intellectual development of the law it is far
too early to say. For the moment, we must deal with the main trends as
they have unfolded for most of the history of the policy.

Perhaps little need be said about the modern tendency of the federal
judiciary to arrogate to itself political judgments that properly belong
to democratic processes and popular assemblies. The existence and
strength of that tendency are widely acknowledged. The fact that it runs
strong in antitrust is undeniable, and the practice of judicial legislation
there merely reflects the practice of courts in all fields of law. Though
this activism came to the fore in the years of the Warren Court and is
popularly identified with that era, it has by no means passed away. Our
legal culture appears to have changed in the past quarter century, and
the judiciary continues to reach out in order to assert primacy over other
branches of government. Whatever else may be said of that development,
it certainly represents an incursion into the traditional area of democratic
government. This occurs, most obviously and dramatically in the modern
expansion of constitutional law—a holding of unconstitutionality explic-

itly denies the power of the legislature and the executive to govern—but
the same tendency is observable in statutory and common law fields as
well. It occurs, for example, through the skewed interpretation of statutes
in order to reach results more to the liking of the judge. In antitrust
it occurs not only through the misuse of economics but also, more obviously, through the introduction of values in conflict with consumer
welfare, so that courts, inadvertently or not, require themselves to make
grossly political choices.

The movement from the ideal of free markets to that of regulated
markets has been documented throughout this book. That trend is so
pervasive that it would hardly be worth remarking in antitrust, were it
not that this law is (or was) the major symbol in public policy of
belief in free markets and that it has a great educative impact. The law
now proceeds on so many mistaken notions of market "inadequacies"
that it teaches the necessity for government intervention when no such
necessity exists, and even when intervention is positively harmful.

This miseducation has been possible, and particularly insidious, because antitrust's doctrinal progression is gradual and because both the
doctrine and its application are inconsistent. If the doctrines the law has
developed were logically and rigorously applied, their perniciousness
would become at once apparent, for the damage done to the economy
all at once would be enormous. The inconsistency both of doctrine and
of application is well known to antitrust lawyers. It makes their practices
lucrative and their clients' lives wretched. The lawyer must repeatedly
tell clients planning a course of business conduct that some decided
cases read against it but it is not clear the government will bring an
action or, if it should, whether the court will apply the precedent in that
fashion. This is ordinarily followed, to the client's chagrin, by an im-
pressionistic statement of the odds for and against, capped by the buck-
passing observation that now the decision whether to proceed has become a question of business rather than legal judgment.

One may be inclined, at first, to be thankful for the law's inconsistency, for it seems to save the economy from much worse damage than
has already been inflicted. But perhaps the truth is that what is saved is
not the economy but the law. If an attempt were made to apply existing
principles completely and consistently, the demand for law reform would
be overwhelming. We would not stand for the sudden, catastrophic
destruction of wealth that would be entailed.

Yet, in the long run, we may stand for too much of it. Wrong ideas,
repeated often enough, lodge themselves in the culture as well as the law,
and then proceed to expand according to their inner logic. Today we

accept results that were seen to be preposterous a few decades ago. A decade or so hence we may accept much worse. Antitrust is now applied to only a fraction of the full range of business structures and practices existing in our economy, but the law's tendency is expansionist, continually framing stricter rules for areas it has reached and always reaching out for new areas. There is an inbuilt thrust toward greater severity or further extension, either through legislation or judicial decision, because the logical extrapolation of existing principles calls for it. The law pushes opinion ahead of it, and opinion then draws law after it. We see clearly the impropriety of extrapolating antitrust's principles to areas distant from the law's present reach, but it seems reasonable to extend them to areas that lie adjacent. Eventually the distant field becomes adjacent, and in the meantime we have become accustomed to the idea that it too should be reached by the law.

This process has no obvious stopping point. It may be seen at work today. In the beginning, antitrust approached large corporate size warily, fearing to destroy efficiencies. Before it would risk dissolution, the law required the size to have been built either by merger or by the use of predatory practices. Large size, even monopolistic size achieved by internal growth, was completely safe, seen to be the result of superior efficiency. By judicial interpretation, however, amended Section 7 of the Clayton Act came to strike at very small horizontal mergers, and other provisions were brought to bear on an increasingly wide variety of practices thought, mistakenly, to be by their nature improperly exclusionary. As antitrust forgot the importance of efficiency, size by merger came to seem no different from size by growth, and ordinary business practices came to seem improper. Gradually, any practice that accounted for large size became suspect. The adjacent category now is large market size attained by internal growth. Not so very long ago it would have seemed fantastic to most people that antitrust should threaten the existence of our most successful corporations, even though they have succeeded only by pleasing customers better. It *is* fantastic, but to many people it no longer seems so.

Since, out of all proportion to its direct economic importance, antitrust is a potent educative force, the worrisome question is the lesson it imparts. The real premises and effects of the law may be little known, but its surface appearance, its official pretenses and claims, are widely publicized. As A. V. Dicey said, "Every law or rule of conduct must, whether its author perceives the fact or not, lay down or rest upon some general principle, and must therefore, if it succeeds in attaining its end, commend this principle to public attention or imitation, and thus affect legislative opinion." [2] Dicey noted that the law need not even succeed in order to have this effect, since a principle gains prestige from its mere recognition, and in any case, "if a law fails in attaining its object the argument lies ready to hand that failure was due to the law not going far enough, i.e., to its not carrying out the principle on which it is founded to its full logical consequences." A distinguished economist once remarked that though there was no economic case for the breakup of great industrial corporations in concentrated industries, he favored it. His reason was that the public would never understand the large corporations' superior performance, and their dissolution would at least show that the free market is to be regarded as important and worth preserving. I replied then, and believe now, that the more likely lesson drawn from such a step would be that continuous and drastic government interventions are required because the free market is not to be trusted.

That, I think, is increasingly the lesson taught by antitrust as a whole. The public does not understand the merits of the various cases. In a busy world it has neither the time nor the inclination to do so. The public observes, however, that the government and the federal courts find that business is continually behaving in ways contrary to the public interest. That lesson, endlessly repeated, even though it is quite erroneous, steadily erodes the intellectual and moral legitimacy of capitalism.

Because the ideas at work in antitrust are merely special forms of larger ideas contending for domination in the society at large, the presence of the two other trends mentioned—toward concern for group rather than general welfare and toward a vague but strong egalitarian philosophy—should come as no surprise. Competition in open markets reflects the ideal of equality of opportunity, while antitrust's longstanding and growing concern for the small and the less efficient reflects a preference for equality of outcome. Outcomes are not equal in open competition, hence the pressure for more intervention by law. Nor can equality of outcome be achieved by making the slow faster, that being beyond the powers of legal compulsion, but only by holding the faster back. That may be the reason antitrust in the modern era for so long refused to recognize the claims of superior efficiency; the reason why, indeed, some opinions have stated explicitly that increases in efficiency are allowable only in very small or struggling companies. Increases in efficiency by successful companies are labeled "competitive advantages" or "barriers to entry" and are barred if they occur through a means within the reach of antitrust law.

The egalitarian ideology that suffuses antitrust has become institutionalized. It is built into doctrine under other names, so enforcement agencies and courts need never admit to a leveling urge, indeed need never realize that they are engaged in leveling. When an ideology is institutionalized it becomes, paradoxically, less visible—even to those who implement it. The basic ideas are no longer apprehended or controverted, and hence it becomes easier to move further along the lines implied by those ideas. Particular developments in the movement may be disliked and resisted, but our capacity to resist effectively is diminished if we fail to recognize that the trouble lies at the source.

Egalitarianism in the sense of a desire for equality of outcome rather than of opportunity is, of course, a prominent feature in many fields of law in our era, as it is in the social philosophy of our time. We need not list all of the laws and social programs whose aim is redistribution of wealth or the minimization of difference; the fact that they have abundantly multiplied in recent years is well known.

There is no prospect either in antitrust or in the society generally that equality of condition will be achieved, but antitrust demonstrates some of the costs of moving toward it. The first and most obvious cost is the destruction of wealth through the inhibition of efficiency. The second is the accumulation of power in government, because of the necessity for increased governmental incursions into the private sphere if greater equality of condition is to be achieved. The third is the replacement of free markets with government-regulated markets. The fourth is the shift of lawmaking from elected representatives to courts and bureaucracies. The reason for the last cost is that detailed interventions require more governmental decisions than can be made by elected officials, so that lawmaking by bureaucracies and courts becomes inevitable. So massive and widespread are these developments that it seems apparent we are faced, not with intellectual failure and institutional inadequacy alone, but with some positive force.

To study antitrust at length, to wonder at the manifold errors of economics and logic displayed, to see that the errors move the law always in one direction, is to begin to suspect that a process much deeper than mere mistaken reasoning is at work. It seems as though the intellectual terrain is regarded as important not in and for itself but as a field of action upon which the political order moves against the private order. The trends just discussed are in various ways manifestations of that movement both in antitrust and in larger fields of policy.

I will not attempt here an examination of that deeper process, but there is an apparent paradox in the movements of law that gives some support to one explanation of these trends. Many observers have suggested that much in modern political life is explicable by the recent enormous growth in size of an intellectual class—using the term broadly to include academics, journalists, lawyers, government officials, and others whose jobs center on ideas and words—and the apparent affinity of that class for expansions of the public sector at the expense of the private sector. This hypothesis says more than that intellectuals are indispensable to the making and implementation of policy; it states that intellectuals as a class have distinctive interests and tastes, and are disproportionately able to move law in the direction of their interests and tastes. The intellectuals' preference for government economic regulation is attributed to a desire to shift power and prestige from the business class to themselves. If this hypothesis were to some degree accurate, one would expect to see the law become less restrictive where it impinges on the intellectual class's interests. Freedom of speech is, of course, the sine qua non of an intellectual class.

It is interesting, therefore, and possibly relevant to the hypothesis stated, that intellectuals who speak to the subject regularly commit the logical fallacy of praising the antitrust laws as the economic counterpart of the First Amendment, designed to keep economic markets free even as the First Amendment keeps the market for speech and ideas free. The analogy, of course, reverses the true relationship of the two laws in a way compatible with intellectual class tastes. The First Amendment has become a severe limitation on the power of government to intervene in the competition of speech and ideas. Intervention is permitted only in the most serious and imminent cases of threatened market failure— when, for example, private groups use speech in an attempt to seize governmental power and close out adverse speech. The antitrust laws, on the other hand, do not curb government; they are themselves governmental interventions in a marketplace, justified on the theory that competition is not to be trusted there, as it is to be trusted in the speech market. Thus, the First Amendment and the antitrust laws stand in philosophic opposition to one another. The counterparts of the antitrust laws in the speech marketplace are the Smith Act and the various criminal syndicalism statutes that attempt to punish advocacy of the violent overthrow of the government. These laws are enormously unpopular with intellectuals. Thus, it may not be surprising that the courts have tended over time to expand the scope both of the First Amendment and of the antitrust laws. It would be well if the similarity of the case for limited government involvement in both markets could be brought home.

If the hypothesis of the influence of the intellectual class is correct, or even partially so, then the future of antitrust, as of much else in our polity, depends heavily on the state of opinion within that class, and particularly its academic core. Recently there have been signs of a new stirring in the intellectual community, a new distrust of statist solutions, a new willingness to reconsider old economic policies and pieties. This is true in antitrust debate as elsewhere. Twenty, perhaps even ten years ago, for example, the argument of this book would have appeared merely idiosyncratic. Today its position might be agreed to, at least in its general outlines, by a not altogether insignificant number—albeit a minority—of economists and academic lawyers.

The debate is worth continuing. I have argued the case for the reform of antitrust law on grounds of consumer welfare and the integrity of law. It is upon those considerations that the argument must turn, and they seem to me sufficient matters for concern. Yet it has also seemed worth suggesting that this policy relates in complicated ways to more general questions of the way we make and apply law, and, still more generally, to larger movements within our society. Because it deals directly and explicitly with the functioning of markets, antitrust has a unique symbolic and educative influence over public attitudes toward free markets and capitalism. That lends the discussion of this law an added degree of importance. The regime of capitalism brings with it not merely unexampled economic performance and a social and cultural atmosphere that stresses the worth of the individual, but, because of the bourgeois class it creates, trains, and raises to power, the possibility of stable, liberal, and democratic government. Antitrust goes to the heart of capitalist ideology, and since the law's fate will have much to do with the fate of that ideology, one may be forgiven for thinking that the outcome of the debate is of more than legal interest.

APPENDIX

NOTES

TABLE OF CASES

INDEX

APPENDIX TO CHAPTERS 13 AND 14: THE EFFICIENCIES OF PRICE FIXING AND MARKET DIVISION

Chapters 13 and 14 argued that horizontal ancillary restraints can never restrict output when the parties lack market power, and that vertical restraints can never restrict output no matter what the market share of the party imposing the restraint. That demonstration, if accepted, should be enough for antitrust purposes. Yet the entire concept of efficiency-creating price-fixing and market-division agreements is so novel to many persons interested in antitrust that it is probably advisable to suggest some of the ways in which these agreements benefit consumers.

This appendix will analyze market division and price fixing separately. Though they are equally means of eliminating unwanted rivalry, they display mechanical differences that make one or the other more useful in particular situations. On the other hand, the analysis here does not distinguish sharply between horizontal and vertical restraints because there is little difference in the ways they create efficiency. Some familiar cases are used as examples and to indicate how the law has misperceived the nature of those situations. This discussion is not intended to be exhaustive but merely illustrative.

EFFICIENCIES FROM
MARKET-DIVISION AGREEMENTS

Though there are certainly other methods which will be discovered through analysis or the study of particular marketing situations, the most obvious ways in which market-division agreements are capable of enhancing the efficiency of contract integrations include:

(1) Optimizing local sales effort (the "free ride" problem);
(2) Optimizing local sales effort (the size-of-the-market problem);
(3) Encouraging exchanges of information;
(4) Minimizing the costs of providing postsales service and minimizing the risks of customer dissatisfaction; and
(5) Preventing overlapping use of a service whose cost is shared.

These points are listed according to the specific benefit that is being sought or the cost that is being avoided. It would have been possible to classify the efficiencies differently. For example, the first and third points and part of the analysis under the fourth point illustrate the general "free ride" problem in different contexts.

LOCAL SALES EFFORT: THE "FREE RIDE" PROBLEM

The *Sealy* case has already been analyzed as a horizontal contract integration in which market division was employed to solve the "free ride" problem and thereby bring the level of local sales effort up to that which a single nationwide seller would find optimal. *Schwinn* appears to present the use of vertical market division for the same purpose. Some indication that vertical market division was employed to secure similar efficiencies was also present in *White Motor* and *Sandura*.

At issue in *White Motor* [1] were the conditions imposed by White, a truck manufacturer, in its distributor and dealer contracts: each reseller had to deal only with customers located within a designated territory, and certain customers, reserved for direct sale by White, could not be dealt with at all. The case thus involved closed dealer and distributor territories and customer allocations, both subspecies of market division. Because the district court awarded summary judgment to the government and the trial ordered by the Supreme Court was avoided by a consent decree, we do not know a great deal about White's purposes in imposing these conditions. Yet in opposing summary judgment, White raised considerations that suggest these conditions were aimed at preventing what is called here the "free ride." Thus, White justified its territorial restrictions on the ground it had "to insist that its distributors and dealers concentrate on trying to take sales away from other competing truck manufacturers in their respective territories rather than on cutting each other's throats in other territories." [2]

White relied heavily upon the sales efforts of its dealers and distributors. These resellers, for example, had to provide considerable technical advice to potential customers, studying their needs and advising on the features that would be desirable in the trucks they purchased. The trucks were assembled at the factory in accordance with the specifications arrived at in this fashion, so that customers received trucks that were close to being custom-built. Dealers and distributors could cut each other's throats, and White's throat, by underbidding on the trucks after some other dealer or distributor had devised the specifications and convinced the customer. If that practice became at all widespread, the amount of this expensive sales effort provided would certainly decline drastically, and White would have lost a valuable service it wanted its resellers to provide.

The customer allocation clauses prevented resellers from dealing with the federal government, any state government, or any department or political subdivision of any such government. White contended that these accounts required special handling: "The size of the orders, the technicalities of bidding and delivery, and other factors all play a part in this decision" [3] to reserve such accounts to White. The customer allocation clause may very well have prevented the dealers and distributors from taking a free ride on White's selling efforts. Customer allocation rather than territorial division would be appropriate if White felt the complexities of serving this class of customers required a scale of sales operation or expertise that could be provided economically only by the manufacturer.

The *Sandura* opinion, though it does not use the same terminology, is quite explicit about the problem of the free ride. Sandura, as the Federal Trade Commission said, was "a small, shortline manufacturer in a field dominated by giant firms producing a full line of hard-surface floor coverings." [4] One of its vinyl floor coverings, Sandran, had at first met with considerable success, but sales fell off disastrously as defects in the product appeared. When the defects had been cured, Sandura faced the problem of resuscitating the product's reputation, and it chose the method of distributor sales effort. "But," the Commission found, "before they would make the necessary heavy investment of capital, prospective distributors required the special inducement of a closed, exclusive territory. They would not spend to advertise and promote an unpopular product without assurance that resulting sales accrued to them."

The Commission nevertheless held the market division illegal. The Court of Appeals for the Sixth Circuit reversed, however, viewing Sandura's resurgence with the aid of its distributors as a contribution to competition.[5] The court put the problem succinctly:

> Certainly it is not difficult to understand either the need for advertising a product whose only reputation was unfavorable, or the unwillingness of distributors to undertake such advertising if it would be possible for one distributor to make the sales and take the profits promoted by another's advertising. Particularly is this so since the distributors uniformly advertise Sandran as a product, rather than themselves as distributors.

The efficiency correctly perceived by the court in *Sandura* is, of course, in no way dependent upon the special facts of a bad product reputation or a small manufacturer. It can be created by market-division agreements in any case where separate firms are promoting and selling an identical product, in *Sealy, Schwinn,* and *White Motor,* as well as *Sandura.*

LOCAL SALES EFFORT: THE SIZE-OF-THE-MARKET PROBLEM

Local sales effort may fall below optimal levels when particular markets are too small to repay the efforts of two sellers of a single brand. Market division, in either a horizontal or a vertical system, is a way of solving this problem by assigning the market or account to a single seller. Testimony in the *Sandura* case also suggests the reality of this hypothesis. The Court of Appeals opinion states:

> Distributor testimony . . . illustrates that closed territories are responsible for more thorough coverage of dealer accounts than Sandura would otherwise enjoy. In the words of one distributor who testified that the Sandura system avoided duplication of effort and resulted in greater coverage of a given territory, "this way we are able to concentrate, and we do a lot of business in little towns, small towns. We don't bypass them. We can back into the hinterland."

This suggestion makes economic sense if there are a number of towns of such small size that they will not repay cultivation by more than one distributor. Where two distributors are able to reach such towns, neither may find it worthwhile to cultivate them intensively, since even occasional visits by the other would diminish the first distributor's returns below the point at which cultivation is worthwhile. Such markets are then likely to be reached only sporadically, as when other business requires a representative of the distributor to pass through the area. Assignment of the town to a single distributor would make proper cultivation worthwhile by eliminating the random visits of the other distributor. This is not the same as the "free ride" problem, for the additional distributor may not be capitalizing on the efforts of the first or charging a lower price, but merely picking off enough of the sales to make the scale of operation the market would repay unprofitable for either.

EXCHANGES OF INFORMATION

A major source of efficiency in any integration is the transmission of information within the organization. This efficiency may be impaired if the unit receiving the information can use it to injure the unit supplying it. This manifestation of the "free ride" problem has obvious application to distributive systems like those in *White Motor, Sandura,* and *Sealy.* The reseller of White trucks or the manufacturer of Sealy mattresses is less likely to make known to the others in the system any new selling or manufacturing techniques if the information may then be used competitively against it. Market division makes the system more efficient by removing this disincentive to disclosure.

This form of efficiency may also be served by a division-of-fields agreement to prevent the problem of a free ride that arises when firms with complementary technologies cooperate. A partial insight of this sort seems to form the basis of the district court's decision in *United States* v. *Bausch & Lomb Optical Co.*[6] The Soft-Lite Lens Co., a distributor of unpatented, pink-tinted lenses, originally bought the necessary glass abroad and had it ground in the United States. Later it turned to Bausch & Lomb, first as a grinder, later as sole manufacturer of the glass. The parties agreed that Bausch & Lomb would make pink-tinted glass for

Soft-Lite alone, and that it would not itself compete with Soft-Lite in the sale of pink-tinted lenses. The government attacked this agreement as violative of the Sherman Act, but the district court sustained the restraint as reasonable and ancillary:

> The main purpose of the contract is to provide a source of supply for Soft-Lite. The restraining covenant is for the protection of the purchaser who is spending large sums to develop his good will and enlarge the public patronage of a relatively new article of commerce. The arrangement, though not a partnership in legal form, is functionally a joint enterprise in which one will produce and the other market the commodity.

The court's explanation of the covenant not to compete is incomplete. Soft-Lite's expenditures to develop goodwill accruing to its trade name are not endangered by sales of glass to firms using other names, nor would expenditures to develop demand for a new product be protected by the restraint if rival distributors could get the glass from other suppliers. The restraint does make sense, however, if Soft-Lite had unique specifications for the glass and, in return for disclosing these to Bausch & Lomb, demanded that such glass not be sold to others. The record of the case suggests that this may well have been the situation. A related hypothesis is that Soft-Lite knew techniques that reduced the cost of making pink-tinted glass and, though not a manufacturer, wished to gain the benefit of its superior information by requiring Bausch & Lomb not to sell the glass to other distributors or go into distribution itself.

An additional hypothesis, also suggested by the record, is that the information Soft-Lite wished to protect related also to its business plans and techniques. Had Bausch & Lomb wished to enter distribution itself or to aid other customers in doing so, information about Soft-Lite's customer lists, methods of pricing, techniques of "missionary work," etc., could have been used to obtain a free ride at Soft-Lite's expense.

Were none of these things true, Soft-Lite could have gained nothing by the restrictive covenant it exacted from Bausch & Lomb. Other suppliers of glass were available, so that Soft-Lite could not avoid their competition and would have had to pay Bausch & Lomb for giving up customers. We must conclude that some explanation of the sort offered is correct, and that the restraint made possible the use of valuable information. The outlawing of such restraints would encourage parties to keep information to themselves, so that either the information would be less efficiently employed or there would be a decline in the incentive to develop or locate knowledge of this type. Either tendency would be a loss to consumers.

POSTSALE SERVICE

The provision of postsale service is likely to be important for somewhat complicated products. When the cost of service is included in the price of the product, the problem of the free ride may arise in either horizontal or vertical systems. If dealers sell to customers from distant locations, tension is likely to arise between the selling dealer and the dealer closest to the customer about the provision of postsale service, while the customer, who thinks he is dealing with a single organization, becomes dissatisfied with the service provided. The selling dealer, who finds the provision of servicing at a distance expensive, will wish to hold it to a minimum and will, in any event, be likely to experience delays, whereas the local dealer, who has not received the purchase price, will feel no incentive to provide service. Market division cures this problem. The local dealer then has an incentive to provide good service because he has been paid for it, and there will be a close connection between the degree of the customer's satisfaction and the likelihood of selling equipment to him in the future.

The same situation may arise between a manufacturer and a reseller with respect to classes of customers that require special expertise in the provision of postsale service. The manufacturer may then find that a customer allocation agreement with his dealers will permit him to offer proper service and charge for it in the purchase price.

There are alternative methods of handling these problems, of course, but where the situation is such that restriction of output is not a realistic motive for the market-division agreement, the manufacturer's or the group's election not to use the alternative must be deemed motivated by a belief that market division is less costly. Thus, one alternative might be to sell servicing separately from the product, but this may give rise to several problems. Selling service separately may be more costly than selling the composite product of equipment plus service. This is true of efforts to sell a number of products in their components. Moreover, the selling dealer, who gets a flat price and is not responsible for later adjustments, is thereby given an incentive to skimp on predelivery adjustments and services, increasing the cost of postsale service. The servicing dealer then loses if a flat fee for service is prescribed, or the total price of equipment plus service is raised if the real cost of such service is charged. The solution of having the servicing dealer reimbursed either by the manufacturer or by the selling dealer also creates incentives for cutting corners and for disputes about what servicing was really required and how much it ought to cost. Market division eliminates such problems, which add costs or risk customer dissatisfaction.

EFFECTIVENESS OF A SERVICE OR FACILITY WHOSE COST IS SHARED

An example is suggested by the reported cooperation of three regional breweries to share the costs of radio and television commercial production through a common advertising agency. One brewer marketed its beer in the Gulf states, one in New England, and the third in the Midwest—each, of course, under separate marks and brand names. This arrangement made commercially feasible the use of nationally known actors, and each commercial was used in all three regions, only the name of the beer being changed. This sharing of efforts was said to reduce production costs of the commercials by as much as a third; moreover, by taking turns testing the commercials, the group was able to achieve the benefits of regional testing usually available only to a national concern. The invasion of each other's markets with identical commercials would have destroyed the value of this system. An agreement by the parties specifying the areas in which each might use the commercials would assist in the preservation of the efficiencies created by this contract integration.

EFFICIENCIES FROM
PRICE-FIXING AGREEMENTS

The efficiencies that may be achieved by a price-fixing agreement include:

(1) Optimizing local sales effort (the "free ride" problem);
(2) Optimizing local sales effort (product uniformity);
(3) Reinforcing a market-division agreement;
(4) Providing the mechanism for the transfer of information;
(5) Assisting the achievement of advertising economies of scale;
(6) Protecting one party to a joint venture against the fraud of the other; and
(7) Breaking down reseller cartels and preventing the misuse of local reseller monopolies.

LOCAL SALES EFFORT: THE "FREE RIDE" PROBLEM

Price fixing can be a method of eliminating free rides in either a vertical or a horizontal contract integration. The argument is very similar to that made in connection with market division. When prices are fixed, no purchaser is able to obtain the information he wants from one seller and then purchase from another at a lower price. Each seller of the brand, therefore, is free to provide the optimal amount of selling effort without fear of a free rider. Where the seller's price is maintained, he is forced by rivals, whether offering the same or other brands, to compete by other means, and this forces him to provide the local sales effort desired by the manufacturer or the group to which he belongs. Market division has the same effect where there is rivalry from other brands. Price fixing is likely to be preferred to market division as the means of attaining this efficiency in situations where effective marketing requires thorough coverage of an area through numerous sellers rather than use of a single outlet.

LOCAL SALES EFFORT: PRODUCT UNIFORMITY

Even where the free ride is not possible because the provision of sales effort and services necessarily occurs at the time of and in conjunction with the sale, price fixing may be an important means of ensuring the provision of sales effort and services. A good example is the provision of services in conjunction with the sale of gasoline. The importance of sales effort in such markets is too often overlooked, but it is clearly present. Much national refiner advertising of gasoline stresses the extra services, conveniences, and courtesies that the local dealers provide. That there is a real concern about this local sales effort is demonstrated by the common refiner policy of instructing their dealers about such matters and policing dealer performance.

The attempt to ensure the provision of such services seems to account, in part, for the persistent efforts of refiners to control the prices charged by their dealers. The question that naturally arises, however, is why refiners do not allow individual dealers to determine for themselves whether a price or a service appeal would be most effective in their particular markets. The answer may be twofold. The refiner may feel that its marketing acumen is significantly greater than that of the general run of the people it can attract as dealers. More important, perhaps, is the fact that a large part of the refiner's brand appeal to motorists rests on the uniformity of the product sold at its stations. This uniformity does not depend on the physical qualities of the gasoline alone. The station also offers a number of services that may be classified as local sales effort: the availability and cleanliness of washroom facilities; the cleanliness of the station and the neatness of the attendants; the politeness or geniality with which service is given; the giving of travel directions; the availability of a range of services for the car (lubrication, tire and battery replacement, and minor repairs); recognition of credit cards; and the provision, often without being asked, of such free services as wiping windows, checking the pressure of tires, pumping air into tires, checking water and oil levels, etc. These are as much a part of the product sold and paid for as is the gasoline.

Since consumers of gasoline are mobile, they will patronize many different dealers. A refiner wishing to appeal to those consumers who value a high degree of service must establish the uniformity of his product, so that consumers can rely on getting approximately the same combination of physical product and services at any station carrying the brand. The deviation of any significant number of stations from the product standard will lessen the effectiveness of the refiner's advertising and reduce the appeal that uniformity makes in itself. A line of Supreme Court decisions has destroyed the refiners' ability to control station prices, and has thus destroyed this efficiency.[7]

REINFORCEMENT OF MARKET DIVISION

Market division may tend to break down where the parties to the agreement sell to resellers. In a system like Sealy's, the existence of wholesalers or retailers would make the territorial division hard to police, and it would be difficult to know whether the manufacturer whose reseller sold across territorial lines had given a lower price with that end in view. The market division could be reinforced either by an agreement on the prices at which the member manufacturers should sell to resellers or by an agreement that the manufacturers should maintain the resale prices of their resellers. The Sealy group did agree to maintain resale prices, and there are some indications in the record that this served to reinforce the manufacturers' market-division agreement. This reinforcement, of course, involves the "aggregation of trade restraints" that the Supreme Court found offensive, but such reasoning is beside the point. If any of the restraints is harmful, it should be unlawful regardless of its "aggregation" with others. If all the restraints are merely methods of creating efficiency, then their "aggregation" merely enhances their beneficial effect.

TRANSFER OF INFORMATION

The suggesting or setting of prices is a means of transferring information about proper market behavior from those whose competence or information is superior to others. It is a familiar device within corporations and partnerships, and there is no reason to believe that it is not a useful device for looser systems.

This efficiency seems, for example, to provide the explanation for the "price fixing" held per se illegal by the district court in the *Nationwide Trailer Rental System (NTRS)* case.[8] NTRS was an organization of automobile trailer rental operations engaged in the one-way rental trade. The system was created to facilitate the exchange of trailers, so that persons renting them for one-way movements did not have to pay the expense of returning the trailers to the renting operator. Trailers involved in NTRS's one-way system continued to be owned by the operators who first put them into the system, but could be rented out successively by the various operators into whose hands the chances of business brought them. The renting operator divided the rental fee with the operator who held title to each particular trailer.

Among other restraints contained in the system, the NTRS Board of Directors, composed of trailer rental operators, adopted a suggested rate schedule that was circulated to the member firms, and also adopted a uniform lease agreement for members' use that specified the charge for overtime use of trailers. Since the members were located in different cities and were not in competition with each other, it is difficult to see how either of these actions relating to prices could have been designed to eliminate a competition that did not exist. NTRS argued, in fact, that the function of the suggested price schedule was to transfer information to its members:

> It was essential to the intelligent conduct of a one-way trailer business by the numerous small businessmen—filling station operators and the like who are members of NTRS—that they have an estimate of what rates would prove profitable and reasonable in areas to which they send trailers. Without this information it was impossible for them to bargain intelligently with their customers.[9]

The district court, however, held that both the circulation of the suggested rate and the form lease with its overtime rate were forbidden tamperings with price under Section 1 of the Sherman Act. It did not explain what competition was suppressed.

ECONOMIES OF SCALE IN ADVERTISING

Either market division or price fixing may be essential to the realization of economies of scale in advertising. It will be recalled that the Supreme Court's *Sealy* opinion rather inconsistently left open the possibility that it might not be per se unlawful for "a number of small grocers" to "allocate territory among themselves on an exclusive basis as incident to the use of a common name and common advertisements." The Federal Trade Commission, however, has issued an advisory opinion that a proposed similar arrangement would be per se illegal.[10]

A number of retail druggists proposed to pool the cooperative advertising allowances given them by suppliers to pay for joint newspaper advertising that would not have been worthwhile for any druggist individually. The advertisements were to list the stores selling products at prices agreed upon by a committee of participating druggists. In this way, the several druggists could have achieved the advertising economies of scale already available to chain drug stores.

The Commission appears to have misperceived the issue, for much of the members' discussion concerned the undesirability of relaxing the per se concept to allow small businessmen to compete more effectively with larger competitors. An exception to the law in favor of small business would of course be improper, but the claim of the proposed agreement to legality need rest on no such foundation. If, as the Commission seemed to assume and as the facts make likely, the agreement on prices was necessary to joint advertising, and if the advertising contributed to the competitive effectiveness of the participating druggists, there was no justification for the application of the per se rule. That rule, as we have seen, can be justified only in types of cases (typically involving naked restraints) in which only restriction of output and not efficiency is to be expected. The Commission should, therefore, have advised that the per se rule was not applicable and that legality would turn upon the market share of the group.

This form of advertising efficiency is more common than we usually suppose, e.g., franchisors often fix prices on food items in franchised drive-in restaurants, and individual manufacturers sometimes fix retail prices of advertised goods.

PROTECTION AGAINST THE FRAUD OF A JOINT VENTURER

Price fixing as a means of protecting one joint venturer against the possibility of fraud by the other usually does not eliminate any competition but merely ensures that the power to set prices that has been vested in one of the parties shall be exercised in a stated way. This sort of price fixing was upheld by the district court in *United States* v. *Columbia Pictures Corp.*[11] The pertinent part of that case involved the government's challenge of agreements by which Screen Gems, Inc., a wholly owned subsidiary of Columbia Pictures, was granted by Universal Pictures Co., Inc., a fourteen-year exclusive license to distribute for television exhibition approximately 600 Universal feature films.

The government objected to the provision for the advance classification of each Columbia and Universal film and to the provision that Universal films should not be sublicensed by Screen Gems for less than Columbia features classified as of comparable quality. This latter term, of course, had the effect of fixing the price of Universal films in relation to Columbia films. Without these provisions it would have been possible for Screen Gems to shift income from Universal to Columbia by offering licenses for Universal films at lower rates, on the tacit understanding that the licensees would take Columbia films at correspondingly higher rates. Classification and price fixing prevented this, facilitated the division of receipts when Universal and Columbia films were licensed together for a single fee, and saved disputes afterward. The government made no showing that the agreements had any likely effect upon general market prices, and the district court properly upheld the provisions under attack.

RESELLER CARTELS AND LOCAL RESELLER MONOPOLIES

Resale price fixing may be employed by a manufacturer to break down reseller cartels or to control the behavior of a local reseller monopolist. The manufacturer's control is, of course, beneficial to consumers in both situations. The *Kiefer-Stewart* case illustrates the first use of vertical price control, and the *Albrecht* case the second. Unfortunately, in both cases the Supreme Court, adhering to the semantic rigors of the per se rule without economic analysis, found the manufacturer guilty of violating the Sherman Act.

In *Kiefer-Stewart* [12] two commonly-owned liquor manufacturers, Seagram and Calvert, agreed to sell only to those Indiana wholesalers who did not resell above stipulated maximum prices. In response to a price-fixing charge brought by a wholesaler, the manufacturers offered the defense that their price fixing was intended to counteract a wholesaler cartel that had agreed on minimum prices. The Supreme Court held this defense invalid, thus destroying without reason a valuable pro-consumer tactic. If a manufacturer knows, or suspects but cannot prove, that resellers have cartelized, he can provide a powerful incentive for resellers to defect from the cartel by refusing to sell to those who comply with the cartel's price agreement.

In *Albrecht* [13] a newspaper publisher was found to have violated the Sherman Act by attempting to hold down the price charged by a dealer making home deliveries. The explanation for the publisher's action seems simple. Revenue is derived partly from the price subscribers pay, but also, and usually more importantly, from rates paid by advertisers. The latter form of revenue tends to rise as circulation rises. The publisher, therefore, finds it in his interest to hold the subscription price below the level he might choose if subscriptions were his only source of revenue. The dealer is given an exclusive territory to encourage his sales effort, but since the dealer is not interested in the publisher's advertising revenue (and may therefore price in a way inimical to the interests of the publisher), the latter finds it wise to control the dealer's price. There is nothing harmful in this to anyone. If dealers generally take advantage of the Court's ruling to reap monopoly profits out of the exclusive territories the publishers give them and the relatively low price at which the publishers sell to them, then the publishers will have to take counteraction, such as abolishing closed territories for dealers or raising the price to dealers. That will injure both publishers and consumers, and will not benefit dealers because they will receive only the competitive rates of return they enjoyed under the prior system.

ALTERNATIVE MEANS OF
CREATING EFFICIENCY

It is sometimes suggested that the benefits of price fixing and market division can be obtained by "less restrictive" means. Thus, it is said that a manufacturer who cannot fix his resellers' prices may suggest such prices, or that a manufacturer who cannot assign his dealers closed territories can use exclusive franchises, profit pass-over systems, or area-of-primary-responsibility clauses. The fallacy inherent in all these suggestions is that these devices are not capable of creating all the efficiencies that manufacturer control of reseller prices and territories can create. Since we are sure the manufacturer has only the motive of creating distributive efficiency, we should leave the choice of means to him. He will make that choice by comparing the relative costs and benefits of each technique. There is no occasion for the law to replace his judgment on such a standard business question with its own.

NOTES

PREFACE

1. Bowman, *Patent and Antitrust Law: A Legal and Economic Appraisal* (Chicago: University of Chicago Press, 1973).
2. Rowe, *Price Discrimination Under the Robinson-Patman Act* (Boston: Little, Brown, 1962).

INTRODUCTION: THE CRISIS IN ANTITRUST

1. Hofstadter, "What Happened to the Antitrust Movement," in *The Paranoid Style in American Politics and Other Essays* (New York: Alfred A. Knopf, 1965), pp. 188, 189, 192–93, 195.
2. Green, Moore, and Wasserstein, *The Closed Enterprise System* (New York: Grossman, 1972).
3. Posner, "Nader on Antitrust: The Closed Enterprise System," *New Republic* 164, June 26, 1971, pp. 11, 13–14.
4. Bork and Bowman, "The Crisis in Antitrust," *Fortune* 68, December 1963, p. 138.
5. *Continental T.V., Inc. v. GTE Sylvania Inc.*, 97 S. Ct. 2549 (1977).

CHAPTER I: THE HISTORICAL FOUNDATIONS OF ANTITRUST POLICY

1. *White Motor Co. v. United States* 372 U.S. 253, 265 (1963).
2. *United States v. Container Corp. of America*, 393 U.S. 333, 341 (1969) (Marshall, J., dissenting).
3. 26 Stat. 209, 15 U.S.C. §§ 1–2 (1890).
4. For a fuller discussion of this entire subject, and detailed citations to the supporting legislative history, see Bork, "Legislative Intent and the Policy of the Sherman Act," 9 *J. Law and Econ.* 7 (1966).
5. The opinions of these judges are analyzed in more detail than is here necessary in Bork, "The Rule of Reason and the Per Se Concept: Price Fixing and Market Division," Part I, 74 *Yale L. J.* 775 (1965).
6. *United States v. Trans-Missouri Freight Ass'n.*, 166 U.S. 290 (1897).
7. *United States v. Trans-Missouri Freight Ass'n.*, 58 Fed. 58, 72 (8th Cir. 1893).
8. *United States v. Trans-Missouri Freight Ass'n.*, 166 U.S. 290 327–28, 329, 331–32, 339, 341–42 (1897).

9. *United States* v. *Joint Traffic Ass'n.*, 171 U.S. 505, 567–68 (1898).

10. *United States* v. *Trans-Missouri Freight Ass'n.*, 166 U.S. 290, 343, 351 (1897).

11. Id. at 323.

12. *United States* v. *Addyston Pipe & Steel Co.*, 85 Fed. 271, 283–84, 284, 283, 281, 280, 282, 287, 291 (1898). ··

13. 139 U.S. 79 (1891).

14. *Northern Securities Co.* v. *United States*, 193 U.S. 197, 320, 331, 326 (1904).

15. Id. at 400, 403, 410, 410–11, 411, 407.

16. *Dr. Miles Medical Co.* v. *John D. Park & Sons Co.*, 220 U.S. 373, 408–09 (1911).

17. *Standard Oil Co. of New Jersey* v. *United States*, 221 U.S. 1 (1911).

18. *United States* v. *American Tobacco Co.*, 221 U.S. 106 (1911).

19. See Letwin, *Law and Economic Policy in America: The Evolution of the Sherman Antitrust Act* (New York: Random House, 1965), pp. 265–270.

20. *Standard Oil Co. of New Jersey* v. *United States*, 221 U.S. 1, 59, 51, 52, 56 (1911).

21. *United States* v. *American Tobacco Co.*, 221 U.S. 106, 179 (1911).

22. *Standard Oil Co. of New Jersey* v. *United States*, 221 U.S. 1, 64–68, 75, 75–77, 76 (1911).

23. *United States* v. *American Tobacco Co.*, 221 U.S. 106, 181–83 (1911).

24. McGee, "Predatory Price Cutting: The Standard Oil (N.J.) Case," 1 *J. Law and Econ.* 137, 168 (1958).

25. *Standard Oil Co. of New Jersey* v. *United States*, 221 U.S. 1, 76, 77 (1911).

26. *United States* v. *American Tobacco Co.*, 221 U.S. 106, 170, 183 (1911).

27. *Chicago Board of Trade* v. *United States*, 246 U.S. 231, 238, 238–39, 241 (1918).

28. Brief for the United States, pp. 9, 14–16.

29. Handler, *Antitrust in Perspective* (New York: Columbia University Press, 1957), p. 94, n. 130.

30. 38 Stat. 730 (1914).

31. 38 Stat. 717 (1914).

32. 49 Stat. 1526 (1936).

CHAPTER 2: THE GOALS OF ANTITRUST: THE INTENTIONS OF CONGRESS

1. Blake and Jones, "In Defense of Antitrust," 65 *Col. L. Rev.* 377 (1965); "Toward a Three-Dimensional Antitrust Policy," id. at 422.

2. Dewey, "The Economic Theory of Antitrust: Science or Religion?" 50 *Va. L. Rev.* 413, 434 (1964).

3. *United States* v. *Aluminum Co. of America*, 148 F. 2d 416, 428, 429 (2d Cir. 1945).

4. *United States* v. *Associated Press*, 52 F. Supp. 362, 370, 370–72 (S.D.N.Y. 1943).

5. *Brown Shoe Co.* v. *United States*, 370 U.S. 294 (1962).

6. Neal, "A Law Professor's View," in *Competition, Efficiency, and Antitrust* (Conference Board, 1969), pp. 7, 9, 8, 9, 9–10.

7. Kaysen and Turner, *Antitrust Policy* (Cambridge: Harvard University Press, 1959), p. 17.

8. *Brown Shoe Co.* v. *United States*, 370 U.S. 294, 344 (1962).

9. *Perma-Life Mufflers, Inc.* v. *International Parts Corp.*, 392 U.S. 134, 140 (1968).

10. *Appalachian Coals, Inc.* v. *United States*, 288 U.S. 344 (1933).

11. *Brown Shoe Co.* v. *United States*, 370 U.S. 294 (1962).

12. *Federal Trade Commission* v. *Procter & Gamble Co.*, 382 U.S. 568 (1967).

13. *United States* v. *Von's Grocery Co.*, 384 U.S. 270 (1966).

14. *White Motor Co.* v. *United States*, 372 U.S. 253, 281 (1963).

15. Stigler, *The Theory of Price*, 3d ed. (New York: Macmillan, 1966), pp. 87–88.

16. The argument is set forth in greater detail in Bork, "Legislative Intent and the Policy of the Sherman Act," 9 *J. Law and Econ.* 7 (1966).

17. Rowe, *Price Discrimination Under the Robinson-Patman Act* (Boston: Little, Brown, 1962), pp. 13, n. 47, 15, 20, 20–21, 21–22.

18. Bok, "Section 7 of the Clayton Act and the Merging of Law and Economics," 74 *Harv. L. Rev.* 226, 233–38 (1960).

19. Turner, "Conglomerate Mergers and Section 7 of the Clayton Act," 78 *Harv. L. Rev.* 1313, 1326 (1965).

20. Jaffe and Tobriner, "The Legality of Price-Fixing Agreements," 45 *Harv. L. Rev.* 1164 (1932).

CHAPTER 3: THE GOALS OF ANTITRUST: THE RESPONSIBILITY
OF THE COURTS

1. 229 U.S. 373, 376, 377, 376 (1913).

2. 234 U.S. 216, 221, 223 (1914).

3. 255 U.S. 81, 89 (1921).

4. 274 U.S. 445, 457–58, 461–62 (1927).

5. 273 U.S. 392, 397–98 (1927).

6. Amsterdam, "The Void-for-Vagueness Doctrine in the Supreme Court," 109 *U. Pa. L. Rev.* 67, 75, 77 (1960).

7. 372 U.S. 29, 35, 35–36, 36, 37–38 (1963).

8. Bickel, *The Least Dangerous Branch* (Indianapolis: Bobbs-Merrill, 1962), p. 152. (Emphasis in original.)

9. See Winter, "Collective Bargaining and Competition: The Application of Antitrust Standards to Union Activities," 73 *Yale L. J.* 14 (1963).

10. *Baker* v. *Carr*, 369 U.S. 186, 268, 289 (1962) (Frankfurter, J., dissenting).

11. See Neal, "Baker v. Carr: Politics in Search of Law," 1962 *Sup. Ct. Rev.* 252.

12. *Standard Oil Co. of California and Standard Stations, Inc.* v. *United States*, 337 U.S. 293 (1949).

13. 310 U.S. 469, 493 (1940).

14. 317 U.S. 111, 129 (1942).

CHAPTER 4: BUSINESS BEHAVIOR AND THE CONSUMER INTEREST

1. Knight, *The Economic Organization* (University of Chicago Press, 1933), p. 9.

2. Id. at 8.

CHAPTER 5: THE CONSUMER WELFARE MODEL

1. Williamson, "Economies as an Antitrust Defense: The Welfare Tradeoffs," 58 *Am. Econ. Rev.* 18, 21 (1968).

2. Id. at 34.

3. Id. at 27–28, 23–24.

4. Id. at 27–28.

5. Id. at 28.

6. Posner, *Antitrust Law: An Economic Perspective* (Chicago and London: University of Chicago Press, 1976), p. 11.

7. Id. at 13–14.

CHAPTER 6: THE METHOD OF ANTITRUST ANALYSIS

1. Friedman, "The Methodology of Positive Economics," in *Readings In Microeconomics*, edited by Breit and Hochman (New York: Holt, Rinehart and Winston, 1968), p. 33; reprinted from Friedman, *Essays in Positive Economics* (Chicago: University of Chicago Press, 1953).

2. Id. at 34–35.

3. Ibid.

4. Alchian, "Uncertainty, Evolution, and Economic Theory," in *Readings in Industrial Organization and Public Policy* (Homewood, Ill.: Richard D. Irwin, 1958), p. 210; reprinted from 58 *J. of Pol. Econ.* 211 (1950).

5. Stigler, *The Theory of Price*, 3d ed. (New York: Macmillan, 1966), p. 177, n. 1.

6. Alchian, *supra* n. 4, at 215.

7. Arthur Conan Doyle, *The Sign of the Four*, Chap. VI.

8. Williamson, "Allocative Efficiency and the Limits of Antitrust," 59 *Am. Econ. Rev.*, Proceedings, 105, 117 (1969).

9. Kaysen and Turner, *Antitrust Policy* (Cambridge: Harvard University Press, 1959), pp. 111, 112.

10. White House Task Force on Antitrust Policy, *Report* 1 (in Trade Reg. Rep., supp. to no. 415, May 26, 1969).

11. Williamson, "Economies as an Antitrust Defense: The Welfare Trade-off," 58 *Am. Econ. Rev.* 18 (1968).

12. Robinson, *The Structure of Competitive Industry* (Chicago: University of Chicago Press, 1958), p. 12.

13. Williamson, *supra* n. 8, at 113.

14. Williamson, *supra* n. 11, at 24.

15. Id. at 20.

16. Id. at 24.

17. Id. at 25.

18. Bork and Bowman, "The Crisis on Antitrust," *Fortune* 68, December 1963, pp.

19. Williamson, *supra* n. 11, at 27.

20. Id. at 27, n. 6.

21. Id. at 27.

22. Williamson, *supra* n. 8, at 107.

23. Bork, "The Goals of Antitrust Policy," 57 *Am. Econ. Rev.* 242, 251 (1967).

24. Williamson, *supra* n. 11, at 29.

CHAPTER 7: INJURY TO COMPETITION

1. *United States* v. *Trans-Missouri Freight Ass'n.*, 166 U.S. 290 (1897), discussed at pp. 22–26, supra.

2. *United States* v. *Addyston Pipe & Steel Co.*, 85 Fed. 271 (6th Cir. 1898), aff'd., 175 U.S. 211 (1899), discussed at pp. 26–30, supra.

3. *Standard Oil Co. of New Jersey* v. *United States*, 221 U.S. 1 (1911), discussed at pp. 33–41, supra.

4. *Northern Securities Co.* v. *United States*, 193 U.S. 197, 400, 410–11 (1904), discussed at pp. 30–32, supra.

5. 110 F. Supp. 295, 345, 341, 344–45 (D. Mass. 1953), aff'd per curiam, 347 U.S. 521 (1954).

6. 334 U.S. 100, 102, 106, 108 (1948).

7. McGee, "Predatory Price Cutting: The Standard Oil (N.J.) Case," 1 *J. of Law and Econ.* 137, 168 (1958).

8. Adelman, *A&P: A Study in Price-Cost Behavior and Public Policy* (Cambridge: Harvard University Press, 1966), pp. 14, 362–79, 390, 394–97, 407–10.

9. *United States* v. *New York Great Atlantic & Pacific Tea Co.*, 67 F. Supp. 626 (E.D. Ill. 1946), aff'd, 173 F.2d 79 (7th Cir. 1949).

10. Elzinga, "Predatory Pricing: The Case of the Gunpowder Trust," 13 *J. Law and Econ.* 223, 236 (1970).

11. Telser, "Cutthroat Competition and the Long Purse," 9 *J. Law and Econ.* 259, 264, 267 (1966).

12. Stigler, "Imperfections in the Capital Market," 75 *J. of Pol. Econ.* 287, 290 (1967).

13. McGee, "Predatory Price Cutting," supra n. 7, at 155.

14. Areeda and Turner, "Predatory Pricing and Related Practices Under Section 2 of the Sherman Act," 88 *Harv. L. Rev.* 697 (1975).

15. Scherer, "Predatory Pricing and the Sherman Act: A Comment," 89 *Harv. L. Rev.* 869, 890 (1976).

16. Koller, "The Myth of Predatory Pricing: An Empirical Study," 4 *Antitrust L. & Econ. Rev.* 105 (Summer 1971).

17. *Chicago Board of Trade* v. *United States*, 246 U.S. 231, 237, 240 (1918).

CHAPTER 8: MONOPOLY AND OLIGOPOLY

1. Testimony on *Planning, Regulation, and Competition in the Automobile Industry,* Cong. Rec., July 17, 1968. S. 8785, 8787.

2. Kaysen and Turner, *Antitrust Policy* (Cambridge: Harvard University Press, 1959), chs. 3–4.

3. White House Task Force on Antitrust Policy, *Report* 1 (in Trade Reg. Reps., supp. to no. 415, May 26, 1969).

4. 21 Cong. Rec. 3152 (1890).

5. *Standard Oil Co. of New Jersey* v. *United States,* 221 U.S. 1, 62 (1911).

6. *United States* v. *Aluminum Co. of America,* 148 F. 2d 416, 422–23, 425, 424, 427–28, 429, 429–30, 430, 422–23, 429, 430, 431, 424–25 (2nd Cir. 1945).

7. *United States* v. *United States Steel Corp.,* 251 U.S. 417 (1920).

8. *United States* v. *International Harvester Co.,* 274 U.S. 693 (1927).

9. *United States* v. *Swift & Co.,* 286 U.S. 106 (1932).

10. Director and Levi, "Law and the Future: Trade Regulation," 51 *Nw. U. L. Rev.* 281, 286 (1956).

11. *United States* v. *United Shoe Machinery Corp.,* 110 F. Supp. 295, 344, 341, 351–54, 346, 350 (D. Mass. 1953).

12. 266 F. Supp. 328 (D. Mass. 1967).

13. *United States* v. *United Shoe Machinery Corp.,* 391 U.S. 244 (1968).

14. Posner, *Antitrust Law: An Economic Perspective* (Chicago and London: University of Chicago Press, 1976), pp. 31, 47–77.

15. Kaysen and Turner, *Antitrust Policy,* p. 27.

16. White House Task Force, supra n. 3.

17. Williamson, "Economies as an Antitrust Defense: The Welfare Tradeoff," 58 *Am. Econ. Rev.* 18, 22–23 (1968).

18. Demsetz, "Why Regulate Utilities," 11 *J. Law & Econ.* 55, 59–60 (1968).

19. The latest exchange is Brozen, "The Concentration-Collusion Doctrine," and Scherer, "Structure-Performance Relationships and Antitrust Policy," Issue No. 3, 46 Antitrust L. J. (1977). See also Demsetz, "Two Systems of Belief About Monopoly," in *Industrial Concentration: The New Learning,* Goldschmid, Mann, and Weston, eds. (Boston: Little Brown, 1974), p. 164; Weiss, "The Concentration-Profits Relationship and Antitrust," id. at 184; and the articles listed, id. at 245.

20. McGee, *In Defense of Industrial Concentration* (New York: Praeger, 1971), p. 95.

21. *United States* v. *United Shoe Machinery Corp.* 110 F. Supp. 295, 325, 326 (D. Mass. 1953).

22. *Telex Corp.* v. *International Business Machines Corp.,* 367 F. Supp. 258 (N.D. Okla. 1973), *reversed in part,* 510 F. 2d 894 (10th Cir. 1975).

23. *American Tobacco Co.* v. *United States,* 328 U.S. 781 (1946).

24. Jordan, "Producer Protection, Prior Market Structure and the Effects of Government Regulation," 15 *J. Law and Econ.* 151, 167, 164 (1972).

25. Memorandum, Hearings on *Planning, Regulation, and Competition: Automobile Industry—1968* before Subcommittees of the Select Committee on Small Business, U.S. Senate, 90th Cong. 2nd Sess., July 10 and 23, 1968, pp. 910, 912.

26. Dorfman, *The Price System* (Englewood Cliffs, N.J.: Prentice-Hall, 1964), p. 100.

27. *The Automobile Industry: A Case Study of Competition,* A Statement by General Motors Corporation (Prepared for the Subcommittee on Retailing, Distribution and Marketing Practices and the Subcommittee on Monopoly of the Select Committee on Small Business of the United States Senate, October 1968), p. 17. *Competition and the Motor Vehicle Industry,* A Study by General Motors Corporation (Submitted to the Subcommittee on Antitrust and Monopoly of the Committee on the Judiciary of the United States Senate and included in the record of the Subcommittee's Hearings on April 10, 1974), pp. 20–21.

28. Dorfman, *Price System,* pp. 102, 102 n. 11, 99, 99–100, 100 n. 10.

29. Telser, "Advertising and Competition," 72 *J. Pol. Econ.* 537 (1964).

30. Stigler, *The Organization of Industry* (Homewood, Ill.: Richard D. Irwin, 1968), pp. 71, 73, 88.

31. Stigler, *The Theory of Price,* 3d ed. (New York: Macmillan, 1966), p. 223.

32. Id. at 220.

CHAPTER 9: THE CRASH OF MERGER POLICY:
THE *Brown Shoe* DECISION

1. *Brown Shoe Co.* v. *United States,* 370 U.S. 294 (1962).

2. Turner, "Conglomerate Mergers and Section 7 of the Clayton Act," 78 *Harv. L. Rev.* 1313, 1317 (1965).

3. *United States* v. *Von's Grocery Co.,* 384 U.S. 270, 301 (1966).

4. *Brown Shoe Co.* v. *United States,* 370 U.S. 294, 316 n. 29, 315, 315–16, 317, 315–16, 345 n. 72 (1962).

5. B. Bock, "New Numbers on Concentration: Fears and Facts," The Conference Board Record, March 1976, p. 22; Farkas and Weinberger, *The Relativity of Concentration Observations;* A Research Report, The Conference Board (to be published, 1978).

6. Turner, supra n. 2 at 1326, 1327–28.

7. *Federal Trade Commission* v. *Procter & Gamble Co.,* 386 U.S. 568, 580 (1967).

8. Adelman, "Problems and Prospects in Antitrust Policy—II," in Phillips, ed., *Perspectives on Antitrust Policy* (Princeton: Princeton University Press, 1965), pp. 32, 36.

9. *United States* v. *E. I. du Pont de Nemours and Co.,* 353 U.S. 586, 597–98 (1957).

10. *Reynolds Metal Co.,* Docket 7009, 56 F.T.C. 743, 776 (1960).

11. *Fortner Enterprises, Inc.* v. *United States Steel Corp.,* 394 U.S. 495

12. *Utah Pie Co.* v. *Continental Baking Co.,* 386 U.S. 685 (1967).

13. *United States* v. *Sealy, Inc.,* 388 U.S. 350 (1967).

14. *United States* v. *Arnold, Schwinn & Co.,* 388 U.S. 365 (1967).

15. *Federal Trade Commission* v. *Procter & Gamble Co.,* 386 U.S. 568 (1967).

16. *United States* v. *Von's Grocery Co.,* 384 U.S. 270 (1966).

17. 370 U.S. 294, 328–29, 331–32, 330, 334, 304 n. 8, 302–04, 343–44, 344, 346 (1962).
18. Adelman, supra. n. 8, at 37.

CHAPTER 10: HORIZONTAL MERGERS

1. *United States* v. *Pabst Brewing Co.*, 384 U.S. 546, 548–50 (1966).
2. *United States* v. *Von's Grocery Co.*, 384 U.S. 270, 278, 283 (1966).
3. 415 U.S. 486 (1974).
4. 418 U.S. 602 (1974).
5. 418 U.S. 656 (1974).
6. 422 U.S. 86 (1975).
7. Williamson, "Economies as an Antitrust Defense: The Welfare Tradeoff," 58 *Am. Econ. Rev.* 18 (1968); DePrano and Nugent, "Economies as an Antitrust Defense: Comment," 59 *Am. Econ. Rev.* 947, 952–53 (1969).
8. *United States* v. *E. I. du Pont de Nemours and Co.*, 353 U.S. 586 (1957).
9. *Reynolds Metals Co.* v. *Federal Trade Commission*, 309 F.2d 223 (1962). See discussion in Bork, "Anticompetitive Enforcement Doctrines under Section 7 of the Clayton Act," 39 *Tex. L.Rev.* 832, 838–39 (1961).

CHAPTER 11: VERTICAL MERGERS

1. *United States* v. *American Tobacco Co.*, 221 U.S. 106 (1911). See Chapter 1.
2. *United States* v. *Yellow Cab Co.*, 332 U.S. 218 (1947).
3. See Bork, "Vertical Integration and the Sherman Act: The Legal History of an Economic Misconception," 22 *U. Chi. L. Rev.* 157 (1954).
4. *Brown Shoe Co.* v. *United States*, 370 U.S. 294 (1962).
5. Merger Guidelines of the Department of Justice (Released May 30, 1968), contained in 1 *Trade Reg. Rep.* 4510.
6. Adelman, "Integration and Antitrust Policy," 63 *Harv. L. Rev.* 27 (1949).
7. See Coase, "The Nature of the Firm," *Economica*, New Series, vol. 4 (1937), p. 386.
8. McGee and Bassett, "Vertical Integration Revisited," 19 *J. of Law & Econ.* 17, 19–20 (1976).
9. *A. G. Spalding & Bros., Inc.* 56 F.T.C. 1125, 1169 (1960).
10. 405 U.S. 562, 568 (1972).
11. Areeda, *Antitrust Analysis: Problems, Text, Cases*, 2d ed. (Boston: Little, Brown, 1974), pp. 675 (footnote omitted, paragraphing added), 676.
12. *Permanente Cement Co.*, Docket No. 7939, 65 F.T.C. 410 (1964), 66 F.T.C. 1587 (1964), 67 F.T.C. 334 (1965).

CHAPTER 12: CONGLOMERATE MERGERS

1. Edwards, "Conglomerate Bigness as a Source of Power," in *Business Concentration and Price Policy* (National Bureau of Economic Research, 1955), p. 331.
2. H. R. Rep. No. 1191, 81st. Cong., 1st Sess., p. 11 (1949).
3. *Reynolds Metal Co.*, Docket 7009, 56 F.T.C. 743, 776 (1960), aff'd.,

Reynolds Metal Co. v. *Federal Trade Commission,* 309 F.2d 223, 229–30 (D.C. Cir. 1962).

4. Docket 6495, 60 F.T.C. 944, 1084 (1962).

5. Docket 6559, 63 F.T.C. 2240, 2247, 2247–48 (1963).

6. *Procter & Gamble Co.,* Docket 6901, 63 F.T.C. 1465, 1580 (1963); *Federal Trade Commission* v. *Proctor & Gamble Co.,* 386 U.S. 568, 583, 572, 578 (1967).

7. See Peterman, "The Clorox Case and the Television Rate Structures," 11 *J. of Law & Econ.* 321 (1968); Blank, "Television Advertising: The Great Discount Illusion, or Tonypandy Revisited," 41 *J. Bus. Univ. Chi.* 10 (1968).

8. Turner, "Conglomerate Mergers and Section 7 of the Clayton Act," 78 *Harv. L. Rev.* 1313, 1352–53, 1355–56, 1346 (1965).

9. *Federal Trade Commission* v. *Consolidated Foods Corp.,* 380 U.S. 592, (1965).

10. Turner, supra n. 8, at 1363.

11. White House Task Force on Antitrust Policy, *Report* 1 (in Trade Reg. Reps., supp. to no. 415, May 26, 1969).

12. *Bendix Corp.,* Docket 8738, 77 F.T.C. 731, *vacated and remanded, Bendix Corp.* v. *Federal Trade Commission,* 450 F.2d 534 (6th Cir. 1971).

13. *Kennecott Copper Corp.,* Docket 8765, 78 F.T.C. 744 (1971).

CHAPTER 13: HORIZONTAL PRICE FIXING AND MARKET DIVISION

1. *United States* v. *Trenton Potteries,* 273 U.S. 392 (1927).

2. *United States* v. *Socony-Vacuum Oil Co.,* 310 U.S. 150 (1940).

3. *United States* v. *Joint Traffic Ass'n.,* 171 U.S. 505, 567–68 (1898).

4. *Northern Securities Co.* v. *United States,* 193 U.S. 197, 400, 410–11 (1904).

5. *United States* v. *Addyston Pipe & Steel Co.,* 85 Fed. 271, 281, 282–83, 280 (6th Cir. 1898).

6. *United States* v. *Container Corp. of America,* 393 U.S. 333, 341 (1969).

7. 338 U.S. 350, 354, 355, 356, 357 (1967).

8. *United States* v. *Sealy:* Post Trial Brief for Plantiff, p. 24.

9. 1964 Trade Case ¶ 71, 258 at 80, 076–77, Finding 84.

10. *Timken Roller Bearing Co.* v. *United States,* 341 U.S. 593 (1951).

11. 405 U.S. 596, 600 n. 3, 604, 604–5, 608, 609 n. 9, 609 n. 10, 609–10, 611–12 (1972).

CHAPTER 14: RESALE PRICE MAINTENANCE AND VERTICAL MARKET DIVISION

1. *Dr. Miles Medical Co.* v. *John D. Park & Sons Co.,* 220 U.S. 373 (1911).

2. *United States* v. *Colgate Co.,* 250 U.S. 300 (1919).

3. *United States* v. *Parke, Davis and Co.,* 362 U.S. 29 (1960).

4. *Simpson* v. *Union Oil Co.,* 377 U.S. 13 (1964).

5. *Kiefer-Stewart Co.* v. *Joseph E. Seagram & Sons, Inc.,* 340 U.S. 211 (1951).

6. 390 U.S. 145 (1968).

7. *White Motor Co.* v. *United States,* 372 U.S. 253, 261, 263 (1963).

8. *United States* v. *Arnold, Schwinn & Co.,* 388 U.S. 365, 372, 378–79, 379–80, 380 (1967).

9. 97 S. Ct. 2549, 2558–59, 2560 (1977).

10. *United States* v. *Addyston Pipe & Steel Co.,* 85 Fed. 271, 287 (6th Cir. 1898).

11. Comanor, "Vertical Territorial and Customer Restrictions: White Motor and Its Aftermath," 81 *Harv. L. Rev.* 1419 (1968).

12. See Telser, "Why Should Manufacturers Want Fair Trade?" 3 *J. Law & Econ.* 86, 96–104 (1960). For a critical analysis of the theory, see Bowman, "The Prerequisites and Effects of Resale Price Maintenance," 22 *U. Chi. L. Rev.* 825, 838–39 (1955).

13. Professors Gould and Yamey were answering an article I had written which set out the arguments made in this and the preceding chapter and in the Appendix to those chapters. I, in turn, answered them. The exchange consists of Bork, "The Rule of Reason and the Per Se Concept: Price Fixing and Market Division, II," 75 *Yale L. J.* 373 (1966); Gould and Yamey, "Professor Bork on Vertical Price Fixing," 76 *Yale L. J.* 722 (1967); Bork, "A Reply to Professors Gould and Yamey," 76 *Yale L. J.* 731 (1967); Gould and Yamey, "Professor Bork on Vertical Price Fixing: A Rejoinder," 77 *Yale L. J.* 936 (1968); and Bork, "Resale Price Maintenance and Consumer Welfare," 77 *Yale L. J.* 950 (1968).

CHAPTER 15: EXCLUSIVE DEALING AND REQUIREMENTS CONTRACTS

1. *Standard Oil Co. of California (Standard Stations)* v. *United States,* 337 U.S. 293, 299, 304–10 (1949).

2. *International Salt Co.* v. *United States,* 332 U.S. 392 (1947).

3. *Tampa Electric Co.* v. *Nashville Coal Co.,* 365 U.S. 320 (1961).

4. *Brown Shoe Co.,* 62 F.T.C. 679 (1963).

5. *Federal Trade Commission* v. *Brown Shoe Co.,* 384 U.S. 316, 321, 322 (1966).

6. Areeda, *Antitrust Analysis: Problems, Text, Cases,* 2d ed. (Boston: Little, Brown, 1974), p. 635.

7. Blake and Jones, "Toward a Three-Dimensional Antitrust Policy," 65 *Colum. L. Rev.* 422, 441, 442, 443, 444, 445 (1965).

8. *Standard Fashion Co.* v. *Magrane-Houston Co.,* 258 U.S. 346, 357 (1922).

9. 344 U.S. 392, 393, 398–99 (1953).

CHAPTER 16: "BARRIERS TO ENTRY"

1. Bain, *Barriers to New Competition* (Cambridge: Harvard University Press, 1956), Chap. 1.

2. Snell, "Annual Style Change in the Automobile Industry as an Unfair Method of Competition," 80 *Yale L. J.* 567 (1971).

3. Bain, supra. n. 1 at 114–115.

4. Telser, "Advertising and Competition," 72 *J. Political Econ.* 537, 556 (1964).

5. Ferguson, "Advertising and Liquor," 40 *J. of Bus.* 419 (1967).

6. Brozen, "Entry Barriers: Advertising and Product Differentiation," in *Industrial Concentration: The New Learning* (Boston: Little, Brown, 1974), p. 115.

7. Turner, "Conglomerate Mergers and Section 7 of the Clayton Act," 78 *Harv. L. R.* 1313, 1361 (1965).

8. Brozen, "The FTC Attack on Advertising," 5 Relig. and Society 12, 22 (1972). See also, Brozen, "Entry Barriers: Advertising and Product Differentiation," in *Industrial Concentration: The New Learning,* Goldschmid, Mann, and Weston, eds. (Boston: Little, Brown, 1974), p. 115.

9. Benham, "The Effect of Advertising on the Price of Eyeglasses," 15 *J. of Law & Econ.* 337, 344 (1972).

10. Blake and Jones, "In Defense of Antitrust," 65 *Col. L. Rev.* 377, 392 (1965).

11. McGee, *In Defense of Industrial Concentration* (New York: Praeger, 1971), p. 51.

12. Bain, supra. n. 1 at 300–2.

13. *United States* v. *United Shoe Machinery Corp.,* 110 F. Supp. 295, 340 (D. Mass. 1953).

14. Schupack, *Statement Regarding Competition in the Automobile Industry,* Hearings on *Planning, Regulation, and Competition: Automobile Industry—* 1968, before Subcommittees of the Select Committee on Small Business, U.S. Senate, 90th Cong., 2nd Sess., July 10 and 25, pp. 917, 923–924.

CHAPTER 17: BOYCOTTS AND INDIVIDUAL REFUSALS TO DEAL

1. 359 U.S. 207, 212–13 (1959).

2. 1956 Trade Cases ¶ 68, 495, p. 72, 048 (N.D. Cal.).

3. 255 F.2d 214, 233 (9th Cir. 1958).

4. 358 F.2nd 165 (9th Cir. 1966), *cert. denied,* 385 U.S. 846.

5. 190 F. Supp. 241 (S.D.N.Y. 1961).

6. Rahl, "Per Se Rules and Boycotts Under the Sherman Act: Some Reflections on the Klor's Case," 45 *Va. L. Rev.* 1165 (1959).

7. 156 F. Supp. 800, 805, 807 (D. Kan. 1957).

8. 355 U.S. 10 (1957).

9. Jurisdictional Statement of Nationwide Trailer Rental System, Inc., pp. 8–9.

10. 234 U.S. 600 (1914).

11. 1953 Trade Cases § 67, 470 (N.D. Okla.).

12. 194 F.2nd 484, 487–88 (1st Cir., 1952) cert. deni. ed., 344 U.S. 817.

13. *United States* v. *Sealy, Inc.,* 388 U.S. 350 (1967). The case is analyzed in Chapter 13.

14. *United States* v. *Topco Associates, Inc.,* 405 U.S. 596 (1972). The case is analyzed in Chapter 13.

15. 312 U.S. 457 (1941).

16. 326 U.S. 1, 16, 14, 34, 15, 17–18 (1945).

17. 373 U.S. 341, 347, 361 (1963).

18. 342 U.S. 143, 147, 152 (1951).

19. 243 F2d. 418, 420, 421 (D.C. Cir. 1957).

CHAPTER 18: PREDATION THROUGH GOVERNMENTAL PROCESSES

1. 365 U.S. 127, 129, 129–30, 136, 137, 138, 144 (1961).

2. 381 U.S. 657, 671 (1965).

3. 382 U.S. 172, 174 (1965).

4. 404 U.S. 508, 510, 515, 516, 518 (1972).

5. 410 U.S. 366 (1973), and 417 U.S. 901 (1974), summarily affirming 360 F. Supp. 451 (D. Minn. 1973).

6. 307 U.S. 533 (1939).

7. 317 U.S. 341 (1943).

8. Familiar examples of government's inherent power to protect its functions may be found in such cases as *McCulloch* v. *Maryland,* 4 Wheat. 316 (1819); *Crandall* v. *Nevada,* 6 Wall. 35 (1868); and *In re Neagle,* 135 U.S. 1 (1890).

9. *Trucking Unlimited* v. *California Motor Transport Co.,* 432 F.2nd 755, 759 n. 6 (9th Cir. 1970).

10. 371 U.S. 415 (1963).

11. 377 U.S. 1 (1964).

12. 389 U.S. 217 (1967).

13. 401 U.S. 576 (1971).

14. 1 Cranch 137, 170 (1803).

15. Wechsler, "The Courts and the Constitution," 65 *Col. L. Rev.* 1001, 1008 (1965).

CHAPTER 19: TYING ARRANGEMENTS AND RECIPROCAL DEALING

1. Aaron Director first exploded the law's theory of tying arrangements. See also, Bork & Bowman, "The Crisis in Antitrust," *Fortune,* Dec. 1963, at 138; Bowman, "Tying Arrangements and the Leverage Problem," 67 *Yale L. J.* 19 (1957); "Law and the Future: Trade Regulation," 51 *Nw. U. L. Rev.* 251 (1956). Anderson, "Reciprocal Dealing," 76 *Yale L. J.* 1020 (1967): Markovits, "Tie-ins, Leverage, and the American Antitrust Laws," 80 *Yale L. J.* 195 (1970).

2. *Henry* v. *A. B. Dick Co.,* 224 U.S. 1, 49 (1912).

3. *Motion Picture Patents Co.* v. *Universal Film Manufacturing Co.,* 243 U.S. 502 (1917).

4. *International Salt Co.* v. *United States,* 332 U.S. 392, 396 (1947).

5. *Standard Oil Co. of California and Standard Stations, Inc.,* v. *United States,* 337 U.S. 293, 305 (1949).

6. *Northern Pacific Railway Co.* v. *United States,* 356 U.S. 1, 6, 8–9, 10 n. 8 (1958).

7. 394 U.S. 495, 505, 507 (1969).

8. *United States Steel Corp.* v. *Fortner Enterprises Inc.,* 429 U.S. 610, 621–22, 622 (1977).

9. 187 F. Supp. 545, 559, 560 (E.D. Pa. 1960), affirmed per curiam, 365 U.S. 567 (1961).

10. *Federal Trade Commission* v. *Consolidated Foods Corp.*, 380 U.S. 592 (1965).

11. *United States* v. *Loew's, Inc.*, 371 U.S. 38 (1962).

12. Stigler, "United States v. Loew's, Inc.: A Note on Block Booking," 1963 *Sup. Ct. Rev.* 152, 152–53 (1963).

13. Kaysen and Turner, *Antitrust Policy* (Cambridge: Harvard University Press, 1959), p. 157.

14. Burstein, "A Theory of Full-Line Forcing," 55 *Nw. U. L. Rev.* 62 (1960); Ferguson, "Tying Arrangements and Reciprocity: An Economic Analysis," 30 *L. & Contemp. Prob.* 552 (1965).

15. See the articles cited *supra* n. 1.

16. Bowman, "Tying Arrangements and the Leverage Problem, 67 *Yale L. J.* 19, 27–28, 28 (1957).

CHAPTER 20: PRICE DISCRIMINATION

1. Rowe, *Price Discrimination Under the Robinson-Patman Act* (Boston: Little, Brown, 1962), Chap. 1.

2. Id. at 93.

3. Id. at pp. 551–55.

4. 386 U.S. 685 (1967).

5. Adelman, "Book Review," 50 Amer. Econ. Rev. 790, 792 (1960).

6. *Federal Trade Commission* v. *Morton Salt Co.*, 334 U.S. 37, 45 (1948).

7. Adelman. "A&P: A Study in Price-Cost Behavior and Public Policy (Cambridge: Harvard University Press, 1959), pp. 164–165.

8. Stigler, *The Theory of Price* (New York: Macmillan, 3rd ed., 1966), p. 105.

9. Edwards, *Maintaining Competition* (New York: McGraw-Hill, 1949), p. 161.

10. Alchian, "Costs and Output," in Abramovitz et. al., *The Allocation of Economic Resources: Essays in Honor of Bernard F. Haley* (Palo Alto: Stanford University Press, 1959).

11. Adelman, *supra* n. 7 at 172.

12. Posner, *Economic Analysis of Law* (Boston: Little, Brown, 1972) § 7.8.

13. Robinson, *The Economics of Imperfect Competition* (London: MacMillan, 1st ed., 1933), pp. 188–95.

14. Stigler. *The Theory of Price* (New York: MacMillan, 3d ed., 1966}, pp. 213–14.

CHAPTER 22: FINAL THOUGHTS

1. *United States* v. *United Shoe Machinery Corp.*, 110 F. Supp. 295, 348 (D. Mass. 1953).

2. Dicey, *Lectures on the Relation Between Law and Public Opinion in England During the Nineteenth Century*, 2d ed. (London: Macmillan, 1962), pp. 41–42.

APPENDIX TO CHAPTERS 13 AND 14

1. *White Motor Co.* v. *United States*, 372 U.S. 253 (1963).

2. *United States* v. *White Motor Co.*, 194 F. Supp. 562, 578 (N.D. Ohio, 1961).

3. Brief for Appellant (in the Supreme Court), p. 18.

4. *Sandura Co.*, Docket 7042, 61 F.T.C. 756, 809 (1962).

5. *Sandura Co.* v. *Federal Trade Commission*, 339 F.2d 847, 852, 853, (6th Cir. 1964).

6. 45 F. Supp. 387, 398 (S.D.N.Y. 1942), affirmed on the point discussed by an equally divided Court, 321 U.S. 707, 719 (1944).

7. Resale price maintenance was first outlawed by *Dr. Miles Medical Co.* v. *John D. Park & Sons Co.*, 220 U.S. 373 (1911), and the use of consignment contracts to accomplish refiner control of retail prices was struck down in *Simpson* v. *Union Oil Co.*, 377 U.S. 13 (1964).

8. *United States* v. *Nationwide Trailer Rental System, Inc.*, 156 F. Supp. 800 (D. Kan. 1957), affirmed, 355 U.S. 10 (1954).

9. NTRS Jurisdictional Statement, p. 11, 355 U.S. 10.

10. BNA, Antitrust & Trade Reg. Rep. No. 91, April 9, 1963, p. x–l.

11. 189 F. Supp. 153 (S.D.N.Y. 1960).

12. *Kiefer-Stewart Co.* v. *Joseph E. Seagram & Sons, Inc.*, 340 U.S. 211 (1951).

13. *Albrecht* v. *The Herald Co.*, 390 U.S. 145 (1968).

INDEX OF CASES

SUBJECT INDEX